SKEPTICISM

SKEPTICISM
AN ANTHOLOGY

Edited by
RICHARD H. POPKIN
JOSÉ R. MAIA NETO

 Prometheus Books

59 John Glenn Drive
Amherst, New York 14228–2197

Published 2007 by Prometheus Books

Inquiries should be addressed to
Prometheus Books
59 John Glenn Drive
Amherst, New York 14228–2197
VOICE: 716–691–0133, ext. 207
FAX: 716–564–2711
WWW.PROMETHEUSBOOKS.COM

11 10 09 08 07   5 4 3 2 1

Library of Congress Cataloging-in-Publication Data

Skepticism : an anthology / edited by Richard H. Popkin & José R. Maia Neto.
    p. cm.
Includes bibliographical references.
ISBN 978–1–59102–474–3 (alk. paper)
    1. Skepticism. I. Popkin, Richard H. (Richard Henry), 1923–2005. II. Maia Neto, José Raimundo, 1959–

BD201.S54 2007
149'.73—dc22

2006035407

Printed in the United States of America on acid-free paper

CONTENTS

ACKNOWLEDGMENTS

W e would like to thank, first of all, three assistants who worked intensely in the preparation of this volume: Flávio F. Loque, who assisted José Maia Neto in Belo Horizonte, and Knox Paden and Peter K. J. Park, who assisted Richard Popkin in Los Angeles. We would also like to thank the colleagues who advised us in the selection of texts: Gian Mario Cao (Pico), Bernardo Jefferson de Oliveira (Bacon), Stuart Brown (Leibniz), Rogério Lopes (Nietzsche), and Avrum Stroll (Wittgenstein). We thank very much the colleagues who translated selections specially for this anthology: Gian Mario Cao (Pico), Leonardo Alves Vieira (Schulze), and, in particular, Richard A. Watson (Hervet, La Mothe Le Vayer, Crousaz, and Diderot). We thank Jean-Robert Armogathe for providing Hervet's text, Niall Martin and Rosemary Boch for allowing us to use their translations of, respectively, Leibniz and Stäudlin, and John Christian Laursen for revising the translation of the selection from Stäudlin. We also thank the Staatsbibliotek zu Berlin (STABI), the Bibliothèque Nationale de France (BNF), the university libraries of UCLA and the library of the School of Philosophy and the Social Sciences (FAFICH) of the Federal University of Minas Gerais (UFMG). José Maia Neto thanks CNPq-Brazil for a research grant and Elene and Frederico for their patience and support during the final phase of the edition of the volume.

PERMISSIONS
AND CREDITS

1. PLATO

Apology. Translated by H. N. Fowler. Cambridge, MA: Harvard University Press, 1995. Loeb
Classical Library [20c–23d].
Theaetetus. Translated by H. N. Fowler. Cambridge, MA: Harvard University Press, 1996.
Loeb Classical Library [150b–152d, 156a–c, 157a–160e, 183a–b, 210b–d].
Selections reprinted by permission of the publisher and the Trustees of the Loeb Classical
Library from PLATO: VOLUME I, Loeb Classical Library® Volume 36, translated by
H. N. Fowler, Cambridge, Mass.: Harvard University Press, Copyright ©1914 by the
President and Fellows of Harvard College, and PLATO: VOLUME VII, Loeb Classical
Library® Volume 123, translated by N. H. Fowler, Cambridge, Mass.: Harvard Univer-
sity Press, Copyright ©1921. The Loeb Classical Library® is a registered trademark of
the President and Fellows of Harvard College.

2. PYRRHO

Diogenes Laertius. *Lives of Eminent Philosophers*, vol. 2, translated by R. D. Hicks. Cambridge,
MA: Harvard University Press, 1943. Loeb Classical Library [9. 61–69]. Reprinted by permission of the publishers and the Trustees of the Loeb Classical Library from DIOGENES
LAERTIUS: VOLUME II, Loeb Classical Library® Volume 185, translated by R. D.
Hicks, Cambridge, Mass.: Harvard University Press, Copyright ©1925 by the President
and Fellows of Harvard College. The Loeb Classical Library® is a registered trademark of
the President and Fellows of Harvard College.
A. Long and D. Sedley. *The Hellenistic Philosophers*, vol. 1. Cambridge: Cambridge University Press, 1997, pp. 14–15 (Aristocles [Eusebius 14.18.1–5]).

3. THE ACADEMICS

Cicero. *Academica*. Translated by H. Rackham. Cambridge, MA: Harvard University Press,
1994. Loeb Classical Library [I. 44–46, 2.7–9, 47–48, 76–78, 83, 88–90, 99–101,
103–104].
Sextus Empiricus. *Against the Logicians*. Translated by R. G. Bury. Cambridge, MA: Harvard
University Press, 1987. Loeb Classical Library [*Adversus Mathematicos* VII 166–89].
Selections reprinted by permission of the publishers and the Trustees of the Loeb Classical

4. SEXTUS EMPIRICUS

Sextus Empiricus. *Outlines of Pyrrhonism*. Translated by R. G. Bury. Cambridge, MA: Harvard University Press, 1987. Loeb Classical Library [1.1–17, 19–35, 36–40, 50–51, 59, 62–69, 73–75, 79, 85, 87, 91, 94–99, 100–104, 108, 118, 124, 129, 135, 141, 145, 148–55, 164–75, 177], [2.18–20, 72–75], [3.280–81].

Sextus Empiricus. *Adversus Mathematicos*. Translated by R. G. Bury. Cambridge, MA: Harvard University Press, 1987. Loeb Classical Library [*Adversus Mathematicos* 8. 480–81].

5. AUGUSTINE

Against the Academics. Translated by J. J. O'Meara, Westminster, MD: Newman Press, 1950. [3.23–26, 35–36].

6. ERASMUS

In Praise of Folly. Translated by Leonard Dean (with minor revisions) in *Philosophy of the 16th and 17th Centuries*, edited by Richard Popkin. Toronto: Collier-Macmillan, 1966, pp. 32–34. Readings in the History of Philosophy series, general editors: Paul Edwards and Richard H. Popkin.

7. GIANFRANCESCO PICO DELLA MIRANDOLA

Examen vanitatis doctrinae gentium et veritatis christianae disciplinae. (Mirandola: 1520), bk. 1, ch. 2, fol. 8^r. Translated by Charles B. Schmitt in *Gianfrancesco Pico della Mirandola (1469–1533) and his Critique of Aristotle*. The Hague: Martinus Nijhoff, 1967, p. 48.

Bk. 2, ch. 20, fols. 50^r–51^r. Translated by Gian Mario Cao.

8. HERVET

Dedicatory letter of *Adversus Mathematicos* to the Cardinal of Lorraine. Translated to English by Richard A. Watson from the French translation by Alain Legros, revised against the Latin original by José R. Maia Neto, *Bulletin de la Societé des Amis de Montaigne* 8 (1999): 51–72.

9. MONTAIGNE

The Apology for Raymond Sebond. Translated by Donald M. Frame in *The Philosophy of the 16th and 17th Centuries*, edited by Richard H. Popkin. Toronto: Collier-Macmillan, 1966, pp. 70–81. Readings in the History of Philosophy series, general editors: Paul Edwards and Richard H. Popkin.

10. CHARRON

Of Wisdom. Translated by Samson Lennard. London: Edward Blount & William Aspley, 1608, bk. 2, ch. 2, pars [1], [5–7]. Translation revised by José R. Maia Neto.

11. SANCHEZ

That Nothing Is Known. Introduction, notes, and bibliography by Elaine Limbrick. Translation by Douglas Thomson. Cambridge: Cambridge University Press, 1988, pp. 195–204, 289–90.

12. BACON

Of the Dignity and Advancement of Learning in *The Works of F. Bacon*. Edited by James Spedding, Robert L. Ellis, and Douglas D. Heath. London: Longman and Co., 1858, vol. 5, bk. 5, ch. 2, v. 4, pp. 411–13.

Novum Organum in *The Works of F. Bacon*. Edited by James Spedding, Robert L. Ellis, and Douglas D. Heath. London: Longman and Co., 1858, v. 4, pars. 67 and 126, pp. 68–69, 111–12.

13. GASSENDI

Exercises against the Aristotelians (selections). Translated and edited by Craig B. Brush in *The Selected Works of Pierre Gassendi*. London and New York: Johnson Reprint, 1972), bk. 2, exercise 5—That proof, as it is commonly defined, does not exist, Article 4: Nor is there any "difference" in the Aristotelian sense of the word, pp. 68–74.

Syntagama philosophicum. The Logic (selections). Edited and translated by Craig B. Brush in
The Selected Works of Pierre Gassendi. London and New York: Johnson Reprint, 1972,
bk. II, pp. 341–49 (selection from ch. 5) and 362–64 (selection from ch. 6).

14. LA MOTHE LE VAYER

Of Divinity. Translated by Richard A. Watson from the original French published in *Dialogues
faits à l'imitation des anciens*. Paris: Fayard, 1988, pp. 330–31, 350–51.
On Being Opinionated. Translated by Richard A. Watson from the original French published
in *Dialogues faits à l'imitation des anciens*. Paris: Fayard, 1988, pp. 378–79, 384–86.

15. DESCARTES

Meditations on First Philosophy. Edited by Richard H. Popkin and translated by John Veitch
in *The Philosophy of the 16th and 17th Centuries*. Toronto: Collier-Macmillan, 1966, pp.
129–34, 141–43, 153–54, 172–73. Readings in the History of Philosophy series, general
editors: Paul Edwards and Richard H. Popkin.

16. PASCAL

Pensées (selections). Translated by W. F. Trotter in Pascal, *Selections*. Edited by Richard H.
Popkin. New York: Macmillan, 1989, fragments La 131 and La 835, pp. 62–66, 211–13,
263.
Preface to the Treatise on the Vacuum. Translated by Richard H. Popkin, in Pascal, *Selections*.
Edited by Richard H. Popkin (New York: Macmillan, 1989), pp. 62–66.

17. GLANVILL

Essays on Several Important Subjects in Philosophy and Religion. Reprint of the London,
1676 edition. Hildesheim: Olms, 1979, pp. 47–50, 20–21.

18. FOUCHER

Critique [of Nicolas Malebranche's] of the Search for the Truth. Translated by Richard A.
Watson. Journal of the History of Philosophy Monograph Series. Carbondale and
Edwardsville: Southern Illinois University Press, 1995, pp. 16–17, 30, 38.
*Dissertation on the Search for the Truth, with an apology for the Academics, where it is shown
that their manner of philosophizing is the most useful to religion, and the most in agree-
ment with good sense*. Paris Estienne Michallet, 1687, pp. 75–83, 122–23. Translated by
José R. Maia Neto.

19. HUET

An Essay concerning the Weakness of Human Understanding. Translated by Edward Combe. London: Matthew de Varenne, 1725, bk. 1, pp. 19–22, 25–28, 30–31, 33–36, 54–55, 59–60, 63–64, 123–24.

Against Cartesian Philosophy. Translated by Thomas M. Lennon. Amherst, NY: Humanity Books, 2003. Excerpts from ch. 1: An Exposition of Descartes' View on Doubt, and the Argument 'I am thinking, therefore I am,' pp. 68, 71–72, 75–76, 109–12.

20. LOCKE

An Essay concerning Human Understanding. Edited with an introduction by Peter H. Nidditch. Oxford: Clarendon Press, 1975, bk. 2, ch. 23, pars. 1–3; bk. 4, ch. 2, pars. 1–4, 7; ch. 3, pars. 1–6; and ch. 9, pars. 1–10,12.

21. BAYLE

Historical and Critical Dictionary: Selections. Edited and translated by Richard H. Popkin. Indianapolis: Hackett, 1991, article "Manicheans," remark D (pp. 145–52); article "Pyrrho," remarks B and C (pp. 194–206); article "Zeno of Elea," remarks G (pp. 364–65) and H (pp. 373, 377); and "Third Clarification" (pp. 422–23, 428–32).

22. LEIBNIZ

Extract from a letter written in 1675 to Foucher. Translated by Leroy E. Loemker in *The Philosophy of the 16th and 17th Centuries*, edited by Richard H. Popkin. Toronto: Collier-Macmillan, 1966, pp. 306–10. Readings in the History of Philosophy series, general editors: Paul Edwards and Richard H. Popkin.

Extract from a letter written in 1686 to Foucher. Translated by Niall Martin from C. J. Gerhardt's edition of Leibniz's *Philosophische Schriften*, vol. 1, pp. 381–82.

23. CROUSAZ

Examen du Pyrrhonisme Ancien et Moderne, 2 vols. Paris: Fayard, 2003–2004, vol. pt. 1, sec. 1, pars III, VI, and XV (pp. 24–30, 49–50). Translated by Richard A. Watson.

24. BERKELEY

Three Dialogues between Hylas and Philonous in *Philosophical Works*. Edited by Michael R. Ayers. London: Everyman, 1st ed. 1975, reissued with revisions in 1993, pp. 162–67.

25. RAMSAY

The Philosophical Principles of Natural and Revealed Religion Unfolded in a Geometrical Order. Glasgow: Robert Foulis, 1748, pp. 278–80.

26. HUME

A Treatise of Human Nature. Edited by L. A. Selby-Bigge. Oxford: Clarendon Press, 1964; 1st ed., 1888), bk. 1 (Of the Understanding), pt. 3 (Of knowledge and probability), secs. 8 (Of the causes of belief), p. 103, and 15 (Rules by which to judge of causes and effects), p. 173; part 4 (Of the skeptical and other systems of philosophy), secs. 1 (Of skepticism with regard to reason), pp. 180–87, 2 (Of skepticism with regard to the senses), p. 187 and 7 (Conclusion of this book), pp. 265–74.

Dialogues concerning Natural Religion. Edited with an introduction by Richard H. Popkin. Indianapolis/Cambridge: Hackett, 1980, pt. 12, pp. 81–82, 88–89.

27. VOLTAIRE

"Soul," in *Philosophical Dictionary*, translated by Peter Gay. New York: Basic Books, 1962, pp. 63–71. Used with permission of Peter Gay.

28. DIDEROT

Encyclopédie in *Oeuvres Completes.* Critical and annotated edition by John Lough and Jacques Proust. Paris: Hermann, 1976, vol. 8, pp. 138–60, article "Pyrrhonienne ou Sceptique."

29. ROUSSEAU

Émile or Education. Translated by Barbara Foxley (London: J. M. Dent and Toronto: E. P. Dutton, 1911), bk. 4, "The Creed of a Savoyard Priest," pp. 228–32, 234, 236, 239.

30. KANT

Critique of Pure Reason. Translated by J. M. D. Meiklejohn. London: J. M. Dent and New York: E. P. Dutton, 1950, 1st ed. 1934, preface to the first edition (1781), pp. 1–2.

Prolegomena to Any Future Metaphysics. Translated and edited by Gary Hatfield. Cambridge: Cambridge University Press, 1997, preface, pp. 5–10. Reprinted with the permission of Cambridge University Press.

31. SCHULZE

Aenesidemus oder uber die Fundamente der von dem Herrn Prof. Reinhold in Jena gelieferten Elementar-Philosophie; nebst einer Vertheidigung des Skepticismus gegen die Anmaasungen der Vernunft (Aenesidemus, or on the Foundations of the Elementary Philosophy Propounded in Jena by Prof. Reinhold, including a defense of Skepticism against the pretensions of the Critique of Pure Reason), first published in 1792, republished with the same pagination by the Kant Society, Neudrucke seltener philosophischer Werke, vol. 1 (Berlin, 1991), pp. 263–67, 269–72. Translated by Leonardo Alves Vieira.

32. STÄUDLIN

Geschichte und Geist der Skepticismus, vorzüglich in Rücksicht auf Moral und Religion (History and Spirit of Skepticism, especially with respect to religion and morals), 2 vols. Leipzig: 1794, "Introduction: On the Spirit, Types, Sources, Effects, and History of Skepticism and Means of Opposing It." Translated by Rosemary Boch and revised by John Christian Laursen.

33. HEGEL

Phenomenology of Spirit. Translated by A. V. Miller. Oxford: Oxford University Press, 1977, secs. 202–206, pp. 123–26.

The Encyclopaedia Logic: Part 1 of the Encyclopaedia of Philosophical Sciences with the Zusätze, translated by T. F. Geraets, W. A. Suchting, and H. S. Harris (Indianapolis: Hackett Publishing Company, 1991), pp. 128–31. Conception and Division of Logic, par. 81, (β), (1) and Addition 2. Copyright © 1991 by Theodore F. Geraets, W. A. Suchting, H. S. Harris. Reprinted by permission of Hackett Publishing Company. All rights reserved.

34. KIERKEGAARD

Fear and Trembling. Edited and translated by Howard V. Hong and Edna H. Hong. Princeton, NJ: Princeton University Press, 1983, preface, pp. 5–8. Selection from Søren Kierkegaard, *Kierkegaard's Writings, VI.* © 1983 Princeton University Press. Reprinted by permission of Princeton University Press.

Philosophical Fragments. Translated by Howard V. Hong and Edna H. Hong. Princeton, NJ: Princeton University Press, 1985, interlude, pp. 81–86. Selection from Søren Kierkegaard, *Concluding Unscientific Postscript to Philosophical Fragments (2 vols.)* © 1992 Princeton University Press. Reprinted by permission of Princeton University Press.

Concluding Unscientific Postscript by Søren Kierkegaard. Translated by David F. Swenson and Walter Lowrie. Princeton, NJ: Princeton University Press, 1974, pp. 182–89. © 1941 Princeton University Press, 1969 renewed. Reprinted by permission of Princeton University Press.

35. NIETZSCHE

Texts extracted from the Web site http://turn.to/nietzsche.

36. JAMES

"The Will to Believe" in *Essays on Faith and Morals*, selected by Ralph Barton Perry. Chicago: Meridian Books, 1962, pp. 42–48.

37. SANTAYANA

Skepticism and Animal Faith: Introduction to a System of Philosophy. New York: Dover, 1955, pp. 6–10, 34–41, 186.

38. SHESTOV

In Job's Balances: On the Sources of the Eternal Truths. Translated from German by Camilla Coventry and C. A. Macartney. Athens: Ohio University Press, 1975. "The Conquest of the Self-Evident; Dostoevsky's Philosophy," pp. 33–35, 42–43. Reprinted with permission of Ohio University Press, Athens, Ohio (www.ohioswallow.com).

39. WITTGENSTEIN

Zettel. Edited by G. E. M. Anscombe and G. H. von Wright, translated by G. E. M. Anscombe. Berkeley: University of California Press, 1967, pars. 394–408, pp. 70–73.

40. RUSSELL

Human Knowledge: Its Scope and Limits. London: George Allen and Unwin Ltd., 1961; 1st ed., 1948, introduction, pp. 9–11, 13.

41. POPPER

"On the Sources of Knowledge and Ignorance," in *Conjectures and Refutations: The Growth of Scientific Knowledge*. London and New York: Rutledge, 1989; 1st ed., 1963, pp. 5–6, 13, 14–16, 25–26, 28–30.

42. FEYERABEND

Farewell to Reason. London: Verso, 1987, ch. 1, "Notes on Relativism," pp. 20, 39, 40, 43, 44, 45, 48, 59, 61, 72–73, 74–77, 78–79.

43. DERRIDA

Writing and Difference. Translated by A. Bass. London: Rutledge, 1978, pp. 44, 49–58.

44. POPKIN

Richard H. Popkin and Avrum Stroll. "Skepticism Today: A Debate between Avrum Stroll and Richard H. Popkin," in *Skeptical Philosophy for Everyone.* Amherst, NY: Prometheus Books, 2002, pp. 317–23.

45. FOGELIN

Text unpublished.

INTRODUCTION

"Skepticism" and "skeptic" have different meanings in philosophy and ordinary life. In common life "skeptic" often means "distrustful," usually referring to distrust of some particular kind of belief such as political views or, more often, religious convictions. This anthology, however, focuses its attention on philosophical skepticism, offering excerpts from some of the major texts of Western philosophy that deal with efforts to question the many claims that have been made regarding what can be known and how we come to have knowledge, however that term might be defined. The German philosopher Georg Wilhelm Friedrich Hegel (1770–1831) said that skepticism is the driving force of philosophical activity. This is at least one way of explaining why the editors of an anthology of skeptical texts might not wish to restrict its contents to a particular period but instead choose to cover the entire history of Western philosophy. However, skepticism has been ascribed different meanings throughout history and among various philosophers within a particular historical period. In the Hellenistic period, skepticism was a way of life. In contemporary philosophy, skepticism is an epistemological challenge to philosophers. In the writings of Hegel, skepticism represents the negation of any determined thing in the dialectical movement of the mind or spirit. In those of Schulze, Hegel's contemporary, skepticism is the triumph of Berkeley's idealism against Kant's critical philosophy.

The variety of meanings of philosophical skepticism can be divided into two kinds. The first concerns different ways skepticism has been viewed as a philosophical school. The label "skepticism" first appeared in the Hellenistic period (from the fourth to the first century BCE) naming a specific philosophical school that rivaled other schools of thought that were vying for the attention of the intellectuals of the day. These skeptics deployed a variety of arguments and techniques to expose what they considered the rashness of dogmatists (Stoics, Epicureans, Aristotelians, etc.) who pretended to have found or established the truth. The members of this school of skeptics no doubt differed among themselves regarding methodological subtleties or even about their broader objectives. And it is equally without doubt that their philosophical adversaries harbored divergent attitudes toward these skeptics and their intentions. Yet from the Hellenistic period to the present, philosophers have adapted the methods of skepticism to the particular philosophical questions and puzzles they ponder. (It appears that the only historical time during which apparently there was no philosopher who considered himself or herself as belonging to a skeptical tradition is the medieval period. However, our knowledge of skepticism in medieval philosophy has grown dramatically in the last few years, which could bode well for discovering a branch of skepticism even during this period.)

The second way of viewing philosophical skepticism is as an epistemological position. Here, too, the ways of construing the position are diverse, but we can say, roughly, that skepticism is the philosophical position that challenges our ability to know either something specific—for instance, the existence of God, or some kind of domain such as religion, which is a restricted kind of skepticism—or anything at all—what is called general or universal skepticism. Of course these two kinds of philosophical skepticism (historical and epistemological) overlap. Basically, a philosopher who sees himself or herself as belonging to the skeptical tradition also holds an epistemological skeptical position of some sort. The contrary, however, is not usually the case. A philosopher may advance a skeptical argument in order to investigate epistemological issues, in particular, in order to show how skepticism can be either refuted or avoided. Even if such a philosopher advocates or expresses a skeptical position, he or she may be unaware of the skeptical tradition, although this possibility tends to diminish with our growing knowledge of the role of skepticism in the history of philosophy.

The main focus of this anthology is not that of skepticism as an epistemological problem. For this we refer the reader to Landesman and Meeks 2003 (see bibliography), who edited an anthology containing some texts of the skeptical tradition but mainly those which give the historical background for contemporary epistemological skeptical problems. The focus of the present anthology is on skepticism as a philosophical tradition. All texts of the philosophers here included, with four exceptions—one ancient, one modern, and two contemporary—not only deal with skeptical issues, but also relate them to previous philosophers in the skeptical tradition.

The first exception is Plato, who does not refer to a previous skeptical tradition because this tradition begins only after him. He is included in the anthology because some of his dialogues, in particular the *Theaetetus*, are crucial for the later development of Hellenistic and modern skepticism. The *Theaetetus* contains Plato's main statement of Socrates' *maieutics* (dialectical method—from the Greek word for *midwife*). Socrates' philosophical practice, claiming to hold no views of his own, but only to submit the views of others to rational criticism, is crucial for the later development of ancient skepticism. Socrates' learned ignorance and *maieutics* is the main source of Academic skepticism and a major influence for such outstanding philosophers such as Michel de Montaigne, Søren Kierkegaard, and Karl Popper. Second, the *Theaetetus* presents a detailed discussion of perceptual knowledge, examining issues that become crucial in the skeptical tradition, such as relativism and sense illusions, and raising the problem of distinguishing veridical wakeful experiences from illusory dream-induced ones.

The second exception is René Descartes. Although there is no reference to the skeptical tradition in Descartes's selection (from the *Meditations*) included in this anthology, Descartes does build on the skeptical tradition and acknowledges this in his *Second*, *Third*, and *Fifth Replies* to the *Objections to the Meditations*. Moreover, Descartes's use of skepticism and the skeptical arguments he construes are crucial for the subsequent history of the skeptical tradition—as they are to the whole history of modern and contemporary philosophy.

The two other exceptions are Ludwig Wittgenstein and Bertrand Russell. They are very important in the construction of—and attempts to solve—the skeptical problem in contemporary analytic philosophy. Furthermore, the first has been interpreted as related in a variety of ways to previous skeptics and models of skepticism (Watson 1969, Kripke 1982, Sousa Filho 1996, De Pierris 1996) and the second was one of the most eminent exponents of contemporary religious skepticism.

There were two schools of ancient skepticism, the Pyrrhonian and the Academic. Only the Pyrrhonians called themselves skeptics, but since the Academics also exhibited a general suspension of judgment (*epoché*), their philosophy is also considered skeptic. Although the Academic skeptics claimed that the "skeptical" tradition began before Socrates with Democritus, Anaxagoras, and Empedocles (Cicero *Academica* 1.44), these philosophers—like Plato—should be considered as sources of the skeptical tradition and not as skeptics themselves. Their philosophies contained elements—the main one being criticism of sense knowledge—which were skeptically interpreted during the Hellenistic period. Ancient and contemporary sources attribute the beginning of the skeptical tradition to Pyrrho of Elis (ca. 360–274 BCE). According to our sources, Pyrrho wrote nothing. We know about him and his philosophy only through other ancient sources, some of whom were his contemporaries, such as his disciple Timon of Phlius (ca. 325–235 BCE), and others from the later Hellenistic and post-Hellenistic periods. Most of these sources were collected by Diogenes Laertius (third century CE) who used them in a chapter on Pyrrho in his *Lives of Eminent Philosophers*. Laertius's text has been the most influential source for Pyrrho's philosophy. It contains a number of anecdotes that have contributed to the view that skepticism—at least Pyrrhonian skepticism—is not a philosophy viable in ordinary life. This view was first raised by the Stoics and Epicureans, then by Descartes, Blaise Pascal, David Hume, and a number of other modern philosophers, and has been renewed in an influential article by Myles Burnyeat (1980). An extremist version of this kind of antiskepticism is represented in the present anthology by a selection from Jean-Pierre Crousaz (1663–1750). Pyrrho is depicted as a man in constant need of being accompanied by friends (presumably not skeptics) to divert him from dangerous cliffs, since he doubted his own sense perceptions. Other anecdotes underline—probably exaggerating and caricaturing—Pyrrho's indifference. One source relates that he could suffer the cut of a surgeon's knife without frowning (*Lives* 9.67). Pyrrho's control over his body, together with other aspects of his skepticism and life, such as the fact that he traveled with Alexander the Great to India where he met Eastern wise men (*Lives* 9.61), has led to the view that his skepticism has Hindu and Buddhist threads among its sources (Flintoff 1980). This interpretation of the origins of Pyrrho's skepticism has been criticized by Bett (2000) in favor of Western sources, including Plato's *Theaetetus* (Bett 2000). Whatever the case, it at least shows that there were forms of skepticism in India both before and at the time when it began to develop as a school of philosophical thought in the Hellenistic world.

The proliferation of a number of conflicting philosophical schools during the Hellenistic period created an intellectual environment fertile for the development of skeptical views. The doctrines held by the members of one school were challenged by the members of a rival one and vice versa, leading to wide-scale criticism of philosophical doctrines. By the time of Pyrrho, the Academy founded by Plato became skeptical when Arcesilaus of Pitane (316–241 BCE) became its head. Arcesilaus struggled with Zeno of Citium (ca. 335–ca. 263 BCE), the founder of Stoicism, who proposed as the criterion of truth what he called the cognitive impression: an impression caused by a real object and exactly like this object. This led Arcesilaus to develop a number of skeptical arguments—such as the dream argument—in order to challenge the existence and discernability of such an impression, in the absence of which the wise man would have to suspend judgment to avoid assenting to what could be false. Academic skepticism has been mainly interpreted as parasitic on Stoicism (Couissin [1929] was the first proponent of this view), and skepticism generally (whether Academic or Pyrrhonian) has been widely interpreted as parasitic on dogmatic philosophy—see for instance the selection from Popkin in this volume. The main Academic notions—inapprehensibility, *epoché*, probability (an important notion introduced by another later Academic: Carneades [ca. 217–129 BCE])—are, according to this view, dialectically derived from Stoicism, implying no commitment from the Academic philosopher to any doctrine whatsoever, that is, according to this interpretation the Academic skeptic holds no position at all. Ioppolo (1986) has contested this view, holding that the Academic skeptics did hold positions of their own, such as the views of the obscurity of things and that to avoid error is more important than to find the truth. These positions did not commit the Academics to dogmatism because they did not give assent to them as true.

Returning to Pyrrho, there is no attested continuity of his skepticism in the period ranging from his and his follower Timon's deaths up to Aenesidemus of Cnossos (ca. 100–40 BCE), who founded a skeptical philosophical school and traced it two hundred years back to Pyrrho. This was the moment the term "skepticism" was first associated with the school, which was then called skeptical or Pyrrhonian. The works of Aenesidemus disappeared, but those of another Pyrrhonian, Sextus Empiricus (ca. 200 CE), have survived. In the first chapters of the first book of his *Outlines of Pyrrhonism*, Sextus reports how one becomes a skeptic or Pyrrhonian (PH 1.12). Disturbed by the perception of some anomaly in things, the philosopher begins to examine them in order to determine what is true and what is false. This investigation is the *zetesis*, which originates the name skeptic (*skepticos*). Sextus's skepticism thus appears different from Pyrrho's since investigation is basic in his modality of skepticism. The investigation does not end with the inquirer finding the truth (which is what the skeptics technically call "dogmatism"), but in a situation of equipollence between the doctrines or phenomena examined (that is, one doctrine does not appear as more credible than a conflicting one) and so, unable to assent to either of them, the Pyrrhonian suspends judgment (*epoché*). Contrary to the initial perspective of getting rid of the disturbance by finding the truth, it is when the inquirer suspends judgment that he or she finds the tranquility being sought. Sextus Empiricus was a doctor. His skepticism is therapeutic—it aims at curing one from the disease the skeptics called dogmatism, a disturbance that arises from affirmative or negative judgments about the nature of things. While this concern with tranquility was specifically Pyrrhonian, followers of this school and Academic skeptics charged the dogmatic philosophers with failing to remain committed to the rational standards of philosophical inquiry. They were accused of arriving too quickly at a conclusion, before a fuller consideration could be made of the issues involved, and are prejudiced by previous commitments to the doctrines of some particular school. The skeptics, on the contrary, consciously rejecting any such commitment, can engage in a more rigorous rational inquiry. This is a basic feature of the skeptical tradition, present in Socrates' *maieutics*, Descartes's first methodical rule ("carefully to avoid precipitate conclusions and preconceptions" [Descartes 1985, 2:120]), and Popper's critical rationalism.

Skepticism as a living philosophical tradition disappears during the Middle Ages. This is not to say that the tradition was not known and discussed, and even less that skepticism as a philosophical problem was not an issue. Although Pyrrhonian skepticism was little known, medieval scholars were aware of Academic skepticism through Cicero's works and those of the Church Fathers, in particular through Lactantius (ca. 260–323), who makes an apologetic use of Academic skepticism in book 3 of his *Divine Institutes*, and Augustine (383–430), later bishop of Hippo, who was close to Academic skepticism before converting to Christianity. Skepticism becomes a major philosophical issue in late scholasticism, above all after William of Ockham's (ca. 1280–1349) view of the radical contingency of the created world and that one can have intuitive cognition of objects that do not exist. This led to the skeptical views on causality held by Ockham's follower Nicholas of Autrecourt (ca. 1300–1350) and discussions about the possibility that God causes illusions or even violates logical principles in the writings of Jean de Mirecourt, Pierre d'Ailly, Gregory of Rimini, and Gabriel Biel. These discussions probably played a role in the reappraisal of skepticism by Montaigne and in the development of modern skepticism by Descartes (Gregory 1974, Funkenstein 1987).

The interest in ancient skepticism grew considerably during the Renaissance (1300–1600). A number of cultural factors favored the dissemination of this ancient philosophy throughout the fifteenth century, particularly Pyrrhonism. First, Sextus's ancient skeptical texts contain much information about a large number of ancient philosophical schools—in particular from the Hellenistic period—which Humanist scholars were eager to recover (Granada 2001, Floridi 2002). Second, the cultural impact in Europe caused by the encounter with the indigenous communities of the new world was the shattering of medieval certainties. Religious, moral, and political beliefs considered as natural and necessary in any human society in Europe were totally ignored in these recently discovered societies without any damage to their proper functioning. Cultural relativism was skeptically exploited by the ancient Pyrrhonians, who adopted as one of their modes of suspension of judgment the conflict of different customs, beliefs, and laws held in different societies. A third factor was the crisis of Aristotelianism and the rejection of authority in philosophy. Philosophers opposing Aristotelian philosophy could find in the Academic and Pyrrhonian sources skeptical arguments against dogmatism in general and specific arguments against particular kinds of dogmatism that could easily be turned against Aristotelianism. Moreover, philosophical freedom and independence from authority were valued by the Academic skeptics, who exhibited them in their philosophical practice. A fourth factor, associated with the crisis of Aristotelianism, was the development of a religiously motivated anti-intellectualism in the Renaissance, a spiritual Christian renewal whose main manifestation was the Reformation of the sixteenth century. This movement was often associated with the rejection of scholastic learning, the view that true piety is not achieved through science. The valuation of primitive Christianity against scholastic science and learning "pedantism" led some to interpret ancient skepticism as a philosophy fitted to combat intellectual pride and worldly learning, indirectly favoring Christian humility and piety. A fifth factor that contributed specifically to making ancient Pyrrhonism a living issue at the time was the intellectual crisis caused by the Reformation. This established a religious controversy over the rule of faith, disputed by Roman Catholics and Reformers, introducing in the religious field the Pyrrhonian exposition of the conflict of philosophies and the difficulty of deciding what is true given the existence of conflicting views on the very criterion of truth that might decide the controversy. Finally, and as a consequence of the previous, the translation into Latin and the publication of Sextus's works by Henri Estienne in 1562 and Gentien Hervet in 1569 greatly increased the diffusion and influence of Pyrrhonian skepticism during the late sixteenth and the seventeenth centuries. These factors contributed in varying degrees to the discussion and reappraisal of ancient skepticism by, among others, Desiderius Erasmus (1467–1536), Gianfrancesco Pico della Mirandola (1469–1533), Cornelius Agripa de Nettesheim (1486–1535), Juan Luis Vives (1493–1540), Omer Talon (ca. 1510–1562), Sebastian Castellio (1515–1563), Michel de Montaigne (1533–1592), Pierre Charron (1541–1603), Francisco Sanches (1551–1623), Pedro de Valencia (1555–1620?), and Francis Bacon (1561–1626). The influence of skepticism in the Renaissance was not limited to philosophy and religion. It was also present in literature, as recently shown in France by Emanuel Naya (forthcoming) and in England by Hamlin (2005). Because the present anthology covers the whole history of Western philosophy, we could include only the most influential of these Renaissance figures who dealt with skepticism.

Of those who reappraised skepticism in the Renaissance, Montaigne was the one who most integrally adopted a skeptical viewpoint, who explored most deeply the philosophical challenges posed by the ancient skeptics, and who was by far the most influential in modern and contemporary philosophy. In the longest and most philosophical of his essays, "The Apology for Raymond Sebond," Montaigne builds on Pyrrhonian (Sextus's) and Academic (Cicero's and Plutarch's) skeptical texts to develop a thorough skepticism. He dethrones reason from the place where the philosophical dogmatic tradition had put it. Rather than a trustful instrument to find the truth, reason is "an instrument of lead and of wax, stretchable, pliable, and adaptable to all biases and all measures" (Montaigne 1965, 425). Reappraising the flux doctrine exhibited in Plato's *Theaetetus* and *Cratylus*, Montaigne holds that our reason like everything else except God, is constantly changing. Whatever human reason establishes, this is always from a particular situation, contingent and precarious. Human beings impose their form on everything they deal with so that we cannot claim to have knowledge of the things themselves, independently of how they appear to us in particular and constantly moving states. Montaigne further says that this happens with his own *Essays*, which reflect his own mutability, in which one would look in vain for coherence. This has led some contemporary readers to interpret Montaigne's skepticism as a precursor of postmodern skepticism, in particular of Jacques Derrida's deconstructionism (see Derrida's [1930–2004] selection in this volume in which Montaigne appears as a source): reason is remitted to the order of contingency, the great traditional philosophical doctrines about the soul and reason are "deconstructed," the very text is self-deconstructed with the denial of authorial presence as a center of unity and meaning.

Some early modern thinkers, often called "libertines" (Pintard 2000), were quite influenced by Montaigne's skepticism. Some of them, La Mothe Le Vayer (1588–1672), for example, considered themselves to be genuine skeptics. They saw that if reason was impotent to construe philosophical systems, it was quite apt to destroy not only philosophical but also religious systems. Despite the "fideistic" claims of Montaigne and most other Renaissance and early modern thinkers who revived ancient skepticism ("fideism" is an anachronistic term but catches well one of the main justifications for the reappraisal of skepticism in the period: the elimination of all human belief in order to make room for supernatural faith), the skeptical criticism of the sciences and of reason allowed the emancipation of the latter from traditional dogmatic philosophies (mainly Aristotle's) and the rejection of any form of authority over reason and belief. This was of course easily extended to the criticism of every form of religion, including Christianity. Unlike ancient skepticism—Academic and Pyrrhonian—which was neutral with respect to religion (for they fought rational theology but respected cultural or state religion), early modern skepticism derived from Montaigne (or having Montaigne's views as its main source) had, therefore, both a religious and an antireligious use. These contrary uses of skepticism in the seventeenth century reappeared in a more sophisticated and passionate way in the nineteenth century with the philosophies of Kierkegaard (1813–1855) and Friedrich Nietzsche (1844–1900). Both were aware of the ancient, Renaissance, and modern skeptical tradition, which they rehearsed, reacting to recent philosophical developments (post-Kantian German philosophy). The results were arguably the most forceful cases ever constructed in the history of philosophy for Christian (Kierkegaard's) and anti-Christian (Nietzsche's) skepticism.

The most influential philosopher in the skeptical tradition was not a skeptic himself. René Descartes (1596–1650) endeavored to fight the skepticism of his time but belonged to this intellectual movement of self-liberation through doubt that occurred in the early part of the seventeenth century. He drank from the same sources (Montaigne and Pierre Charron, [1541–1603]) as did libertine skeptics such as La Mothe Le Vayer, but not in view of developing a skeptical criticism of Christianity as a revealed religion—this would be one of the tasks of the skeptic David Hume (1711–1776)—but in view of founding a new philosophy. Building on Charron (Popkin 1954, Maia Neto 2003), Descartes doubted what were believed to be sources of knowledge in order to recover the integrity of the intellect untainted by any previous beliefs and worked out the difference between philosophy and theology in order to keep philosophy free and autonomous to develop along strictly rational lines.

Descartes accepted the Academic view revived by Charron that truth is hidden, but not the view that to avoid error is more important than to find the truth. To get this truth, grounding his new natural philosophy on an unshakable metaphysical certainty, Descartes radicalized skeptical doubt to a point never reached by previous skeptics. He doubted the existence of an external material world, including his own body with its senses. Most scholars on ancient and modern skepticism agree that the ancient skeptics did not entertain such a radical doubt (Burnyeat 1982, and for a dissenting view, Groarke 1991). Descartes himself oscillates between affirming that he differs from the ancient skeptics merely in using skeptical arguments to achieve certainty and in saying that his more skeptical argument (the deceiver) is really original. In the First Meditation and in other works, Descartes argues that in order to know that the sense perceptions we have at any given time may possibly be true (that is, be caused by real material objects outside our minds), we must first be certain that we are not dreaming, that these perceptions are not dream perceptions. The difficulty is that we cannot be certain that our most clear and vivid sense perceptions are awake perceptions because we may have dream perceptions as vivid and clear as the awake ones. This argument already appears in the ancients, in Plato's *Theaetetus*, in Cicero's *Academics*, in Sextus's *Outlines*, and in Montaigne's *Essays*, but it is not clear that in all these cases the argument challenges the existence of an external material world, even if they can be reconstructed by contemporary interpreters as having this implication. Descartes added the argument that we cannot exclude the possibility that the simplest mental operations we ordinarily experience are caused by a powerful evil genius who can deceive us in instances in which we are absolutely convinced of being right, such as when we add 2 plus 2. Besides reinforcing the dream argument—all our perceptions of an external material world may be mere illusions caused by this powerful deceiver—the argument also puts in doubt all purely rational knowledge. The goal of Descartes with these arguments is to establish a real distinction between the mind and the body. The fact that the body can be doubted but the mind cannot (for the doubting of the body is an action of the mind), that the mind is therefore directly known (unlike the body), and that it is ontologically independent from the body (for we can have a clear and distinct conception of the mind in abstraction of anything belonging to the body) allows Descartes to ground his view that the physical world is deprived of any secondary qualities such as tastes, colors, etc. (which belong to the mind), thereby justifying a purely mechanical and mathematical new science. The skeptical price of this effort was soon exploited by post-Cartesian philosophers. Descartes's main legacy was not the elimination of skepticism from philosophy and science but a much more fundamental doubt. How can we be sure that there is an external material world if we have no access to this world except through the very perceptions put in doubt by the skeptical scenarios?

This problem dominates a considerable part of post-Cartesian philosophy to this day. Some of the first critics of Descartes—Joseph Glanvill (1636–1680), Pierre-Daniel Huet (1630–1721), Simon Foucher (1644–1696), Gottfried Wilhelm Leibniz (1646–1716), and Pierre Bayle (1647–1706)—built on Cartesian doubt to renovate and enforce the ancient and pre-Cartesian skeptical tradition. The selections from John Locke (1632–1704), George Berkeley (1685–1753), and David Hume (1711–1776) included here show that late seventeenth-century Cartesian skepticism and Pierre Gassendi's (1592–1655) mitigated skepticism played a very important role in the development of British empiricism (Lennon 1993).

It was mainly through the British empiricists that skepticism remained a major philosophical force during the Enlightenment, despite the belief in human progress during this period. François-Marie Arouet de Voltaire (1694–1778), Denis Diderot (1713–1784), Jean-Jacques Rousseau (1712–1778), and Marie-Jean-Antoine-Nicolas de Caritat, marquis de Condorcet (1743–1794) combined anti-Cartesian skeptical views—often inspired in Gassendi and Locke—with their criticism of superstition and revealed religion. Skepticism was a major issue in German philosophy when Immanuel Kant (1724–1804) was awakened from his dogmatic slumber by Hume's skepticism about induction and the exterior world and developed his critical philosophy, which led immediately to skeptical reactions in Germany, for example, by Gottlob Schulze (1761–1833). The greatest Western philosophers—Plato, Descartes, Kant, and Wittgenstein—who not only were not skeptics, but who according to many scholars combated different kinds of skepticism, were crucial for the continuity, renewal, and strengthening of the skeptical tradition.

The problem of the external world raised by Descartes is the main epistemological problem tackled by contemporary Anglo-American analytical epistemologists. Some—the minority—are contemporary epistemological skeptics in the sense that for them this problem cannot be resolved. These upholders of skepticism usually employ an arsenal of sophisticated philosophical analyses to strengthen or reconstruct Descartes's and Hume's doubt about the possibility of rationally justifying the existence of a world external to the mind and Hume's doubt about the possibility of rationally justifying the derivation of effects from causes (i.e., the problem of induction). Barry Stroud's defense of the cogency of the Cartesian dream argument (among others) in his *The Significance of Philosophical Skepticism* (Oxford 1984) and Robert

Fogelin's analysis of contemporary epistemology as failing to reply to Descartes's and Hume's skeptical arguments (see Fogelin's text in this anthology) have been a major challenge to contemporary epistemologists. The skeptical arguments have been updated. Contemporary skeptical literature rarely mentions the possibility of a deceiver God or an evil genius. Instead they offer science-fiction scenarios like the one exhibited in the movie *Matrix Revolutions* to raise the possibility of global illusion; for example, the possibility of a brain being kept in a vat hooked up to a computer supplying this brain with all experiences we ordinarily have.

Most contemporary epistemologists reject skepticism, although this usually does not translate into actual refutations of the skeptical arguments. The foundational Cartesian-type of response to skepticism is out of fashion. It has been replaced by "linguistic" kinds of response, reflecting the linguistic turn in contemporary philosophy, for which Wittgenstein (1889–1951) is chiefly responsible. These are some of the main arguments offered against skepticism: that the skeptical position involves a performative contradiction (Apel 1987), usually of a linguistic kind; that the skeptic's standards of knowledge and certainty are beyond scientific and ordinary practice and therefore should be ignored by the philosopher; and that skeptical scenarios such as Descartes's or that exhibited in the movie *Matrix Revolutions*, although possible, are not relevant in most ordinary cognitive situations and therefore should be disregarded. These responses to skepticism strike more at practical aspects of skepticism than at the skeptical arguments themselves. One basic practical presupposition of skepticism—which we can already identify in the *Theaetetus* and which becomes crucial above all in the Academic skeptical tradition—is directly challenged by many antiskeptical contemporary philosophers. They, often influenced by William James's (1842–1910) pragmatist reply to skepticism, contest the skeptic's strict commitment to intellectual integrity, that is, to the view that assent should be given only to what is fully warranted by reason. A contemporary original and influential answer to skepticism, that provided by Stanley Cavell (1979), challenges precisely this commitment. The skeptical quest for certainty about the existence of an external material world and of other minds is interpreted by Cavell as a lack of acknowledgment of the world and others. Cavell's views on skepticism, as Derrida's deconstruction, have greatly influenced literary studies.

Wishing to keep this anthology to a manageable size, we were unable to include every skeptical trend in contemporary philosophy. The same limitation holds, of course, for the other periods of the history of philosophy, to say nothing of non-Western traditions. We have attempted to compensate for some of the lacunae by adding a comprehensive bibliography of the most significant philosophers (given our present knowledge) connected with the skeptical tradition. In the bibliography we have also included skeptical works by other philosophers who also belong to the skeptical tradition but could not be included in the volume. The bibliography also contains a significant number of studies of the philosophers included in the anthology and general studies on ancient, Renaissance, early modern, and eighteenth- and nineteenth-century skepticism. We have given priority to publications in English but hope to have also included the most relevant publications in Italian and French. There is an amazing number of studies that demonstrate the historical vitality of the skeptical tradition. This is occurring worldwide, covers all periods of the history of philosophy, and relates a tremendous number of philosophers to the skeptical tradition, both the main figures already known for other philosophical interests and lesser-known figures who remained little known precisely because there were more visible skeptics and so were considered not entitled to figure in the canon of the history of philosophy.

Several reasons indicate that in the near future philosophical skepticism will no longer be viewed chiefly as an abstract epistemological position, but as a dynamic and fertile tradition in Western—and perhaps also in Eastern—philosophy, running almost without interruption from ancient times to the present.

The first reason is that some contemporary epistemologists are realizing that the skeptical questions they deal with have a long history, the knowledge of which can only help them understand and find solutions to contemporary philosophical problems. Robert Fogelin's work in North America and Porchat Pereira's in Brazil are eminent illustrations of this direction.

Second, scholarship on ancient skepticism has been quite intense since the 1970s and has been carried out by scholars well trained in analytical philosophy. Not only have they interpreted ancient skepticism in its historical context, they have also brought to light its philosophical value and relevance to modern and contemporary epistemological and ethical debates.

Third, there is an increasing number of studies showing the relevance of skeptical issues in a number of medieval philosophers, in particular in the late Scholastics. These studies tend to spread to other medieval philosophers from different periods of scholasticism.

Finally, recent studies of the skeptical arguments and views in Descartes and Hume are increasingly taking in account other varieties of skepticism in antiquity and modernity. The present expansion of scholarship on early modern skepticism will sooner or later lead to the recognition that modern skepticism cannot be reduced to "Cartesian" and "Humean" skepticism, concepts that will be revised with our better understanding of the skeptical roots and connections of Descartes and Hume.

The bibliography and the texts—which give the primary material for most of the philosophers whose views have been examined by contemporary scholarship on skepticism—gathered in this volume attest well to the tremendous shift that has taken place in the historiography of skepticism since Richard Popkin began, almost sixty years ago, his inquiry on whether there was a connection between Hume and Sextus. Today we have not only a good picture of the skeptical stream that runs from Sextus to Hume—to a large extent thanks to Popkin's research and the conferences and books he organized—but also from Plato to Sextus and from Hume to Wittgenstein and Derrida. It is sad that Popkin passed away before the completion of this anthology, the main condition for which—the worldwide research that began in the 1960s after the publication of the first edition of his *History of Skepticism* and which continues to grow—he was greatly responsible.

1

PLATO

It may appear strange that a skeptical anthology begins with Plato (ca. 428–347 BCE). Indeed, very few today, after a long and influential tradition of reading Plato's dialogues under the influence of Neoplatonism, would associate Plato's philosophy with any form of skepticism. Our perception of Plato is, however, quite different from the ancients', in particular during the Hellenistic period when the issue of whether Plato was a skeptic philosopher was a living one. The view of Plato's philosophy as more skeptical than dogmatic was held by eminent philosophers in the seventeenth century such as Descartes and, in particular, by early modern skeptics such as Montaigne and Foucher. The skeptical reading of Plato was favored by some of the dialogues, in particular the aporetic early ones (*Laches, Lysis, Euthypro*), in which Socrates appears questioning his interlocutors on the nature of courage, friendship, piety, etc., without arriving at any conclusion. The character of Socrates, both in his conception of human wisdom as awareness of ignorance and in his practice of helping others to achieve this awareness, was one of the most important influences on Hellenistic skepticism, in particular in its Academic version, and also in various versions of modern skepticism, from Charron's through Kierkegaard's to Popper's. The passages of the two texts here underline Socrates' practical attitude toward philosophy, which is foundational for the skeptical standpoint. In the *Theaetetus*, a crucial dialogue for those who read Plato as a kind of skeptic, we see not only the theory and practice of Socrates' attitude, but also the examination of sense knowledge and the epistemological problems it poses, including the first known version of the skeptical dream argument. Plato's association of these kinds of skeptical problems with Heraclitism and Protagoreanism was also important in the later development of ancient and modern skepticism.

FROM PLATO'S *APOLOGY**

[20c] Now perhaps someone might rejoin: "But, Socrates, what is the trouble about you? Whence have these prejudices against you arisen? For certainly this great report and talk has not arisen while you were doing nothing more out of the way than the rest, unless you were doing something other than most people; [20d] so tell us what it is,

---

*Editorial notes were omitted.

that we may not act unadvisedly in your case." The man who says this seems to me to be right, and I will try to show you what it is that has brought about my reputation and aroused the prejudice against me. So listen. And perhaps I shall seem to some of you to be joking; be assured, however, I shall speak perfect truth to you.

The fact is, men of Athens, that I have acquired this reputation on account of nothing else than a sort of wisdom. What kind of wisdom is this? Just that which is perhaps human wisdom. For perhaps I really am wise in this wisdom; [20e] and these men, perhaps, of whom I was just speaking, might be wise in some wisdom greater than human, or I don't know what to say; for I do not understand it, and whoever says I do, is lying and speaking to arouse prejudice against me. And, men of Athens, do not interrupt me with noise, even if I seem to you to be boasting; for the word which I speak is not mine, but the speaker to whom I shall refer it is a person of weight. For of my wisdom—if it is wisdom at all—and of its nature, I will offer you the god of Delphi as a witness. You know Chaerephon, I fancy. [21a] He was my comrade from a youth and the comrade of your democratic party, and shared in the recent exile and came back with you. And you know the kind of man Chaerephon was, how impetuous in whatever he undertook. Well, once he went to Delphi and made so bold as to ask the oracle this question; and, gentlemen, don't make a disturbance at what I say; for he asked if there were anyone wiser than I. Now the Pythia replied that there was no one wiser. And about these things his brother here will bear you witness, since Chaerephon is dead.

[21b] But see why I say these things; for I am going to tell you whence the prejudice against me has arisen. For when I heard this, I thought to myself: "What in the world does the god mean, and what riddle is he propounding? For I am conscious that I am not wise either much or little. What then does he mean by declaring that I am the wisest? He certainly cannot be lying, for that is not possible for him." And for a long time I was at a loss as to what he meant; then with great reluctance I proceeded to investigate him somewhat as follows.

[21c] I went to one of those who had a reputation for wisdom, thinking that there, if anywhere, I should prove the utterance wrong and should show the oracle "This man is wiser than I, but you said I was wisest." So examining this man—for I need not call him by name, but it was one of the public men with regard to whom I had this kind of experience, men of Athens—and conversing with him, this man seemed to me to seem to be wise to many other people and especially to himself, but not to be so; and then I tried to show him that he thought he was wise, but was not. [21d] As a result, I became hateful to him and to many of those present; and so, as I went away, I thought to myself, "I am wiser than this man; for neither of us really knows anything fine and good, but this man thinks he knows something when he does not, whereas I, as I do not know anything, do not think I do either. I seem, then, in just this little thing to be wiser than this man at any rate, that what I do not know I do not think I know either." [21e] From him I went to another of those who were reputed to be wiser than he, and these same things seemed to me to be true; and there I became hateful both to him and to many others.

After this then I went on from one to another, perceiving that I was hated, and grieving and fearing, but nevertheless I thought I must consider the god's business of the highest importance. So I had to go, investigating the meaning of the oracle, to all those who were reputed to know anything. [22a] And by the Dog, men of Athens—for I must speak the truth to you—this, I do declare, was my experience: those who had the most reputation seemed to me to be almost the most deficient, as I investigated at the god's behest, and others who were of less repute seemed to be superior men in the matter of being sensible. So I must relate to you my wandering as I performed my Herculean labors, so to speak, in order that the oracle might be proved to be irrefutable. For after the public men I went to the poets, those of tragedies, and those of dithyrambs, and the rest, [22b] thinking that there I should prove by actual test that I was less learned than they. So, taking up the poems of theirs that seemed to me to have been most carefully elaborated by them, I asked them what they meant, that I might at the same time learn something from them. Now I am ashamed to tell you the truth, gentlemen; but still it must be told. For there was hardly a man present, one might say, who would not speak better than they about the poems they themselves had composed. [22c] So again in the case of the poets also I presently recognized this, that what they composed they composed not by wisdom, but by nature and because they were inspired, like the prophets and givers of oracles; for these also say many fine things, but know none of the things they say; it was evident to me that the poets too had experienced something of this same sort. And at the same time I perceived that they, on account of their poetry, thought that they were the wisest of men in other things as well, in which they were not. So I went away from them also thinking that I was superior to them in the same thing in which I excelled the public men.

Finally then I went to the hand-workers. [22d] For I was conscious that I knew practically nothing, but I knew I should find that they knew many fine things. And in this I was not deceived; they did know what I did not, and in this way they were wiser than I. But, men of Athens, the good artisans also seemed to me to have the same failing as the poets; because of practicing his art well, each one thought he was very wise in the other most important matters, and this folly of theirs obscured that wisdom, [22e] so that I asked myself in behalf of the oracle whether I should prefer to be as I am, neither wise in their wisdom nor foolish in their folly, or to be in both respects as they are. I replied then to myself and to the oracle that it was better for me to be as I am.

[23a] Now from this investigation, men of Athens, many enmities have arisen against me, and such as are most harsh and grievous, so that many prejudices have resulted from them and I am called a wise man. For on each occasion those who are present think I am wise in the matters in which I confute someone else; but the fact is, gentlemen, it is likely that the god is really wise and by his oracle means this: "Human wisdom is of little or no value." And it appears that he does not really say this of Socrates, [23b] but merely uses my name, and makes me an example, as if lie were to say: "This one of you, O human beings, is wisest, who, like Socrates, recognizes that he is in truth of no account in respect to wisdom."

Therefore I am still even now going about and searching and investigating at the god's behest anyone, whether citizen or foreigner, who I think is wise; and when he does not seem so to me, I give aid to the god and show that he is not wise. And by reason of this occupation I have no leisure to attend to any of the affairs of the state worth mentioning, or of my own, [23c] but am in vast poverty on account of my service to the god.

And in addition to these things, the young men who have the most leisure, the sons of the richest men, accompany me of their own accord, find pleasure in hearing people being examined, and often imitate me themselves, and then they undertake to examine others; and then, I fancy, they find a great plenty of people who think they know something, but know little or nothing. As a result, therefore, those who are examined by them are angry with me, instead of being angry with themselves, and say that "Socrates is a most abominable person and is corrupting the youth."

[23d] And when anyone asks them "by doing or teaching what?" they have nothing to say, but they do not know, and that they may not seem to be at a loss, they say these things that are handy to say against all the philosophers, "the things in the air and the things beneath the earth" and "not to believe in the gods" and "to make the weaker argument the stronger." For they would not, I fancy, care to say the truth, that it is being made very clear that they pretend to know, but know nothing. Since, then, they are jealous of their honor and energetic and numerous and speak concertedly and persuasively about me, they have filled your ears both long ago and now with vehement slanders.

FROM PLATO'S *THEAETETUS**

[150b] SOC. All that is true of their art of midwifery is true also of mine, but mine differs from theirs in being practiced upon men, not women, and in lending their souls in labor, not their bodies. But the greatest thing about my art is this, [150c] that it can test in every way whether the mind of the young man is bringing forth a mere image, an imposture, or a real and genuine offspring. For I have this in common with the midwives: I am sterile in point of wisdom, and the reproach which has often been brought against me, that I question others but make no reply myself about anything, because I have no wisdom in me, is a true reproach; and the reason of it is this: the god compels me to act as midwife, but has never allowed me to bring forth. I am, then, not at all a wise person myself, [150d] nor have I any wise invention, the offspring born of my own soul; but those who associate with me, although at first some of them seem very ignorant, yet, as our acquaintance advances, all of them to whom the god is gracious make wonderful progress, not only in their own opinion, but in that of others as well. And it is clear that they do this, not because they have ever learned anything from me, but because they have found in themselves many fair things and have brought them forth. But the delivery is due to the god and me. And the proof of it is this: [150e] many

---

*Editorial notes were omitted.

before now, being ignorant of this fact and thinking that they were themselves the cause of their success, but despising me, have gone away from me sooner than they ought, whether of their own accord or because others persuaded them to do so. Then, after they have gone away, they have miscarried thenceforth on account of evil companionship, and the offspring which they had brought forth through my assistance they have reared so badly that they have lost it; they have considered impostures and images of more importance than the truth, and at last it was evident to themselves, as well as to others, that they were ignorant. . . . [151a] Now those who associate with me are in this matter also like women in childbirth; they are in pain and are full of trouble night and day, much more than are the women; and my art can arouse this pain and cause it to cease. Well, that is what happens to them. [151b] But in some cases, Theaetetus, when they do not seem to me to be exactly pregnant, since I see that they have no need of me, I act with perfect goodwill as match-maker and, under God, I guess very successfully with whom they can associate profitably, and I have handed over many of them to Prodicus, and many to other wise and inspired men.

Now I have said all this to you at such length, my dear boy, because I suspect that you, as you yourself believe, is in pain because you are pregnant with something within you. Apply, then, to me, remembering [151c] that I am the son of a midwife and have myself a midwife's gifts, and do your best to answer the questions I ask as I ask them. And if, when I have examined any of the things you say, it should prove that I think it is a mere image and not real, and therefore quietly take it from you and throw it away, do not be angry as women are when they are deprived of their first offspring. For many, my dear friend, before this have got into such a state of mind towards me that they are actually ready to bite me, if I take some foolish notion away from them, and they do not believe that I do this in kindness, since they are far from knowing that no god is unkind to mortals, [151d] and that I do nothing of this sort from unkindness, either, and that it is quite out of the question for me to allow an imposture or to destroy the true. And so, Theaetetus, begin again and try to tell us what knowledge is. And never say that you are unable to do so; for if God wills it and gives you courage, you will be able.

THEAET. Well then, Socrates, since you are so urgent it would be disgraceful for anyone not to exert himself in every way to say what he can. [151e] I think, then, that he who knows anything perceives that which he knows, and, as it appears at present, knowledge is nothing else than perception.

SOC. Good! Excellent, my boy! That is the way one ought to speak out. But come now, let us examine your utterance together, and see whether it is a real offspring or a mere wind-egg. Perception, you say, is knowledge?

THEAET. Yes.

SOC. And, indeed, if I may venture to say so, it is not a bad description of knowledge that you have given, [152a] but one which Protagoras also used to give. Only, he has said the same thing in a different way. For he says somewhere that man is "the measure of all things, of the existence of the things that are and the non-existence of the things that are not." You have read that, I suppose?

THEAET. Yes, I have read it often.

SOC. Well, is not this about what he means, that individual things are for me such as they appear to me, and for you in turn such as they appear to you—you and I being "man"?

THEAET. Yes, that is what he says.

SOC. [152b] It is likely that a wise man is not talking nonsense; so let us follow after him. Is it not true that sometimes, when the same wind blows, one of us feels cold, and the other does not? Or one feels slightly and the other exceedingly cold?

THEAET. Certainly.

SOC. Then in that case, shall we say that the wind is in itself cold or not cold; or shall we accept Protagoras' saying that it is cold for him who feels cold and not for him who does not?

THEAET. Apparently we shall accept that.

SOC. Then it also seems cold, or not, to each of the two?

THEAET. Yes.

SOC. But "seems" denotes perceiving?

THEAET. It does.

SOC. [152c] Then seeming and perception are the same thing in matters of warmth and everything of that sort. For as each person perceives things, such they are to each person.

THEAET. Apparently.

SOC. Perception, then, is always of that which exists and, since it is knowledge, cannot be false.

THEAET. So it seems.

SOC. By the Graces! I wonder if Protagoras, who was a very wise man, did not utter this dark saying to the common herd like ourselves, and tell the truth in secret to his pupils.

THEAET. [152d] Why, Socrates, what do you mean by that?

SOC. I will tell you and it is not a bad description, either, that nothing is one and invariable, and you could not rightly ascribe any quality whatsoever to anything, but if you call it large it will also appear to be small, and light if you call it heavy, and everything else in the same way, since nothing whatever is one, either a particular thing or of a particular quality; but it is out of movement and motion and mixture with one another that all those things become which we wrongly say "are"—wrongly, because nothing ever is, but is always becoming. . . .

. . . SOC. . . . [156a] But others are more clever, whose secret doctrines I am going to disclose to you. For them the beginning, upon which all the things we were just now speaking of depend, is the assumption that everything is really motion and that there is nothing besides this, but that there are two kinds of motion, each infinite in the number of its manifestations, and of these kinds one has an active, the other a passive force. From the union and friction of these two are born offspring, infinite in number, but always twins, [156b] the object of sense and the sense which is always born and brought forth together with the object of sense. Now we give the senses names like these: sight and hearing and smell, and the sense of cold and of heat, and pleasures and pains and desires and fears and so forth. Those that have names are very numerous, and those that are unnamed are innumerable. Now the class of objects of sense is akin to each of these; all sorts of colors are akin to all sorts of acts of vision, and in the same way sounds to acts of hearing, [156c] and the other objects of sense spring forth akin to the other senses. . . .

. . . [157a] And so it results from all this, as we said in the beginning, that nothing exists as invariably one, itself by itself, but everything is always becoming in relation to something, [157b] and "being" should be altogether abolished, though we have often—and even just now—been compelled by custom and ignorance to use the word. But we ought not, the wise men say, to permit the use of "something" or "somebody's" or "mine" or "this" or "that" or any other word that implies making things stand still, but in accordance with nature we should speak of things as "becoming" and "being made" and "being destroyed" and "changing"; for anyone who by his mode of speech makes things stand still is easily refuted. And we must use such expressions in relation both to particular objects and collective designations, [157c] among which are "mankind" and "stone" and the names of every animal and class. Do these doctrines seem pleasant to you, Theaetetus, and do you find their taste agreeable?

THEAET. I don't know, Socrates; besides, I can't tell about you, either, whether you are preaching them because you believe them or to test me.

SOC. You forget, my friend, that I myself know nothing about such things, and claim none of them as mine, but am incapable of bearing them and am merely acting as a midwife to you, and for that reason am uttering incantations and giving you a taste of each of the philosophical theories, [157d] until I may help to bring your own opinion to light. And when it is brought to light, I will examine it and see whether it is a mere wind-egg or a real offspring. So be brave and patient, and in good and manly fashion tell what you think in reply to my questions.

THEAET. Very well; ask them.

SOC. Then say once more whether the doctrine pleases you that nothing is, but is always becoming—good or beautiful or any of the other qualities we were just enumerating.

THEAET. Why, when I hear you telling about it as you did, it seems to me that it is wonderfully reasonable and ought to be accepted as you have presented it.

SOC. [157e] Let us, then, not neglect a point in which it is defective. The defect is found in connection with dreams and diseases, including insanity, and everything else that is said to cause illusions of sight and hearing and the other senses. For of course you know that in all these the doctrine we were just presenting seems admittedly to be refuted, [158a] because in them we certainly have false perceptions, and it is by no means true that everything is to each man which appears to him; on the contrary, nothing is which appears.

THEAET. What you say is very true, Socrates.

SOC. What argument is left, then, my boy, for the man who says that perception is knowledge and that in each case the things which appear are to the one to whom they appear?

THEAET. I hesitate to say, Socrates, that I have no reply to make, because you scolded me just now when I said that. [158b] But really I cannot dispute that those who are insane or dreaming have false opinions, when some of them think they are gods and others fancy in their sleep that they have wings and are flying.

SOC. Don't you remember, either, the similar dispute about these errors, especially about sleeping and waking?

THEAET. What dispute?

SOC. One which I fancy you have often heard. The question is asked, what proof you could give if anyone should ask us now, at the present moment, whether we are asleep and our thoughts are a dream, [158c] or whether we are awake and talking with each other in a waking condition.

THEAET. Really, Socrates, I don't see what proof can be given; for there is an exact correspondence in all particulars, as between the strophe and antistrophe of a choral song. Take, for instance, the conversation we have just had: there is nothing to prevent us from imagining in our sleep also that we are carrying on this conversation with each other, and when in a dream we imagine that we are relating dreams, the likeness between the one talk and the other is remarkable.

SOC. So you see it is not hard to dispute the point, since it is even open to dispute whether we are awake or in a dream. [158d] Now since the time during which we are asleep is equal to that during which we are awake, in each state our spirit contends that the semblances that appear to it at any time are certainly true, so that for half the time we say that this is true, and for half the time the other, and we maintain each with equal confidence.

THEAET. Certainly.

SOC. And may not, then, the same be said about insanity and the other diseases, except that the time is not equal?

THEAET. Yes.

SOC. Well, then, shall truth be determined by the length or shortness of time?

THEAET. [158e] That would be absurd in many ways.

SOC. But can you show clearly in any other way which of the two sets of opinions is true?

THEAET. I do not think I can.

SOC. Listen, then, while I tell you what would be said about them by those who maintain that what appears at any time is true for him to whom it appears. They begin, I imagine, by asking this question: "Theaetetus, can that which is wholly other have in any way the same quality as its alternative? And we must not assume that the thing in question is partially the same and partially other, but wholly other."

THEAET. It is impossible for it to be the same in anything, [159a] either in quality or in any other respect whatsoever, when it is wholly other.

SOC. Must we not, then, necessarily agree that such a thing is also unlike?

THEAET. It seems so to me.

SOC. Then if anything happens to become like or unlike anything—either itself or anything else—we shall say that when it becomes like it becomes the same, and when it becomes unlike it becomes other?

THEAET. We must.

SOC. Well, we said before, did we not, that the active elements were many—infinite in fact—and likewise the passive elements?

THEAET. Yes.

SOC. And furthermore, that any given element, by uniting at different times with different partners, will beget, not the same, but other results?

THEAET. [159b] Certainly.

SOC. Well, then, let us take me, or you, or anything else at hand, and apply the same principle—say Socrates in health and Socrates in illness. Shall we say the one is like the other, or unlike?

THEAET. When you say "Socrates in illness" do you mean to compare that Socrates as a whole with Socrates in health as a whole?

SOC. You understand perfectly; that is just what I mean.

THEAET. Unlike, I imagine.

SOC. And therefore other, inasmuch as unlike?

THEAET. Necessarily.

SOC. [159c] And you would say the same of Socrates asleep or in any of the other states we enumerated just now?

THEAET. Yes.

SOC. Then each of those elements which by the law of their nature act upon something else, will, when it gets hold of Socrates in health, find me one object to act upon, and when it gets hold of me in illness, another?

THEAET. How can it help it?

SOC. And so, in the two cases, that active element and I, who am the passive element shall each produce a different object?

THEAET. Of course.

SOC. So, then, when I am in health and drink wine, it seems pleasant and sweet to me?

THEAET. Yes.

SOC. The reason is, in fact, that according to the principles we accepted a while ago, [159d] the active and passive elements produce sweetness and perception, both of which are simultaneously moving from one place to another, and the perception, which comes from the passive element, makes the tongue perceptive, and the sweetness, which comes from the wine and pervades it, passes over and makes the wine both to be and to seem sweet to the tongue that is in health.

THEAET. Certainly, such are the principles we accepted a while ago.

SOC. But when it gets hold of me in illness, in the first place, it really doesn't get hold of the same man, does it? For he to whom it comes is certainly unlike.

THEAET. True.

SOC. [159e] Therefore the union of the Socrates who is ill and the draught of wine produces other results: in the tongue the sensation or perception of bitterness and in the wine—a bitterness which is engendered there and passes over into the other; the wine is made, not bitterness, but bitter, and I am made, not perception, but perceptive.

THEAET. Certainly.

SOC. Then I shall never have this perception of any other thing; for a perception of another thing is another perception, [160a] and makes the percipient different and other: nor can that which acts on me ever by union with another produce the same result or become the same in kind; for by producing another result from another passive element it will become different in kind.

THEAET. That is true.

SOC. And neither shall I, furthermore, ever again become the same as I am, nor will that ever become the same as it is.

THEAET. No.

SOC. And yet, when I become percipient, I must necessarily become percipient of something, for it is impossible to become percipient and perceive nothing; and that which is perceived must become so to someone, [160b] when it becomes sweet or bitter or the like; for to become sweet, but sweet to no one, is impossible.

THEAET. Perfectly true.

SOC. The result, then, I think, is that we (the active and the passive elements) are or become, whichever is the case, in relation to one another, since we are bound to one another by the inevitable law of our being, but to nothing else, not even to ourselves. The result, then, is that we are bound to one another; and so if a man says anything "is," he must say it is to or of or in relation to something, and similarly if he says it "becomes"; [160c] but he must not say it is or becomes absolutely, nor can he accept such a statement from anyone else. That is the meaning of the doctrine we have been describing.

THEAET. Yes, quite so, Socrates.

SOC. Then, since that which acts on me is to me and to me only, it is also the case that I perceive it, and I only?

THEAET. Of course.

SOC. Then to me my perception is true; for in each case it is always part of my being; and I am, as Protagoras says, the judge of the existence of the things that are to me and of the non-existence of those that are not to me.

THEAET. So it seems.

SOC. [160d] How, then, if I am an infallible judge and my mind never stumbles in regard to the things that are or that become, can I fail to know that which I perceive?

THEAET. You cannot possibly fail.

SOC. Therefore you were quite right in saying that knowledge is nothing else than perception, and there is complete identity between the doctrine of Homer and Heraclitus and all their followers— that all things are in motion, like streams—the doctrine of the great philosopher Protagoras that man is the measure of all things—

[160e] and the doctrine of Theaetetus that, since these things are true, perception is knowledge. Eh, Theaetetus? Shall we say that this is, so to speak, your new-born child and the result of my midwifery? Or what shall we say?

THEAET. We must say that, Socrates. . . .

. . . SOC. [183a] . . . But this, I think, did prove to be true, that if all things are in motion, every answer to any question whatsoever is equally correct, and we may say it is thus or not thus—or, if you prefer, "becomes thus," to avoid giving them the fixity by using the word "is."

THEO. You are right.

SOC. Except, Theodorus, that I said "thus," and "not thus"; but we ought not even to say "thus"; [183b] for "thus" would no longer be in motion; nor, again, "not thus." For there is no motion in "this" either; but some other expression must be supplied for those who maintain this doctrine, since now they have, according to their own hypothesis, no words, unless it be perhaps the word "nohow." That might be most fitting for them, since it is indefinite. . . .

. . . SOC. [210b] Are we then, my friend, still pregnant and in travail with knowledge, or have we brought forth everything?

THEAET. Yes, we have, and, by Zeus, Socrates, with your help I have already said more than there was in me.

SOC. Then does our art of midwifery declare to us that all the offspring that have been born are mere wind-eggs and not worth rearing?

THEAET. It does, decidedly.

SOC. If after this you ever undertake to conceive other thoughts, Theaetetus, and do conceive, [210c] you will be pregnant with better thoughts than these by reason of the present search, and if you remain barren, you will be less harsh and gentler to your associates, for you will have the wisdom not to think you know that which you do not know. So much and no more my art can accomplish; nor do I know aught of the things that are known by others, the great and wonderful men who are today and have been in the past. This art, however, both my mother and I received from God, she for women and I for young and noble men and for all who are fair.

[210d] And now I must go to the Porch of the King, to answer to the suit which Meletus has brought against me. But in the morning, Theodorus, let us meet here again.

FURTHER READINGS

Annas, Julia. "Plato the Skeptic." In *Methods of Interpreting Plato and His Dialogues*, edited by J. Klagge and N. Smith, 43–72. Oxford Studies in Ancient Philosophy, supp. vol. Oxford: Clarendon Press, 1992.

Benitez, Eugenio, and Lívia Guimarães. "Philosophy as Performed in Plato's *Theaetetus*." *Review of Metaphysics* 47 (1993): 297–328.

Burnyeat, Myles. *The Theaetetus of Plato*. Indianapolis and Cambridge: Hackett, 1990.

————. "Protagoras and Self-Refutation in Later Greek Philosophy." *Philosophical Review* 85 (1976): 44–69.

McDowell, John. *Plato: Theaetetus*. Oxford: Clarendon Press, 1973.

Sedley, David. "Three Platonist Interpretations of the *Theaetetus*." In *Form and Argument in Late Plato*, edited by C. Gill and M. M. McGabe, 79–103. Oxford: Oxford University Press, 2000.

2

PYRRHO

Pyrrho of Elis (ca. 360–274 BCE) is considered the first skeptical philosopher. He wrote nothing and our information about him comes from a variety of indirect sources, most of which are of doubtful credibility. One of the two ancient skeptical traditions, Pyrrhonism, is named after him, but there is no attested historical continuity between him and the much later development of the Pyrrhonian school, initiated by Aenesidemus of Cnossos (ca. 100–40 BCE). Some even suspect that the attribution of a skeptical philosophy to Pyrrho is anachronistic and we do have an ancient source— Cicero—who does not present him as a skeptic at all, although Cicero may thus proceed in order to preserve the philosophy of the *epoché* exclusively to the Academics. We have selected two ancient texts about Pyrrho. The first is *The Life of Pyrrho* by Diogenes Laertius. Diogenes relates a number of episodes and anecdotes, relaying on different sources most of which we no longer possess which, although of polemical credibility, were quite influential in the interpretation and reception of Pyrrhonism from antiquity to contemporary philosophy. The other short piece derives from the Aristotelian philosopher Aristocles' (ca. 190 CE) critical examination of Timon's (a disciple of Pyrrho) description of his master's views preserved in Eusebius of Caesarea's *Preparatio Evangelica*. We selected the most important fragment available in our sources concerning the content of Pyrrho's kind of skepticism, known as the fragment on the indifference of things. According to the most-accepted reading of this fragment, Pyrrho's epistemological kind of skepticism is a consequence of the ontological view which denies any difference among existent things.

FROM DIOGENES LAERTIUS IN *LIVES OF EMINENT PHILOSOPHERS**

[61] Pyrrho of Elis was the son of Pleistarchus, as Diocles relates. According to Apollodorus in his *Chronology*, he was first a painter; then he studied under Stilpo's son Bryson: thus Alexander in his *Successions of Philosophers*. Afterwards he joined Anaxarchus, whom he accompanied on his travels everywhere so that he even forgathered with the Indian Gymnosophists and with the Magi. This led him to adopt a most noble philosophy, to quote Ascanius of Abdera, taking the form of agnosti-

---

*Editorial notes were omitted.

cism and suspension of judgment. He denied that anything was honorable or dishonorable, just or unjust. And so, universally, he held that there is nothing really existent, but custom and convention govern human action; for no single thing is in itself any more this than that.

[62] He led a life consistent with this doctrine, going out of his way for nothing, taking no precaution, but facing all risks as they came, whether carts, precipices, dogs, or what not, and, generally, leaving nothing to the arbitrage of the senses; but he was kept out of harm's way by his friends who, as Antigonus of Carystus tells us, used to follow close after him. But Aenesidemus says that it was only his philosophy that was based upon suspension of judgment, and that he did not lack foresight in his everyday acts. He lived to be nearly ninety.

This is what Antigonus of Carystus says of Pyrrho in his book upon him. At first he was a poor and unknown painter, and there are still some indifferent torch-racers of his in the gymnasium at Elis. [63] He would withdraw from the world and live in solitude, rarely showing himself to his relatives; this he did because he had heard an Indian reproach Anaxarchus, telling him that he would never be able to teach others what is good while he himself danced attendance on kings in their courts. He would maintain the same composure at all times, so that, even if you left him when he was in the middle of a speech, he would finish what he had to say with no audience but himself, although in his youth he had been hasty. Often, our informant adds, he would leave his home and, telling no one, would go roaming about with whomsoever he chanced to meet. And once, when Anaxarchus fell into a slough, he passed by without giving him any help, and, while others blamed him, Anaxarchus himself praised his indifference and *sang-froid*.

[64] On being discovered once talking to himself, he answered, when asked the reason, that he was training to be good. In debate he was looked down upon by no one, for he could both discourse at length and also sustain a cross-examination, so that even Nausiphanes when a young man was captivated by him: at all events he used to say that we should follow Pyrrho in disposition but himself in doctrine; and he would often remark that Epicurus, greatly admiring Pyrrho's way of life, regularly asked him for information about Pyrrho; and that he was so respected by his native city that they made him high priest, and on his account they voted that all philosophers should be exempt from taxation.

Moreover, there were many who emulated his abstention from affairs, so that Timon in his *Pytho* and in his *Silli* says:

[65]   O Pyrrho, O aged Pyrrho, whence and how
       Found'st thou escape from servitude to sophists.
       Their dreams and vanities; how didst thou loose
       The bonds of trickery and specious craft?
       Nor reck'st thou to inquire such things as these,
       What breezes circle Hellas, to what end,
       And from what quarter each may chance to blow.

And again in the *Conceits*:

> This, Pyrrho, this my heart is fain to know.
> Whence peace of mind to thee doth freely flow,
> Why among men thou like a god dost show?

Athens honored him with her citizenship, says Diocles, for having slain the Thracian Cotys. [66] He lived in fraternal piety with his sister, a midwife, so says Eratosthenes in his essay *On Wealth and Poverty*, now and then even taking things for sale to market, poultry perchance or pigs, and he would dust the things in the house, quite indifferent as to what he did. They say he showed his indifference by washing a porker. Once he got enraged in his sister's cause (her name was Philista), and he told the man who blamed him that it was not over a weak woman that one should display indifference. When a cur rushed at him and terrified him, he answered his critic that it was not easy entirely to strip oneself of human weakness; but one should strive with all one's might against facts, by deeds if possible, and if not, in word.

[67] They say that, when septic salves and surgical and caustic remedies were applied to a wound he had sustained, he did not so much as frown. Timon also portrays his disposition in the full account which he gives of him in *Pytho*. Philo of Athens, a friend of his, used to say that he was most fond of Democritus and then of Homer, admiring him and continually repeating the line

> As leaves on trees, such is the life of man.

He also admired Homer because he likened men to wasps, flies, and birds, and would quote these verses as well:

> Ay, friend, die thou; why thus thy fate deplore?
> Patroclus too, thy better, is no more,

and all the passages which dwell on the unstable purpose, vain pursuits, and childish folly of man.

[68] Posidonius, too, relates of him a story of this sort. When his fellow-passengers on board a ship were all unnerved by a storm, he kept calm and confident, pointing to a little pig in the ship that went on eating, and telling them that such was the unperturbed state in which the wise man should keep himself. Numenius alone attributes to him positive tenets. He had pupils of repute, in particular one Eurylochus, who fell short of his professions; for they say that he was once so angry that he seized the spit with the meat on it and chased his cook right into the market-place. [69] Once in Elis he was so hard pressed by his pupils' questions that he stripped and swam across the Alpheus. Now he was, as Timon too says, most hostile to Sophists.

FROM *THE HELLENISTIC PHILOSOPHERS*

It is supremely necessary to investigate our own capacity for knowledge. For if we are so constituted that we know nothing, there is no need to continue enquiry into other things. Among the ancients too there have been people who made this pronouncement, and Aristotle has argued against them. Pyrrho of Elis was also a powerful spokesman of such a position. He himself has left nothing in writing, but his pupil Timon says that whoever wants to be happy must consider these three questions: first, how are things by nature? Secondly, what attitude should we adopt towards them? Thirdly, what will be the outcome for those who have this attitude? According to Timon, Pyrrho declared that things are equally indifferent, unmeasurable and inarbitrable. For this reason neither our sensations nor our opinions tell us truths or falsehoods. Therefore for this reason we should not put our trust in them one bit, but we should be unopinionated, uncommitted, and unwavering, saying concerning each individual thing that it no more is than is not, or it both is and is not, or it neither is or is not. The outcome for those who actually adopt this attitude, says Timon, will be first speechlessness, and then freedom from disturbance; and Aenesidemus says pleasure. These are the main points of what they say.

FURTHER READINGS

Bett, Richard. *Pyrrho: His Antecedents, and His Legacy.* Oxford: Oxford University Press, 2000.

Caizzi, Fernanda Decleva. *Pirrone Testimonianze.* Naples: Bibliopolis, 1981.

Conche, Marcel. *Pyrrhon ou l'apparence.* Paris: Presses Universitaires de France, 1994.

Flintoff, Everard. "Pyrrho and India." *Phronesis* 25 (1980): 88–108.

Long, A. "Timon of Phlius: Pyrrhonist and Satirist." *Proceedings of the Cambridge Philosophical Society* 24 (1978): 68–91.

Robin, L. *Pyrrhon et le scepticisme grec.* Paris: Presses Universitaires de France, 1944.

3

THE ACADEMICS

Plato's Academy went through a skeptical phase from around 273 BCE, when Arcesilaus of Pitane (316–241 BCE) became its leader, to the first century BCE, when Philo of Larissa was succeeded by the Stoic Antiochus of Ascalon. Although these Academics (also known as the New Academics) did not call themselves skeptics—a term peculiar to the Pyrrhonians—they held that things could not be apprehended with the certainty pretended by the philosophers, notably the Stoics, and suspended judgment. The two greatest Academic skeptics were Arcesilaus, who engaged with Zeno of Cintium, the founder of Stoicism, in a memorable epistemological debate over the Stoic criterion of truth (the cognitive impression) and, about fifty years later, Carneades (ca. 217–129 BCE), who carried through the debate with the Stoics—at this time led first by Chrysippus, than by Zeno of Tarsus, than by Diogenes of Babylon, and finally by Antipater of Tarsus—and developed a theory of probabilism as an answer to the Stoic objection that suspension of judgment makes life unlivable. This theory played a major role in the development of modern philosophy. Cicero (106–43 BCE), our main source for the skeptical Academy, was a disciple of Philo and defended the skeptical Academic standpoint against Antiochus's criticisms—although Philo, whom he followed, had already departed from the pure suspension of judgment held by Arcesilaus and Carneades. This appears above all in his book on the Academics, from which we extracted passages which exhibit: (a) Arcesilaus's debate with Zeno; (b) the main skeptical arguments deployed by the Academics (the *sorites*, the dream argument, and an argument which has been pointed out as a possible source for Descartes's deceiver argument in the First Meditation); and (c) Carneades' probabilism. Another very important source for the Academic skeptics is Sextus Empiricus. We reproduce a passage from *Adversus Mathematicos* VII (also known as *Against the Logicians*), which is the most complete and detailed account available of Carneades' probabilism.

FROM *ACADEMICA**

[1.44] "It was entirely with Zeno, so we have been told," I replied, "that Arcesilaus set on foot his battle, not from obstinacy or desire for victory, as it seems to me at all

---

*The editorial notes were omitted.

events, but because of the obscurity of the facts that had led Socrates to a confession of ignorance, as also previously his predecessors Democritus, Anaxagoras, Empedocles, and almost all the old philosophers, who utterly denied all possibility of cognition or perception or knowledge, and maintained that the senses are limited, the mind feeble, the span of live short, and that truth (in Democritus' phrase) is sunk in as abyss, opinion, and custom are all-prevailing, no place is left for truth, all things successively are wrapped in darkness. [1.45] Accordingly Arcesilaus said that there is nothing that can be known, not even that residuum of knowledge that Socrates had left himself— the truth of this very dictum: so hidden in obscurity did he believe everything lies, nor is there anything that can be perceived or understood, and for these reasons, he said, no one must make any positive statement or affirmation or give the approval of his assent to any proposition, and a man must always restrain his rashness and hold it back from every slip, as it would be glaring rashness to give assent either to a falsehood or to something not certainly known, and nothing is more disgraceful than for assent and approval to outstrip knowledge and perception. His practice was consistent with his theory—he led most of his hearers to accept it by arguing against the opinions of all men, so that when equally weighty reasons were found on opposite sides on the same subject, it was easier to withhold assent from either side. [1.46] They call this school the New Academy,—to me it seems old, at all events if we count Plato a member of the Old Academy, in whose books nothing is stated positively and there is much arguing both *pro* and *contra*, all things are inquired into and no certain statement is made; but nevertheless let the Academy that you expounded be named the Old and this one the New; and right down to Carneades, who was fourth in succession from Arcesilaus, it continued to remain true to the same theory of Arcesilaus. . . ."

[2.7] . . . There remains one class of adverse critics who do not approve the Academic system of philosophy. This would trouble us more if anybody approved any set of doctrines except the one of which he himself was a follower. But for our part, since it is our habit to put forward our views in conflict with all schools, we cannot refuse to allow others to differ from us; although we at all events have an easy brief to argue, who desire to discover the truth without any contention, and who pursue it with the fullest diligence and devotion. For even though many difficulties hinder every branch of knowledge, and both the subjects themselves and our faculties of judgment involve such a lack of certainty that the most ancient and learned thinkers had good reason for distrusting their ability to discover what they desired, nevertheless they did not give up, nor yet will we abandon in exhaustion our zeal for research; and the sole object of our discussions is by arguing on both sides to draw out and give shape to some result that may be either true or the nearest possible approximation to the truth. [2.8] Nor is there any difference between ourselves and those who think that they have positive knowledge except that they have no doubt that their tenets are true, whereas we hold many doctrines as probable, which we can easily act upon but can scarcely advance as certain; yet we are more free and untrammeled in that we possess our power of judgment uncurtailed, and are bound by no compulsion to support all the dogmas laid down for us almost as edicts by certain masters. For all other people in the first place are held in close bondage placed upon them before they were able to judge what doctrine was the best, and secondly they form judgments about matters as to which they know nothing at the most incompetent period of life, either under the guidance of some friend or under the influence of a single harangue from the first lecturer that they attended, and cling as to a rock to whatever theory they are carried to by stress of weather. [2.9] For as to their assertion that the teacher whom they judge to have been a wise man commands their absolute trust, I would agree to this if to make that judgment could actually have lain within the power of unlearned novices (for to decide who is a wise man seems to be a task that specially requires a wise man to undertake it); but granting that it lay within their power, it was only possible for them after hearing all the facts and ascertaining the views of all the other schools as well, whereas they gave their verdict after a single hearing of the case, and enrolled themselves under the authority of a single master. But somehow or other most men prefer to go wrong, and to defend tooth and nail the system for which they have come to feel an affection, rather than to lay aside obstinacy and seek for the doctrine that is most consistent. . . .

[2.47] I will therefore set out their arguments in classified form, since even they themselves make a practice of orderly exposition. They first attempt to show the possibility that many things may appear to exist that are absolutely non-existent, since the mind is deceptively affected by non-existent objects in the same manner as it is affected by real ones. For, they say, when your school asserts that some presentations are sent by the deity—dreams for example, and the revelations furnished by oracles, auspices, and sacrifices (for they assert that the Stoics against whom they are arguing accept these manifestations)—how possibly, they ask, can the deity have the power to render false presentations probable and not have the power to render probable those which approximate absolutely most closely to the truth? or else, if he is able to render these also probable, why cannot he render probable those which are distinguishable, although only with extreme difficulty, from false presentations? and if these, why not those which do not differ from them at all? [2.48] Then, since the mind is capable of entirely self-originated motion, as is manifest by our faculty of mental imagination and by the visions that sometimes appear to men either when asleep or mad, it is probable that the mind may also be set in motion in such a manner that not only it cannot distinguish whether the presentations in question are true or false but that there really is no difference at all between them: just as if people were to shiver and turn pale either of themselves as a result of some mental emotion or in consequence of encountering some terrifying external object, with nothing to distinguish between the two kinds of shivering and pallor, and without any difference between the internal state of feeling and the one that came from without. Lastly, if no false presentations at all are probable, it is another story; but if some are, why are not even those that are difficult to distinguish? why not those that are so much like true ones that there is absolutely no difference between them? especially as you yourselves say that the wise man when in a state of frenzy restrains himself from all assent because no distinction between presentations is visible to him. . . .

[2.76] ... "Enough about authority—although you had put the question to me whether I did not think that with so many able minds carrying on the search with such zealous energy, after so many ages since the old philosophers mentioned, the truth might possibly have been discovered. What actually has been discovered permit me to consider a little later, with you yourself indeed as umpire. But that Arcesilaus did not do battle with Zeno merely for the sake of criticizing him, but really wished to discover the truth, is gathered from what follows. [2.77] That it is possible for a human being to hold no opinions, and not only that it is possible but that it is the duty of the wise man, had not only never been distinctly formulated but had never even been stated by any of his predecessors; but Arcesilaus deemed this view both true and also honorable and worthy of a wise man. We may suppose him putting the question to Zeno, what would happen if the wise man was unable to perceive anything and if also it was the mark of the wise man not to form an opinion. Zeno no doubt replied that the wise man's reason for abstaining from forming an opinion would be that there was something that could be perceived. What then was this? asked Arcesilaus. A presentation, was doubtless the answer. Then what sort of a presentation? Hereupon no doubt Zeno defined it as follows, a presentation impressed and sealed and molded from a real object, in conformity with its reality. There followed the further question, did this hold good even if a true presentation was of exactly the same form as a false one? At this I imagine Zeno was sharp enough to see that if a presentation proceeding from a real thing was of such a nature that one proceeding from a non-existent thing could be of the same form, there was no presentation that could be perceived. Arcesilaus agreed that this addition to the definition was correct, for it was impossible to perceive either a false presentation or a true one if a true one had such a character as even a false one might have; but he pressed the points at issue further in order to show that no presentation proceeding from a true object is such that a presentation proceeding from a false one might not also be of the same form. [2.78] This is the one argument that has held the field down to the present day. . . .

[2.83] ... There are four heads of arguments intended to prove that there is nothing that can be known, perceived, or comprehended, which is the subject of all this debate: the first of these arguments is that there is such a thing as a false presentation; the second, that a false presentation cannot be perceived; the third, that of presentations between which there is no difference it is impossible for some to be able to be perceived and others not; the fourth, that there is no true presentation originating from sensation with which there is not ranged another presentation that precisely corresponds to it and that cannot be perceived. The second and third of these four arguments are admitted by everybody; the first is not granted by Epicurus, but you with whom we are dealing admit that one too; the entire battle is about the fourth. . . .

[2.88] ... My points are of the sort that have been handled very industriously by you. Your assertion was that presentations seen by people asleep and tipsy and mad are feebler than those of persons awake and sober and sane. How? Because, you said, when Ennius had woken up he did not say that he had seen Homer but that he had seemed to see him, while his Alcmaeon says

But my mind agrees in no wise . . .

There are similar passages about men tipsy. As if anybody would deny that a man that has woken up thinks that he has been dreaming, or that one whose madness has sub-sided thinks that the things that he saw during his madness were no true! But that is not the point at issue; what we are asking is what theses things looked like at the time when they were seen. Unless indeed we think that, if Ennius merely dreamt that passage

O piety of spirit . . .

he did not hear the whole of it in the same way as if he had been listening to it when awake; for when he had woken up he was able to think those appearances dreams, as they were, but he accepted them as real while he was asleep just as much as he would have done if awake. Again, in that dream of Iliona,

Mother, on thee I call . . . ,

did she not so firmly believe that her son had spoken, that she believed it even after waking up? For what is the cause of her saying

Come, stand by me, stay and hear me; say those words
To me again—?

does she seem to have less faith in her visual presentations than people have when they are awake? . . .

[2.90] . . . But all these things are brought forward in order to prove what is the most certain fact possible, that in respect of the mind's assent there is no difference between true presentations and false ones. But your school achieve nothing when you refute those false presentations by appealing to the recollection of madmen or dreamers; for the question is not what sort of recollection is usually experienced by those who have woken up or have ceased to be mad, but what was the nature of the visual perception of men mad or dreaming at the moment when their experience was taking place . . .

[2.99] Carneades holds that there are two classifications of presentations, which under one are divided into those that can be perceived and those that cannot, and under the other into those that are probable and those that are not probable; and that accordingly those presentations that are styled by the Academy contrary to the senses and contrary to perspicuity belong to the former division, whereas the latter division must not be impugned; and that consequently his view is that there is no presentation of such a sort to result in perception, but many that result in a judgment of probability. For it is contrary to nature for nothing to be probable, and entails that entire subversion of life of which you, Lucullus, were speaking; accordingly even many sense-percepts must be deemed probable, if only it be held in mind that no sense-presentation has such a character as a false presentation could not also have without differing from it at all. Thus the wise man will make use of whatever apparently probable presentation he encounters, if nothing presents itself that is contrary to that probability, and his whole plan of life will be charted out in this manner. In fact even the person whom your school brings on the stage as the wise man follows many things probable, that he has not grasped nor perceived nor assented to but that possess verisimilitude; and if he were not to approve them, all life would be done away with. [2.100] Another point: when a wise man is going on board a ship surely he has not got the knowledge already grasped in his mind and perceived that he will make the voyage as he intends? how can he have it? But if for instance he were setting out from here to Puteoli, a distance of four miles, with a reliable crew and a good helmsman and in the present calm weather, it would appear probable that he would get there safe. He will therefore be guided by presentations of this sort to adopt plans of action and of inaction, and will be readier at proving that snow is white than Anaxagoras was (who not only denied that this was so, but asserted that to him snow did not even appear white, because he knew that it was made of water solidified and that water was black); [2.101] and whatever object comes in contact with him in such a way that the presentation is probable, and unhindered by anything, he will be set in motion. For he is not a statue carved out of stone or hewn out of timber; he has a body and a mind, a mobile intellect and mobile senses, so that many things seem to him to be true, although nevertheless they do not seem to him to possess that distinct and peculiar mark leading to perception, and hence the doctrine that the wise man does not assent, for the reason that it is possible for a false presentation to occur that has the same character as a given true one. Nor does our pronouncement against the senses differ from that of the Stoics, who say that many things are false and widely different from what they appear to the senses. . . .

[2.103] [Clitomachus wrote that] "The Academic school holds that there are dissimilarities between things of such a nature that some of them seem probable and others the contrary; but this is not an adequate ground for saying that some things can be perceived and others cannot, because many false objects are probable but nothing false can be perceived and known." And accordingly he asserts that those who say that the Academy robs us of our senses are violently mistaken, as that school never said that color, taste, or sound was non-existent, but their contention was that these presentations do not contain a mark of truth and certainty peculiar to themselves and found nowhere else. [2.104] After setting out these points, he adds that the formula "the wise man withholds assent" is used in two ways, one when the meaning is that he gives absolute assent to no presentation at all, the other when he restrains himself from replying so as to convey approval or disapproval of something, with the consequence that he neither makes a negation nor an affirmation; and that this being so, he holds the one plan in theory, so that he never assents, but the other in practice, so that he is guided by probability, and wherever this confronts him or is wanting he can answer "yes" or "no" accordingly. In fact as we hold that he who restrains himself from assent about all things nevertheless does move and does act, the view is that there remain presentations of a sort that arouse us to action, and also answers that we can give in the affirmative or the negative in reply to questions, merely following a corresponding presentation, provided that we answer without actual assent but that nevertheless not all presentations of this character were actually approved, but those that nothing hindered.

FROM SEXTUS EMPIRICUS'S *AGAINST THE LOGICIANS**

[166] . . . yet as he [Carneades], too, himself requires a criterion for the conduct of life and for the attainment of happiness, he is practically compelled on his own account to frame a theory about it, and to adopt both the probable presentation and that which is at once probable and irreversible and tested. [167] What the distinction is between these must briefly be indicated. The presentation, then, is a presentation of something—of that, for instance, from which it comes and of that which it occurs; that from which it comes being, say, the externally existent sensible object, and that in which it occurs, say, a man. [168] And, such being its nature, it will have two aspects, one in its relation to the object presented, the second in its relation to the subject experiencing the presentation. Now in regard to its aspect in relation to the object presented it is either true or false—true when it is in accord with the object presented, but false when it is not in accord. [169] But in regard to its aspect in relation to the subject experiencing the presentation, the one kind of presentation is apparently true, the other apparently false; and of these the apparently true is termed by the Academics "emphasis" and probability and probable presentation, while the not apparently true is denominated "ap-emphasis" and unconvincing and improbable presentation; for neither that which itself appears false, nor that which though true does not appear so to us, is naturally convincing to us. [170] And of these presentations that which is evidently false, or not apparently true, is to be ruled out and is not a criterion whether (it be derived from a non-existent object or) from an object which exists, but not in accord with that object and not representing the actual object—such as was the presentation derived from Electra which Orestes experienced, when he supposed her to be one of the Furies and cried out—

Avaunt! For of my Furies thou art one.

[171] And of the apparently true kind of presentation, one sort is obscure—the sort, for instance, that is found in the case of those who have a perception that is confused and not distinct owing to the smallness of the object viewed or owing to the extent of the interval or even owing to the weakness of the sense of sight,—while the other sort, in addition to being apparently true, possesses this appearance of truth to an intense degree. [172] And of these, again, the presentation which is obscure and

---

*The editorial notes were omitted.

vague will not be a criterion; for because of its not indicating clearly either itself or that which caused it, it is not of such a nature as to persuade us or to induce us to assent. [173] But that which appears true, and appears so vividly, is the criterion of truth according to the School of Carneades. And, being the criterion, it has a large extension, and when extended one presentation reveals itself as more probable and more vivid than another. [174] Probability, in the present instance, is used in three senses—in the first, of that which both is and appears true; in the second, of that which is really false but appears true; in the third, of that which is at once both true and false. Hence the criterion will be the apparently true presentation, which the Academics called "probable"; [175] but sometimes the impression it makes is actually false, so that we are compelled at times to make use of the presentation which is at once both true and false. But the rare occurrence of this kind—the kind I mean which imitates the truth—should not make us distrust the kind which "as a general rule" reports truly; for the fact is that both our judgments and our actions are regulated by the standard of "the general rule."

Such then is the first and general criterion according to Carneades. [176] But since no presentation is ever simple in form but, like links in a chain, one hangs from another, we have to add, as a second criterion, the presentation which is at once both probable and "irreversible." For example, he who receives the presentation of a man necessarily receives the presentation both of his personal qualities and of the external conditions—[177] of his personal qualities, such as color, size, shape, motion, speech, dress, foot-gear; and of the external conditions, such as air, light, day, heaven, earth, friends, and all the rest. So whenever none of these presentations disturbs our faith by appearing false, but all with one accord appear true, our belief is the greater. [178] For we believe that this man is Socrates from the fact that he possesses all his customary qualities—color, size, shape, converse, coat, and his position in a place where there is no one exactly like him. [179] And just as some doctors do not deduce that it is a true case of fever from one symptom only—such as too quick a pulse or a very high temperature—but from a concurrence, such as that of a high temperature with a rapid pulse and soreness to the touch and flushing and thirst and analogous symptoms; so also the Academic forms his judgment of truth by the concurrence of presentations, and when none of the presentations in the concurrence provokes in him a suspicion of its falsity he asserts that the impression is true. [180] And that the "irreversible" presentation is a concurrence capable of implanting belief is plain from the case of Menelaus; for when he had left behind him on the ship the wraith of Helen—which he had brought with him from Troy, thinking it to be the true Helen—and had landed on the island of Pharos, he beheld the true Helen, but though he received from her a true presentation, yet he did not believe that presentation owing to his mind being warped by that other impression from which he derived the knowledge that he had left Helen behind in the ship. [181] Such then is the "irreversible" presentation; and it too seems to possess extension inasmuch as one is found to be more irreversible than another.

Still more trustworthy than the irreversible presentation and supremely perfect is that which creates judgment; for it, in addition to being irreversible, is also "tested." [182] What the distinctive feature of this presentation is we must next explain. Now in the case of the irreversible presentation it is merely required that none of the presentations in the concurrence should disturb us by a suspicion of its falsity but all should be apparently true and not improbable; but in the case of the concurrence which involves the "tested" presentation, we scrutinize attentively each of the presentations in the concurrence—, just as the practice is at assembly-meetings, when the People makes inquiry about each of those who desire to be magistrates or judges, to see whether he is worthy to be entrusted with the magistracy or the judgeship. [183] Thus, for example, as there are present at the seat of judgment both the subject that judges and the object that is being judged and the medium through which judgment is effected, and distance and interval, place, time, mood, disposition, activity, we judge the distinctive character of each of these factors—as regards the subject judging, whether its vision be not dimmed (for vision of that kind is unfitted for judging); and as regards the object judged, whether it be not excessively small; and as regards the medium through which the judgment is effected, whether the atmosphere be not dark; and as to distance, whether it be not excessively great; and as to interval, whether it be not too short; and as to place, whether it be not immense; and as to time, whether it be not brief; and as to disposition, whether it is not found to be insane; and as to activity, whether it be not unacceptable.

[184] For all these factors together form the criterion—namely, the probable presentation, and that which is at once both probable and irreversible and besides these that which is at once probable and irreversible and tested. And it is because of this that, just as in ordinary life when we are investigating a small matter we question a single witness, but in a greater matter several, and when the matter investigated is still more important we cross-question each of the witnesses on the testimony of the others,—so likewise, says Carneades, in trivial matters we employ as criterion only the probable presentation, but in greater matters the irreversible, and in matters which contribute to happiness the tested presentation. [185] Moreover, just as they adopt, they say, a different presentation to suit different cases, so also in different circumstances they do not cling to the same presentation. For they declare that they attend to the immediately probable in cases where the circumstances do not afford time for an accurate consideration of the matter. [186] A man, for example, is being pursued by enemies, and coming to a ditch he receives a presentation which suggests that there, too, enemies are lying in wait for him; then being carried away by this presentation, as a probability, he turns aside and avoids the ditch, being led by the probability of the presentation, before he has exactly ascertained whether or not there really is an ambush of the enemy at the spot. [187] But they follow the probable and tested presentation in cases where time is afforded for using their judgment on the object presented with deliberation and thorough examination. For example, on seeing a coil of rope in an unlighted room a man jumps over it, conceiving it for the moment to be a snake, but turning back afterwards he inquires into the truth, and on finding it motionless he is already inclined to think that it is not a

snake, [188] but as he reckons, all the same, that snakes too are motionless at times when numbed by winter's frost, he prods at the coiled mass with a stick, and then, after thus testing the presentation received, he assents to the fact that it is false to suppose that the body presented to him is a snake. And once again, as I said before, when we see a thing very plainly we assent to its being true when we have previously proved by testing that we have our senses in good order, and that we see it when wide awake and not asleep, and that there exists at the same time a clear atmosphere and a moderate distance and immobility on the part of the object perceived, [189] so that because of these conditions the presentation is trustworthy, we having had sufficient time for the scrutiny of the facts observed at the seat of the presentation. The same account is to be given of the irreversible presentation as well; for they accept it whenever there is nothing capable of controverting it, as was said above in the case of Menelaus.

FURTHER READINGS

Bett, Richard. "Carneades' Distinction Between Assent and Approval," *Monist* 73, no. 1 (1990): 3–20.

———. "Carneades' *Pythanon*: A Reappraisal of Its Role and Status." *Oxford Studies in Ancient Philosophy* 7 (1989): 59–94.

Brittain, Charles. *Philo of Larissa: The Last of the Academic Sceptics.* Oxford: Oxford University Press, 2001.

Couissin, Pierre. "The Stoicism of the New Academy." In *The Skeptical Tradition*, edited by Myles Burnyeat, 31–63. Berkeley: University of California Press, 1983.

———. "L'origine et l'évolution de l'*époche*." *Revue des études grecques* 42 (1929): 373–97.

Frede, Michael. "The Sceptic's Two Kinds of Assent and the Question of the Possibility of Knowledge." In *Philosophy in History: Essays on the Historiography of Philosophy*, edited by Richard Rorty, J. B. Schneewind, and Quentin Skinner, 255–78. Cambridge: Cambridge University Press, 1984.

Glucker, John. *Antiochus and the Late Academy.* Göttingen: Vandenhoeck & Ruprecht, 1978.

Ioppolo, A. M. *Opinione e Scienza: Il dibattio tra Stoici e Accademici nel III e nel II secolo a. c.* 2 vols. Naples: Bibliopolis, 1986.

Levy, Carlos. *Cicero Academicus: recherches sur les Académiques et sur la philosophie ciceronienne.* Rome: Ecole Française de Rome, 1992.

Powell, J. G. F., ed. *Cicero the Philosopher: Twelve Papers.* Oxford: Clarendon Press, 1995.

Schofield, M., Myles Burnyeat, and Jonathan Barnes, eds. *Doubt and Dogmatism: Studies in Hellenistic Epistemology.* Oxford: Oxford University Press, 1986.

Tarrant, Harold. *Scepticism or Platonism? The Philosophy of the Fourth Academy.* Cambridge: Cambridge University Press, 1985.

4

SEXTUS EMPIRICUS

Only two books written by the ancient Pyrrhonians were preserved, both by Sextus Empiricus: *Outlines of Pyrrhonism* (in three books) and *Against the Professors* (in eleven books). Pyrrhonism, named after Pyrrho of Elis, developed in Alexandria where its practitioners constructed arguments for and against everything. They claimed to be interested in curing people of a disease called dogmatism by leading the infected to suspend judgment. We know very little about Sextus, only that he was a physician of the Methodical school of medicine who lived around 200 CE. The prominent ancient Pyrrhonians were Aenesidemus of Cnossos (ca. 100–40 BCE), who founded the school probably as a reaction to the increasingly dogmatic developments in the Academy to which he probably belonged, and Agrippa, of whom almost nothing is known except that he probably lived around the first century CE—certainly some time between Aenesidemus and Sextus Empiricus—and elaborated the five modes of suspension of judgment (conflict, infinite regress, *dialelus*, hypothesis, and relativity). There is some controversy about the originality of Sextus. Although Aenesidemus's books are Sextus's main sources, he disagrees from him on a number of issues and, however original he was, he eventually became crucial to later philosophers to the extent that his was the only extant version of ancient Pyrrhonism from one of its members. Most of the text below comes from book 1 of the *Outlines*, where Sextus gives, as he says (PH 1.5), the "general" position of the school, namely, its specific features such as method, motivation, goals, and sets of modes that lead to suspension of judgment. This comprehends the most influential and discussed part of ancient Pyrrhonism and corresponds roughly to another systematic—but much more resumed and defective—account of ancient Pyrrhonism we have, that given by Diogenes Laertius in his chapter on Pyrrho in his *Lifes* (9.69–108). We have also included short passages from books 2 and 3 of the *Outlines* and from book 8 of *Against the Professors* that deal with the problem of the criterion of truth and with the Pyrrhonian argumentative and therapeutic approaches. Books 2 and 3 of *Outlines* give in a more summary way—and *Against the Professors* in a more detailed way—what Sextus calls the "special" branch of the school, namely the refutation of the various philosophical doctrines in epistemology, ethics, physics, and—in the case of *Against the Professors*—the liberal arts (grammar, rhetoric, geometry, arithmetic, astrology, and music). Flávio Loque assisted in the selection of the texts below.

FROM *OUTLINES OF PYRRHONISM**

Chapter 1: Of the Main Differences between Philosophic Systems

[1] The natural result of any investigation is that the investigators either discover the object of search or deny that it is discoverable and confess it to be inapprehensible or persist in their search. [2] So, too, with regard to the objects investigated by philosophy, this is probably why some have claimed to have discovered the truth, others have asserted that it cannot be apprehended, while others again go on inquiring. [3] Those who believe they have discovered it are the "Dogmatists," specially so called—Aristotle, for example, and Epicurus and the Stoics and certain others; Clitomachus and Carneades and other Academics treat it as inapprehensible: the Skeptics keep on searching. [4] Hence it seems reasonable to hold that the main types of philosophy are three—the Dogmatic, the Academic, and the Skeptic. Of the other systems it will best become others to speak: our task at present is to describe in outline the Skeptic doctrine, first premising that of none of our future statements do we positively affirm that the fact is exactly as we state it, but we simply record each fact, like a chronicler, as it appears to us at the moment.

Chapter 2: Of the Arguments of Skepticism

[5] Of the Skeptic philosophy one argument (or branch of exposition) is called "general," the other "special." In the general argument we set forth the distinctive features of Skepticism, stating its purport and principles, its logical methods, criterion, and end or aim; the "Tropes," also, or "Modes," which lead to suspension of judgment, and in what sense we adopt the Skeptic formulae, and the distinction between Skepticism and the philosophies which stand next to it. [6] In the special argument we state our objections regarding the several divisions of so-called philosophy. Let us, then, deal first with the general argument, beginning our description with the names given to the Skeptic School.

Chapter 3: Of the Nomenclature of Skepticism

[7] The Skeptic School, then, is also called "Zetetic" from its activity in investigation and inquiry, and "Ephectic" or Suspensive from the state of mind produced in the inquirer after his search, and "Aporetic" or Dubitative either from its habit of doubting and seeking, as some say, or from its indecision as regards assent and denial, and "Pyrrhonian" from the fact that Pyrrho appears to us to have applied himself to Skepticism more thoroughly and more conspicuously than his predecessors.

---

*Editorial notes were omitted.

Chapter 4: What Skepticism Is

[8] Skepticism is an ability, or mental attitude, which opposes appearances to judgments in any way whatsoever, with the result that, owing to the equipollence of the objects and reasons thus opposed, we are brought firstly to a state of mental suspense and next to a state of "unperturbedness" or quietude. [9] Now we call it an "ability" not in any subtle sense, but simply in respect of its "being able." By "appearances" we now mean the objects of sense-perception, whence we contrast them with the objects of thought or "judgments." The phrase "in any way whatsoever" can be connected either with the word "ability," to make us take the word "ability," as we said, in its simple sense, or with the phrase "opposing appearances to judgments"; for inasmuch as we oppose these in a variety of ways—appearances to appearances or judgments to judgments, or *alternando* appearances to judgments,—in order to ensure the inclusion of all these antitheses we employ the phrase "in any way whatsoever." Or, again, we join "in any way whatsoever" to "appearances and judgments" in order that we may not have to inquire how the appearances appear or how the thought-objects are judged, but may take these terms in the simple sense. [10] The phrase "opposed judgments" we do not employ in the sense of negations and affirmations only but simply as equivalent to "conflicting judgments." "Equipollence" we use of equality in respect of probability and improbability, to indicate that no one of the conflicting judgments takes precedence of any other as being more probable. "Suspense" is a state of mental rest owing to which we neither deny nor affirm anything. "Quietude" is an untroubled and tranquil condition of soul. And how quietude enters the soul along with suspension of judgment we shall explain in our chapter (12) "Concerning the End."

Chapter 5: Of the Skeptic

[11] In the definition of the Skeptic system there is also implicitly included that of the Pyrrhonian philosopher: he is the man who participates in this "ability."

Chapter 6: Of the Principles of Skepticism

[12] The originating cause of Skepticism is, we say, the hope of attaining quietude. Men of talent, who were perturbed by the contradictions in things and in doubt as to which of the alternatives they ought to accept, were led on to inquire what is true in things and what false, hoping by the settlement of this question to attain quietude. The main basic principle of the Skeptic system is that of opposing to every proposition an equal proposition; for we believe that as a consequence of this we end by ceasing to dogmatize.

Chapter 7: Does the Skeptic Dogmatize?

[13] When we say that the Skeptic refrains from dogmatizing we do not use the term "dogma," as some do, in the broader sense of "approval of a thing" (for the Skeptic gives assent to the feelings which are the necessary results of sense-impressions, and he would not, for example, say when feeling hot or cold "I believe that I am not hot or cold"); but we say that "he does not dogmatize" using "dogma" in the sense, which some give it, of "assent to one of the non-evident objects of scientific inquiry" for the Pyrrhonian philosopher assents to nothing that is non-evident. [14] Moreover, even in the act of enunciating the Skeptic formulae concerning things non-evident—such as the formula "No more (one thing than another)," or the formula "I determine nothing," or any of the others which we shall presently mention,—he does not dogmatize. For whereas the dogmatizer posits the things about which he is said to be dogmatizing as really existent, the Skeptic does not posit these formulae in any absolute sense; for he conceives that, just as the formula "All things are false" asserts the falsity of itself as well as of everything else, as does the formulae "Nothing is true," so also the formula "No more" asserts that itself, like all the rest, is "No more (this than that)," and thus cancels itself along with the rest. And of the other formulae we say the same. [15] If then, while the dogmatizer posits the matter of his dogma as substantial truth, the Skeptic enunciates his formulae so that they are virtually cancelled by themselves, he should not be said to dogmatize in his enunciation of them. And, most important of all, in his enunciation of these formulae he states what appears to himself and announces his own impression in an undogmatic way, without making any positive assertion regarding the external realities.

Chapter 8: Has the Skeptic a Doctrinal Rule?

[16] We follow the same lines in replying to the question "Has the Skeptical a doctrinal rule?" For if one defines a "doctrinal rule" as "adherence to a number of dogmas which are dependent both on one another and on appearances," and defines "dogma" as "assent to a non-evident proposition," then we shall say that he has not a doctrinal rule. [17] But if one defines "doctrinal rule" as "procedure which, in accordance with appearance, follows a certain line of reasoning, that reasoning indicating how it is possible to seem to live rightly (the word 'rightly' being taken, not as referring to virtue only, but in a wider sense) and tending to enable one to suspend judgment," then we say that he has a doctrinal rule. For we follow a line of reasoning which, in accordance with appearances, points us to a life conformable to the customs of our country and its laws and institutions, and to our own instinctive feelings.

Chapter 10: Do the Skeptics Abolish Appearances?

[19] Those who say that "the Skeptics abolish appearances," or phenomena, seem to me to be unacquainted with the statements of our School. For, as we said above, we do not overthrow the affective sense-impressions which induce our assent involun-

tarily; and these impressions are "the appearances." And when we question whether the underlying object is such as it appears, we grant the fact that it appears, and our doubt does not concern the appearance itself but the account given of that appearance,—and that is a different thing from questioning the appearance itself. [20] For example, honey appears to us to be sweet (and this we grant, for we perceive sweetness through the senses), but whether it is also sweet in its essence is for us a matter of doubt, since this is not an appearance but a judgment regarding the appearance. And even if we do actually argue against the appearances, we do not propound such arguments with the intention of abolishing appearances, but by way of pointing out the rashness of the Dogmatists; for if reason is such a trickster as to all but snatch away the appearances from under our very eyes, surely we should view it with suspicion in the case of things non-evident so as not to display rashness by following it.

Chapter 11: Of the Criterion of Skepticism

[21] That we adhere to appearances is plain from what we say about the Criterion of the Skeptic School. The word "Criterion" is used in two senses: in the one it means "the standard regulating belief in reality or unreality" (and this we shall discuss in our refutation); in the other it denotes the standard of action by conforming to which in the conduct of life we perform some actions and abstain from others; and it is of the latter that we are now speaking. [22] The criterion, then, of the Skeptic School is, we say, the appearance, giving this name to what is virtually the sense-presentation. For since this lies in feeling and involuntary affection, it is not open to question. Consequently, no one, I suppose, disputes that the underlying object has this or that appearance; the point in dispute is whether the object is in reality such as it appears to be. [23] Adhering, then, to appearances we live in accordance with the normal rules of life, undogmatically, seeing that we cannot remain wholly inactive. And it would seem that this regulation of life is fourfold, and that one part of it lies in the guidance of Nature, another in the constraint of the passions, another in the tradition of laws and customs, another in the instruction of the arts. [24] Nature's guidance is that by which we are naturally capable of sensation and thought; constraint of the passions is that whereby hunger drives us to food and thirst to drink; tradition of customs and laws, that whereby we regard piety in the conduct of life as good, but impiety as evil; instruction of the arts, that whereby we are not inactive in such arts as we adopt. But we make all these statements undogmatically.

Chapter 12: What Is the End of Skepticism?

[25] Our next subject will be the End of the Skeptic system. Now an "End" is that for which all actions or reasonings are undertaken, while it exists for the sake of none; or, otherwise, "the ultimate object of appetency." We assert still that the Skeptic's End is quietude in respect of matters of opinion and moderate feeling in respect of things unavoidable. [26] For the Skeptic, having set out to philosophize with the object of

passing judgment on the sense-impressions and ascertaining which of them are true and which false, so as to attain quietude thereby, found himself involved in contradictions of equal weight, and being unable to decide between them suspended judgment; and as he was thus in suspense there followed, as it happened, the state of quietude in respect of matters of opinion. [27] For the man who opines that anything is by nature good or bad is for ever being disquieted: when he is without the things which he deems good he believes himself to be tormented by things naturally bad and he pursues after the things which are, as he thinks, good; which when he has obtained he keeps falling into still more perturbations because of his irrational and immoderate elation, and in his dread of a change of fortune he uses every endeavor to avoid losing the things which he deems good. [28] On the other hand, the man who determines nothing as to what is naturally good or bad neither shuns nor pursues anything eagerly; and, in consequence, he is unperturbed. The Skeptic, in fact, had the same experience which is said to have befallen the painter Apelles. Once, they say, when he was painting a horse and wished to represent in the painting the horse's foam, he was so unsuccessful that he gave up the attempt and flung at the picture the sponge on which he used to wipe the paints off his brush, and the mark of the sponge produced the effect of a horse's foam. [29] So, too, the Skeptics were in hopes of gaining quietude by means of a decision regarding the disparity of the objects of sense and of thought, and being unable to effect this they suspended judgment; and they found that quietude, as if by chance, followed upon their suspense, even as a shadow follows its substance. We do not, however, suppose that the Skeptic is wholly untroubled; but we say that he is troubled by things unavoidable; for we grant that he is cold at times and thirsty, and suffers various affections of that kind. [30] But even in these cases, whereas ordinary people are afflicted by two circumstances,—namely, by the affections themselves and, in no less a degree, by the belief that these conditions are evil by nature,—the Skeptic, by his rejection of the added belief in the natural badness of all these conditions, escapes here too with less discomfort. Hence we say that, while in regard to matters of opinion the Skeptic's End is quietude, in regard to things unavoidable it is "moderate affection." But some notable Skeptics have added the further definition "suspension of judgment in investigations."

Chapter 13: Of the General Modes Leading to Suspension of Judgment

[31] Now that we have being saying that tranquility follows on suspension of judgment, it will be our next task to explain how we arrive at this suspension. Speaking generally, one may say that it is the result of setting things in opposition. We oppose either appearances to appearances or objects of thought to objects of thought or *alternando*. [32] For instance, we oppose appearances to appearances when we say "The same tower appears round from a distance, but square from close at hand"; and thoughts to thoughts, when in answer to him who argues the existence of the Providence from the order of the heavenly bodies we oppose the fact that often the good fare ill and the bad fare well, and draw from this the inference that Providence does

not exist. [33] And thoughts we oppose to appearances, as when Anaxagoras countered the notion that snow is white with the argument, "Snow is frozen water, and water is black." With a different idea we oppose things present sometimes to things present, as in the foregoing examples, and sometimes to things past or future, as, for instance, when someone propounds to us a theory which we are unable to refute, we say to him in reply, [34] "Just as, before the birth of the founder of the School to which you belong, the theory it holds was not as yet apparent as a sound theory, although it was really in existence, so likewise it is possible that the opposite theory to that which you now propound is already really existent, though not yet apparent to us, so that we ought not as yet to yield assent to this theory which at the moment seems to be valid."

[35] But in order that we may have a more exact understanding of these antithesis I will describe the Modes by which suspension of judgment is brought about, but without making any positive assertion regarding either their number or their validity; for it is possible that they may be unsound or there may be more of them than I shall enumerate.

Chapter 14: Concerning the Ten Modes

[36] The usual tradition amongst the older Skeptics is that the "modes" by which "suspension" is supposed to be brought about are ten in number; and they also give them the synonymous names of "arguments" and "positions." They are these: the first, based on the variety in animals; the second, on the differences in human beings; the third, on the different structures of the organs of sense; the fourth, on the circumstantial conditions; the fifth, on positions and intervals and locations; [37] the sixth, on intermixtures; the seventh, on the quantities and formations of the underlying objects; the eighth, on the fact of relativity; the ninth, on the frequency or rarity of occurrence; the tenth, on the disciplines and customs and laws, the legendary beliefs and the dogmatic convictions. [38] This order, however, we adopt without prejudice.

As superordinate to these there stand three Modes—that based on the subject who judges, that on the object judged, and that based on both. The first four of the ten Modes are subordinate to the Mode based on the subject (for the subject which judges is either an animal or a man or a sense, and existent in some condition): the seventh and tenth Modes are referred to that based on the object judged: the fifth, sixth, eighth, and ninth are referred to the Mode based on both subject and object. [39] Furthermore, these three Modes are also referred to that of relation, so that the Mode of relation stands as the highest *genus*, and the three as *species*, and the ten as subordinate *sub-species*. We give this as the probable account of their numbers; and as to their argumentative force what we say is this:

[40] The *First* argument (or *Trope*) is that which shows that the same impressions are not produced by the same objects owing to the differences in animals. This we infer both from the differences in their origins and from the variety of their bodily structures. . . .

[50] . . . Thus, in respect of touch, how could one maintain that creatures covered with shells, with flesh, with prickles, with feathers, with scales, are all similarly affected? And as for the sense of hearing, how could we say that its perceptions are alike in animals with a very narrow auditory passage and those with a very wide one, or in animals with hairy ears and those with smooth ears? For, as regards this sense, even we ourselves find our hearing affected in one way when we have our ears plugged and in another way when we use they just as they are. [51] Smell also will differ because of the variety in animals. For if we ourselves are affected in one way when we have a cold and our internal phlegm is excessive, and in another way when the parts about our head are filled with an excess of blood, feeling an aversion to smells which seem sweet to everyone else and regarding them as noxious it is reasonable to suppose that animals too—since some are flaccid by nature and rich in phlegm, others rich in blood, others marked by a predominant excess of yellow or of black gall—are in each case impressed in different ways by the objects of smell. . . .

[59] But if the same things appear different owing to the variety in animals, we shall, indeed, be able to state our own impressions of the real object, but as to its essential nature we shall suspend judgment. For we cannot ourselves judge between our own impressions and those of the other animals, since we ourselves are involved in the dispute and are, therefore, rather in need of a judge than competent to pass judgment ourselves. . . .

[62] By way of supper-addition too, we draw comparisons between mankind and the so-called irrational animals in respect of their sense-impressions. For, after our solid arguments, we deem it quite proper to poke fun at those conceited braggarts, the Dogmatists. As a rule, our School compares the irrational animals in the mass with mankind; [63] but since the Dogmatists captiously assert that the comparison is unequal, we—super-adding yet more—will carry our ridicule further and base our argument on one animal only, the dog for instance if you like, which is held to be the most worthless of animals. For even in this case we shall find that the animals we are discussing are no wise inferior to ourselves in respect of the credibility of their impressions.

[64] Now it is allowed by the Dogmatists that this animal, the dog, excels us in point of sensation: as to smell it is more sensitive than we are, since by this sense it tracks beasts that it cannot see; and with its eyes it sees them more quickly than we do; and with its ears it is keen of perception. [65] Next let us proceed to the reasoning faculty. Of reason one kind is internal, implanted in the soul, the other externally expressed. Let us consider first the internal reason. Now according to those Dogmatists who are, at present, our chief opponents—I mean the Stoics—internal reason is supposed to be occupied with the following matters: the choice of things congenial and the avoidance of things alien; the knowledge of the arts contributing thereto; the apprehension of the virtues pertaining to one's proper nature and of those relating to the passions. [66] Now the dog—the animal upon which, by way of example, we have decided to base our argument—exercises choice of the congenial and avoidance of the harmful, in that it hunts after food and slinks away from a raised whip. More-

over, it possesses an art which supplies what is congenial, namely hunting. [67] Nor is it devoid even of virtue; for certainly if justice consists in rendering to each his due, the dog, that welcomes and guards its friends and benefactors but drives off strangers and evil-doers, cannot be lacking in justice. [68] But if he possesses this virtue, then, since the virtues are interdependent, he possesses also all the other virtues; and these, say the philosophers, the majority of men do not possess. That the dog is also valiant we see by the way he repels attacks, and intelligent as well, as Homer too testified when he sang how Odysseus went unrecognized by all the people of his own household and was recognized only by the dog Argus, who neither was deceived by the bodily alterations of the hero nor had lost his original apprehensive impression, which indeed he evidently retained better than the men. [69] And according to Chrysippus, who shows special interest in irrational animals, the dog even shares in the far-famed "Dialectic." This person, at any rate, declares that the dog makes use of the fifth complex indemonstrable syllogism when, on arriving at a spot where three ways meet, after smelling at the two roads by which the quarry did not pass, he rushes off at once by the third without stopping to smell. For, says the old writer, the dog implicitly reasons thus: "The creature went either by this road, or by that, or by the other but it did not go by this road or by that: therefore it went by the other." . . .

[73] Concerning external reason, or speech, it is unnecessary for the present to inquire; for it has been rejected even by some of the Dogmatists as being a hindrance to the acquisition of virtue, for which reason they used to practice silence during the period of instruction; and besides, supposing that a man is dumb, no one will therefore call him irrational. But to pass over these cases, we certainly see animals—the subject of our argument—uttering quite human cries,—jays, for instance, and others. [74] And, leaving this point also aside, even if we do not understand the utterances of the so-called irrational animals, still it is not improbable that they converse although we fail to understand them; for in fact when we listen to the talk of barbarians we do not understand it, and it seems to us a kind of uniform chatter. [75] Moreover, we hear dogs uttering one sound when they are driving people off, another when they are howling, and one sound when beaten, and a quite different sound when fawning. And so in general, in the case of all other animals as well as the dog, whoever examines the matter carefully will find a great variety of utterance according to the different circumstances, so that, in consequence, the so-called irrational animals may justly be said to participate in external reason. . . .

[79] . . . The *Second Mode* is that based on the differences in men; for even if we grant for the sake of the argument that men are more worthy of credence than irrational animals, we shall find that even our own differences of themselves lead to suspense. For man, you know, is said to be compounded of two things, soul and body, and in both these we differ one from another.

Thus, as regards to the *body*, we differ in our figures and "idiosyncrasies," or constitutional peculiarities. . . .

[85] . . . [M]en probably also differ from one another in respect of the *soul* itself; for the body is a kind of expression of the soul, as in fact is proved by the sci-

ence of Physiognomy. But the greatest proof of the vast and endless differences in men's intelligence is the discrepancy in the statements of the dogmatists concerning the right objects of choice and avoidance, as well as other things. . . .

[87] Seeing, then, that choice and avoidance depend on pleasure and displeasure, while pleasure depend on sensation and sense-impression, whenever some men choose the very things which are avoided by others, it is logical for us to conclude that they are also differently affected by the same things, since otherwise they would all alike have chosen and avoided the same things. But if the same objects affect men differently owing to the differences in the men, then, on this ground also, we shall reasonably be led to suspension of judgment. . . .

[91] The *Third Mode* is based on differences in the senses. That the senses differ from one another is obvious. . . .

[94] A longer list of examples might be given, but to avoid prolixity, in view of the plan of our treatise, we will say just this. Each of the phenomena perceived by the senses seems to be a complex: the apple, for example, seems smooth, odorous, sweet, and yellow. But it is non-evident whether it really possesses these qualities only; or whether it has but one quality but appears varied owing to the varying structure of the sense-organs; or whether, again, it has more qualities than are apparent, some of which elude our perception. [95] That the apple has but one quality might be argued from what we said above regarding the food absorbed by bodies, and the water sucked up by trees, and the breath in flutes and pipes and similar instruments; for the apple likewise may be all of one sort but appear different owing to differences in the sense-organs in which perception takes place. [96] And that the apple may possibly possess more qualities than those apparent to us we argue in this way. Let us imagine a man who possesses from birth the senses of touch, taste, and smell, but can neither hear nor see. This man, then, will assume that nothing visible or audible has any existence, but only those three kinds of qualities which he is able to apprehend. [97] Possibly, then, we also, having only our five senses, perceive only such of the apple's qualities as we are capable of apprehending; and possibly it may possess other underlying qualities which affect other sense-organs, though we, not being endowed with those organs, fail to apprehend the sense-objects which come through them.

[98] "But," it may be objected, "Nature made the senses commensurate with the objects of sense." What kind of "Nature"? we ask, seeing that there exists so much unresolved controversy amongst the Dogmatists concerning the reality which belongs to Nature. For he who decides the question as to the existence of Nature will be discredited by them if he is an ordinary person, while if he is a philosopher he will be a party to the controversy and therefore himself subject to judgment and not a judge. [99] If, however, it is possible that only those qualities which we seem to perceive subsist in the apple, or that a greater number subsist, or, again, that not even the qualities which affect us subsist, then it will be non-evident to us what the nature of the apple really is. And the same argument applies to all the other objects of sense. But if the senses do not apprehend external objects, neither can the mind apprehend them; hence, because of this argument also, we shall be driven, it seems, to suspend

judgment regarding the external underlying objects.

[100] In order that we may finally reach suspension by basing our argument on each sense singly, or even by disregarding the senses, we further adopt the *Fourth Mode* of suspension. This is the Mode based on the "circumstances," meaning by "circumstances" conditions and dispositions. And this Mode, we say, deals with states that are natural or unnatural, with waking or sleeping, with conditions due to age, motion or rest, hatred or love, emptiness or fullness, drunkenness or soberness, predispositions, confidence or fear, grief or joy. [101] Thus, according as the mental state is natural or unnatural, objects produce dissimilar impressions, as when men in a frenzy or in a state of ecstasy believe they hear demons' voices, while we do not. . . . And the same honey seems to me sweet, but bitter to men with jaundice. [102] Now should anyone say that it is an intermixture of certain humors which produces in those who are in an unnatural state improper impressions from the underlying objects, we have to reply that, since healthy persons also have mixed humors, these humors too are capable of causing the external objects—which really are such as they appear to those who said to be in an unnatural state—to appear other than they are to healthy persons. [103] For to ascribe the power of altering the underlying objects to those humors, and not to these, is purely fanciful; since just as healthy men are in a state that is natural for the healthy but unnatural for the sick, so also sick men are in a state that is unnatural for the healthy but natural for the sick, so that to these last also we must give credence as being, relatively speaking, in a natural state.

[104] Sleeping and waking, too, give rise to different impressions, since we do not imagine when awake what we imagine in sleep, nor when asleep what we imagine when awake; so that the existence or non-existence of our impressions is not absolute but relative, being in relation to our sleeping or waking condition. Probably, then, in dreams we see things which to our waking state are unreal, although not wholly unreal; for they exist in our dreams, just as waking realities exist although non-existent in dreams. . . .

[108] Love and hatred are a cause, as when some have an extreme aversion to pork while others greatly enjoy eating it. . . . Many lovers, too, who have ugly mistresses think them most beautiful. . . .

[118] The *Fifth Argument* (or *Trope*) is that based on positions, distances, and locations; for owing to each of these the same objects appear different; for example, the same porch when viewed from one of its corners appears curtailed, but viewed from the middle symmetrical on all sides; and the same ship seems at a distance to be small and stationary, but from close at hand large and in motion; and the same tower from a distance appears round but from a near point quadrangular. . . .

[124] The *Sixth Mode* is that based on admixtures, by which we conclude that, because none of the real objects affects our senses by itself but always in conjunction with something else, though we may possibly be able to state the nature of the resultant mixture formed by the external object and that along with which it is perceived, we shall not be able to say what is the exact nature of the external reality itself. . . .

[129] The *Seventh Mode* is that based on the quantity and constitution of the

underlying objects, meaning generally by "constitution" the manner of the composition. . . . Thus, for example, the filings of a goat's horn appear white when viewed simply by themselves and without combination, but when combined in the substance of the horn they look black. And silver filings appear black when they are by themselves, but when united to the whole mass they are sensed as white. . . .

[135] The *Eighth Mode* is that based on relativity; and by it we conclude that, since all things are relative, we shall suspend judgment as to what things are absolutely and really existent. But this we must notice—that here as elsewhere we use the term "are" for the term "appear," and what we virtually mean is "all things appear relative." And this statement is twofold, implying, firstly, relation to the thing which judges (for the external object which is judged appears in relation to that thing), and, in a second sense, relation to the accompanying percepts, for instance the right side in relation to the left. . . .

[141] The *Mode* which comes *Ninth* in order is based on constancy or rarity of occurrence, and we shall explain it as follows. The sun is, of course, much more amazing than a comet; yet because we see the sun constantly but the comet rarely we are so amazed by the comet that we even regard it as a divine portent, while the sun causes no amazement at all. If, however, we were to conceive of the sun as appearing but rarely and setting rarely, and illuminating everything all at once and throwing everything into shadow suddenly, then we should experience much amazement at the sight. . . .

[145] There is a *Tenth Mode,* which is mainly concerned with Ethics, being based on rules of conduct, habits, laws, legendary beliefs, and dogmatic conceptions. . . .

[148] And each of these we oppose now to itself, and now to each of the others. For example, we oppose habit to habit in this way: some of the Ethiopians tattoo their children, but we do not; and while the Persians think it seemly to wear a brightly dyed dress reaching to the feet, we think it unseemly; and whereas the Indians have intercourse with their women in public, most other races regard this as shameful. [149] And law we oppose to law in this way: among the Romans the man who renounces his father's property does not pay his father's debts, but among the Rhodians he always pays them; and among the Scythian Tauri it was a law that strangers should be sacrificed to Artemis, but with us it is forbidden to slay a human being at the altar. [150] And we oppose rule of conduct to rule of conduct, as when we oppose the rule of Diogenes to that of Aristippus or that of the Laconians to that of the Italians. And we oppose legendary belief to legendary belief when we say that whereas in one story the father of men and gods is alleged to be Zeus, in another he is Oceanos—"Ocean sire of the gods, and Tethys the mother that bare them." [151] And we oppose dogmatic conceptions to one another when we say that some declare that there is one element only, others an infinite number; some that the soul is mortal, others that it is immortal; and some that human affairs are controlled by divine Providence, others without Providence.

[152] And we oppose habit to the other things, as for instance to law when we say that amongst the Persians it is the habit to indulge in intercourse with males, but

amongst the Romans it is forbidden by law to do so; and that, whereas with us adultery is forbidden, amongst the Massagetae it is traditionally regarded as an indifferent custom, as Eudoxus of Cnidos relates in the first book of his *Travels*; and that, whereas intercourse with a mother is forbidden in our country, in Persia it is the general custom to form such marriages; and also among the Egyptians men marry their sisters, a thing forbidden by law amongst us. [153] And habit is opposed to rule of conduct when, whereas most men have intercourse with their own wives in retirement, Crates did it in public with Hipparchia; and Diogenes went about with one shoulder bare, whereas we dress in the customary manner. [154] It is opposed also to legendary belief, as when the legends say that Cronos devoured his own children, though it is our habit to protect our children; and whereas it is customary with us to revere the gods as being good and immune from evil, they are presented by the poets as suffering wounds and envying one another. [155] And habit is opposed to dogmatic conception when, whereas it is our habit to pray to the gods for good things, Epicurus declares that the Divinity pays no heed to us; and when Aristippus considers the wearing of feminine attire a matter of indifference, though we consider it a disgraceful thing. . . .

Chapter 15: Of the Five Modes

[164] The later Skeptics hand down Five Modes leading to suspension, namely these: the first based on discrepancy, the second on regress *ad infinitum*, the third on relativity, the fourth on hypothesis, the fifth on circular reasoning. [165] That based on discrepancy leads us to find that with regard to the object presented there has arisen both amongst ordinary people and amongst the philosophers an interminable conflict because of which we are unable either to choose a thing or reject it, and so fall back on suspension. [166] The Mode based upon regress *ad infinitum* is that whereby we assert that the thing adduced as a proof of the matter proposed needs a further proof, and this again another, and so on *ad infinitum*, so that the consequence is suspension, as we possess no starting-point for our argument. [167] The Mode based upon relativity, as we have already said, is that whereby the object has such or such an appearance in relation to the subject judging and to the concomitant percepts, but as to its real nature we suspend judgment. [168] We have the Mode based on hypothesis when the Dogmatists, being forced to recede *ad infinitum*, take as their starting-point something which they do not establish by argument but claim to assume as granted simply and without demonstration. [169] The Mode of circular reasoning is the form used when the proof itself which ought to establish the matter of inquiry requires confirmation derived from that matter; in this case, being unable to assume either in order to establish the other, we suspend judgment about both.

That every matter of inquiry admits of being brought under these Modes we shall show briefly in this way. [170] The matter proposed is either a sense-object or a thought-object, but whichever it is, it is an object of controversy; for some say that only sensibles are true, others only intelligibles, others that some sensible and some intelligible objects are true. Will they then assert that the controversy can or cannot be decided? If they say it cannot, we have it granted that we must suspend judgment; for concerning matters of dispute which admit of no decision it is impossible to make an assertion. But if they say that it can be decided, we ask by what is it to be decided. [171] For example, in the case of the sense-object (for we shall base our argument on it first), is it to be decided by a sense-object or a thought-object? For if they say by a sense-object, since we are inquiring about sensibles that object itself also will require another to confirm it; and if that too is to be a sense-object, it likewise will require another for its confirmation, and so on *ad infinitum*. [172] And if the sense-object shall have to be decided by a thought-object, then, since thought-objects also are controverted, this being an object of thought will need examination and confirmation. Whence then will it gain confirmation? If from an intelligible object, it will suffer a similar regress *ad infinitum*; and if from a sensible object, since an intelligible was adduced to establish the sensible and a sensible to establish the intelligible, the Mode of circular reasoning is brought in.

[173] If, however, our disputant, by way of escape from this conclusion, should claim to assume as granted and without demonstration some postulate for the demonstration of the next steps of his argument, then the Mode of hypothesis will be brought in, which allows no escape. For if the author of the hypothesis is worthy of credence, we shall be no less worthy of credence every time that we make the opposite hypothesis. Moreover, if the author of the hypothesis assumes what is true he causes it to be suspected by assuming it by hypothesis rather than after proof; while if it is false, the foundation of his argument will be rotten. [174] Further, if hypothesis conduces at all to proof, let the subject of inquiry itself be assumed and not some other thing which is merely a means to establish the actual subject of the argument; but if it is absurd to assume the subject of inquiry, it will also be absurd to assume that upon which it depends.

[175] It is also plain that all sensibles are relative; for they are relative to those who have the sensations. Therefore it is apparent that whatever sensible object is presented can easily be referred to one of the Five Modes. And concerning the intelligible object we argue similarly. . . .

[177] Such then are the Five Modes handed down amongst the later Skeptics; but they propound these not by way of superseding the Ten Modes but in order to expose the rashness of the Dogmatists with more variety and completeness by means of the Five in conjunction with the Ten.

Book 2, Chapter 4—Does a Criterion of Truth Really Exist?

[18] Of those, then, who have treated of the criterion some have declared that a criterion exists—the Stoics, for example, and certain others—while by some its existence is denied, as by the Corinthian Xeniades, amongst others, and by Xenophanes of Colophon, who says—"Over all things opinion bears sway"; while we have adopted suspension of judgment as to whether it does or does not exist. [19] This dispute, then, they will declare to be either capable or incapable of decision; and if

they shall say it is incapable of decision they will be granting on the spot the propriety of suspension of judgment, while if they say it admits of decision, let them tell us whereby it is to be decided, since we have no accepted criterion, and do not even know, but are still inquiring, whether any criterion exists. [20] Besides, in order to decide the dispute which has arisen about the criterion, we must possess an accepted criterion by which we shall be able to judge the dispute; and in order to possess an accepted criterion, the dispute about the criterion must first be decided. And when the argument thus reduces itself to a form of circular reasoning the discovery of the criterion becomes impracticable, since we do not allow them to adopt a criterion by assumption, while if they offer to judge the criterion by a criterion we force them to a regress *ad infinitum*. And furthermore, since demonstration requires a demonstrated criterion, while the criterion requires an approved demonstration, they are forced into circular reasoning. . . .

Book 2, Chapter 7—Of the Criterion "According to Which"

. . . [72] Further, even were we to grant that the "presentation" is apprehended, objects cannot be judged according to it; for the intellect, as they assert, does not make contact with external objects and receive presentations by means of itself but by means of the senses, and the senses do not apprehend external real objects but only, if at all, their own affections. So then the presentation will be that of the affection of the sense, which is different from the external reality; for honey is not the same as my feeling of sweetness nor gall the same as my feeling of bitterness, but a different thing. [73] And if this affection differs from the external real object, the presentation will not be that of the external reality but of something else which is different therefrom. If, therefore, the intellect judges according to this, it judges badly and not accordingly to reality. Consequently, it is absurd to say that external objects are judged according to the presentation.

[74] Nor, again, is it possible to assert that the soul apprehends external realities by means of the affections of sense owing to the similarity of the affections of the senses to the external real objects. For how is the intellect to know whether the affections of the senses are similar to the objects of sense when it has not itself encountered the external objects, and the senses do not inform it about their real nature but only about their own affections, as I have argued from the Modes of Suspension. [75] For just as the man who does not know Socrates but has seen a picture of him does not know whether the picture is like Socrates, so also the intellect when it gazes on the affections of the senses but does not behold the external objects will not so much as know whether the affections of the senses are similar to the external realities. So that not even on the ground of resemblance will he be able to judge these objects according to the presentation. . . .

Book 3, Chapter 32—Why the Skeptic Sometimes Purposely Propounds Arguments which Are Lacking in Power of Persuasion

[280] The Skeptic, being a lover of his kind, desires to cure by speech, as best he can, the self-conceit and rashness of the Dogmatists. So, just as the physicians who cure bodily ailments have remedies which differ in strength, and apply the severe ones to those whose ailments are severe and the milder to those mildly affected,—so too the Skeptic propounds arguments which differ in strength, [281] and employs those which are weighty and capable by their stringency of disposing of the Dogmatists' ailment, self-conceit, in cases where the mischief is due to a severe attack of rashness, while he employs the milder arguments in the case of those whose ailment of conceit is superficial and easy to cure, and whom it is possible to restore to health by milder methods of persuasion. Hence the adherent of Skeptic principles does not scruple to propound at one time arguments that are weighty in their persuasiveness, and at another time such as appear less impressive,—and he does so on purpose, as the latter are frequently sufficient to enable him to effect his object.

FROM *ADVERSUS MATHEMATICOS*

[480] . . . For there are many things which produce the same effect on themselves as they produce on other things. Just as, for example, fire after consuming the fuel destroys also itself, and like as purgatives after driving the fluids out of the bodies expel themselves as well, so too the argument against proof, after abolishing every proof, can cancel itself also. And again, just as it is not impossible for the man who has ascended to a high place by a ladder to overturn the ladder with his foot after his ascent, so also it is not unlikely that the Skeptic after he has arrived at the demonstration of his thesis by means of the argument proving the non-existence of proof, as it were by a step-ladder, should then abolish this very argument.

FURTHER READINGS

Annas, Julia. "Doing without Objective Values: Ancient and Modern Strategies." In *The Norms of Nature*, edited by M. Schofield and Gisela Striker, 3–29. Cambridge: Cambridge University Press, 1986.

Annas, Julia, and Jonathan Barnes. *The Modes of Skepticism*. Cambridge: Cambridge University Press, 1985.

Bailey, Alan. *Sextus Empiricus and Pyrrhonian Skepticism*. Oxford: Oxford University Press, 2002.

Barnes, Jonathan. *The Toils of Skepticism*. Cambridge: Cambridge University Press, 1990.

———. "The Beliefs of a Pyrrhonist." *Elenchos* 4 (1983): 5–43.

Brochard, Victor. *Les Sceptiques grecs*. Paris: Vrin, 1959 (first edition, 1887).

Burnyeat, Myles. "Can the Sceptic Live His Scepticism?" In *Doubt and Dogmatism: Studies in Hellenistic Epistemology*, edited by M. Schofield, M. Burnyeat, and J. Barnes, 20–53. Oxford: Clarendon Press, 1980.

Frede, Michael. "The Sceptic's Beliefs." In *Essays in Ancient Philosophy*, edited by Michael Frede, chap. 10. Minneapolis: University of Minnesota Press, 1989.

House, D. K. "The Life of Sextus Empiricus." *Classical Quarterly* 30 (1980): 227–38.

Janácek, K. *Sextus Empiricus' Sceptical Methods*. Prague: Karlova University, 1972.

Mates, Benson. *The Skeptic Way*. Oxford: Oxford University Press, 1996.

5

AUGUSTINE

*A*gainst the Academics is the first philosophical work written by Augustine of Hippo (383–430) after his conversion to Christianity. In *Confessions* 5.14 and in *Retractions* 1.1, he says he was influenced by the Academics when he abandoned the Manichean sect. *Against the Academics* is a response to Academic skepticism at a time Augustine considered crucial to dissociate wisdom from suspension of judgment. The book is a direct reply to Cicero's *Academics*, the main source for his view of ancient skepticism. (Augustine apparently had no knowledge of Pyrrhonism.) *Against the Academics* is not the only place where he objects to Academic skepticism. For instance, his famous *cogito* is stated much clearer in *De Trinitate* 10.10.14. In the present selection we have included Augustine's main arguments against the Academics and also his concern with the immoral consequences of Carneades' probabilism. Augustine's position with respect to the Academic skeptics is not completely negative though. Maybe considering his own experience, he claims that if, contrary to his view of Cicero's version of Academic skepticism, suspension of judgment does not mean the end of the search for the truth, it can help one to keep oneself free from the materialist and sensualist philosophies that prevailed in the Hellenistic period. Augustine even gives credit to the legend—today largely denied by scholars—that the Academics supported an esoteric form of doctrinal Platonism. In *Against the Academics* 2.24 and 3.37 Augustine explains what he thinks was the real thought of the Academics and why they hid their true views. Their suspension of judgment was in a way necessary to preserve a truth that could only be fully displayed after the advent of the Christian revelation.

FROM *AGAINST THE ACADEMICS*

23. You say that in philosophy nothing can be perceived, and so that you may give your contention wide publicity, you seize upon the disputes and disagreements of philosophers and think with them to furnish arms to yourself against the philosophers themselves. For how, you argue, shall we be able to settle the dispute between Democritus and his predecessors in physics as to whether there is one or innumerable worlds, when Democritus himself and his heir, Epicurus, could not agree? When this latter voluptuary allows the atoms, as it were his little handmaids, those

little bodies which he joyfully embraces in the dark, to deviate from their course and turn aside wherever they like into the domains of others, he is quarrelling and he has thus dissipated all his patrimony.

But this is no concern of mine. If it is part of wisdom to know something of these things, then all this will certainly not escape the attention of the wise man. But if wisdom consists in something different, then it is *that* that the wise man knows and the other is despised by him. Even I, however, who am still far from being anyway near being a wise man, know something at any rate in Physics. I am certain, for instance, that there is one world or not one. If there is not one world, then the number of worlds is finite or infinite. Carneades may say, if he likes, that this opinion is like one that is not true. Likewise, I know that this world of ours is ordered as it is, either by the intrinsic nature of corporeal matter, or by some providence; that it either always was and always will be, or began to be and will never cease, or never began in time but will end, or began to exist and will not exist forever. I know countless things about physics after this manner. These disjunctions are true, and no one can refute them by pointing to any likeness in them to what is not true.

"But elect for one member of the disjunction," bids the Academic. No. I shall not. You are asking me not to assert what I do know, and assert what I do not know. "But your assertion hangs in the air." It is better that it should hang there than that it should be dashed to the ground. You see, it is adequate for our purpose; that is to say, as an assertion it can be pronounced either true or not true. I assert that this is something that I know. Let you, who cannot deny that such matter pertains to philosophy, and who assert that none of these things can be known, demonstrate to me that I do not know these things. Assert that these disjunctions are either not true or have something in common with what is not true, so that, as a consequence, they are incapable of being distinguished from what is not true.

Chapter 11. Something Can Be Perceived

24. "But," he asks, "how do you know that the world you speak of exists at all? The senses may deceive." No matter how you argued, you were never able to repudiate the value of the senses to the extent that you could convince us that nothing appears to us to be. Indeed, you have never in any way ventured to try to do so. But you have done your very best to convince us that the reality could be different from the appearance. By the term "world," then, I mean all this, whatever kind of thing it be, which surrounds and nourishes us and which presents itself to my eyes and seems to me to hold earth and sky or quasi-earth and quasi-sky. If you say that non-reality presents itself to me, I shall still be free from error. It is he who rashly judges that which presents itself to him to be actual reality that falls into error. But while you do say that what is not true can present itself to sentient beings, you do not say that non-reality so presents itself. Indeed, all ground for disputation—wherein you love to reign supreme—is entirely removed if not only we know nothing, but if no appearance presents itself to us. If, however, you deny that that which presents itself to me

is the world, you are raising a question merely about a word; for I have stated that I do call that appearance the "world."

25. But you will ask me: "If you are asleep, does the world which you now see exist?" I have already said that whatever presents itself to me in that way, I call "world." But if you wish that only to be called "world" which presents itself to those who are awake or, even better, those who are sane, then maintain also, if you can, that those who are asleep or insane are not insane and asleep in the world! Accordingly, I make this statement: all that mass and contrivance in which we are, whether we be sleeping, or insane, or awake, or sane, is either one or not one. Explain how that judgment can be not true. If I am asleep, possibly I have made no statement at all. Or, if in my sleep the words have, as happens, escaped my mouth, possibly I have not spoken them here, sitting as I am, and with this audience. But the proposition itself that I have mentioned cannot be not true.

And I am not saying that I have perceived this on condition of my being awake. For you could say that in my sleep, too, this could have presented itself to me, and, consequently, can be very like what is not true. But it is manifest that no matter in what condition I am, if there is one world and six worlds, there are in all seven worlds, and I unhesitatingly assert that I know this. Now, then, convince me that this combination or the above-mentioned disjunctions can be not true by reason of sleep, madness, or the unreliability of the senses; and if being awakened from my slumber I recall them, I shall allow that I am vanquished. I feel sure that it is now sufficiently clear what appearances, although not true, can because of sleep or insanity present themselves as true: they are those which pertain to bodily senses. For that three times three makes nine, and that this is the squaring of rational numbers, must be true even though the human race were snoring! All the same, I notice that much can be said in defence even of the senses themselves—things which we do not find to be questioned by the Academics. The senses are not, I take it, blamed for the fact that insane people have illusions, or that we see in our dreams things that are not true. If the senses give reports that are true to those who are awake and sane, then they will not be involved in what the mind of one who is asleep or insane, conjures up.

26. There remains to ask if, when the senses report, they report what is true. Now, then, if an Epicurean says: "I have no complaint to make about the senses. It is unjust to demand from them more than that of which they are capable. When the eyes see anything, they see what is true": is, then, what the eyes see of an oar in water, true? Certainly, it is true. A cause has intervened so that it should present itself so. If when an oar was dipped under water it presented itself as straight, then in that case I would convict my eyes of giving a report that was not true. For they would not see what, given the existing circumstances, should have been seen. What need is there of developing the theme? The same thing can be said of towers that appear to move, of the changing colors on the feathers of birds, and of countless other cases.

"But," says someone, "I am deceived, if I give my assent." Do not assent more than that you know that it appears so to you. There is then no deception. I do not see how the Academic can refute him who says: I know that this presents itself to me as white; I know that this delights my ear; I know that this has a sweet smell for me; I know that this has a pleasant taste for me; I know that this feels cold to me. "Tell me, rather, if the leaves of the wild olive tree, of which the goat is so passionately fond, are *per se* bitter?" You rascal! The goat himself is more reasonable! I do not know how cattle find them. Anyway, I find them bitter. Does that satisfy you? "But there is perhaps among men one to whom they are not bitter." You are trying to make a nuisance of yourself. Have I said that all men found them bitter? I said that I found them bitter now, and I do not even assert that they will always be so for me. Could it not happen that at different times and for different reasons a thing could taste in one's mouth now sweet, now bitter? This I do assert that when a man tastes something, he can swear in all good faith that he knows that to his palate a given thing is sweet or the contrary. No Greek sophistry can steal such knowledge from him. Who would be so impertinent as to say to me as I savour with delight the taste of something: "Perhaps there is nothing to taste; you are only dreaming"? Do I stop my savouring? No! I reply that even though I were dreaming, it would still delight me. Accordingly, no likeness to what is not true can prove that that which I said I knew was wrong. Moreover, an Epicurean or the Cyrenaics may perhaps say many other things in defence of the senses, and I am not aware that the Academics have said anything to refute them. But what is that to me? If they want to, and if they can, let them refute these things. I shall even help them.

Certainly, their arguments against sense perception are not valid against all philosophers. There are some philosophers, for example, who maintain that whatever the spirit receives by way of bodily sense can generate opinion indeed, but not knowledge. They insist that the latter is found only in the intelligence and, far removed from the senses, abides in the mind. Perhaps the wise man whom we seek is to be found in their midst. But we shall talk about this at another time. Now let us turn to the points that remain. In view of what has already been said, we shall, if I mistake not, be able to deal with them in a few words. . . .

Chapter 16

35. It may be, indeed, that not everyone who errs, commits sin. It is conceded, however, that everyone who sins, either errs or does something worse. Well, then, if some young man, hearing the Academics say: "It is shameful to err, and, consequently, we ought not to assent to anything; when, however, a man does what seems probable to him, he neither sins, nor errs. All he need remember is that he is not to assent to as true anything that comes before his mind or senses"—if, I say, he hears this, what if the young man will lay siege to the chastity of another's wife?

I am asking you, Marcus Tullius—yes, you—for your opinion. We are dealing with the morals and lives of young men, with whose formation and instruction all your writings are concerned. What can you say but that it is not probable to *you*, that the young man would do such a thing? But to *him*, it is probable. For if we were to live by what seemed probable to another, you ought not to have governed in the state, since Epicurus thought that one should not do such a thing. That young man will, then, commit adultery with another's wife. If he is caught, where will he find you to defend him? And even if he does find you, what will you say? You will deny outright that the thing happened. But if it is so clear that it is useless to deny it? Of course, you will try to convince your opponents, as if you were in a scholastic establishment at Cumae or Naples, that he had committed no sin, in fact, had not even erred. He did not assent to the proposition that "I should commit adultery" as true. But then it occurred to him as probable: he followed it—he did the deed. Or, perhaps he did not do it, but thinks he has done it! The husband in his simplicity is causing general confusion by his litigation and the clamour he raises about his wife's chastity—with whom he is perhaps now sleeping without being aware of it!

If the jury is able to follow this, they will either ignore the Academics and mete out punishment on the crime as having been actually committed, or, being convinced by the same gentlemen, they will, acting according to what is likely and probable, condemn the man, so that his advocate will now be at a complete loss as to what course to take. He will not have cause to get angry with any of them, since all say that they have not fallen into an error. For, while not assenting, they had done what seemed probable. In these circumstances he will lay aside the role of advocate and assume that of the consoling philosopher. He can thus readily persuade the young man, who has already made such progress in the Academy, to think that he is condemned only in a dream.

But you think I am making fun! I am prepared to swear by all that is holy that I am completely at a loss to know how that young man sinned, if one who does what seems probable to him, does not sin. The only possible answer I find is that they may say that to err and to sin are two entirely different things and that by their principles they had in mind that we should not err, while they considered sinning itself to be of no great consequence.

36. I pass over homicide, parricide, sacrilege, and every type of crime and evildoing that can be committed or thought of—all can be justified by a few words, and, what is worse, before judges that are wise: "I did not assent, and therefore I did not err. How could I not have done what seemed probable?" If anyone thinks that such arguments cannot be made to seem probably conclusive, let him read the speech of Catiline wherein he sought to commend the parricide of one's country, in which is embodied all crime.

But what follows is merely ridiculous. The Academics themselves say that they act only on the probable. Nevertheless, they make great efforts in searching for truth, although they have already made up their minds that it is probable that it cannot be found. What a marvellous absurdity! But let us forget about it: it does not affect us or endanger our lives or belongings. But the other point is of the greatest importance: it is fraught with the most serious consequences and must cause the greatest anxiety to every upright man. For if this reasoning of the Academics is probable, then one may commit every crime not only without being blamed for the sin, but also without being blamed for an error—since one thought that one should act on the probable without assenting to anything as true. Well, then, did the Academics not see this? Indeed, they did see it—for they were clever and careful. I would never think of claiming that I came anyway near Marcus Tullius in hard work, prudence, capacity, or learning. Yet, when he says that a man cannot know anything, if this only were replied: "I know that it seems to me that he can," he would not be able to refute it.

FURTHER READINGS

Alven, M. N. *Augustine: Skepticism and Philosophy*. Notre Dame, IN: University of Notre Dame Press, 1978.

Augustine. *Confessions*. Translated by F. J. Sheed. Indianapolis, IN: Hackett, 1993.

———. *The Trinity*. Translated by Edmund Hill. New York: New City Press, 1991.

Curley, Edwin. *Augustine's Critique of Skepticism: A Study of "Contra Academicos."* New York: Peter Lang, 1997.

Kirwan, Christopher. "Augustine against the Skeptics." In *The Skeptical Tradition*, edited by Myles Burnyeat, 205–23. Berkeley: University of California Press, 1983.

Mosher, D. "The Arguments of St. Augustine's *Contra Academicos.*" *Augustinian Studies* 12 (1981): 89–113.

6

ERASMUS

In including Desiderius Erasmus (1467–1536) in this anthology we do not mean to claim that he was a skeptic or particularly engaged in discussing skepticism. Erasmus's place in the history of skepticism is threefold. First, in debating with Luther on the problem of reconciling grace with free will (*De Libero Arbitrio*), Erasmus opened up a skeptical line of argumentation of the Counter Reformation, holding the view that human beings cannot reach certainty in theological matters, a view that Luther considered skeptical. This association of skepticism with the theological debate opposing Roman Catholics and Reformers greatly contributed to rendering philosophical skepticism a living issue at least up to the end of the seventeenth century. Second, Erasmus was also involved in the transmission of Pyrrhonism during the late sixteenth and early seventeenth centuries. A translation of his from 1526 of Galen's (second half of the second century CE) *De Optime Docendi Genere* was included, along with Traversari's translation of Diogenes' *Life of Pyrrho*, in Gentien Hervet's 1569 edition of Sextus's *Hypotyposes* (translated by Henri Estienne) and *Adversus Mathematicos* (translated by Hervet). Galen's piece is a reply to Favorinus's (his contemporary) defense of skepticism. Although the Pyrrhonians are mentioned only twice in the text, one of the main issues examined by Galen is the typically Pyrrhonian problem of justifying a criterion of truth. Third, Erasmus has also a place in the history of early modern skepticism because of his *In Praise of Folly*, published in 1511, a satire strongly inspired by the work of Lucian of Samosate (second century CE). Although Erasmus does not enter in detailed skeptical argumentation, *In Praise of Folly* presents a skeptical outlook typical of Renaissance skepticism, pointing out the vanity of philosophy and theology and the importance of irrational passions and ignorance in human life. In the passage selected, this outlook is related by "Folly" to Academic skepticism, the sole philosophical school with which "Folly" sympathizes.

FROM *IN PRAISE OF FOLLY*

The notion that happiness comes from a knowledge of things as they really are is wrong. Happiness resides in opinion. Human affairs are so obscure and various that nothing can be clearly known. This was the sound claim of my Academics, the least insolent of all philosophers. At least if something can be truly known, it is rarely anything that adds to the pleasure of life. Anyway, man's mind is much more taken with appearances than with reality. This can be easily and surely tested by going to church. When anything serious is being said, the congregation dozes or squirms. But if the ranter—I mean the reverend—begins some old wives' tale, as often happens, everyone wakes up and strains to hear. You will also see more devotion being paid to such fabulous and poetic saints as George, Christopher, or Barbara than to Peter or Paul or even Christ Himself. But these examples belong elsewhere. . . .

After the lawyers come the philosophers, who are reverenced for their beards and the fur on their gowns. They announce that they alone are wise, and that the rest of men are only passing shadows. Their folly is a pleasant one. They frame count- less worlds, and measure the sun, moon, stars, and spheres as with thumb and line. They unhesitatingly explain the causes of lightning, winds, eclipses, and other inex- plicable things. One would think that they had access to the secrets of nature, who is the maker of all things, or that they had just come from a council of the gods. Actually, nature laughs uproariously at them all the time. The fact that they can never explain why they constantly disagree with each other is sufficient proof that they do not know the truth about anything. They know nothing at all, yet profess to know everything. They are ignorant even of themselves, and are often too absent- minded or near-sighted to see the ditch or stone in front of them. At the same time, they assert that they can see ideas, universals, pure forms, original matter, and essences—things so shadowy that I doubt if Lynceus could perceive them. They show their scorn of the layman whenever they produce their triangles, quadrangles, circles, and other mathematical forms, lay one on another or entangle them into a labyrinth, then maneuver letters as if in battle formation, and presently reverse the arrangement. It is all designed to fool the uninitiated. Among these philosophers are some who predict future events by consulting the stars, and others who promise even greater wonders. And these fortunate fellows find people to believe them.

Perhaps it would be wise to pass over the theologians in silence. That short- tempered and supercilious crew is as unpleasant to deal with as Lake Camarina or *Anagyris foetida*. They may attack me with an army of six hundred syllogisms; and if I do not recant, they will proclaim me a heretic. With this thunderbolt they terrify the people they don't like. They are extremely reluctant to acknowledge my benefits to them, which are nevertheless considerable. Their opinion of themselves is so great that they behave as if they were already in heaven; they look down pityingly on other men as so many worms. A wall of imposing definitions, conclusions, corol- laries, and explicit and implicit propositions protects them. They have so many hide- outs that even Vulcan could not catch them with his net. They escape through dis- tinctions, and cut knots as easily as with a double-bitted axe from Tenedos. They are full of big words and newly invented terms.

They explain (to suit themselves) the most difficult mysteries: how the world was created and set in order; through what channels original sin has passed to suc- cessive generations; by what means, in what form, and for how long the perfect

Christ was in the womb of the Virgin; and how accidents subsist in the Eucharist without their subject. But these are nothing. Here are questions worthy of these great and reputedly illuminated theologians. If they encounter these questions they will have to extend themselves. Was divine generation at a particular instant? Are there several sonships in Christ? Is this a possible proposition: God the Father hates the Son? Could God have assumed the form of a woman, a devil, an ass, a gourd, a stone? If so, how could the gourd have preached, performed miracles, and been crucified? What would Peter have consecrated if he had administered the sacrament when Christ's body hung on the Cross? And was Christ at that moment a man? After the resurrection will it be forbidden to eat and drink? (They are providing now against hunger and thirst!) These subtleties are countless, and include even more refined propositions dealing with instants of time, opinions, relations, accidents, quiddities, entities, which no one can discern unless, like Lynceus, he can see in blackest darkness things that are not there.

There are in addition those moral maxims, or rather, contradictions, that make the so-called Stoic paradoxes seem like child's play. For example: it is less of a sin to cut the throats of a thousand men than to stitch a poor man's shoe on Sunday; it is better to commit the whole world to destruction than to tell a single lie, even a white one. These subtlest of subtleties are made more subtle by the methods of the scholastic philosophers. It is easier to escape from a maze than from the tangles of Realists, Nominalists, Thomists, Albertists, Occamists, and Scotists, to name the chief ones only. There is so much erudition and obscurity in the various schools that I imagine the apostles themselves would need some other spiritual assistance if they were to argue these topics with modern theologians.

Paul could exhibit faith, but when he said, "Faith is the substance of things hoped for, the evidence of things not seen," he did not define it scholastically. Although he exemplified charity supremely well, he analyzed and defined it with little logical subtlety in his first epistle to the Corinthians, Chapter Thirteen. No doubt the apostles consecrated the Eucharist devoutly; but suppose you had examined them about the *terminus ad quo* and the *terminus ad quem*, or about transubstantiation: in what way the body is in many places at once; the difference between the body of Christ in heaven, on the Cross, and in the sacrament; and the point at which transubstantiation takes place, considering the fact that the prayer effecting it is a distinct quantity in time. I rather doubt if they would have answered you as acutely as the Scotists do. The apostles knew the mother of Jesus, but who among them has demonstrated philosophically how she was kept free from the sin of Adam, as our theologians have done? Peter received the keys, and from Him who did not entrust them to an unworthy person; yet I suspect that he never understood—since he never became very sophisticated—how a person may have the key to wisdom without first having wisdom himself. The apostles baptized many, although they were never taught the formal, material, efficient, and final causes of baptism, nor do they observe that it has a delible and an indelible character. They certainly worshipped, but spiritually, following only the Gospel: "God is a spirit, and they that worship Him must worship Him in spirit and in truth." It does not appear to have been revealed to them that one should worship a charcoal picture on the wall as if it were Christ Himself—that is, if it has two fingers extended, the hair unshorn, and three rays in the halo behind the head. After all, who could comprehend these things if he had not devoted thirty-six years to the physics and metaphysics of Aristotle and the Scotists?

FURTHER READINGS

Backus, Irena. "The Issue of Reformation Skepticism Revisited: What Sebastian Castellio Did or Did Not Know." In *Renaissance Skepticisms*, edited by Gianni Paganini, and José R. Maia Neto. Forthcoming.

Caccia, N. *Note sulla fortuna di Luciano nel Rinascimento. Le versioni e I dialoghi satirici di Erasmo da Rotterdam e di Ulrico Hutten.* Milan: Signorelli, 1914.

Margolin, Jean-Claude. "D'Érasme à Montaigne: l'écriture de l'opinion et la double voie de la croyance." In *L'Écriture du scepticisme chez Montaigne*, edited by M-L Demonet and A. Legros, 109–30. Geneva: Droz, 2004.

Nehels, B. "Erasmus von Rotterdam: Das für und wider die Skepsis." In *Renaissance-Humanismus, Jugäng zur Bildungstheorie der frühen Neuzit*, edited by Jörg Ruhloff. Essen: Die Blaue Eule, 1989.

GIANFRANCESCO PICO DELLA MIRANDOLA

The nephew of the famous humanist Giovani Pico, Gianfrancesco Pico della Mirandola (1469–1533) was a close associate of the prophet radical Giromalo Savonarola (1452–1498) and supported the latter's opposition to pagan philosophy. There were three manuscript copies of Sextus's work in Florence at the time, and Savonarola wanted another associate, Giorgio Vespucci, to translate it into Latin. The project was not realized probably because of Savonarola's death. Gianfrancesco's *Examen vanitatis doctrinae gentium et veritatis christianae disciplinae* (first published in 1520) is the first systematic use of Sextus's work, which became more widely known only after its translation into Latin in 1562. In this work, Pico introduced the actual skeptical arguments of Sextus Empiricus, plus some newer additions, in order to demolish all philosophical views, especially those of Aristotle, and to show that only Christian knowledge, as stated in scripture, is true and certain. Accordingly, the Pyrrhonian trope he uses most extensively is that of *diaphonia*, showing the interminable and insoluble controversy among different philosophical sects. The texts below were selected by Gian Mario Cao, who also translated the second excerpt. The passages show Pico's indication of the difference between his and his uncle's—the famous Giovani Pico—interest in ancient philosophy. While the author of *De Hominis Dignitate*, as a typical humanist, valued the teachings of the Greek philosophers, his nephew became interested in ancient Pyrrhonism precisely because he saw this philosophy as an involuntary ally of Christianity in the enemy's field. Pico's *Examen* is the first systematic use of ancient Pyrrhonism for Christian apologetic purposes.

FROM *EXAMEN VANITATIS DOCTRINAE GENTIUM ET VERITATIS CHRISTIANAE DISCIPLINAE*

In the interpretation [of philosophy] there are diverse sects, diverse leaders, although there was Giovanni Pico, brother of my father Galeotto. He, by his genius, memory, indefatigable study, his singular learning, his pre-eminent eloquence, in writing the highest things, has gained the wonder and admiration of the men of our time. Whereas it has been believed that this could be accomplished by others more than it has been proven, he promised (and would have carried out his promise) to reconcile the teachings of Aristotle and Plato. But this task has been believed by many to be most difficult, even to the present day, and by some even to be beyond the grasp of human ability. It occurs to me, however, that it is more proper and more useful to render the teachings of the philosophers uncertain than to reconcile them as my uncle wished to do. For, I prefer to follow in this matter those ancient theologians of our faith who held that some action must be taken against the pagan philosophers and that their teachings must be demolished. This I prefer to philosophizing from pagan teachings, as some who have cultivated doctrinal studies in later centuries have done; although, of these later thinkers there are some who have agreed with the teachings of the earlier theologians.

FROM BOOK 2, CHAPTER 20, TRANSLATED BY GIAN MARIO CAO

The ancient philosophers devoted a good deal of work and attention to raising objections, because by so doing they would gain glory, for which they were extremely greedy and which led them to adopt certain arguments or sophisms. Others managed to compile handbooks, as did most rhetoricians and, among the philosophers, Aristotle in his eight books of *Topics*. All of them, however, assumed both the possibility of grasping the truth and its criterion; others claimed this assumption to be false, and were eager to get rid of as much as possible. There were other philosophers, the Skeptics, who made no assertion and nevertheless with all their might contradicted everybody, especially those boasting of their own certainties. They did not claim their arguments to be true, since in fact their arguments and reasons were clearly drawn from others'; the Skeptics, however, rejected them not unlike the purge which expels itself along with the humors. They carried on a continuous examination, always withholding assent and seeking to uproot the foundational principles of other doctrines, so that every building would collapse. Among them Pyrrho of Elis was outstanding; then followed Aenesidemus as well as many other Skeptics, the last of which known to me is Sextus Empiricus. It was Sextus himself, along with several others, who was usually employed within our Church in the exercise of proud and empty inquiring—vices which Gregory of Nazianzus rightly condemned, since they are to be extirpated, rather than cultivated.

The Skeptics can be helpful in contrasting the philosophers' arrogance as well as displaying the superiority of the Christian faith. As I have elsewhere pointed out, this very intention was once shared by great and illustrious men, given that the Skeptics are able to damage the enemies of our [Catholic] Church, whereas they would not be powerful enough to damage the Church itself. In fact, the principles of our faith are not derived from human beings, but from God himself; furthermore, these principles are not drawn from the senses or appearance or any human invention, but rather through divine Revelation; they are not established from technical experiments, but through the light of faith as well as through wonders and miracles, against which no argument could be put forth, either by Pyrrho or Sextus or any other philosopher, no matter how clever and learned. Such is the strength of divine truth, that whatever weapons are raised against it will be neutralized and warded off. Thus the persuasion of the Skeptic philosopher—whose aim was to avoid any disturbance through suspension of judgment—can lead, not so much to demolishing or refuting our doctrine, the Christian one (the most convincing and altogether sublime), as to demolish and refute the pagan philosophy established by the human beings.

In fact, the Skeptics suspended judgment because of the contradiction of both opinions and arguments, as well as the varying nature of things. . . . Various Skeptics (some more than others) provided sets of arguments (*modi*), which they called also tropes (*loci*) or types, to withhold assent because of the diversity of things, and accordingly to raise objections. All this, however, took place not only among the Skeptics, but also the Academics. Cicero ascribes four books on suspension of judgment to Clitomachus, and Aulus Gellius in his tenth [*recte*: 11.5] book reported Favorinus to be the author of ten books entitled *Pyrrhonian Tropes*. As far as I am concerned, however, the Skeptics were the more accurate in the modes of withholding and suspending assent.

FURTHER READINGS

Cao, Gian Mario. "L'eredità pichiana: Gianfrancesco Pico tra Sexto Empirico e Savonarola." In *Pico Poliziano e l'Umanesimo di fine Quattrocento*, edited by P. Viti, 231–45. Florence: Olschki, 1994.

———. "Gianfrancesco Pico and Skepticism." In *Renaissance Skepticisms*, edited by Gianni Paganini and José R. Maia Neto. Dordrecht: Kluwer. Forthcoming.

———. "The Prehistory of Modern Skepticism: Sextus Empiricus in Fifteenth-Century Italy." *Journal of the Warburg and Courtauld Institutes* 64 (2001): 229–79.

Garfagnini, Gian Carlo, ed. *Giovanni Pico della Mirandola: Convegno internazionale di studi nel cinquecentesimo anniversario della morte (1494–1994)*. Florence: Olschki, 1997.

Granada, Miguel. "Apologétique platonicienne et apologétique sceptique: Ficin, Savonarole, Jean-François Pic de la Mirandole." In *Le Scepticisme au XVIe et au XVIIe Siècle*, edited by Pierre-François Moreau, 11–47. Paris: Albin Michel, 2001.

Popkin, Richard H. "Prophecy and Skepticism in the Sixteenth and Seventeenth Century." *British Journal for the History of Philosophy* 4, no. 1 (1996): 1–20.

Schmitt, Charles. *Gianfrancesco Pico della Mirandola (1469–1533) and His Critique of Aristotle*. The Hague: Nijhoof: 1967.

8

HERVET

Although there were a few manuscript copies of Sextus Empiricus's works between the fourteenth and sixteenth centuries, the knowledge of Sextus was quite limited (one exception is Gianfrancesco Pico della Mirandola, who is included in this anthology) until Henri Estienne (1528?–1598) translated *Outlines of Pyrrhonism* in 1562 and Gentien Hervet (1499–1584) translated *Adversus Mathematicos* and published the whole Sextus in Latin in 1569. Like Henri Estienne, Hervet was a humanist scholar—he also translated into Latin works by Aeschylus, Aristotle, Basil of Caesarea, Clement of Alexandria, and Augustine—but he also was secretary to the powerful Cardinal de Lorraine (1525–1574), to whom his translation of Sextus is dedicated, and with whom he was actively engaged in the Roman Catholic reaction to the Reformers. He is thus a key figure in the transition from the humanist scholarly interest in ancient Pyrrhonism to its use as a weapon in the theological struggles of the Counter-Reformation. However, as the recent work of Luciano Floridi and Emmanuel Naya has shown, Sextus's influence in the Renaissance was by no means restricted to the impact caused by Estienne's and Hervet's translations. Floridi has shown that there were a significant number of manuscripts of Sextus's works in European libraries, and Naya has shown a wider and more complex reception of ancient Pyrrhonism in the period. One important factor that led to a wider influence of Pyrrhonism after the publication of Sextus is the fact that the particular version of ancient skepticism found in Sextus Empiricus—unlike those already known at the time available in Diogenes Laertius and Cicero—raised the skeptical problem of the criterion of truth (to justify a truth claim one needs a criterion, but this must be further justified, and so on), which coincided with the issue of justifying the rule of faith (the Bible as interpreted by the tradition of the Roman Catholic Church or the Bible as interpreted by one man's conscience). Hervet's preface to his edition of Sextus, whose first English translation we publish in this volume, underlines this utility of skepticism, which becomes central in the appropriations and discussions of skepticism from Montaigne to Bayle. Besides helping orthodoxy, Hervet also calls attention to the pedagogical value of Sextus Empiricus's works.

DEDICATORY LETTER OF *ADVERSUS MATHEMATICOS* TO THE CARDINAL OF LORRAINE

To the illustrious and very eminent Charles, Cardinal of Lorraine, Gentian Hervet addresses a thousand salutations in Christ.

Having come to the end of a thousand long-winded works of which I had burdened myself by consecrating myself in part to the translation of ancient commentators on the sacred letters, and in part to the refutation of the monstrous errors of the sacramentarians [Protestants], I looked for some charming little diversion with which to recover for a moment from my fatigue and to revivify my spirit, when, in the library, always graciously open to me by your courtesy, I came upon a work by Sextus Empiricus, *Adversus Mathematicos*, that is, *Against those who teach doctrines*. Because of the exquisite pleasure I had in reading this work to its end, I thought it would be useful if I translated it into Latin.

In effect, I am convinced that one can gather from this work the fruit of the very first importance, because it clearly shows that no human discipline has been constructed with such rigor that it cannot be shaken, that no science is certain to the point of holding firm if it is besieged by the arsenal of reason and argument. We satisfy ourselves in superficially going through the human sciences which fill us of pride but do not edify. We apply ourselves to the study of the discipline and science proper to Christians, founding our faith on the revelation that Christ has given us, supporting ourselves with the hope of the good things He has promised us and obeying God's commandments, in order, to be sure, always to conserve and embrace charity. The science that is above all others, the truly eminent science, is that according to which God is known by faith and His kingdom is acquired. If we propose to ourselves this goal and assiduously turn ourselves to the contemplation of the first and supreme cause of all things, we will easily comprehend the correctness of the words of the Psalmist: *admirable is the science of God*, not *from our point of view* (according to the Vulgate version), but *in comparison to us* (according to the truth of the Hebrew text), that is, in comparison to our science which is completely nonexistent compared to that of God. Moreover, considered in itself, it does not even deserve the name of science. In helping us powerfully refute the foreigner and pagan philosophers, this work also furnishes us with a multitude of arguments against the heretics of our time. Measuring with natural arguments what is above nature and can be known and grasped only by faith, they do not comprehend because they do not believe. In fact, given that things that are purely natural are so difficult to know that everything one could think or say about them can easily be reversed, what is astonishing about the fact that supernatural things exceed the grasp of the human mind? If nothing else, this book should at least persuade Calvinists to return to the simple word of God without in any way seeking to know how what it professes could be realized, as did the people of Capharnatim. If this were done, they would not cast themselves so precipitously into such an abyss of impiety that they battle with temerity against Christ Himself in taking from His words their dignity and efficacy. Furthermore, Franciscus Picus Mirandulanus [Gianfrancesco Pico della Mirandola] marvelously teaches us, in his book where he defends Christianity against the dogmas of foreign philosophers, how much use one can make of the commentary of Sextus Empiricus to defend the dogmas of the Christian religion against foreign philosophers. I am greatly astonished that our epoch has seen the appearance of these new Academicians, who think they can attain glory in scorning the ancient and true religion of Christ by making themselves disciples of a new and false doctrine.

But Sextus Empiricus's commentary can serve not solely to defend the dogmas of the Christian religion. It can serve also to improve the learning and comprehension of the philosophy taught today in the schools and the entire circle of the so-called disciplines. The best way to learn is to treat the object of study under the form of disputations among opposing points of view. In their commentaries, dogmatists consolidate dogmas to the point that the authors themselves would not be able to support better and more forcibly. But the skeptics attack in such a way that almost nothing remains to be said by the dogmatists to defend their position. It follows necessarily that this exercise is very effective in stimulating and sharpening intelligence of young people, who only then will be able to distinguish the truth from the probable and likely, thereby extracting the truth that the probable and likely had concealed. If, as happens, the reasons weigh equal for both one side and the other, so that one can determine nothing certain about the controversial subject, this will be due to human weakness, which makes that men remain in the dark even in full light, and not due to dogmatic or skeptical doctrines, which do what they can to preponderate. But in this situation, I find that it is best to adopt the attitude the skeptics call *epoché*, that suspension of judgment that saves them from sliding so thoughtlessly and easily into error. Notwithstanding my approval [of Pyrrhonism], that one does not deviate even the width of a fingernail from the true doctrine of Christ and the morals that should be practiced in conformity with that doctrine! Once this condition is fulfilled, this commentary will be of the greatest utility on all other questions.

This is what drove me to translate Sextus Empiricus into Latin while I repaired my nearly depleted forces so I could undertake greater work. This that now sees the light of day anticipates from no one a warmer greeting than it will receive from you, illustrious prince, because it is well known that you have always encouraged letters and the learned. There is no doubt in the milieu of the most important activities that are incumbent on you, one day you will have the leisure to hear spoken out loud in Latin what was written in Greek and was until now locked in its box, devoted to silence. If you do this and give your mind a rest, this work is so short among all the other studies on sacred letters that I have good hope that you will not regret in the least that you have consecrated a few hours to read it.

Adieu, from Paris, the 16th of Calendes of March, in the year 1567.

FURTHER READINGS

Carabin, Denise. *Henri Estienne, érudit, novateur, polémiste.* Paris: Honoré Champion, 2006.

Feugère, F. *Essai sur la vie et les ouvrages de Henri Estienne.* Paris: J. Delalain, 1853.

Floridi, Luciano. *Sextus Empiricus: The Transmission and Recovery of Pyrrhonism.* Oxford: Oxford University Press, 2002.

————. "The Diffusion of Sextus Empiricus' Works in the Renaissance." *Journal of the History of Ideas* 56, no. 1 (1995): 63–85.

Guillemin, J. J. *Le Cardinal de Lorraine, son influence politique et religieuse au XVIe siècle.* Paris, 1847.

Joukovsky, F. "Le Commentaire d'Henri Estienne aux *Hypotyposes* de Sextus Empiricus." In *Henri Estienne*, 129–45. Paris: Centre V. L. Saunier, 1988.

Legros, A. "La Dédicace de l'*Adversus Mathematicos* au Cardinal de Lorraine, ou du bon usage de Sextus Empiricus selon Gracien Hervet et Montaigne." *Bulletin de la Société Internationale des Amis de Montaigne* 8 (1999): 15–16, 41–72.

Naya, Emmanuel. "Renaissant Pyrrhonism: A Relative Phenomenon." In *Renaissance Skepticisms*, edited by Gianni Paganini and José R. Maia Neto. Dordrecht: Kluwer. Forthcoming.

————. "Sextus à Genève: La Réforme du doute." *Libertinage et Philosophie au XVIIe siècle* (2004): 7–30.

9

MONTAIGNE

Michel de Montaigne (1533–1592) is the most important of all Renaissance thinkers who diffused skeptical views. Montaigne was very impressed by the text of Sextus Empiricus and had mottos from it carved into the beams of his study. More than any other Renaissance skeptic, Montaigne's personal philosophical views have strong affinities with both the Pyrrhonian and the Academic branches of ancient skepticism. While most other Renaissance authors used ancient skepticism for some end alien to skepticism itself (humanist scholarship, attack on pagan philosophy to vindicate Christian revelation, criticism of Aristotelian science in view of a new one, etc.), Montaigne articulates a personal form of skepticism in his *Essays* (in particular in books 2 and 3), which is both theoretical and practical in the sense that it is intrinsically bound to his own life and the very writing of the *Essays*. Montaigne does argue that skepticism is useful to combat heresy (the Reformers) and to embrace faith, but based on ancient and scholastic sources (the skepticism, nominalism, and voluntarism held by some of William of Ockham's [ca. 1285–1349] disciples) and his own personal experience, he articulates a sophisticated form of skepticism, bringing in skeptical arguments (mostly Pyrrhonian) that play a crucial role when taken up by Descartes, Pascal, and other philosophers. Besides the skeptical arguments, Montaigne contributes significantly to the skeptical tradition by construing this philosophy as an experience of intellectual autonomy and freedom. We have included in this anthology the central parts of the longest and most philosophical of Montaigne's essays, the "Apology for Raymond Sebond" (book 2, chapter 12). It is a rambling presentation of all sorts of skeptical views, from the most minor to the most significant. The reader will find in this selection the outline of some of the skeptical problems that are central in early modern philosophy (the veil of ideas and the problem of global illusion, among others). Raymond Sebond was a fifteenth-century Spanish theologian admired by Montaigne's father, who asked Montaigne to translate Sebond's book *Liber creaturarum* (also known as *Theologia naturalis*) into French. In the *Apology*, Montaigne replies to the critics who claim that Sebond's philosophical defense of Christianity is not cogent through a skeptical "tactics of war," as he says, which shows that no knowledge claim whatsoever in any field can be sufficiently established by reason. He thus presents a view of humanity and religion quite opposite to Sebond's humanist and rationalist one.

FROM *THE APOLOGY FOR RAYMOND SEBOND*

. . . Now it is nevertheless a great consolation to the Christian to see our frail mortal tools so properly suited to our holy and divine faith, that when they are used on subjects that are by their nature frail and mortal, they are no more completely and powerfully appropriate. Let us see then if man has within his power other reasons more powerful than those of Sebond, or indeed if it is in him to arrive at any certainty by argument and reason. . . .

What does truth preach to us when she exhorts us to flee worldly philosophy, when she so often inculcates in us that our wisdom is but folly before God; that of all vanities the vainest is man; that the man who is presumptuous of his knowledge does not yet know what knowledge is; and that man, who is nothing, if he thinks he is something, seduces and deceives himself? . . .

Let us then consider for the moment man alone, without outside assistance, armed solely with his own weapons, and deprived of divine grace and knowledge, which is his whole honor, his strength, and the foundation of his being. Let us see how much presence he has in this fine array. Let him help me to understand, by the force of his reason, on what foundations he has built these great advantages that he thinks he has over other creatures. Who has persuaded him that the admirable motion of the celestial vault, the eternal light of those torches rolling so proudly above his head, the fearful movements of that infinite sea, were established and have lasted so many centuries for his convenience and his service? Is it possible to imagine anything so ridiculous as that this miserable and puny creature, who is not even master of himself, exposed to the attacks of all things, should call himself master and emperor of the universe, the least part of which it is not in his power to know, much less to command? . . .

Presumption is our natural and original malady. The most vulnerable and frail of all creatures is man, and at the same time the most arrogant. He feels and sees himself lodged here, amid the mire and dung of the world, nailed and riveted to the worst, the deadest, and the most stagnant part of the universe, on the lowest story of the house and the farthest from the vault of heaven, with the animals of the worst condition of the three, and in his imagination he goes planting himself above the circle of the moon, and bringing the sky down beneath his feet. It is by the vanity of this same imagination that he equals himself to God, attributes to himself divine characteristics, picks himself out and separates himself from the horde of other creatures, carves out their shares to his fellows and companions the animals, and distributes among them such portions of faculties and powers as he sees fit. How does he know, by the force of his intelligence, the secret internal stirrings of animals? By what comparison between them and us does he infer the stupidity that he attributes to them?

When I play with my cat, who knows if I am not a pastime to her more than she is to me? . . .

But even if knowledge would actually do what they say, blunt and lessen the keenness of the misfortunes that pursue us, what does it do but what ignorance does much more purely and more evidently? The philosopher Pyrrho, incurring the peril of a great storm at sea, offered those who were with him nothing better to imitate than the assurance of a pig that was traveling with them, and that was looking at this tempest without fear. Philosophy, at the end of her precepts, sends us back to the examples of an athlete or a muleteer, in whom we ordinarily see much less feeling of death, pain, and other discomforts, and more firmness than knowledge ever supplied to any man who had not been born and prepared for it on his own by natural habit. . . .

What they tell us of the Brazilians, that they died only of old age, which is attributed to the serenity and tranquility of their air, I attribute rather to the tranquility and serenity of their souls, unburdened with any tense or unpleasant passion or thought or occupation, as people who spent their life in admirable simplicity and ignorance, without letters, without law, without king, without religion of any kind. . . .

The participation that we have in the knowledge of truth, whatever it may be, has not been acquired by our own powers. God has taught us that clearly enough by the witnesses that he has chosen from the common people, simple and ignorant, to instruct us in his admirable secrets. Our faith is not of our own acquiring, it is a pure present of another's liberality. It is not by reasoning or by our understanding that we have received our religion; it is by external authority and command. The weakness of our judgment helps us more in this than its strength, and our blindness more than our clear-sightedness. It is by the mediation of our ignorance more than of our knowledge that we are learned with that divine learning. It is no wonder if our natural and earthly powers cannot conceive that supernatural and heavenly knowledge; let us bring to it nothing of our own but obedience and submission. For, as it is written, "I will destroy the wisdom of the wise, and will bring to nothing the understanding of the prudent. Where is the wise? where is the scribe? where is the disputer of this world? hath not God made foolish the wisdom of this world? For after that the world by wisdom knew not God, it pleased God by the foolishness of preaching to save them that believe" [Corinthians 1:19].

Yet must I see at last whether it is in the power of man to find what he seeks, and whether that quest that he has been making for so many centuries has enriched him with any new power and any solid truth.

I think he will confess to me, if he speaks in all conscience, that all the profit he has gained from so long a pursuit is to have learned to acknowledge his weakness. The ignorance that was naturally in us we have by long study confirmed and verified. . . .

Ignorance that knows itself, that judges itself and condemns itself, is not complete ignorance: to be that, it must be ignorant of itself. So to be sure of nothing, to answer for nothing. . . .

. . . They [the skeptics] do not fear contradiction in their discussion. When they say that heavy things go down, they would be very sorry to have anyone take their word for it; and they seek to be contradicted, so as to create doubt and suspension of judgment, which is their goal. They advance their propositions only to combat those they think we believe in. . . .

Why, they say, since among the dogmatists one is allowed to say green, the other yellow, are they not also allowed to doubt? Is there anything that can be proposed for you to admit or deny, which is not legitimate to consider ambiguous? And where others are swept—either by the custom of their country, or by their parental upbringing, or by chance—as by a tempest, without judgment or choice, indeed most often before the age of discretion, to such or such an opinion, to the Stoic or Epicurean sect, to which they find themselves pledged, enslaved, and fastened as to prey they have bitten into and cannot shake loose—"to whatever doctrine they have been driven, as by a storm, to it they cling as to a rock" [Cicero *Academica* 2.8]— why shall it not be granted similarly to these men to maintain their liberty, and to consider things without obligation and servitude? "The more free and independent because their power to judge is intact" [Cicero *Academica* 2.8].

. . . Is it not better to remain in suspense than to entangle yourself in the many errors that the human fancy has produced? Is it not better to suspend your conviction than to get mixed up in these seditious and quarrelsome divisions?

What am I to choose? What you like, provided you choose! There is a stupid answer, to which nevertheless all dogmatism seems to come, by which we are not allowed not to know what we do not know.

Take the most famous theory, it will never be so sure but that in order to defend it you will have to attack and combat hundreds of contrary theories. Is it not better to keep out of this melee? . . .

The Pyrrhonians have kept themselves a wonderful advantage in combat, having rid themselves of the need to cover up. It does not matter to them that they are struck, provided they strike; and they do their work with everything. If they win, your proposition is lame; if you win, theirs is. If they lose, they confirm ignorance; if you lose, you confirm it. . . . They use their reason to inquire and debate, but not to conclude and choose. Whoever will imagine a perpetual confession of ignorance, a judgment without leaning or inclination, on any occasion whatever, he has a conception of Pyrrhonism. . . .

There is nothing in man's invention that has so much verisimilitude and usefulness. It presents man naked and empty, acknowledging his natural weakness, fit to receive from above some outside power; stripped of human knowledge, and all the more apt to lodge divine knowledge in himself, annihilating his judgment to make more room for faith neither disbelieving nor setting up any doctrine against the common observances; humble, obedient, teachable, zealous; a sworn enemy of heresy, and consequently free from the vain and irreligious opinions introduced by the false sects. He is a blank tablet prepared to take from the finger of God such forms as he shall be pleased to engrave on it . . .

Nothing of us can be related in anyway whatsoever to divine nature without maculating it with imperfection. How can infinite beauty, power and goodness suffer any correspondence and similitude with such an abject being as we are without greatly compromising divine greatness? . . .

However, we prescribe limits to God, we hold his power besieged by our reasons (I am calling reason our reveries and dreams, with the dispensation of philosophy, which says that even the crazy man and the wicked man are mad with reason, but it is a particular sort of reason); we want to enslave him to the vain and feeble approximations of our understanding, him who has made both us and our knowledge. "Because nothing is made of nothing, God cannot have built the world without material." What! Has God placed in our hands the keys and ultimate springs of his power? Has he pledged himself not to overstep the bounds of our knowledge? Assuming, O man, that you have been able to observe here some traces of his deeds; do you think that he has used all his power and put all his forms and all his ideas into this work? You see only the order and government of this little cave you dwell in, at least if you do see it. His divinity has infinite jurisdiction beyond; this part is nothing in comparison with the whole. . . .It is a municipal law that you allege; you do not know what the universal law is. Attach yourself to what you are subjected to, but not him; he is not your colleague, or fellow citizen, or companion; if he has communicated himself at all to you, it is not in order to lower himself to your smallness, nor to give you surveillance over his power . . .

. . . I can see why the Pyrrhonian philosophers cannot express their general conception in any manner of speaking; for they would need a new language. Ours is wholly formed of affirmative propositions, which to them are utterly repugnant; so that when they say "I doubt," immediately you have them by the throat to make them admit that at least they know and are sure of this fact, that they doubt. Thus they have been constrained to take refuge in this comparison from medicine, without which their attitude would be inexplicable: when they declare "I do not know" or "I doubt," they say that this proposition carries itself away with the rest, no more nor less than rhubarb, which expels evil humors and carries itself off with them.

This idea is more firmly grasped in the form of interrogation: "What do I know?"—the words I bear as a motto, inscribed over a pair of scales.

See how people take advantage of this wholly irreverent way of speaking. In the disputes we have at present in our religion, if you press your adversaries too hard, they will tell you quite shamelessly that it is not in God's power to make his body be in paradise and on earth, and in several places at the same time. And that ancient scoffer, how he takes advantage of it! At least, he says, it is no slight consolation to man to see that God cannot do everything: for he cannot kill himself even if he wished, which is the greatest privilege we have in our condition; he cannot make mortals immortal, or the dead live again, nor can he arrange that the man who has lived shall not have lived, or that the man who has had honors shall not have had them; having no other power over the past than that of oblivion. And, to bind this association of man to God further by comical examples, he cannot make that two times ten not be twenty. That is what he says, and what a Christian should avoid having pass out of his mouth. Whereas, on the contrary, men seem to seek out this mad arrogance of speech, to bring God down to their measure. . . . When we say that the infinity of the centuries both past and to come is to God but an instant, that his goodness, wisdom, power, are the same thing as his essence—our tongue say it, but our intelligence does not apprehend it. And yet our overweening arrogance would pass the deity through our sieve. And from that are born all the delusions and errors with which the world is possessed, reducing and weighing in its scales a thing so far from its measure . . .

It is very easy, upon accepted foundations, to build what you please; for according to the law and ordering of this beginning, the rest of the parts of the building are easily done, without contradictions. By this path we find our reason well founded, and we argue with great ease. For our masters occupy and win beforehand as much room in our belief as they need in order to conclude afterward whatever they wish, in the manner of the geometricians with their axioms; the consent and approval that we lend them giving them the wherewithal to drag us left or right, and to spin us around at their will. Whoever is believed in his presuppositions, he is our master and our God. . . . For each science has its presupposed principles, by which human judgment is bridled on all sides. If you happen to crash this barrier in which lies the principal error, immediately they have this maxim in their mouth, that there is no arguing against people who deny first principles.

Now there cannot be first principles for men, unless the Divinity has revealed them; all the rest—beginning, middle, and end—is nothing but dreams and smoke. To those who fight by presupposition, we must presuppose the opposite of the same axiom we are disputing about. For every human presupposition and every enuncia-tion has as much authority as another, unless reason shows the difference between them. Thus they must all be put in the scales, and first of all the general ones, and those which tyrannize over us. The impression of certainty is a certain token of folly and extreme uncertainty . . .

That things do not lodge in us in their own form and essence, or make their entry into us by their own power and authority, we see clearly enough. Because, if that were so, we should receive them in the same way: wine would be the same in the mouth of a sick man as in the mouth of a healthy man; he who has chapped or numb fingers would find the same hardness in the wood or iron he handles as does another. Thus external objects surrender to our mercy; they dwell in us as we please. Now if for our part we received anything without alteration, if the human grip was capable and firm enough to grasp the truth by our own means; these means being common to all men, this truth would be bandied from hand to hand, from one man to another; and at least there would be one thing in the world, out of all there are, that would be believed by all men with universal consent. But this fact, that no proposition can be seen which is not debated and controverted among us, or which may not be, well shows that our natural judgment does not grasp very clearly what it grasps. For my judgment cannot make my companion's judgment accept it; which is a sign that I have grasped it by some other means than by a natural power that is in me and in all men.

Let us leave aside that infinite confusion of opinions that is seen among the philosophers themselves, and that perpetual and universal debate over the knowl-edge of things. For this is a very true presupposition: that men are in agreement about nothing. I mean even the most gifted and ablest scholars, not even that the sky is over our head. For those who doubt everything also doubt that; and those who deny that we can understand anything say that we have not understood that the sky is over our head; and these two views are incomparably the strongest in number.

Besides this infinite diversity and division, it is easy to see by the confusion that our judgment gives to our own selves, and the uncertainty that each man feels within himself, that it has a very insecure seat. How diversely we judge things! How many times we change our notions! What I hold today and what I believe, I hold and believe it with all my belief; all my tools and all my springs of action grip this opinion and sponsor it for me in every way they can. I could not embrace or preserve any truth with more strength than this one. I belong to it entirely, I belong to it truly. But has it not happened to me, not once, but a hundred times, a thousand times, and every day, to have embraced with these same instruments, in this same condition, something else that I have since judged false? . . .

Now from the knowledge of this mobility of mine I have accidentally engendered in myself a certain constancy of opinions, and have scarcely altered my original and natural ones. For whatever appearance of truth there may be in novelty, I do not change easily, for fear of losing in the change. And since I am not capable of choosing, I accept other people's choice and stay in the position where God put me. Otherwise I could not keep myself from rolling about incessantly. Thus I have, by the grace of God, kept myself intact, without agitation or disturbance of conscience, in the ancient beliefs of our religion, in the midst of so many sects and divisions that our century has produced. The writings of the ancients, I mean the good writings, full and solid, tempt me and move me almost wherever they please; the one I am listening to always seems to me the strongest; I find each one right in his turn, although they contradict each other. . . . The sky and the stars have been moving for three thousand years; everybody had so believed, until it occurred to Cleanthes of Samos, or (according to Theophrastus) to Nicetas of Syracuse, to maintain that it was the earth that moved, through the oblique circle of the Zodiac; turning about its axis; and in our day Copernicus has grounded this doctrine so well that he uses it very systematically for all astronomical deductions. What are we to get out of that, unless that we should not bother which of the two is so? And who knows whether a third opinion, a thousand years from now, will not overthrow the preceding two? . . .

Thus when some new doctrine is offered to us, we have great occasion to distrust it, and to consider that before it was produced its opposite was in vogue; and, as it was overthrown by this one, there may arise in the future a third invention that will likewise smash the second. Before the principles which Aristotle introduced were in credit, other principles satisfied human reason, as his satisfy us at this moment. What letters-patent have these, what special privilege, that the course of our invention stops at them, and that to them belongs possession of our belief for all time to come? They are no more exempt from being thrown out than were their predecessors. . . .

How long is it that medicine has been in the world? They say that a newcomer, whom they call Paracelsus, is changing and overthrowing the whole order of the ancient rules, and maintaining that up to this moment it has been good for nothing but killing men. I think he will easily prove that; but as for putting my life to the test of his new experience, I think that would not be great wisdom.

We must not believe every man, says the maxim, because any man may say anything.

A man of that profession of novelties and of reforms in physics was saying to me not long ago that all the ancients had evidently been mistaken about the nature and movements of the winds, which fact he would make so palpable that I could touch it, if I would hear him out. After I had taken some patience to listen to his arguments, which were full of likelihood: "What?" I said to him. "Then did those who navigated under the laws of Theophrastus go west when they headed east? Did they go sideways, or backward?" "That was luck," he replied; "at all events they miscalculated." I then replied to him that I would rather follow facts than reason . . .

Ptolemy, who was a great man, had established the limits of our world; all the ancient philosophers thought they had its measure, except for a few remote islands that might escape their knowledge. It would have been Pyrrhonizing, a thousand years ago, to cast in doubt the science of cosmography, and the opinions that were accepted about it by one and all; it was heresy to admit the existence of the Antipodes. Behold in our century an infinite extent of terra firma, not an island or one particular country, but a portion nearly equal in size to the one we know, which has just been discovered. The geographers of the present time do not fail to assure us that now all is discovered and all is seen . . .

The question is, if Ptolemy was once mistaken on the grounds of his reason, whether it would not be stupid for me now to trust what these people say about it; and whether it is not more likely that this great body that we call the world is something quite different from what we judge . . .

This subject has brought me to the consideration of the senses, in which lies the greatest foundation and proof of our ignorance. All that is known, is doubtless known through the faculty of the knower; for since judgment comes from the operation of him who judges, it stands to reason that he performs this operation by his means and will, not by the constraint of others, as would happen if we knew things through the power and according to the law of their own essence.

Now all knowledge makes its way into us through the senses; they are our masters. . . . Knowledge begins through them and is resolved into them.

After all, we would know no more than a stone, if we did not know that there is sound, smell, light, taste, measure, weight, softness, hardness, roughness, color, smoothness, breadth, depth. These are the base and the principles of the whole edifice of our knowledge. And according to some, knowledge is nothing else but sensation. Whoever can force me to contradict the senses has me by the throat; he could not make me retreat any further. The senses are the beginning and the end of human knowledge . . .

Attribute to them as little as you can, still you must grant them this, that by way of them and by their mediation proceeds all our instruction . . .

The first consideration that I offer on the subject of the senses is that I have my doubts whether man is provided with all the senses of nature. I see many animals that live a complete and perfect life, some without sight, others without hearing; who knows whether we too do not still lack one, two, three, or many other senses? For if any one is lacking, our reason cannot discover its absence. It is the privilege of the senses to be the extreme limit of our perception. There is nothing beyond them that can help us to discover them; no, nor can one sense discover the other . . .

It is impossible to make a man who was born blind conceive that he does not see; impossible to make him desire sight and regret its absence. Wherefore we should take no assurance from the fact that our soul is content and satisfied with those senses we have, seeing that it has no means of feeling its malady and imperfection therein, if any there be . . .

. . . The properties that we call occult in many things, as that of the magnet to attract iron—is it not likely that there are sensory faculties in nature suitable to judge them and perceive them, and that the lack of such faculties causes our ignorance of the true essence of such things? Perhaps it is some particular sense that reveals to cocks the hours of morning and midnight, and moves them to crow . . .

We have formed a truth by the consultation and concurrence of our five senses; but perhaps we needed the agreement of eight or ten senses, and their contribution, to perceive it certainly and in its essence . . .

As for the error and uncertainty of the operation of the senses, each man can furnish himself with as many examples as he pleases, so ordinary are the mistakes and deceptions that they offer us. At the echo in a valley, the sound of a trumpet seems to come from in front of us, when it comes from a league behind . . .

. . . For that the senses are many a time masters of reason, and constrain it to receive impressions that it knows and judges to be false, is seen at every turn . . .

Put a philosopher in a cage of thin wire in large meshes, and hang it from the top of the towers of Notre Dame of Paris: he will see by evident reason that it is impossible for him to fall, and yet (unless he is used to the trade of the steeplejacks) he cannot keep the sight of this extreme height from terrifying and paralyzing him . . .

This same deception that the senses convey to our understanding they receive in their turn. Our souls at times take a like revenge; they compete in lying and deceiving each other. What we see and hear when stirred with anger, we do not hear as it is. . . . The object that we love seems to us more beautiful than it is . . . and uglier the one that we loathe. To a man vexed and afflicted the brightness of the day seems darkened and gloomy. Our senses are not only altered, but often completely stupefied by the passions of the soul . . .

Those who have compared our life to a dream were perhaps more right than they thought. When we dream, our soul lives, acts, exercises all her faculties, neither more nor less than when she is awake; but if more loosely and obscurely, still surely not so much so that the difference is as between night and bright daylight; rather as between night and shade. There she sleeps, here she slumbers: more and less. It is always darkness, and Cimmerian darkness.

Sleeping we are awake, and waking asleep. I do not see so clearly in sleep; but my wakefulness I never find pure and cloudless enough. Moreover sleep in its depth sometimes puts dreams to sleep. But our wakefulness is never so awake as to purge and properly dissipate reveries, which are the dreams of the waking, and worse than dreams.

Since our reason and our soul accept the fancies and opinions which arise in it while sleeping, and authorize the actions of our dreams with the same approbation as they do those of the day, why do we not consider the possibility that our thinking, our acting, may be another sort of dreaming, and our waking another kind of sleep?

If the senses are our first judges, it is not ours alone that must be consulted, for in this faculty the animals have as much right as we have, or more. It is certain that some have hearing keener than man's, others sight, others smell, others touch or taste. Democritus said that the gods and the animals had much more perfect sensitive faculties than man . . .

Those who have jaundice see all things as yellowish and paler than we do . . . Those who have that malady that the doctors call hyposphagma, which is a suffusion of blood under the skin, see everything as red and bloody. These humors which thus change the operations of our sight, how do we know but that they predominate in animals and are the ordinary thing with them? For we see some that have yellow eyes like our sufferers from jaundice, others that have them red and bloodshot. It is probable that to them the color of objects appears different than to us. Which of the two is the true judgment? . . .

To judge the action of the senses, then, we should first of all be in agreement with the animals, and second, among ourselves. Which we are not in the least; and we get into disputes at every turn because one man hears, sees, or tastes something differently from someone else; and we dispute about the diversity of the images that the senses bring us as much as about anything else. By the ordinary rule of nature, a child hears, sees, and tastes otherwise than a man of thirty, and he otherwise than a sexagenarian.

The senses are in some people more obscure and dim, in others more open and acute. We receive things in one way and another, according to what we are and what they seem to us. Now since our seeming is so uncertain and controversial, it is no longer a miracle if we are told that we can admit that snow appears white to us, but that we cannot be responsible for proving that it is so of its essence and in truth; and, with this starting point shaken, all the knowledge in the world necessarily goes by the board . . .

. . . Moreover since the accidents of illnesses, madness, or sleep make things appear to us otherwise than they appear to healthy people, wise men, and waking people, is it not likely that our normal state and our natural disposition can also assign to things an essence corresponding to our condition, and accommodate them to us as our disordered states do? And that our health is as capable of giving them its own appearance as sickness? Why should the temperate man not have some vision of things related to himself, like the intemperate man, and likewise imprint his own character on them? . . .

Now, since our condition accommodates things to itself and transforms them according to itself, we no longer know what things are in truth; for nothing comes to us except falsified and altered by our senses. When the compass, the square, and the ruler are off, all the proportions drawn from them, all the buildings erected by their measure, are also necessarily imperfect and defective. The uncertainty of our senses makes everything they produce uncertain. . . . Furthermore who shall be fit to judge these differences? As we say in disputes about religion that we need a judge not attached to either party, free from preference and passion, which is impossible among Christians, so it is in this. For if he is old, he cannot judge the sense perception of old age, being himself a party in this dispute; if he is young, likewise; healthy, likewise; likewise sick, asleep, or awake. We would need someone exempt from all these qualities, so that with an unprejudiced judgment he might judge of these propositions as of things indifferent to him; and by that score we would need a judge that never was.

To judge the appearances that we receive of objects, we would need a judicatory instrument; to verify this instrument, we need a demonstration; to verify the demonstration, an instrument: there we are in a circle.

Since the senses cannot decide our dispute, being themselves full of uncertainty, it must be reason that does so. No reason can be established without another reason: there we go retreating back to infinity.

Our conception is not itself applied to foreign objects, but is conceived through the mediation of the senses; and the senses do not comprehend the foreign object, but only their own impressions. And thus the conception and semblance we form is not of the object, but only of the impression and effect made on the sense; which impression and the object are different things. Wherefore whoever judges by appearances judges by something other than the object.

And as for saying that the impressions of the senses convey to the soul the quality of the foreign objects by resemblance, how can the soul and understanding make sure of this resemblance, having of itself no communication with foreign objects? Just as a man who does not know Socrates, seeing his portrait, cannot say that it resembles him.

Now if anyone should want to judge by appearances anyway, to judge by all appearances is impossible, for they clash with one another by their contradictions and discrepancies, as we see by experience. Shall some selected appearances rule the others? We shall have to verify this selection by another selection, the second by a third; and thus it will never be finished.

Finally, there is no existence that is constant, either of our being or of that of objects. And we, and our judgment, and all mortal things go on flowing and rolling unceasingly. Thus nothing certain can be established about one thing by another, both the judging and the judged being in continual change and motion.

We have no communication with being, because every human nature is always midway between birth and death, offering only a dim semblance and shadow of itself, and an uncertain and feeble opinion. And if by chance you fix your thought on trying to grasp its essence, it will be neither more nor less than if someone tried to grasp water: for the more he squeezes and presses what by its nature flows all over, the more he will lose what he was trying to hold and grasp. Thus, all things being subject to pass from one change to another, reason, seeking a real stability in them, is baffled, being unable to apprehend anything stable and permanent; because everything is either coming into being and not yet fully existent, or beginning to die before it is born . . .

. . . Wherefore we must conclude that God alone *is*—not at all according to any measure of time, but according to an eternity immutable and immobile, not measured by time or subjected to any decline; before whom there is nothing, nor will there be after, nor is there anything more new or more recent; but one who really is—who by one single *now* fills the *ever*; and there is nothing that really is but he alone—nor can we say "He has been," or "He will be"—without beginning and without end.

To this most religious conclusion of a pagan I want to add only this remark of a witness of the same condition, for an ending to this long and boring discourse, which would give me material without end: "O what a vile and abject thing is man," he says, "if he does not raise himself above humanity!" [Seneca, *Natural Questions* I.17]. That is a good statement and a useful desire, but equally absurd. For to make the handful bigger than the hand, the armful bigger than the arm, and to hope to straddle more than the reach of our legs, is impossible and unnatural. Nor can man raise himself above himself and humanity; for he can see only with his own eyes, and seize only with his own grasp. He will rise, if God by exception lends him a hand; he will rise by abandoning and renouncing his own means, and letting himself be raised and uplifted by purely celestial means.

It is for our Christian faith, not for his Stoical virtue, to aspire to that divine and miraculous metamorphosis.

FURTHER READINGS

Brahami, Frédéric. *Le Scepticisme de Montaigne*. Paris: Presses Universitaires de France, 1997.

Brush, Craig. *Montaigne and Bayle: Variations on the Theme of Skepticism*. The Hague: Martinus Nijhoof, 1966.

Carraud, Vincent, and Jean-Luc Marion, eds. *Montaigne: scepticisme, métaphysique, théologie*. Paris: Presses Universitaires de France, 2004.

Comparot, Andrée. "Montaigne et Sanchez ou les exigencies de la pensée scientifique." In *Montaigne et la Grèce: 1588–1988. Actes du colloque de Calamata*, edited by K. Christodoulou, 206–16. Paris: Aux Amateurs des Livres, 1990.

Demonet, Marie-Luce, and Alain Legros, eds. *L'Écriture du scepticisme chez Montaigne: actes des journées d'étude (15–16 novembre 2001)*. Geneva: Droz, 2004.

Laursen, John Christian. *The Politics of Skepticism in the Ancients, Montaigne, Hume and Kant*. Leiden: J. Brill, 1992.

Limbrick, Elaine. "Was Montaigne Really a Pyrrhonian?" *Bibliothèque d'Humanisme et Renaissance* 39 (1977): 67–80.

Maia Neto, José R. "*Epoche* as Perfection: Montaigne's View of Ancient Skepticism." In *Skepticism in Renaissance and Post-Renaissance Thought: New Interpretations*, edited by José R. Maia Neto and Richard H. Popkin, 13–42. Amherst, NY: Humanity Books, 2004.

Montaigne, Michel de. *The Complete Essays*. Translated by Donald M. Frame. Stanford, CA: Stanford University Press, 1965.

Panichi, Nicola. "A Skepticism That Conquers the Mind: Montaigne and Plutarch." In *Renaissance Skepticisms*, edited by Gianni Paganini and José R. Maia Neto. Dordrecht: Kluwer. Forthcoming.

Schiffman, Z. S. "Montaigne and the Rise of Skepticism in Early Modern Europe: A Reappraisal." *Journal of the History of Ideas* 45 (1984): 499–516.

Villey, Pierre. *Les Sources et l'évolution des Essais de Montaigne*. Paris: Hachette, 1908.

10

CHARRON

Pierre Charron (1541–1603) was an influential philosopher during the seventeenth century who fell into oblivion chiefly because his main work—*Of Wisdom*—was considered merely a patchwork of other Renaissance works—Montaigne's *Essays* in particular. Charron lived in Bordeaux, France, where he met and became a disciple of Montaigne. But Montaigne is not the only Renaissance source of Charron's skepticism. He studied in Paris at the time Petrus Ramus (1515–1572) provoked a crisis at the University of Paris for his criticism of Aristotle. Ramus's associate, Omer Talon (ca. 1510–1562), presented the New Academy (*Academica*, 1548) as the champion of philosophical freedom. This view is one of the pillars of Charron's conception of wisdom. More recently, with more detailed analysis of the *Essays* and *Of Wisdom*, scholars have pointed out important differences between Montaigne's and Charron's views. One such difference is Charron's proposal of a methodic doubt, the main source of Descartes's, although doubt is used by Charron for moral purposes— to achieve wisdom—whereas Descartes's aim is metaphysical—the foundation of a new science. Charron's *Wisdom* has generated from the time of its publication to the present a great deal of divergence among its readers. The main polemical issue is whether Charron's wisdom is consistent or not with Christianity. Although some consider it quite orthodox, the fact of the matter is that the thinkers most influenced by Charron were free thinkers from the early seventeenth century up to Nietzsche.

Charron divides his book *Of Wisdom* in three parts. The first, dealing with self-knowledge, is presented as a precondition for wisdom (the Delphic precept: Know yourself). The second contains the "general rules of wisdom," and the third presents the application of wisdom in the various circumstances of life. We have selected a central chapter of book 2, which presents the most basic features of wisdom according to Charron.

FROM *OF WISDOM*

An entire and universal liberty of the mind; the second disposition to wisdom.

[1] The other disposition to wisdom, which in truth is a natural consequence and improvement of the former [namely, "exemption and freedom from the passions and the errors and vices of the world, first disposition to wisdom," bk. 2, chap. 1], is

(after we have delivered ourselves from the bondage and captivity of popular opinions from without, and our own passions from within) to attain to a full, entire, and
generous liberty of mind; and this is of two sorts, according to the two great faculties concerned in the pursuit of wisdom, implying first, a liberty of judgment, and
then a liberty of the will.

The former of these, which regards the judgment, consists in considering,
judging, and examining all things; yet not tying one up to any, but remaining still
free, and at one's own disposal; of a large universal spirit, open and ready to anything. This is the highest pitch of soul, the most peculiar and distinguishing privilege
of a truly great and wise man; but such a one I confess it is, as all people are not
capable of understanding, and much less still of attaining to it. Upon which account
I think myself obliged to establish this point, against the objections of those vulgar
souls, which are not of capacity large enough for true wisdom.

And first of all, to prevent all mistakes and unreasonable cavils upon words, I
will explain the terms made use of here, and give the true meaning of them. Now
this description consists of three things, which mutually produce, and support one
another. And these are, *judging everything, being wedded or tied up to nothing*; and
preserving a largeness of soul, being open and universal with respect of everything.

By *judging* in the first of these particulars, it is plain I cannot mean resolving,
determining, or positively affirming; because this would imply a direct contradiction
to the second branch of the description. And therefore no more can possibly be
understood by it, than examining and weighing all matters that come before us;
putting the arguments for either side of the question into the balance, considering the
pros and contras of all sides, their weight and merit, thus searching the truth.

Then again, *by not espousing, or being bound up to anything*, I do not mean to
stop and remain still, floating in the air; never acting and proceeding in the actions
and deliberations which are required. For I would have my philosopher conform to
the customs of the world, and in all the external and common passages of human
life, act like other men. The rules prescribed here have nothing at all to do with any
man's commerce or outward behavior; their business is only to regulate the mind;
and to set the thoughts and judgment secret within. Nay, and even in this inward regulation too, I am content, that men should assent and follow what seems most probable, honest, useful, and convenient. But still that this should be done with some sort
of modesty and reserve; without any resolution, positiveness, and stiffness; all cen-
sures and contemptuous usage of those who think otherwise: treating the contrary
opinions, be they never so distant, be they new, or old, with candor and caution; dis-
daining nothing that can be offered, but ready and content to hear the arguments of
those that oppose us. Nay, not only content, but desirous, that they should oppose us,
and allege whatever they have to say against our notions; because this will put us
upon a more accurate exercise of the first of these qualifications, which is to judge
and to always be in search after the truth.

Now these three qualities I affirm to preserve, and mutually to support each
other; for he that examines things carefully and without passion, will find somewhat

of reason and probability on every side; so much at least as will preserve him, not only from rashness and precipitation, but from peremptoriness and obstinacy; and this puts the mind in that state of ingenuity, and indifference, which I mean by openness, and universality of soul. Whereas on the contrary, the man who comes to a conclusion cuts himself out from farther examination, he is fastened down to the notions already entertained by him; and makes himself of a party, resolved to maintain his opinion, despite of all sense and reason to the contrary.

Simple and weak and foolish men are defective in the first of these qualifications; obstinate dogmatists are faulty in the second point; and both the one and the other sort, to the extent that they are factious, and espouse a party, offend against the third. But all these rules are practiced by the wise, modest, discreet, tempered, true philosopher whose only aim is truth.

It is farther necessary, for the giving a true state of the matter I am now upon, to add, that by the *all things* to be examined, and the *no one thing* to be espoused (for he says: judge all things but assent to any), do not concern divine truths which were revealed to us. For these we are obliged to receive with an entire submission and most profound humility. These are not matters for discussion and controversy; we have nothing to do here, but to bow down the head and worship; to check and captivate our minds, and *resign our understandings to the obedience of faith*. But, we mean all other things without exception.

This short explanation of the terms might perhaps suffice for men of equity and good sense to accept this rule of wisdom; but because I see plainly that there are a party of men in the world, of a positive, fierce, and domineering spirit, who are for leading all mankind after them in a very magisterial manner; and, having first inviolably engaged in some particular principles and opinions themselves, take the confidence to expect, that everybody else should come in upon their authority, thereby opposing themselves to this noble freedom of the mind, I think myself under some necessity to prove, and confirm what has been here advanced; and will therefore consider each branch of this proposition distinctly, as the parts lie before us. . . .

[5] The other branch then of this absolute liberty of soul, consists in a sort of indifference, and a suspending one's judgment and final resolution. By this the wise man preserves his temper; his affections are not engaged, and so he can consider everything without heat or passion: He is not at all committed, obliged, or attached to any notion; but always ready to receive either the truth, or that which appears to him as most probable, saying internally and secretly to himself, "it looks like this," "this side appears probable": but still he can hear it contradicted without any disorder, and satisfy himself to know all that can be said against it; and if what is offered preponderates, he makes no scruple to change his mind; and constantly, even of that opinion which stuck last by him, he goes no farther in vindication, than that possibly there may be some other better grounded, but this is the best that he has met with. Now this suspension and indifference I speak of, is built upon several famous maxims entertained and propagated by the wise men; saying, that there is nothing certain; that we know nothing; that all nature was full of doubts; that nothing was

more certain than uncertainty; that there was scarce anything so plain, but an ingenious man might bring plausible and almost equal arguments for either side of the
question; that all things may be equally disputed; that we do nothing but inquiry and
touch around the appearances; that truth is not within our reach, that even if it fell
upon our hands we could not vindicate nor possess nor assure it; that we receive
truth and error through the same door and both are equally sustained; that there is no
opinion sustained by everybody, none that is not disputed and contested, which does
not have a contrary one held and sustained by somebody; that everything has two
sides and views; that there is reason everywhere, and none which does not have a
contrary one, it is made of plumb, turning and accommodating itself to anything we
want. In summary, it is the doctrine and practice of all wise men and the noblest
philosophers who professed ignorance, doubt, and inquiry. . . .

[6] Those who come later, men of a pedantic, and presumptuous temper, who
make Aristotle and others say whatever they want, and hold to their opinions more
dogmatically than the older philosophers had held to them. They would not accept
them as disciples if they returned. They condemn and detest this rule of wisdom, this
Academic modesty and suspension. They glorify themselves in dogmatizing around
a party and are fonder of a hotheaded peremptory fellow though contrary to their
own party and judgment than of a peaceable, sedate, and modest man, who contents
himself with doubting, and suspends judgment, against whom thy blunt their blows.
Briefly, they esteem a rash fool, more than a cautious wise man. (Like women, who
take it ill not to be contradicted, and had rather be answered rudely, than not at all.
Because they think the coldness and indifference of silence argues greater contempt
and disdain, than it is possible for the most injurious language to express.) In which
they betray great perverseness and injustice. For what reason can be given, why a
man should not be allowed to suspend his judgment, and still to deliberate upon
things as doubtful, without venturing to affirm on either side; when they at the same
time take a privilege of determining as they see fit? Why is it not permitted to frankly
confess oneself ignorant, when he is really so; and to suspend judgment about that
which we are not assured and against which there are many reasons and oppositions?

It is certain, according to all wise men, that we are ignorant of a great deal more
than we know; nay, that our knowledge is not comparable, not fit to be mentioned in
competition with our ignorance. The causes of which are infinite; for we may be
mistaken in the objects of our inquiry, by reason of their being too near or too distant; too great or too small; of too long, or too short duration; and in perpetual flux
and uncertainty. These causes of error proceed from the object, but then there are
infinite others owing to ourselves, and our manner of perception; which in truth is
not yet universally agreed upon, nor perfectly well understood. What we think ourselves sure of we do not really know, nor can we be secure of continuing in our present opinion any time. For how often do we see fresh arguments extort it from us?
or, if our obstinacy will hold it fast, despite of all reasons to the contrary; yet at least
they raise a dust, and disturb us in the possession of it. Now I would be glad to know,
which way a man shall ever be capable of improving his judgment, if he fasten him-

self down to some certain notions; resolving to look and examine no farther, nor enduring to hear anything offered in prejudice of an opinion, which he fancied himself abundantly satisfied in already. They are ashamed of this suspense I am treating of and consider it as a weakness because they have a wrong notion of it and are unaware that the greatest philosophers suspended judgment. They would be ashamed and would never have the heart to say frankly "I do not know." The idea of positiveness and presumption has taken such fast hold of them, that there is no persuading them, that there is a sort of ignorance and doubt, more learned, more generous; and consistent with better assurance, and more accurate knowledge, than all their boasted science and certainty. This gave that great renown to Socrates, and entitled him to the character of the wisest man of his age. This is the fruit of study, and deep inquiry; it is a modest, candid, innocent, and hearty acknowledgment, of the sublime mysterious nature of truth; and the defects and poverty of our own understanding; so weak within, so beset with mists and darkness without, and from both so uncertain, and unsteady in its resolutions. . . .

And I have ordered this motto, *I know not: Je ne sais,* to be engraved over the gate of my little house which I built at Condom in 1600.

Now there is a sort of persons, who take it ill, that men should not submit themselves absolutely, and fix on some certain principles; which ought, they tell you, never to be examined or controverted at all, which is an unjust tyranny. Now I allow, that they be employed in all judgment, that we consider them, but if they will not admit me to try whether they be sterling or counterfeit, before I take them for current coin; this is a condition full of hardship and such as I can never yield to. For who has power to give law to our thoughts, to enslave our minds, and set up principles, which it shall not be lawful to inquire into; or admit any manner of doubt concerning them? I can own no such power in any but God; and He has it upon the account of his being the sovereign spirit and the true principle itself, the only one to be believed upon his bare word. All other [alleged principle] is subject to inquiry and opposition. It is weakness to submit to them.

If a man requires my belief to what are commonly styled by the name of principles, my answer shall be the same with that of a parish priest to his parishioners. . . . "Agree among yourselves first, and then I will give my consent too." Now the controversies are really as great about these principles, as they are concerning the conclusions advanced upon them; as many doubts upon the generals as the particulars; so that in the midst of so many contending parties, there is no coming in to any one without giving offense, and proclaiming war upon all the rest.

They tell us farther, that it is a horrid uneasy state of mind; to be always thus upon the float; and never coming to any settled resolution, to live in eternal doubt and perplexity of thought; nay, that it is not only painful, but very difficult, and almost impracticable, to continue long in such uncertainty. They speak this, I suppose, from their own experience; and tell us what they feel themselves: but this is an uneasiness peculiar to foolish and weak people. To the former, because fools are presumptuous, and passionate, and violent espousers of parties and opinions; full of prejudices, and strong possessions; fierce condemners of all that differ from them; never yielding the cause, nor living out the dispute, though they be really convinced; and supplying the want of reason by heat and anger, instead of ingenuous acknowledgments of their error. If they find themselves obliged to change their opinion, you have them then as peremptory and furious in their new choice, as ever they were in their first principles. In short, they know not what it is to maintain an argument, without passion; and when they dispute, it is nor for the sake of truth or improvement, but purely to sustain what they have already wedded to. These men know nothing; not so much as what it is *to know*; so exceeding pert and confident are they; and insult as if they carried truth about in their pockets, and it was their own incommunicable property.

As for men of weak judgments, and such as are not able to stand upon their own legs, but need to be supported, they cannot live but in marriage, not keeping themselves free. They are people born to servitude, who fear the goblin or being devoured by the wolf were they left alone.

But as for wise men, who are qualified for it, men of modesty and reserve, and prudent candor, it is the most composed state of mind that can be, and puts us into a condition of firmness, and freedom, of stable and uninterrupted happiness. *We are so much less under constraint than other men, by how much more our minds enlarge themselves, and the liberty of judging is preserved entire* [*Academica* 2.8]. This is a quite pleasant and sweet home, where we do not fear to fail nor to be unsatisfied. One is in a safe harbor free from all dangers of the so many errors produced by human fantasy of which the world is plain. It delivers us from quarrels and disputes, and from engaging in, or becoming offensive to parties from the precipitation of thinking wrong at first, and the shame of retracting when we come to think better afterwards, for how many times did we not realize after some time that we were wrong and were forced to change our minds? In a word, this suspension of the judgment keeps us snug and under a cover, where the inconveniences and calamities which affect the public will seldom sensibly affect, and scarce can ever involve us; at a distance from those vices and vehement agitations, which ruffle and discompose first men's own minds, and then human society in general. For this fierceness and peremptoriness, is at once the spawn, and the parent of pride and insolence; ambition and vainglory, and immoderate desires; presumption and disdain; love of novelty and change; rebellion and disobedience in the state; heresy and schism in the church; faction, and hatred, and contention in both. These are all of the same lineage and descent. These are begun, fomented, inflamed by your hot, and positive, and opinionative men; not by the modest, indifferent, neutral, suspensive Academics, that is to say, the wise men.

I will advance yet one step farther, and venture to affirm, that the temper of mind I am now recommending, is so far from having any ill influence upon piety, and religion, that it is extremely well calculated to serve and promote it; whether we regard the first propagation among unbelievers, or preserving a due reverence of it, where it is already received. Theology, and especially the mystic, tells us plainly that the mind must be cleansed and purified, in order to receive those heavenly truths, and the impressions of the Holy Spirit. That God will not inhabit our souls, till all corrupt opinions as well as affection are cast out; for, with regard to both, we shall do well to understand those commands of *Purging away the old leaven*, and *putting off the old man*. From whence we may collect, that the most compendious and successful method of planting the Christian religion among infidels, such as today in China, would be a nice method to begin with these following propositions and persuasions: "That all the Knowledge of this world is largely based on vanity and falsehood"; "That the generality of mankind are deluded with fantastical notions, the forgeries of their own brain"; "That God created man to know the truth but that he can know it only through faith, not through any human mean"; "That God himself where truth abides, and who is responsible for man's desire for it, reveals it as he has done, but that in order to dispose and qualify ourselves for being instructed in the Divine Revelations, we must abandon all worldly and carnal opinions, and as it were, bring our minds, a pure blank for God to write his will in." When these points are gained, and men are made like Academics and Pyrrhonians, then it will be time to lay the foundations, and instill some of the first and plainest principles of Christianity: To show them that these doctrines came down from heaven, that the person, who vouchsafed to bring them was a faithful ambassador, and entire confident of God, that his authority was abundantly confirmed, by infinite testimonies, such as were miraculous, supernatural, and so authentic proofs, because capable of coming from no other hand but God's only. Thus this innocent and candid suspense and unresolvedness of mind, would prove a happy instrument toward the creating, and first begetting a knowledge and belief of the Truth where it is not: Nor would the efficacy of it be less in preserving it, where it is planted, and has taken root already. For such a modest caution and deference would undoubtedly prevent all manner of singularity, and daring extravagance in opinions; but to be sure, it would absolutely put a stop to heresies and public divisions. An Academic or Pyrrhonian never will be a heretic. You will answer me perhaps that neither will he be a Christian or a Catholic. But this is to misunderstand what I said, for there is no suspension, nor judgment, nor freedom, with respect to what concerns God. It is necessary to let Him instill and engrave whatever He wants to and nothing else. I have made a sort of digression here, in honor of the rule I am recommending, that those who profess themselves enemies to it may find their great objection obviated. In which, if I have trespassed upon my reader's patience, I ask his pardon: And now to our business again.

[7] After these two qualities, of judging all things, and suspending all fixing, follows the third qualification, which is, a largeness, or universality of soul. By virtue of this the wise man casts his eyes, expands and stretches out his thoughts over all this vast universe; with Socrates becomes a citizen of the world, and takes in all mankind for his neighbors and country-men. Looks down, like the sun, with an equal, steady, and indifferent eye, upon the changes and vicissitudes here below, as things that cannot reach, nor have the power to change him. This is the security, the privilege of a wise man, that which resembles him to the powers above, and renders

him a sort of God upon earth. . . . The greatest and most beautiful minds are the most universal ones—as the flattest and lowest ones are the most particular. It is a sign of weakness and foolishness to think that one must do, believe, and live everywhere as one does in one's village. . . . Each person calls barbarous that which does not agree with his taste and habit. And it seems that we have no rule of truth and reason but the opinions and costumes of the country were we live. Such people do not judge anything and are slaves of their beliefs. They are entirely possessed by the strong prevention of opinions. . . . But partiality is opposed to liberty. Who has his taste compromised by a particular taste can no longer judge the others. The indifferent person judges all tastes. Who is attached to a place is banished from and deprived of all others. The sheet colored by a particular color is no longer capable of the others; the white one is capable of all. A judge favorable and inclined to a party is no longer a right, full, judge. But one must get free from this brutality and present to oneself, as on a table, this great image of mother nature in its full majesty . . . [and] read on it a so general and constant variety, in everything so many humors, judgments, beliefs, costumes, laws, so many changes in the states, so many changes of fortune, victories, conquests, popes, eminences. By considering this variety one learns to know oneself, to wonder at nothing, to find nothing new or strange, to affirm and resolve oneself in all things. In order to achieve such universal mind, this indifference, one must consider the following four or five points.

First, what you find already insisted upon in the foregoing part of this Treatise, concerning the wonderful variety, and vast difference observable in men; according to those qualities of body and mind, which nature has distributed so very unequally among them.

Secondly, those differences men have made among themselves, by the disagreeing laws and customs, which obtain in several nations, and constitutions.

Thirdly, the strange variety of opinions held by the philosophers concerning the unity and plurality, eternity and temporality, beginning and end . . . of the world and its parties. . . .

Fourthly, how much we have learned by the improvement of navigation, and the discovery lately made of a new world in the East and West Indies. For by this we are plainly convinced that all ancients were in gross error, when they imagined that they knew the utmost extremities of the habitable world; and had comprehended and delineated the whole extent of the earth in their maps and books of cosmography, except only for some few scattered islands. And that they were perfectly in the dark about antipodes; for here, all of a sudden, starts up a new world just like our own old one, placed upon a large continent; inhabited, peopled, governed by laws, and civil constitutions; divided into provinces and kingdoms and empires; adorned with noble cities and towns; larger, more magnificent, more delightful, more wealthy, than any that Asia, Africa, or Europe can show; and such they have been some thousands of years. And have we not reason from hence to presume, that time will hereafter make fresh discoveries of other lands yet unknown? If Ptolemy and the ancient writers were mistaken in their accounts heretofore, I would be very glad to know, what better security any man can have of being the right, who pretends that all is found out, and fully discovered now. If any man shall take the confidence to be positive in this point, I shall take my liberty in believing him.

FURTHER READINGS

Adam, Michel. *Etudes sur Pierre Charron*. Talence: Presses Universitaires de Bordeaux, 1991.

Belin, Christian. *L'Oeuvre de Pierre Charron, 1541–1603: Littérature et théologie de Montaige à Port-Royal*. Paris: Honoré Champion, 1995.

Busson, Henri. *La Pensée religieuse française de Charron à Pascal*. Paris: J. Vrin, 1933.

Charron, Pierre. *Oeuvres*. 2 Vols. Geneva: Slatkine reprints, 1970. Reprint of the Paris 1635 edition.

Charron, Jean D. *The "Wisdom" of Pierre Charron: An Original and Orthodox Code of Morality*. Chapel Hill: University of North Carolina, 1961.

Gregory, Tulio. *Genèse de la raison classique de Charron à Descartes*. Paris: Presses Universitaires de France, 2000.

Harowitz, Maryanne. "Pierre Charron's View of the Source of Wisdom." *Journal of the History of Philosophy* 9 (1971): 443–57.

Maia Neto, José R. "Charron's Academic Skeptical Wisdom." In *Renaissance Skepticisms*, edited by Gianni Paganini and José R. Maia Neto. Dordrecht: Kluwer. Forthcoming.

Nadeau, Christian. "Sagesse 'sceptique' de Charron? L'articulation du scepticisme et du stoïcisme dans *La Sagesse* de Pierre Charron." *Libertinage et philosophie* 7 (2003): 85–104.

Talaeus, Audomarus (Omer Talon). *Academia: Eiusdem in Academicam Ciceronis fragmentum explicatio*. Paris: M. David, 1547.

11

SANCHEZ

Francisco Sanchez (1551–1623) was a Portuguese physician who established himself in Toulouse, France, where he was professor at and, for a period, head of its prestigious Faculty of Medicine. He studied at the College de Guyenne in Bordeaux, the same school that his distant cousin Michel de Montaigne attended. One of the first philosophical writings of Sanchez that has survived is a letter to the Jesuit mathematician Christopher Clavius, who had just edited Euclid's works. Sanchez offered a skeptical attack on the possibility of attaining genuine truth in mathematics. This was followed by his most important work, *Quod Nihil Scitur*, written in 1576 and first published in Lyon in 1581, from which the following text was extracted. The work is a skeptical attack aimed in particular at Aristotle's philosophy and view of knowledge. Sanchez's skeptical attack is dialectical, attempting to point out inconsistencies in Aristotelian philosophy. Although Sextus had already been published (1562 and 1569), Sanchez does not seem to have known his works, though Emmanuel Naya has found echoes of Sextus in *Quod Nihil Scitur*. In the conclusion, Sanchez refers to another work of his own, in which, it seems, he proposes a kind of empirical nondogmatic science, as he says, commensurable with human frailty. This work was either only projected or actually written but lost.

FROM *THAT NOTHING IS KNOWN**

What, I repeat, is "knowing"? We are told that it is "understanding something by means of its causes." This is still not quite satisfactory; the definition is obscure. For it immediately raises the problem of *causes*, which is harder to solve than the first question. In order to understand something, must we understand *all* its causes? Certainly not its *efficient* cause; for what does my father contribute to an understanding of *me*? What, then, of the *final* cause? Then again, if you would like to gain complete understanding of the thing that is caused, you ought also to understand its causes completely. What follows? That nothing can be known, if you should wish to have complete understanding of its efficient and final causes. I shall now demonstrate this. In order to understand me completely, you ought to understand my father

---

*Editorial notes are omitted.

117

completely; and in order to understand him, you must first understand *his* father, and after him another father, and so on *ad infinitum*. Similarly with other objects; and the same may be said of the final cause.

You will maintain that you are not considering particular things, which as such are not objects of knowledge, but universals such as "man," "horse," and so on. But in fact, as I said before, your "knowledge" is knowledge not of the real man but of the "man" whom you invent for yourself; accordingly, you *know* nothing. So be it, then; consider that invented "man" of yours. You will not know him, unless you first know his causes. Has he not an efficient cause? You will not deny that he has. If you wish to know this efficient cause in turn, you must ponder *its* efficient cause. There will be no end to this; hence it will not result in your coming to know what that "man" of yours is. Nor did you previously know what the *real* man was. Therefore, you know nothing. Perhaps you will have recourse to Almighty God, as both the first cause and the final end of all things, and will assert that *there* you must stop, and not proceed to infinity. More of this later; but I would now say: what follows from this? That you know nothing. In avoiding the infinite you fall into what is both infinite and measureless, incomprehensible, ineffable, and beyond the reach of the understanding. Can this Being be known? Certainly not. Yet, by your account, He is the cause of everything; and therefore, according to your definition, understanding of Him is necessary for the understanding of His works. Therefore, you know nothing.

If you do not believe that the efficient cause *and* the final cause are necessary for understanding a thing, why do you not distinguish between causes in your definition? For my part, I supposed that when you said, without reservation, "understand a thing by means of its causes," this meant *all* its causes. (But elsewhere, too, Aristotle comprehensively lists and enumerates all the causes—efficient, material, formal, and final—although he has said that we believe we understand a thing only when we grasp its "first" cause.) Yet suppose I concede to you, even though it neither need be nor could rightly be conceded, that the efficient and the final cause are not necessary; there remain two causes, the material and the formal, which—as I believe you understand the matter—must be comprehended, but this is still less correct. On your definition, should you wish to know the *form*, you ought to know it by its causes; not by the efficient and the final cause, as before; therefore, by the material and the formal cause. But these it does not possess. Therefore you will not know it. But if you do not know this [i.e., the form], you will not know that of which it is the form; for when the parts are unknown, the whole is unknown. I may say the same of the *matter*, which is simpler still, and less of an entity; and it may be that it has no cause—at least, efficient, material, and formal cause, according to Aristotle. As to the final cause, a doubt may be entertained about it. What are you saying? "Any understanding of causes whatever, albeit imperfect, is enough for acquiring knowledge of a thing." This is nonsense.

"It is impossible fully to understand a whole without fully understanding its parts." But if I were to grant that also—I ask whether one can have knowledge of form and matter? You will allow this, inasmuch as you profess to know everything. I ask once more: can one acquire knowledge by means of causes? If you answer no, then your definition is no definition. If yes, I ask again concerning these causes: can they be known? Not less than the other things; nay, more than they; for, by your account, simpler things are by nature more familiarly known, and consequently more knowable in themselves. Knowable by causes, then?—We are entering an infinite regress. Thus, you have no definition. Nay, rather, for these same reasons also, you know nothing. And Aristotle elsewhere raises this very same objection against himself: "If the only knowledge is, in fact, that which is acquired by demonstration, while its first principles are incapable of being demonstrated, then there will be no knowledge of the first principles, and hence there will be no knowledge." But he did not give a satisfactory answer to this objection when he said that not *all* knowledge is demonstrative, but knowledge of those things that have no intermediate terms cannot be demonstrated. For it follows from this that the statement "Knowledge is understanding a thing by means of its causes" is not true in an unqualified sense, nor is that other statement, "Knowledge is an acquired disposition (*habitus*), gained by demonstration," if there is some knowledge that is not gained by demonstration. Now, Aristotle had expressed it better elsewhere, and could have been excused if he had always spoken in the same way, and had once for all given a full account of knowledge. As it is, however, since at all points he is vague, confused, and inconsistent, he has left himself no grounds to be excused. Further, he had said that "knowledge of things depends on understanding their first principles, causes, and elements, where these exist." It is absurd how Aristotle's followers enlarge upon this statement; for, perverting realities into words and syllogisms (lulled to sleep by an ancient mistake, and stagnating under its influence), they identify "first principles" with the primary, familiar, and underlying propositions of each particular science, which they themselves refer to as "first principles" and "axioms"; whereas they identify "causes" with the *intermediate* propositions between the first principles and the fact that is to be proved. As for "elements," these they interpret as subject and predicate, copula, middle term, major and minor "extreme terms." Is not this a clever invention—or rather, delusion? In this way, while their leader is *slightly* mistaken, they—since they do not understand him or follow his thought—do worse than this, to the extent that finally they slip into a multitude of foolish fancies, gradually falling away from the truth. But let us return to Aristotle. In an earlier context he argued that there was knowledge of first principles but it could not be demonstrated. Elsewhere he calls a grasp of first principles "understanding" (*intellectus*), not "knowledge"; but this is a misnomer, since if first principles, like other things, were fully understood then perfect knowledge would exist. As it is, however, since we do not possess understanding of first principles, we do not possess it either in respect of things of which they are first principles. From which it follows that nothing is known. Again, what else is knowledge but understanding an object? For it is only when we understand something that we say we "know" it. But on the other hand it is not true that there are two kinds of knowledge. For knowledge, if any existed, would be one, and single in nature, just as there is only one faculty of seeing, but it would be *acquired* in two ways: one way would be simple, when we comprehended a simple thing (such as matter, form, and spirit, if you like); the other would be complex, so to speak, when we comprehended a complex thing, which it would be necessary first to break down into its parts and comprehend them individually, and then finally to comprehend the whole. Now, this last method is always *preceded* by the first; however, it does not invariably follow it. In all these matters, demonstration is useful only perhaps for pointing out the thing that is to be known. But enough of this, for I have said more than might have appeared suitable to one who knows nothing!

But my remarks were not unreasonable, for up to this point I have occasionally pointed out the ignorance of others in relation to the definition of knowledge and the nature of understanding; I shall now exhibit my own ignorance, just in case it seems that I am alone in knowing *something*. From this you will be able to see how completely we lack knowledge. Now, the doctrines that have hitherto been accepted by the majority appear to me false, as I have already shown, whereas those I am about to formulate appear to me true. Perhaps you will take the opposite view, and it may be that this will be the true one—from which results the confirmation of the proposition that "nothing is known." Accordingly let us now see what "knowing" is, in order that it may as a result become clearer whether anything is known. KNOWLEDGE IS PERFECT UNDERSTANDING OF A THING. There you have an easy, yet true, explanation of the term "knowledge." If you ask me what are its genus and differentia, I will not provide you with these, for these two words are more obscure than the thing that is defined. What is "understanding"? Certainly I could not explain it in any other way; and if I were to define it in any other way, you could again ask the same question about this definition and the parts thereof. Thus there would be no end, and the doubt about names would go on for ever.

Consequently, the sources of our knowledge are both extended to infinity and also completely insecure; for we attempt to demonstrate the natures of things in words, and these words again in other words, which is both hard and impossible. We know nothing. You say that we must come to a halt somewhere in our questioning. True—because we can do nothing else. But I do not know what "understanding" is; define it for me. I should call it comprehension or perception or "intellection" of a thing, and anything else that means what these words mean. If you are still in doubt about this, I will be silent; but I shall ask you for another definition, and if you reply to my request I will raise a doubt about your statement. Thus we are always in difficulties because of our ignorance. What course remains to us? The final remedy: you must think for yourself. You *have* thought, and it may be that you have acquired understanding; but nothing could be less true.

I, too, believe that I have comprehended. What follows? When, afterwards, I discuss understanding with you, *I* suppose it to be such as I have grasped, while *you* suppose it to be such as you have grasped. *I* assert that it is *this*, while *you*, on the other hand, assert that it is *that*. Who is to arbitrate our dispute? Why, one who recognizes what understanding *truly* is. But who is he? He does not exist. Everyone believes himself to be extremely learned; to me, all men seem ignorant. It may be that I am the *only* ignorant man alive; but I should like to *know this* at least, and this

I cannot do. What, therefore, can I go on to say that is free of the suspicion of ignorance? Nothing. Why, then, do I write? What do I know? With fools you will be foolish. I am a human being—what am I to do? It is the same thing exactly. Now I return to my theme.

We know nothing. So, in order that our discussion may proceed, please assume the explanation of the word "knowledge" which I set down; and let us infer from it that nothing can be known—for to assume a supposition is not to know but to invent; consequently it is invention, not knowledge, that will emerge from assumptions. Observe the point to which our discussion has now brought us: all knowledge is invention. This is evident. "Knowledge is acquired by demonstration"; this in turn assumes a definition. Now, definitions cannot be *proved*, but have to be *believed*; therefore demonstration based on assumptions (*ex suppositis*) will produce knowledge of a suppositious kind, not sound and exact knowledge. (All these conclusions are based on statements of your own.) Again, according to you, first principles must be assumed in every branch of knowledge, and Aristotle has no right to challenge these. So the conclusions to be drawn from these first principles will be things assumed, not things known.

What could be more pitiable than our situation? In order to know, we have to be ignorant! For what is making an assumption but admitting things we do not know? Would it not be better to know the first principles beforehand? Say that I deny, to you, the first principles of your science; now prove them. You say that "you need not argue against people who deny your first principles." You do not know how to prove them; then you are an ignorant person, not one who knows. But "it belongs to a higher, or generalized, kind of science to test the first principles of other sciences." So then, he who possesses this generalized science will perhaps know everything, while you know nothing; for he who is ignorant of the first principles is also ignorant of the subject itself. But what *is* that generalized science? It is strange how *your* experts divide their functions among themselves; they draw boundaries between one another, just as the commonalty of fools appropriates and shares out the land. Nay, rather, they have erected an empire of sciences, among which the queen and supreme arbitrator is the "generalized" science; to it disputes are, in the last instance, referred. It lays down rules for the others, rules which they must accept as binding; and to none of the others is it allowed with impunity to encroach on *its* preserves, nor upon one another's either. Thus they quarrel, all their lives long, about the subject-matter of each science, and nobody can adjudicate this suit—or rather this ignorance. Hence if in the realm of physical science anyone argues about the stars, they say he does this either in the capacity of a physical scientist or of an astrologer; and of another, "He borrows this from Arithmetic"; but still another "purloins that from Mathematics." What does this mean?

Surely all of this is childish nonsense. For it is children who in a public place— the square, the forum, or the Campus—build their "gardens" and enclose them with tiles; and each of them forbids anyone else to set foot on his little plot. I can see what this means: since each one could not possibly embrace everything, one man chose *this* part for himself, another seized another part. Hence nothing is known. For since all things that are in this world unite to make up a single collective whole, some of them cannot exist without others, while again some cannot continue in existence along with others; each thing performs its own function, separate and differing from another's function, yet all things contribute to a single whole. Some are the cause of others; and some are caused by the action of others. The links between all of them are inexpressibly complicated. It is not, therefore, surprising if, one of them being unknown, the rest are also unknown. The reason for it may be the following: one who is interested in studying the stars, in considering their motions, and the causes of those motions, takes as proved the statements of a physicist on the questions what a star is, and what motion is; he then has only to study the variety and the multiplicity of motion in stars. Similarly with the other sciences. But this is not knowledge.

For true knowledge is to understand, in the first place the nature of a thing, in the second place its accidents, where it has any. From which it follows that a "demonstration" is not a "syllogism resulting in knowledge"; rather, it is nothing, insofar as it merely demonstrates that the accident inheres in the thing, according to you (since for me, so far is it from demonstrating anything that it rather conceals something, and manages only to confuse the intellect), but takes for granted the definition of the thing itself. Consequently all those who rely on demonstrations, and look for knowledge as a result of them, in fact know nothing; as for those who condemn demonstrations, they too know nothing, as you yourself maintain and as I shall presently prove. Therefore, we all alike know nothing. Accordingly, if you grant my definition, there are three factors in knowledge: the thing that is to be known; understanding (*cognitio*); and the perfection of knowledge. We shall have to consider each of them singly, in order that we may deduce that nothing is known.

First of all, how many *things* are there? Perhaps they are infinite in number, not only as individuals but even in species. You will deny that they are infinite in number; yet you will not prove that they are finite, for you have not been able to count even the least part of them; for myself, I have barely come to identify "man" and "horse" and "dog." Therefore, on this point we already know nothing; for you have not seen the finite limit of all things, yet you say they are finite, whereas *I* have not seen their *in*finity, yet I conjecture that they are infinite. Can anything be more certain? You must decide for yourself, but so far as I am concerned *nothing* is more certain. But how, you will say, can their infinity hamper us in respect to the understanding of one single thing? A very great deal, in your view; for in order to understand the thing, one must understand first principles (matter and form, perhaps), but in the infinite state it may be that infinite quantities of matter are distinct in outward form (and yet *you* would not have matter be distinguished in terms of outward form, inasmuch as you deprive it of form altogether; more of this later). Concerning forms, there is no doubt; but concerning the infinite, there is no knowledge. But, you will say, even infinite numbers of things may share the same matter. This is indeed true, but it is also possible that their matter may not be the same, and so it may be of various kinds. . . .

You have, then, observed the difficulties that place scientific knowledge beyond our reach. I am aware that perhaps much of what I have said will not find favor; but on the other hand, you will say, neither have I *demonstrated* that nothing is known. At least, I have expounded my own opinion as clearly, accurately, and truthfully as I could; for I was not anxious myself to perpetrate the fault I condemn in others, namely to prove my assertion with arguments that were far-fetched, excessively obscure, and perhaps more doubtful than the very problem under investigation. For my purpose is to establish, as far as I am able, a kind of scientific knowledge that is both sound and as easy as possible to attain; but *not* a science that is full of those chimeras and fictions, unconnected with factual truth, which are put together, not to teach facts, but solely to show off the writer's intellectual subtlety. For, like others, I am not devoid of subtleties and clever fictions—and, if my intellect were content with these, I have *more* than they have! But since these notions are far removed from facts, they tend to deceive rather than to instruct the mind, and divert it from truth to fictions. To this I do not give the name of science but of imposture; of a dream, like those made up by wandering char-latans and mountebanks. It will now be for you to judge of these, and to receive in a friendly spirit whatever things seem good to you, but not to pull to pieces, with hostile intent, those that shall seem otherwise; for it would be a far from brotherly act to inflict blows on someone who is trying to be of service. To work, then; and if you know something, then teach me; I shall be extremely grateful to you. In the meantime, as I prepare to examine *Things*, I shall raise the question whether anything is *known*, and if so, how, in the introductory passages of another book, a book in which I will expound, as far as human frailty allows, the *method of knowing*. Farewell.

WHAT IS TAUGHT HAS NO MORE STRENGTH THAN IT DERIVES FROM HIM WHO IS TAUGHT.

WHAT?

FURTHER READINGS

Besnier, Bernard. "Sanchez à moitié endormi." In *Le Scepticisme au XVIe et au XVIIe Siècle*, edited by Pierre-François Moreau, 102–20. Paris: Albin Michel, 2001.

Comparot, Andrée. "Montaigne et Sanchez ou les exigencies de la pensée scientifique." In *Montaigne et la Grèce: 1588–1988: Actes du colloque de Calamata*, edited by K. Christodoulou, 206–16. Paris: Aux Amateurs des Livres, 1990.

Limbrick, Elaine. "Franciscus Sanchez 'Scepticus': Un médicin philosophe précurseur de Descartes (1550–1623)." *Renaissance and Reformation* 6 (1982): 264–72.

Lupoli, Agostino. "*Humanus animus nusquam consistit*: Doctor Sanchez's Diagnosis of Incurable Human Unrest and Ignorance." In *Renaissance Skepticisms*, edited by Gianni Paganini and José R. Maia Neto. Dordrecht: Kluwer. Forthcoming.

Moreau, Joseph. "Doute et savoir chez Francisco Sanchez." *Portugiesische Forschungen des Gorrespgesellschaft*, erste reihe, *Aufsatze zur Portugiesischen Kulturgeschichte* 1 (1960): 24–50.

Sanchez, Francisco. *Opera philosophica*. Edited by Joaquim de Carvalho. Coimbra: Inedita Ac Rediviva, Separata da *Revista da Universidade de Coimbra* 18 (1955).

Senchet, Emilien. *Essai sur la méthode de Francisco Sanchez*. Paris: V. Giard et E. Brière, 1904.

Yrjönsuuri, Mikko. "Self-Knowledge and Renaissance Sceptics." In *Ancient Scepticism and the Sceptical Tradition*, edited by Juha Sihvola, 225–53. Helsinki: Acta Philosophica Fennica, 2000.

12

BACON

Francis Bacon's (1561–1626) search for a new way of understanding nature grew in part out of the discussions of skepticism and dogmatism of his time. He knew Montaigne and Charron, but there is no evidence he read Sextus Empiricus. Although he refers to Pyrrho, the brand of ancient skepticism he chiefly discusses is the Academic, which he knew above all through Cicero. Bacon exhibits a somewhat ambivalent reaction to ancient skepticism, on the one hand criticizing suspension of judgment—which he saw as meaning despair of ever finding new knowledge—but, on the other, recognizing the validity of the skeptical arguments against traditional forms of knowledge. Bacon's texts included here were selected by Bernardo Jefferson de Oliveira. They were extracted from Bacon's two most important and influential philosophical works, namely *Of the Dignity and Advancement of Learning* (1605, 1623) and the *Novum Organum* (1620). In the selection from the former, Bacon attacks the use of syllogism in natural philosophy and recognizes a partial validity in the skeptical position at the same time that he points out where he thinks the skeptics went wrong. In the two paragraphs extracted from the *Novum Organum*, Bacon compares his own epistemological position with that of the skeptics, claiming that it is neither a form of dogmatism nor a kind of skepticism, but a new kind of knowledge immune to the skeptical arguments against traditional forms of dogmatism. The fact that these paragraphs conclude Bacon's exposition of his famous theory of idols is not incidental, given that Bacon's theory is strongly influenced by ancient and Renaissance skeptical views.

FROM *OF THE DIGNITY AND ADVANCEMENT OF LEARNING*

. . . [E]ven if it be granted that the principles of sciences may, by the induction which is in use, or by sense and experience, be rightly established; yet it is very certain that the lower axioms cannot (in things natural, which participate of matter) be rightly and safely deduced from them by syllogism. For in the syllogism propositions are reduced to principles through intermediate propositions. Now this form of invention or of probation may be used in popular sciences, such as ethics, politics, laws, and the like; yea, and in divinity also, because it has pleased God of his goodness to accommodate himself to the capacity of man; but in Physics, where the point is not to master an adversary in argument, but to command nature in operation, truth slips wholly out of our hands, because the subtlety of nature is so much greater than the subtlety of words; so that, syllogism failing, the aid of induction (I mean the true and reformed induction) is wanted everywhere, as well for the more general principles as for intermediate propositions. For syllogisms consist of propositions, and propositions of words; and words are but the current tokens or marks of popular notions of things; wherefore if these notions (which are the souls of words) be grossly and variably collected out of particulars, the whole structure falls to pieces. And it is not the laborious examination either of consequences of arguments or of the truth of propositions that can ever correct the error; being (as the physicians say) in the first digestion; which is not to be rectified by the subsequent functions. And therefore it was not without great and evident reason that so many philosophers (some of them most eminent) became Skeptics and Academics, and denied any certainty of knowledge or comprehension; affirming that the knowledge of man extended only to appearances and probabilities. It is true that Socrates, when he disclaimed certainty of knowledge for himself, is thought by some to have done it only in irony, and to have enhanced his knowledge by dissembling it; pretending not to know that which it was plain he knew, in order that he might be thought to know also that which he knew not. And in the later academy too (which Cicero embraced) that opinion of the incapacity of the mind to comprehend truth was not held very sincerely. For those who excelled in eloquence commonly chose that sect, for the glory of speaking copiously on either side of the question; whereby they were led astray from the straight road, which they ought to have followed in pursuit of truth, into certain pleasant walks laid out for amusement and recreation. It is certain however that there were some here and there in both academies (both old and new) and much more among the Skeptics, who held this opinion in simplicity and integrity. But their great error was, that they laid the blame upon the perceptions of the sense, and thereby pulled up the sciences by the very roots. Now the senses, though they often deceive us or fail us, may nevertheless, with diligent assistance, suffice for knowledge; and that by the help not so much of instruments (though these too are of some use) as of those experiments which produce and urge things which are too subtle for the sense to some effect comprehensible by the sense. But they ought rather to have charged the defect upon the mind—as well its contumacy (whereby it refuses to submit itself to the nature of things) as its errors,—and upon false forms of demonstration, and ill-ordered methods of reasoning and concluding upon the perception of the senses. But this I say not to disable the intellect, or to urge the abandonment of the enterprise; but to stir men to provide the intellect with proper helps for overcoming the difficulties and obscurities of nature. For no steadiness of hand or amount of practice will enable a man to draw a straight line or perfect circle by hand alone, which is easily done by help of a ruler or compass. And this is the very thing which I am preparing and labouring at with all my might,—to make the mind of man by help of art a match for the nature of things; to discover an art of Indication and Direction, whereby all other arts with their axioms and works may be detected and brought to light.

FROM *NOVUM ORGANUM*

LXVII. A caution must also be given to the understanding against the intemperance which systems of philosophy manifest in giving or withholding assent; because intemperance of this kind seems to establish Idols and in some sort to perpetuate them, leaving no way open to reach and dislodge them.

This excess is of two kinds: the first being manifest in those who are ready in deciding, and render sciences dogmatic and magisterial; the other in those who deny that we can know anything, and so introduce a wandering kind of inquiry that leads to nothing; of which kinds the former subdues, the latter weakens the understanding. For the philosophy of Aristotle, after having by hostile confutations destroyed all the rest (as the Ottomans serve their brothers), has laid down the law on all points; which done, he proceeds himself to raise new questions of his own suggestion, and dispose of them likewise; so that nothing may remain that is not certain and decided: a practice which holds and is in use among his successors.

The school of Plato, on the other hand, introduced *Acatalepsia*, at first in jest and irony, and in disdain of the older sophists, Protagoras, Hippias, and the rest, who were of nothing else so much ashamed as of seeming to doubt about anything. But the New Academy made a dogma of it, and held it as a tenet. And though theirs is a fairer seeming way than arbitrary decisions; since they say that they by no means destroy all investigation, like Pyrrho and his Refrainers, but allow of some things to be followed as probable, though of none to be maintained as true; yet still when the human mind has once despaired of finding truth, its interest in all things grows fainter; and the result is that men turn aside to pleasant disputations and discourses and roam as it were from object to object, rather than keep on a course of severe inquisition. But, as I said at the beginning and am ever urging, the human senses and understanding, weak as they are, are not to be deprived of their authority, but to be supplied with helps.

CXXVI. It will also be thought that by forbidding men to pronounce and to set down principles as established until they have duly arrived through the intermediate steps at the highest generalities, I maintain a sort of suspension of the judgment, and bring it to what the Greeks call *Acatalepsia*,—a denial of the capacity of the mind to comprehend truth. But in reality that which I meditate and propound is not *Acatalepsia*, but *Eucatalepsia*; not denial of the capacity to understand, but provision for understanding truly; for I do not take away authority from the senses, but supply them with helps; I do not slight the understanding but govern it. And better surely it is that we should know all we need to know, and yet think our knowledge imperfect, than that we should think our knowledge perfect, and yet not know anything we need to know.

FURTHER READINGS

Oliveira, Bernardo J. de, and José R. Maia Neto. "The Skeptical Evaluation of *Techné* and Baconian Science." In *Renaissance Skepticisms*, edited by Gianni Paganini and José R. Maia Neto. Dordrecht: Kluwer. Forthcoming.

Perez Ramos, Antonio. *Francis Bacon's Idea of Science and the Maker's Knowledge Tradition*. Oxford: Clarendon, 1988.

Urbach, Peter. *Francis Bacon's Philosophy of Science: An Account and a Reappraisal*. La Salle, IL: Open Court, 1987.

Van Leeuwen, Henry. *The Problem of Certainty in English Thought, 1630–1690*. The Hague: Martinus Nijhoff, 1963, pp. 1–12.

Zagorin, Perez. *Francis Bacon*. Princeton, NJ: Princeton University Press, 1998.

13

GASSENDI

Pierre Gassendi (1592–1655) was a Catholic theologian, philosopher, astronomer, and geologist. He interacted with the leading scientists of his day and raised a number of skeptical objections to some of the main philosophical systems of his time. He attacked Herbert of Cherbury's (1583–1648) *De Veritate*, Descartes's metaphysics (he wrote the longest and most polemical of the Objections to Descartes's *Meditations*, a polemics further developed with Gassendi's replies to Descartes's replies in *Disquisitio metaphysica seu dubitationes et instantiae adversus Renati Cartesi metaphysicam et responsa*), and scholastic Aristotelianism in his first published work, *Exercitationes paradoxicae adversus Aristoteleos*, whose first part was published in 1624. In this work against the Aristotelians, Gassendi criticizes Aristotle using a number of skeptical arguments found in Sextus Empiricus and raising a series of skeptical objections to Aristotelianism, most of which—like those here reproduced—are dialectically designed to show inconsistencies in Aristotle's philosophy. He also outlined what he called the "middle way" between skepticism and dogmatism. This middle way is more developed in his later work *Syntagama philosophicum*, from which we extracted the second selection in this anthology. Besides his important role in reviving Pyrrhonism, Gassendi was also mainly responsible for introducing atomism in early modern philosophy and science and for rehabilitating Epicurus. Gassendi's mitigated skepticism and his christianized Epicureanism were influential in the development of modern British empiricism, in particular on the corpuscular hypothesis held by Boyle and Locke.

FROM *EXERCISES AGAINST THE ARISTOTELIANS**

Let us speak now of difference, and at the outset let us propose this paradox, that "if we knew the difference of the least little thing, we would have an intimate knowledge of everything in the whole universe." Some people will perhaps assume that everything can in fact be known with an intimate knowledge, but our concern will be to prove the cogency of the reasoning. Because of its difference, every single thing differs from every other thing in some way, either by reason of its specific dif-

---

*The editor's notes are not included. Gassendi's notes are included in square brackets.

ference, or by reason of its generic difference. But it is still always true that in every single thing there is something by which it is separated from everything else. Therefore, if we are to know the difference of a thing perfectly, we must know everything else perfectly. For if there is something we do not know, or if we do not know it that well, how shall we know whether the thing in question differs from it, and how it does. Might it not be true that the things which are concealed from us tend more to bring things together than to differentiate them? Surely we cannot say that such-and-such is the difference between this thing and that unless we know that there is something lacking in that thing which can be found in this. But how are we to know that something is lacking in that thing unless we have delved into its very most inner recesses? For example, take man; it is certain that he differs in some way from everything else in the universe. You designate the fact that he is rational as his specific and sufficient difference, and you say that man differs from all the other animals because of that fact. That may well be, but in order to distinguish him adequately from all the other animals you must know every animal intimately and perfectly. For if some qualities lie hidden from you, how can you know that that fact is the legitimate and sufficient difference?

You will say that you know it because all other things must be irrational. But must they really? and why must they? Could it be either that you are lazy or that you are groping blindly as you try to know them? Pray, is there any other reason? Unless, perhaps, you are an incompetent wretch absolutely without reason who goes about dogmatically prescribing what the nature of so many animals must be when you have not seen them, or heard them, or had even the slightest hint of acquaintance with the greater part of them. . . .

But, not to linger too long over this, let me ask something else: how do men arrive at a knowledge of the differences? Obviously they cannot get to know them except by the intermediary of the senses, which may provide an account of the common difference from an induction based upon the canvass of every single individual case. But besides the fact that every individual case cannot be passed in review and therefore no absolutely reliable universal statement can be made . . . and besides the fact that all knowledge derived from the senses is unreliable . . . and therefore obviously no certain knowledge of the difference can be achieved through their operation, besides these facts, is it not true, even according to Aristotle, that the senses are limited to the perception of accidents only? How then will they be able to penetrate as far as the difference which is part of the inner essence?

Perhaps you will say that the differences between things are known by the understanding and not by the senses. But since according to the same Aristotle there is nothing in the understanding that has not first been in the senses, just how will the understanding be able to peer into something that has not passed through the senses to it? And do not say that the essence slips in undetected underneath the accidents. For if it slips in secretly, then the understanding must subsequently unveil it in order to recognize it; for otherwise it would never lay hold of the difference, disguised as it is. But if, after dispelling all phantoms, the understanding is capable of knowing the differences between things, and therefore their essences, I ask you why either the difference or the essence of such things as the magnet, the electric eel, and the like remain unknown? Is it not true that their difference or essence, lying concealed under the accidents, very rarely makes its way into our senses? But why speak of those things? Have we yet learned the essence of any other natural being, even the most familiar ones, like the horse, the dog, the apple, the nut, iron, or a pebble despite the fact that their accidents have always been so well known? Just because you have often seen a horse running and whinnying, can you explain the principle of the act of running or whinnying? I am not asking how the whinny is formed, what provokes the act of running, how the internal power is applied to the organs, and why such an action results from such an application; I am merely asking what you imagine to be the nature of a horse's soul, or its substance. How thick or how rarefied is it? . . .

. . . But do you know the inner nature of the rational soul? Do you know how it is created? what its substance is? what sort of existence something without corporeality can have? how it is joined to the body when it is a spirit? how it is affected by the body? how it gives rise to physical action? how it is spread throughout the body? how it is entirely present in the whole and in every part too? how it is not divided, but remains intact in the rest of the body when a member of the body is cut off? how something so insubstantial can move such a thick mass? . . . how does it give rise to vision, the most delightful of all things? in short, since it is incorporeal, how does it know corporeal things? . . . But why do I linger over these matters as if I thought you had some means of grasping them? Alas! such is the fate of our condition. That fine soul, which claims boastfully to know everything does not even know itself! . . .

Moreover, why should I think that those few words that are claimed to be necessary and sufficient for a definition are clear and comprehensible? Dialecticians insist that one of the rules of definition is that the definition must be clearer than the thing defined. Let us see just how well they obey this precept. I shall choose one example. Let the subject to be defined be motion. Here is the Aristotelian definition that is usually given for motion: "the act of a being in potentiality insofar as it is in potentiality." Great god! Is there any stomach strong enough to digest that? The explanation of a rather familiar thing was requested, but this is so complicated that nothing is clear any more. What man, pray, no matter how unschooled, does not conjure up some intelligible idea of motion the minute he hears the word? . . . Need I say how outstandingly the nature of motion has been explained when "act," "being," "potentiality," "insofar as," and "in potentiality" are left in need of definition? And while you expound these particulars, there will be particular parts of the definitions requiring further explanation, from which will follow the need for giving more definitions *ad infinitum*. I shall add just this: in my opinion, when you want to reach a stopping point, it is far better to take your stand at the first, simple understanding of a word than to proceed into neverending digressions and circles. When Democritus saw some philosophers arguing among themselves over the question what is man, he quite rightly uses this definition, which is found in Epicurus: "man is what we all know he is." [See *Against the Logicians* 1.265; also in the *Outlines of Pyrrhonism* 2.23.]

FROM *SYNTAGMA PHILOSOPHICUM, THE LOGIC**

Selection from chapter 5: That some truth can be known
by a sign and determined by a criterion.

. . . But, you will ask, what answer can be given to those modes presented by the
Skeptics? It seems indeed to be the case that the same thing appears different to different men and different animals and even to one man according to his separate
senses and conditions (which are the four first modes) since so many different
images, or appearances, are produced; nevertheless, it can be inferred that there is
some general cause underneath in the thing, or object, that is sufficient to produce
all these manifestations. And so, however much the effects may not be in conformity
with one another, there are still two things which are certain and can be proven true
upon examination: one, that there is a single *cause* in the thing itself, or the object;
and two, that there are different *dispositions* in the receiving faculties. In much the
same way, when we see the sun melt wax and harden clay, it is the same heat from
the sun which produces the effect once it has penetrated each body; however, there
is a different disposition in each body, namely a fatty humor in the wax, which can
be stirred up and disengaged to a certain extent, but still cannot be completely
removed and dispersed on account of its tenacity, with the result that the whole mass
remains softened or even liquefied; but in the clay there is a lean humor which
because of its lack of tenacity can not only be stirred up and disengaged from the dry
particles with which it is mixed but can also be completely detached from them and
go off into the atmosphere, or be evaporated, with the result that the mass that is left
becomes dry and hard. Consequently the only task that remains is the investigation
of the uniformity of the cause and the dissimilarity of the effects; and if someone
should succeed in understanding this, he will be considered to have nothing less than
full acquaintance with the nature of the thing and to share in the knowledge of it. For
no matter how much it is objected that it cannot be stated definitely from these considerations just what the thing is like according to its nature, but only what it is like
in respect to one thing or to another, it may still be said what there is in it which
makes it appear to be this in respect to one thing and that in respect to another; and
consequently it may be said both to be one thing according to its nature and to be
this or that in respect to other things. Likewise, although the sun cannot be said to
be softening rather than hardening according to its nature, it can be said, however,
to be heat-producing by its nature since it provides the heat which according to the
condition of the receiving matter melts it or hardens it. The objection made more frequently than any other concerns the variety of tastes that the same thing can be
thought to have; but it can be firmly established that the general cause of all the
tastes is the salt if it is established that anything becomes tasteless when the salt is
removed; and since salt has a multiple nature, and can be distributed differently in

---

*The editor's notes are not included. Gassendi's notes are included in square brackets.

various mixtures, it can happen that it is distributed in one fashion in honey and another in wormwood, and so, however great a variety of particular flavors it may have, there is a corresponding variety in taste sensations it may produce.

On the other hand, it can also be established that not every palate and not every tongue is formed in the same way; if one admits that it seems highly likely that the same diversity that is found in foreheads, noses, cheeks, and the rest of the face and the entire body should be expected in the palate and the tongue. Then, wherever there was a difference of configuration in them, it cannot happen that the same salt produces the same effect in all of them. For since the particles of salt set free in the liquid and mixed in it have a certain shape, as will be made clear in its proper place, it is inevitable that these particles, when received in the apertures of the organ which also have their own configuration, create an agreeable sensation whenever they are admitted into apertures similarly shaped into which they fit gently, but create a disagreeable one whenever they are admitted into others which they do not caress, but tear instead with their points because of their different configuration. From these considerations it will be obvious how so many different appearances happen to be generated by one and the same cause. Obviously the same can be said of odors, colors, sounds, and other sensations although all these matters depend upon considerations that will be explained explicitly in the section on physics. It is enough at this point if it is granted that the quality which appears to one man cannot be said to be exactly the same as the one that is in the object since other qualities will be apparent to others which might claim the same right; but it can be said that the object has really only one nature and that the various appearances it has exist by the necessity of the nature of the faculties in which they are created.

Concerning the following modes, the same or analogous answers can be given. For indeed position, distance, location, mixture, constitution, quantity, rarity, frequency, and whatever else, do not prevent things from actually being certain things in themselves and creating this appearance because of some physical necessity in some people and that one in others. Moreover, it is impossible not to recognize some necessity of this sort; and causes why things present this appearance or another can be investigated in order that something certain and true may be won and known. For example, to speak of the difference in colors, it depends upon the cognition of a general cause producing the effect of color; and if it has been established that that cause is light, it is only appropriate that it produces a diversity of apparent colors in the eye according to the variations in the degree of light, in the reflections, refractions, and relative presence of shadows. And even that range of colors which is produced by interposing a prism, or triangle of glass, which anyone can procure, conveys quite clearly what the case is. Since the colors displayed in this phenomenon are not in the things, or in the glass itself, or in the medium of the air, it is likely that how they appear to the senses is created in the eye alone and that the eye receives the impression of colors because the rays of light reflected from objects in front of us undergo the same refraction as in the glass, and bearing this refraction as they strike the eye, imprint such-and-such an appearance upon it. And since objects themselves can reflect rays from their surfaces which have been refracted in the same way according to the configuration of the tiny bodies of which they are composed, nothing prevents the colors that appear to be in things from taking their appearances from such a cause. But I shall speak of these things in their place, telling at greater length and in more detail how they occur.

Likewise, by reason of the distance involved it happens inevitably that a thing appears to be large, small, square, round, and so forth. Since any visible thing diffuses rays in every direction from its surfaces and parts which make it perceptible as they strike the eye, the result is that the more rays reach the eye, the more parts of the thing are depicted, and so the thing appears to be bigger, being made up, so to speak, of more parts; and the fewer the rays, the fewer the parts that are depicted, and so the thing appears to be smaller, as if it were made up only of those parts. And since rays spread out in a circle are more densely packed closer up and fall upon the eye in greater numbers, and are less dense at a distance and hence fewer of them reach the eye, the outcome is that a thing appears larger close up, as if it were made up of more parts, and seems smaller from a distance as if it were made up of fewer parts. Add to this the fact that the eye is so situated that in one look it takes in an entire hemisphere made up of various visible things, the nearer of which cover the farther with their bulk; a thing always appears so much the larger as it occupies a greater part of the hemisphere and so much smaller as it occupies a smaller part. Moreover, close up it occupies a larger part since it covers up a greater number of visible things farther out, and at a distance it takes up a smaller part since the farther away it is the greater the number of those things that are uncovered. And this is exactly why it happens that a tower appears square from close up and round or smooth from a distance, since the rays which come from the corners and surfaces close by are numerous and convey the parts distinctly separated from each other by intervals and make it possible for the eye to perceive their differences because of the short distance from them to the eye, but those coming from far away are fewer in number and on the contrary portray the parts which are separate from each other as if they were joined with the intervals suppressed, as it were, and make it impossible because of the great distance to perceive the differences which allow the eye to keep the parts separate. Consequently, the surface of the distant tower appears stretched and even, with indistinguishable corners. But more details about this in their place since it is sufficient for our purposes here that the capacity for error of the senses which is usually given as the reason for this and similar experiences does not prevent the possibility of knowing something true and certain.

I shall pass over the fact that the dispute whether the senses have any capacity for error could seem to be one of words inasmuch as those who say they do not mean that the senses do not make errors because they do not make judgments, or define what a thing is like, but only apprehend the appearance of the thing which is produced in them while those who maintain that they do have the capacity to err understand this matter as if the senses were the occasion of the error in the intellect by their apprehension of the thing. Hence it seems to be the case that properly speaking it is not the senses themselves, but the intellect which makes the error; and when it makes a mistake, it is not the fault of the senses but of the intellect whose responsibility it is as the higher and dominant faculty before it pronounces what a thing is like to inquire which of the different appearances produced in the senses (each one of which is the result of a necessity that produces them as they are) is in conformity with the thing. For this reason, even Epicurus himself, as we related above, ordered that any appearances coming from the senses be held in abeyance, *prosmeirai*, and that judgment be suspended or deferred until all obstacles to a genuine knowledge had been removed and the truth about the thing had been clearly established. If this advice were duly observed, many things would become certain and indubitable about which it would be possible to offer a true judgment; for instance the tower would be square when you came up close to it, the stick would be really straight when taken out of the water and held entirely in the air, and things like that.

The other matters contained in these modes are on a par with the things that have been said about the first modes. The tenth one, which deals with ethics, contains things which, like the rest, depend on physical causes, stemming principally from the fact that the soul is inclined to follow the constitution of the body, the consequence of which is that since such diverse temperaments exist, diverse things will please them, and the same thing will not appeal to everybody.

The three modes appended to the ten deal with the general form of proving and refuting. But in answer to them when the objection is made, for instance, that no truth, no sign, no criterion of the agent, of the instrument, or of the operation exists because whoever says they do exist does so either with a proof or without one, and that in either case, etc.—it can be declared as a general fact that in the first place we do have a proof, not one such as Aristotle requires or one which insists upon a previous inquiry of a most exact sort into the sign, the criterion, and the like, but certainly one that all well-endowed, wise, and intelligent men will generally accept as reasonable and which cannot be denied except for contradiction's sake. For it seems that we can stand firm in this and have no dread of an infinite regress or diallelus or pay any heed to arguments put forth more cleverly than solidly.

To illustrate, it is asked if there is any truth; the answer is that there is; and in order to forestall any subterfuge, one must then say what kind of truth it is, for instance that there are pores in the skin. The question comes whether this is claimed with or without proof. The answer is with a proof, namely the one given above. But is this proof true or false? The answer is that it is true. But it must be proven, in fact with a proof which requires another and then another on to infinity. But this whole argument must be denied on the grounds that the truth of the proof by which it is demonstrated that pores exist is obvious enough by itself, that is that it is firmly established upon propositions which are known in their own right and which the intellect cannot reject and therefore the debate must come to a stop at them. But that is a circular argument since the question was whether any truth exists. But it must be denied that any circle exists on the grounds that a certain truth does exist, namely that there are pores, and this is demonstrated fully, not from the fact that there are pores, but from the fact that if there were not, two bodies would have to be in the same place at the same time. Likewise, when it is asked whether any sign exists, the answer is that they do; and perspiration is immediately presented as an example of a sign that pores exist. But when the further question is raised whether that is claimed with or without proof, the reply is that it is claimed on the basis of the proof of experience itself, which requires no proof. And when it is said that someone denying this argument may legitimately assert the opposite, the answer must be that he may if he wants to, but let him just see whether his experience supports or rejects his assertion.

In the same way, when it is asked if a criterion exists, the answer must be that it does; and an example of the criterion must be given, for instance, the intellect is the instrument; and there is no necessity to fall back on an infinite regress or circular argument. And when it is countered that one cannot be sure to whom to give credence, given the very great diversity among intellects, the answer must be to that man who, having weighed all considerations, presents an argument that cannot be legitimately contradicted, such as the one concerning the existence of pores. Next, it is permissible to say that proof does not count and is not necessary when things are so clear that merely stating them convinces us of them, as is the case not only with specific things that are obvious to the senses and established by experience, but also with general statements against which no counterargument can be brought forth, such as the axioms to which mathematical demonstrations can be reduced like "the whole is greater than its parts," or "if equals are taken from equals, the remainders are equal," and others of the same sort. But when it is countered that someone who simply makes a declaration and does not prove it does not deserve to be believed and that the opposite can be asserted hypothetically and claimed to be true by anyone arguing against him and wishing to maintain the other side, it is clear that this can indeed be done in doubtful matters in which neither experience nor some convincing and reasonable argument comes to our support; but it cannot be done without folly in other cases in which if someone persists in assuming and maintaining the opposite, one might think of applying these verses of Lucretius to him:

> I will not plead my case against a man
> Who follows his traces to find himself.

[*De rerum natura* 4.471–72]

But, to sum up the whole matter in a few words, I take pleasure in making use here of this passage which I quote from Seneca to bring to a conclusion this treatise on truth and the criterion in a final summary: "Let me tell you how much harm too much subtlety does and how inimical it is to the truth. Protagoras says that one can debate equally well on either side of any topic, and even on that very topic, whether all things are debatable on both sides. Nausiphanes says that of the things that seem to exist, nothing has more existence than nonexistence. Parmenides says that of the things that seem to exist, the one is everything. Zeno of Elea removed all difficulties over the difficulty; he says nothing exists. The Pyrrhonians, Megarians, Eretrians,

and Academics, who have introduced a new knowledge—that we know nothing—
are occupied with almost the same matter. Put all these theories in that useless flock
of liberal studies. One man does not offer me any useful knowledge; another takes
away all hope of knowledge. It would be better to know useless nonsense than
nothing at all. One man does not bear any light before me by which my gaze is
directed toward the truth; the other scratches out my eyes. If I believe Protagoras,
there is nothing in the universe that is not doubtful. If I believe Nausiphanes, this one
thing is certain, that nothing is certain. If Parmenides, nothing exists except the one.
If Zeno, not even the one. Then what are we? What are those things that are all
around us, that feed us, that sustain us? The whole universe is a shadow, either
empty or deceptive. "I could not easily say whether I am more angered by those who
believe we know nothing or those who do not even leave us this truth, that we know
nothing." So Seneca. [*Epistle* 88, 43–46]

Selection from chapter 6: What service is logic to the truth,
for the pursuit of which it was devised?

. . . The entire logic of Lord Verulam [Francis Bacon] is directed toward physics in
itself, and therefore toward the truth, or genuine knowledge of things. Moreover, it
consists principally in forming clear ideas since he desires foremost that all preconceived notions be wiped out, and then that new notions, or ideas inferred from new
experiments properly conducted, be formed. Likewise, it consists in expressing
ideas clearly, since he desires that we construct axioms from individual cases duly
examined through experimentation, not by flying off the handle directly up to the
highest, or most general, axioms, but by proceeding gradually in an orderly manner
through intermediate steps. It consists also in making clear deductions, but only universal statements from individual cases since that is done by a legitimate induction,
and not individual truths from universals, since that is done by means of the syllogism, which he does not approve of. However, since the sinew and muscle of all reasoning actually lies in the syllogism, and not even induction proves anything except
by the force of a syllogism because of the general proposition clearly implied [in
inductive reasoning] according to which it is claimed that everything which can be
enumerated individually has been enumerated, or that not one thing can be found
which does not agree with the statement, the syllogism seems to be condemned quite
without reason inasmuch as he can be convicted of using it whenever he reasons at
all, even though he condemns it. Accordingly, he does not seem to have rejected the
syllogism totally but merely the syllogism which is founded on statements that have
not been sufficiently examined and adequately confirmed; therefore, before he
explains the form or uses of the syllogism, he may be expected to have estimated to
what extent general propositions subject to no exceptions may exist. Meanwhile,
however, just this treatise on the syllogism is lacking, and so is any general treatment of method, although he perhaps intended to furnish some such treatment when
he spoke about the partition of the sciences. I shall not try to justify all those words

that may be considered a trifle too affected since the founder of a new system seems to have the right to use new words or words in a new way.

Lastly, Cartesian logic is founded upon a direct imitation of Lord Verulam's since in order to form ideas clearly, it stresses the elimination of malformed preconceived notions and the adoption of true ideas (for that he thinks all of them are to be eliminated, and how they are to be, that is another matter); but since immediately afterward in order to gain a true and real knowledge of things he concludes that the intellect should find help as it proceeds in its judgment not so much from examining things themselves both in themselves and by themselves as from its thoughts alone examined by itself in solitude, it is obvious that his method is less fitting than Bacon's. If there is occasionally something that concerns logic in the whole series of things that follow, it is primarily the principle that the author proposes as follows: "Everything that I perceive clearly and distinctly is true." In fact he proves this laboriously on the grounds that God exists and that he is not a deceiver, that he has imprinted the idea of himself in us, that since he is the cause of all things, he is also the cause of a clear and distinct perception, etc. And it would perhaps be satisfactory if it were proposed in this manner: a wise man must accept nothing as true and unshakable, except on the basis that he perceives it clearly and distinctly. But it is well known that experience teaches us, as he himself confesses in his own case, that it happens from time to time that we learn subsequently something is false which it seemed to us we perceived clearly and distinctly. But even when we have taken every precaution human skill and diligence allow us to take, we still learn with the passage of time that we had been deluded; we may then assign the cause of this merely to human weakness, considering which we cannot be too cautious to prevent something false from insinuating itself upon us sometime.

FURTHER READINGS

Bloch, Olivier. *La Philosophie de Gassendi*. The Hague: Martinus Nijhoff, 1971.

Brundell, Barry. *Pierre Gassendi: From Aristotelianism to a New Natural Philosophy*. Dordrecht: D. Reidel, 1987.

Gassendi, Pierre. *Disquisitio metaphysica seu dubitationes et instantiae adversus Renati Cartesi metaphysicam et responsa*. Bilingual edition and French translation by Bernard Rochot. Paris: J. Vrin, 1962.

———. *Exercitationes Paradoxicae adversus Aristoteleos*. Bilingual edition and French translation by Bernard Rochot. Paris: J. Vrin, 1959.

Gassendi, Pierre. *Vie et moeurs d'Epicure*. Translated and annotated by Sylvie Taussig. Paris: Alive, 2001.

Gregory, Tulio. *Scetticismo ed empirismo: Studio su Gassendi*. Bari: Editori Laterza, 1961.

Jones, Howard. *Pierre Gassendi, 1592–1655: An Intellectual Biography*. Nieuwkoop: Graaf, 1981.

Joy, Lynn. *Gassendi, the Atomist: Advocate of History in an Age of Science*. Cambridge: Cambridge University Press, 1987.

Lennon, Thomas. *The Battle of the Gods and Giants: The Legacies of Descartes and Gassendi: 1655–1715*. Princeton, NJ: Princeton University Press, 1993.

Murr, Sylvia, ed. *Gassendi et l'Europe, 1592–1792*. Paris: J. Vrin, 1997.

Osler, Margaret. *Divine Will and the Mechanical Philosophy: Gassendi and Descartes on Contingency and Necessity in the Created World*. Cambridge: Cambridge University Press, 1994.

———. "Baptizing Epicurean Atomism." In *Religion, Science and Worldview*. Edited by Margaret Osler and P. L. Farber. Cambridge: Cambridge University Press, 1985.

Sarasohn, Lisa T. *Gassendi's Ethics: Freedom in a Mechanistic Universe*. Ithaca, NY: Cornell University Press, 1996.

Walker, Ralph. "Gassendi and Skepticism." In *The Skeptical Tradition*, edited by Myles Burnyeat, 319–36. Berkeley: University of California Press, 1983.

14

LA MOTHE LE VAYER

François de La Mothe Le Vayer (1588–1672) was one of the few self-avowed skeptics after Sextus. He wrote and published a large number of skeptical works: *Problèmes Sceptiques*; *Discours ou Homélies Académiques*; *Du peu de certitude qu'il y a dans l'histoire*; *Petit traité sceptique sur cette commune façon de parler, "n'avoir pas le sens commun"*; *Discours sceptique sur la musique* (dedicated to Mersenne); and *Discours pour montrer que les doutes de la philosophie sceptique sont de grand usage dans les sciences*, among others. His open skepticism, which he always claimed to be not only compatible with but also conductive to Christianity (see the extract below), did not preclude him from being appointed preceptor of the king's brother, the Duc d'Anjou. He was close to Richelieu in favor, for whom he wrote *La Vertu des Payans*, directed at Antoine Arnauld (1612–1694) and the Jansenist movement in France. However, the volumes in which he published the two dialogues from which were taken the extracts below were published anonymously, with a false date of publication and publisher. The possible reason for the secrecy is—as he says in the preface to the book—that his "hand [in these dialogues] is so generous or so libertine, that it can only follow the caprices of its own fancies, and this in a so free and independent way, that it is proud of aiming at nothing but the search after the truth or natural probabilities and of having as subject nothing but my own satisfaction, which consists in these naïf conversations." La Mothe Le Vayer is a marginal figure in the history of philosophy, but recently there has been some interest in his thought with the edition of some of his works other than the *Dialogues*.

FROM *OF DIVINITY*

But when we contemplate like a great ocean the immense and prodigious number of human religions it is then in default of having faith as a compass to guide our soul toward the pole of Divine Grace that it is impossible to evade errors and tempests more lengthy and perilous than those of Ulysses because they carry us finally to a spiritual shipwreck. An old Chinese writing says that since the first man there have been only three hundred and sixty-five religious sects, but one easily sees that this is a number chosen to be equal to the days of the year. And only a little thought allows one to perceive that the number cannot be determined. Whoever has thought humanely of the irreligious, who like Ptolemy or his predecessors invent hypotheses of epicycles, eccentrics or concentrics, and other fantastic mechanisms to give reasons for celestial phenomena or appearances, each could in the same way suppose the mobility of the earth and the repose of the firmament, or something similar, providing that this saves and explains methodically the things in the heavens that fall under our senses. Similarly, all that we apprehend of the gods and religions is only what the most able men have conceived to be the most reasonable according to their discourse on the moral, economic, and civil life to explain the phenomena of customs, actions, and thoughts of poor mortals, to provide them with certain rules for living, exempt as much as possible from all absurdity. It follows that if someone with a better imagination than his predecessors establishes new foundations or hypotheses that better explain all the duties of civil life and in general all that transpires among men, with a little luck this position would be as acceptable as the new systems of Copernicus and others who account for what is observed in the heavens more clearly and briefly than before. So finally, a religion conceived of in this way is only a particular system that renders moral phenomena and all the appearances of our doubtful ethics reasonable. Now in this infinity of religions there is hardly anyone who does not believe that he possesses the true religion, and who does not condemn all the others and who does not combat them *pro aris et focis* to the last drop of his blood. . . .

Therefore, it is neither impertinence nor impiety on my part to maintain that Saint Paul has taught us to believe and not to know, and that by the truly aporetic sentiments, of which all his sacred theology is replete, he has given us lessons expressing the vanity, that is, the nullity of all human sciences, and thus that he has never departed from our skeptical school. I know only one thing, he says ingenuously: Jesus Christ crucified. All natural knowledge, all philosophical demonstrations, are nothing. His spirit acquiesces only to the unique hyperphysical light of Christianity, and submits only to the unique precepts of faith. Also very important is that as the end of our *epoché* is to give us a reasonable moderation in all our passions, and perfect assurance in what concerns opinions, all Christian doctrine will take the same way as that devout *metriopatheia*, which make us submit all our affections to, and yield all our will to, that of the All Powerful. We will acquire that religious *ataraxia* that renders us inflexible and unshakable in our belief. *Justus ex fide vivet.* Make therefore hardy profession of the honorable ignorance of our well-loved skeptic. It is skepticism alone that can prepare for us the way to knowledge revealed by the Divinity. All others philosophic sects only lead us away from this knowledge by making us obstinate with their dogmas and by confusing our spirit with their scientific maxims, rather than clarifying and purifying our understanding. . . .

FROM *ON BEING OPINIONATED*

. . . In examining all the orders of nature in the world, large or small, you will find nothing upon which people have not formed entirely different conceptions. Nor are those who believe that they have penetrated to things that they call metaphysics any less protected from the presumptuous imbecility of the human mind, as shown by the continual controversies they raise concerning what takes place in the heavens. . . . The many volumes of reveries that people argue are revelations, the multiple scholastic chimeras that people try to pass off as articles of faith, so many mortal battles over these matters every day, are just so many signs of our weakness, and witness of our rashness. Some make God the creator of the world; others attribute its creation to evil demons, a view that seems less strange to those who pay attention to the behavior of those who hold this belief. The first revere heaven; the others respect hell. . . . Our devout believers do not eat meat; those in Egypt do not eat fish. . . .

. . . Given that our human nature can penetrate only to the probable, how rash it would be of us to take the doubtful for the certain, and to defend stubbornly today what we will be compelled to retract tomorrow, or not to be more reasonable than those who we complain do these things. It is better that we utilize that excellent suspension of judgment of our cherished skeptic, and that we hold in reserve the parts we cannot commend because we are not sufficiently informed. Because moreover our understanding is in its nature no less subject to variations in its operations than is the moon to change its face. . . . Let us leave it to others this odious profession of knowing everything with certainty . . . and since the gods have not desired that our mind extend its sphere of activity beyond appearances and probabilities, let us be quietly content with the limits that their providence has prescribed for us, which in any case it would be in vain for us to try to surpass. Let us doubt everything, since this is the nature of humanity, and to determine nothing too readily, does not even give us complete assurance about our skeptical doubts. Anaximander estimated that the earth maintains its place in the center of the universe only because it has an equal inclination toward everything that surrounds it and thus does not know which direction to lean . . . just as a hair squarely drawn by its two ends and thus having equal force on all its parts would never break because it would have no more reason to rapture in any one place than in any other. It is, Anaximander adds, like someone starving who is at an equal distance from several foods toward each of which he has an equal propensity, and who would of necessity remain eternally starving because he would remain without any action or movement. . . . But it is even more true when one considers without partiality the probabilities of all things according to the rules of our sect, that one with a mind in such a state of indifference and not knowing which direction to lean would be constrained to remain suspended among the equality of reasons that are found everywhere. . . . The Dogmatists, who are prejudiced, often see things only in a way that favors their expectations, so it is not surprising that they promptly take one side or the other with such determination that one can never move them from it. . . . But as for those of our sort, who make their reflections in accord with the probability of each proposition, instead of weakly allowing themselves to be carried along lock step by a party, they depend liberally on their own strengths, between the extremities of so many different opinions, which is the best and most favorable position that a philosophic mentality can possess. That is, they do not hold the views of Tantalus, who, as remarked, starves while surrounded by food he cannot approach. The skeptic considers and pays attention to everything without prejudicing his judgment and without being opinionated, and so remains an indifferent judge of the many dishes and sauces, as the most notable guest at a table where everything is equally well served. It is in this fine milieu that *ataraxia* is rendered mistress of all our opinions, and *metriopatheia* tempers all our passions by means of our divine *epoché*.

FURTHER READINGS

Beaude, Joseph. "Amplifier le dixième trope, ou la différence culturelle comme argument sceptique." In *Recherches sur le XVII siecle* 5. Paris: Editions du CNRS, 1982, pp. 21–29.

Cavaillé, Jean-Pierre. "Skepticisme, tromperie et mensonge chez La Mothe Le Vayer et Descartes." In *The Return of Skepticism from Hobbes and Descartes to Bayle*, edited by Gianni Paganini, 115–31. Dordrecht: Kluwer, 2003.

Giocanti, Sylvia. *Penser l'irrésolution: Montaigne, Pascal, La Mothe Le Vayer*. Paris: Honoré Champion, 2001.

Gouverneur, Sophie. "La Mothe Le Vayer et la politique, ou l'usage libertin du scepticisme antique." *Libertinage et philosophie* 7 (2003): 189–201.

La Mothe Le Vayer, François. *De la vertu des païens*. Paris: Augustin Courbe, 1647.

———. *Hexameron Rustique*. La Versanne: Encre Marine, 2005.

———. *Oeuvres*. 14 vols. Dresden: M. Groell, 1756–1759.

———. *Petit traité sceptique sur cette commune façon de parler: N'avoir pas le Sens commun*. Mayenne: Le Promeneur, 2003.

Paganini, Gianni. "Pyrrhonisme 'tout pur' ou 'circoncis'? La dynamique du scepticisme chez La Mothe Le Vayer." *Libertinage et Philosophie au XVIIe siècle* 2 (1997): 7–31.

Pintard, René. *Le Libertinage érudit en France dans la première moitié du 17éme siècle*. Nouvelle édition augmentée d'un avant-propos et de notes et réflexions sur les problèmes de l'histoire du libertinage. Réimpression de l'édition de Paris, 1943. Geneva: Slatkine, 2000.

Wetsel, David. "La Mothe Le Vayer and the Subversion of Christian Belief." *Seventeenth-Century French Studies* 21 (1999): 183–93.

Whelan, Ruth. "The Wisdom of Simonides: Bayle and La Mothe Le Vayer." In *Skepticism and Irreligion in the Seventeenth and Eighteenth Centuries*, edited by Richard H. Popkin and Arjo Vanderjagt, 230–53. Leiden: E. J. Brill, 1993.

15

DESCARTES

René Descartes (1596–1650) is the most influential philosopher in modern philosophy. His influence lies, above all, on (1) his proposition of a radical and universal doubt as a method to eradicate previous beliefs in order to establish a new philosophy founded on metaphysical certainty and (2) the main fruit of this radical doubt: the emergence of the *cogito* that led to various forms of idealism in modern—and "internalism" in contemporary—philosophy. With universal radical doubt that challenges the justifications of our belief in the existence of a material world external to our minds, Descartes begins a new epoch in the history of skepticism. After Cartesian doubt, skepticism loses its practical orientation and becomes a major epistemological or metaphysical challenge to be tangled by most of the great philosophers afterward. The use of skeptical doubt for ends alien to skepticism itself is a commonplace after the reappraisal of ancient skepticism at least since Augustine. But it is Descartes's particular philosophical deployment of skeptical doubt to ground a radical separation between mind and body that turns skepticism into a crucial challenge to modern and contemporary philosophy. Although Descartes claimed that one of his goals was to provide a definitive refutation of skepticism, the novelty and difficulty of Descartes's strategy to accomplish this task, namely, to radicalize doubt itself, soon led to the view that what Descartes really accomplished was to foster skepticism. In contemporary epistemology, "modern skepticism," that is, skepticism about the external material world, is also called "Cartesian skepticism." We have included in this selection parts of Descartes's most important philosophical work, the *Meditations on First Philosophy*. We have selected the sections which are most relevant to the setting of the problem of skepticism about the external world, that is, the whole of Meditation I (hyperbolic doubt) and sections from Meditations II (the *cogito*), III (criticism of naïve realism and the argument of the nondeceiver God), and VI (Descartes's polemical proof of the existence of an external material world).

FROM *MEDITATIONS ON FIRST PHILOSOPHY*

Meditation I: Of the Things of Which We May Doubt

Several years have now elapsed since I first became aware that I had accepted, even from my youth, many false opinions for true, and that consequently what I afterwards based on such principles was highly doubtful; and from that time I was convinced of the necessity of undertaking once in my life to rid myself of all the opinions I had adopted, and of commencing anew the work of building from the foundation, if I desired to establish a firm and abiding superstructure in the sciences. But as this enterprise appeared to me to be one of great magnitude, I waited until I had attained an age so mature as to leave me no hope that at any stage of life more advanced I should be better able to execute my design. On this account, I have delayed so long that I should henceforth consider I was doing wrong were I still to consume in deliberation any of the time that now remains for action. To-day, then, since I have opportunely freed my mind from all cares, [and am happily disturbed by no passions], and since I am in the secure possession of leisure in a peaceable retirement, I will at length apply myself earnestly and freely to the general overthrow of all my former opinions. But, to this end, it will not be necessary for me to show that the whole of these are false—a point, perhaps, which I shall never reach; but as even now my reason convinces me that I ought not the less carefully to withhold belief from what is not entirely certain and indubitable, than from what is manifestly false, it will be sufficient to justify the rejection of the whole if I shall find in each some ground for doubt. Nor for this purpose will it be necessary even to deal with each belief individually, which would be truly an endless labor; but, as the removal from below of the foundation necessarily involves the downfall of the whole edifice, I will at once approach the criticism of the principles on which all my former beliefs rested.

All that I have, up to this moment, accepted as possessed of the highest truth and certainty, I received either from or through the senses. I observed, however, that these sometimes misled us; and it is the part of prudence not to place absolute confidence in that by which we have even once been deceived.

But it may be said, perhaps, that, although the senses occasionally mislead us respecting minute objects, and such as are so far removed from us as to be beyond the reach of close observation, there are yet many other of their informations (presentations), of the truth of which it is manifestly impossible to doubt; as for example, that I am in this place, seated by the fire, clothed in a winter dressing-gown, that I hold in my hands this piece of paper, with other intimations of the same nature. But how could I deny that I possess these hands and this body, and withal escape being classed with persons in a state of insanity, whose brains are so disordered and clouded by dark bilious vapors as to cause them pertinaciously to assert that they are monarchs when they are in the greatest poverty; or clothed [in gold] and purple when destitute of any covering; or that their head is made of clay, their body of glass,

or that they are gourds? I should certainly be not less insane than they, were I to regulate my procedure according to examples so extravagant.

Though this be true, I must nevertheless here consider that I am a man, and that,
consequently, I am in the habit of sleeping, and representing to myself in dreams
those same things, or even sometimes others less probable, which the insane think
are presented to them in their waking moments. How often have I dreamt that I was
in these familiar circumstances,—that I was dressed, and occupied this place by the
fire, when I was lying undressed in bed? At the present moment, however, I certainly
look upon this paper with eyes wide awake; the head which I now move is not
asleep; I extend this hand consciously and with express purpose, and I perceive it;
the occurrences in sleep are not so distinct as all this. But I cannot forget that, at
other times, I have been deceived in sleep by similar illusions; and, attentively considering those cases, I perceive so clearly that there exist no certain marks by which
the state of waking can ever be distinguished from sleep, that I feel greatly astonished; and in amazement I almost persuade myself that I am now dreaming.

Let us suppose, then, that we are dreaming, and that all these particulars—
namely, the opening of the eyes, the motion of the head, the forth-putting of the
hands—are merely illusions; and even that we really possess neither an entire body
nor hands such as we see. Nevertheless, it must be admitted at least that the objects
which appear to us in sleep are, as it were, painted representations which could not
have been formed unless in the likeness of realities; and, therefore, that those general objects, at all events,—namely, eyes, a head, hands, and an entire body—are not
simply imaginary, but really existent. For, in truth, painters themselves, even when
they study to represent sirens and satyrs by forms the most fantastic and extraordinary, cannot bestow upon them natures absolutely new, but can only make a certain
medley of the members of different animals; or if they chance to his imagine something so novel that nothing at all similar has ever been seen before, and such as is,
therefore, purely fictitious and absolutely false, it is at least certain that the colors of
which this is composed are real.

And on the same principle, although these general objects, viz. [a body], eyes,
a head, hands, and the like, be imaginary, we are nevertheless absolutely necessi-
tated to admit the reality at least of some other objects still more simple and universal than these, of which, just as of certain real colors, all those images of things,
whether true and real, or false and fantastic, that are found in our consciousness, are
formed.

To this class of objects seem to belong corporeal nature in general and its extension; the figure of extended things, their quantity or magnitude, and their number, as
also the place in, and the time during, which they exist, and other things of the same
sort. We will not, therefore, perhaps reason illegitimately if we conclude from this
that Physics, Astronomy, Medicine, and all the other sciences that have for their end
the consideration of composite objects, are indeed of a doubtful character; but that
Arithmetic, Geometry, and the other sciences of the same class, which regard merely
the simplest and most general objects, and scarcely inquire whether or not these are

really existent, contain somewhat that is certain and indubitable: for whether I am awake or dreaming, it remains true that two and three make five, and that a square has but four sides; nor does it seem possible that truths so apparent can ever fall under a suspicion of falsity [or incertitude].

Nevertheless, the belief that there is a God who is all-powerful, and who created me, such as I am, has, for a long time, obtained steady possession of my mind. How, then, do I know that he has not arranged that there should be neither earth, nor sky, nor any extended thing, nor figure, nor magnitude, nor place, providing at the same time, however, for [the rise in me of the perceptions of all these objects, and] the persuasion that these do not exist otherwise than as I perceive them? And further, as I sometimes think that others are in error respecting matters of which they believe themselves to possess a perfect knowledge, how do I know that I am not also deceived each time I add together two and three, or number the sides of a square, or form some judgment still more simple, if more simple indeed can be imagined? But perhaps Deity has not been willing that I should be thus deceived, for He is said to be supremely good. If, however, it were repugnant to the goodness of Deity to have created me subject to constant deception, it would seem likewise to be contrary to his goodness to allow me to be occasionally deceived; and yet it is clear that this is permitted. Some, indeed, might perhaps be found who would be disposed rather to deny the existence of a Being so powerful than to believe that there is nothing certain. But let us for the present refrain from opposing this opinion, and grant that all which is here said of a Deity is fabulous: nevertheless in whatever way it be supposed that I reached the state in which I exist, whether by fate, or chance, or by an endless series of antecedents and consequents, or by any other means, it is clear (since to be deceived and to err is a certain defect) that the probability of my being so imperfect as to be the constant victim of deception, will be increased exactly in proportion as the power possessed by the cause, to which they assign my origin, is lessened. To these reasonings I have assuredly nothing to reply, but am constrained at last to avow that there is nothing of all that I formerly believed to be true of which it is impossible to doubt, and that not through thoughtlessness or levity, but from cogent and maturely considered reasons; so that henceforward, if I desire to discover anything certain, I ought not the less carefully to refrain from assenting to those same opinions than to what might be shown to be manifestly false.

But it is not sufficient to have made these observations; care must be taken likewise to keep them in remembrance. For those old and customary opinions perpetually Recur—long and familiar usage giving them the right of occupying my mind, even almost against my will, and subduing my belief; nor will I lose the habit of deferring to them and confiding in them so long as I shall consider them to be what in truth they are, viz., opinions to some extent doubtful, as I have already shown, but still highly probable, and such as it is much more reasonable to believe than deny. It is for this reason I am persuaded that I shall not be doing wrong, if, taking an opposite judgment of deliberate design, I become my own deceiver, by supposing, for a time, that all those opinions are entirely false and imaginary, until at length, having thus balanced my old by my new prejudices, my judgment shall no longer be turned aside by perverted usage from the path that may conduct to the perception of truth. For I am assured that, meanwhile, there will arise neither peril nor error from this course, and that I cannot for the present yield too much to distrust, since the end I now seek is not action but knowledge.

I will suppose, then, not that Deity, who is sovereignly good and the fountain of truth, but that some malignant demon, who is at once exceedingly potent and deceitful, has employed all his artifice to deceive me; I will suppose that the sky, the air, the earth, colors, figures, sounds, and all external things, are nothing better than the illusions of dreams, by means of which this being has laid snares for my credulity; I will consider myself as without hands, eyes, flesh, blood, or any of the senses, and as falsely believing that I am possessed of these; I will continue resolutely fixed in this belief, and if indeed by this means it be not in my power to arrive at the knowledge of truth, I shall at least do what is in my power, viz., [suspend my judgment], and guard with settled purpose against giving my assent to what is false, and being imposed upon by this deceiver, whatever be his power and artifice.

But this undertaking is arduous, and a certain indolence insensibly leads me back to my ordinary course of life; and just as the captive, who, perchance, was enjoying in his dreams an imaginary liberty, when he begins to suspect that it is but a vision, dreads awakening, and conspires with the agreeable illusions that the deception may be prolonged; so I, of my own accord, fall back into the train of my former beliefs, and fear to arouse myself from my slumber, lest the time of laborious wakefulness that would succeed this quiet rest, in place of bringing any light of day, should prove inadequate to dispel the darkness that will arise from the difficulties that have now been raised.

Meditation II: Of the Nature of the Human Mind; and That It Is More Easily Known Than the Body

The Meditation of yesterday has filled my mind with so many doubts, that it is no longer in my power to forget them. Nor do I see, meanwhile, any principle on which they can be resolved; and, just as if I had fallen all of a sudden into very deep water, I am so greatly disconcerted as to be unable either to plant my feet firmly on the bottom or sustain myself by swimming on the surface. I will, nevertheless, make an effort, and try anew the same path on which I had entered yesterday, that is, proceed by casting aside all that admits of the slightest doubt, not less than if I had discovered it to be absolutely false; and I will continue always in this track until I shall find something that is certain, or at least, if I can do nothing more, until I shall know with certainty that there is nothing certain. Archimedes, that he might transport the entire globe from the place it occupied to another, demanded only a point that was firm and immovable; so also, I shall be entitled to entertain the highest expectations, if I am fortunate enough to discover only one thing that is certain and indubitable.

I suppose, accordingly, that all the things which I see are false (fictitious); I believe that none of those objects which my fallacious memory represents ever existed; I suppose that I possess no senses; I believe that body, figure, extension, motion, and place are merely fictions of my mind. What is there, then, that can be esteemed true? Perhaps this only, that there is absolutely nothing certain.

But how do I know that there is not something different altogether from the objects I have now enumerated, of which it is impossible to entertain the slightest doubt? Is there not a God, or some being, by whatever name I may designate him, who causes these thoughts to arise in my mind? But why suppose such a being, for it may be I myself am capable of producing them? Am I so dependent on the body and the senses that without these I cannot exist? But I had the persuasion that there was absolutely nothing in the world, that there was no sky and no earth, neither minds nor bodies; was I not, therefore, at the same time, persuaded that I did not exist? Far from it; I assuredly existed, since I was persuaded. But there is I know not what being, who is possessed at once of the highest power and the deepest cunning, who is constantly employing all his ingenuity in deceiving me as he may, he can never bring it about that I am nothing, so long as I shall be conscious that I am something. So that it must, in fine, be maintained, all things being maturely and carefully considered, that this proposition I am, I exist, is necessarily true each time it is expressed by me, or conceived in my mind.

Meditation III: Of God: That He Exists

. . . I am certain that I am a thinking thing; but do I not therefore likewise know what is required to render me certain of the truth? In this first knowledge, doubtless, there is nothing that gives me assurance of its truth except the clear and distinct perception of what I affirm, which would not indeed be sufficient to give me the assurance that what I say is true, if it could ever happen that anything I thus clearly and distinctly perceived should prove false; and accordingly it seems to me that I may now take as a general rule, that all that is very clearly and distinctly apprehended (conceived) is true.

Nevertheless I before received and admitted many things as wholly certain and manifest, which yet I afterwards fond to be doubtful. What, then, were those: They were the earth, the sky, the stars, and all the other objects which I was in the habit of perceiving by the senses. But what was it that I clearly [and distinctly] perceived in them? Nothing more than that the ideas and the thoughts of those objects were presented to my mind. And even now I do not deny that these ideas are found in my mind. But there was yet another thing which I affirmed, and which, from having been accustomed to believe it, I thought I clearly perceived, although, in truth, I did not perceive it at all; I mean the existence of objects external to me, from which those ideas proceeded, and to which they had a perfect resemblance; and it was here I was mistaken, or if I judged correctly, this assuredly was not to be traced to any knowledge I possessed.

But then I considered any matter in arithmetic and geometry, that was very simple and easy, as, for example, that two and three added together make five, and things of this sort, did I not view them with at least sufficient clearness to warrant me in affirming their truth? Indeed, if I afterwards judged that we ought to doubt of these things, it was for no other reason than because it occurred to me that a God might perhaps have given me such a nature as that I should be deceived, even respecting the matters that appeared to me the most evidently true. But as often as this preconceived opinion of the sovereign power of a God presents itself to my mind, I am constrained to admit that it is easy for him, if he wishes it, to cause me to err, even in matters where I think I possess the highest evidence; and, on the other hand, as often as I direct my attention to things which I think I apprehend with great clearness, I am so persuaded of their truth that I naturally break out into expressions such as these: Deceive me who may, no one will yet ever be able to bring it about that I am not, so long as I shall be conscious that I am, or at any future time cause it to be true that I have never been, it being now true that I am, or make two and three more or less than five, in supposing which, and other like absurdities, I discover a manifest contradiction.

. . . I must inquire whether there is a God, as soon as an opportunity of doing so shall present itself; and if I find that there is a God, I must examine likewise whether he can be a deceiver; for; without the knowledge of these two truths, I do not see that I can ever be certain of anything. . . .

. . . There remains only the inquiry as to the way in which I received this idea from God; for I have not drawn it from the senses, nor is it even presented to me unexpectedly, as is usual with the ideas of sensible objects, when these are presented or appear to be presented to the external organs of the senses; it is not even a pure production or fiction of my mind, for it is not in my power to take from or add to it; and consequently there but remains the alternative that it is innate, in the same way as is the idea of myself. And, in truth, it is not to be wondered at that God, at my creation, implanted this idea in me, that it might serve, as it were, for the mark of the workman impressed on his work; and it is not also necessary that the mark should be something different from the work itself; but considering only that God is my creator, it is highly probable that he in some way fashioned me after his own image and likeness, and that I perceived this likeness, in which is contained the idea of God, by the same faculty by which I apprehend myself,—in other words, when I make myself the object of reflection, I not only find that I am an incomplete, [imperfect] and dependent being, and one who unceasingly aspires after something better and greater than he is; but, at the same time, I am assured likewise that he upon whom I am dependent possesses in himself all the goods after which I aspire, [and the ideas of which I find in my mind], and that not merely indefinitely and potentially, but infinitely and actually, and that he is thus God. And the whole force of the argument of which I have here availed myself to establish the existence of God, consists in this, that I perceive I could not possibly be of such a nature as I am, and yet have in my mind the idea of God, if God did not in reality exist,—this same God, I say, whose idea is in my mind—that is, a being who possesses all those lofty perfections, of which the mind may have some slight conception, without, however, being able fully to comprehend them—and who is wholly superior to all defect, [and has nothing that marks imperfection]: whence it is sufficiently manifest that he cannot be a deceiver, since it is a dictate of the natural light that all fraud and deception spring from some defect.

Meditation VI: Of the Existence of Material Things; and of the Real Distinction between the Mind and the Body of Man

. . . I cannot doubt but that there is in me a certain passive faculty of perception, that is, of receiving and taking knowledge of the ideas of sensible things; but this would be useless to me, if there did not also exist in me, or in some other thing, another active faculty capable of forming and producing those ideas. But this active faculty cannot be in me [in as far as I am but a thinking thing], seeing that it does not pre-suppose thought, and also that those ideas are frequently produced in my mind without my contributing to it in any way, and even frequently contrary to my will. This faculty must therefore exist in some difference from me, in which all the objec-tive reality of the ideas that are produced by this faculty, is contained formally or eminently, as I before remarked; and this substance is either a body, that is to say, a corporeal nature in which is contained formally [and in effect] all that is objectively [and by representation] in those ideas; or it is God himself, or some other creature, of a rank superior to body, in which the same is contained eminently. But as God is no deceiver, it is manifest that he does not of himself and immediately communicate those ideas to me, nor even by the intervention of any creature in which their objec-tive reality is not formally, but only eminently, contained. For as he has given me no faculty whereby I can discover this to be the case, but, on the contrary, a very strong inclination to believe that those ideas arise from corporeal objects, I do not see how he could be vindicated from the charge of deceit, if in truth they proceeded from any other source, or were produced by other causes than corporeal things: and accord-ingly it must be concluded, that corporeal objects exist. Nevertheless they are not perhaps exactly such as we perceive by the senses, for their comprehension by the sense is, in many instances, very obscure and confused; but it is at least necessary to admit that all which I clearly and distinctly conceive as in them, that is, generally speaking, all that is comprehended in the object of speculative geometry, really exists external to me.

FURTHER READINGS

Araujo, Marcelo de. *Scepticism, Freedom and Autonomy: A Study of the Moral Foundations of Descartes' Theory of Knowledge*. Berlin: De Gruyter, 2003.
Bracken, Harry M. *Descartes*. Oxford: Oneworld, 2002.
Broughton, Janet. *Descartes' Method of Doubt*. Princeton, NJ: Princeton University Press, 2002.

Curley, Edwin. *Descartes against the Skeptics*. Cambridge, MA: Harvard University Press, 1978.

Davies, Richard. *Descartes: Belief, Scepticism and Virtue*. London: Routledge, 2001.

Descartes, René. *The Philosophical Writings*. Translated by John Cottingham, Robert Stoothoof, and Dugald Murdoch. 2 vols. Cambridge: Cambridge University Press, 1985.

Fine, Gail. "Descartes and Ancient Skepticism: Reheated Cabbage?" *Philosophical Review* 109 (2000): 195–234.

Frankfurt, Harry G. *Demons, Dreamers, and Madmen: The Defense of Reason in Descartes' Meditations*. Indianapolis, IN: Bobbs-Merrill, 1970.

Gouhier, Henri. "Doute metodique ou negation metodique?" *Etudes Philosophiques* 9 (1954): 135–62.

Groake, Leo. "Descartes' First Meditation: Something Old, Something New, Something Borrowed." *Journal of the History of Philosophy* 22 (1984): 281–301.

Kambouchner, Denis. *Les Méditations Metaphysiques de Descartes*. Vol. I: Introduction générale. Première Méditation. Paris: Presses Universitaires de France, 2005.

Maia Neto, José R. "Charron's Epoche and Descartes' Cogito: The Skeptical Base of Descartes' Refutation of Skepticism." In *The Return of Skepticism from Hobbes and Descartes to Bayle*, edited by Gianni Paganini, 81–113. Dordrecht: Kluwer, 2003.

Popkin, Richard H. "Charron and Descartes: The Fruits of Systematic Doubt." *Journal of Philosophy* 51 (1954): 831–37.

Williams, Bernard. *Descartes: The Project of Pure Inquiry*. Harmondsworth: Penguin, 1978.

16

PASCAL

Blaise Pascal (1623–1662) was an experimental scientist, mathematician, philosopher, religious thinker, and controversialist. His most famous work, *Thoughts*, is a collection of fragments he left upon his death, most of which belong to a projected apology for Christianity in which skepticism plays a major role. Pascal was influenced by the two main branches of early modern skepticism. The first is the Renaissance one held by Montaigne, Charron, and La Mothe Le Vayer, which was interpreted both religiously, as preparation for faith, and irreligiously by free thinkers who emphasized the criticism of religion present in this skepticism, which they turned specifically against Christian revelation and doctrine. The second is Descartes's skepticism about the external material world. Although Pascal was strongly impressed with Montaigne's kind of skepticism, he found it dangerous to Christianity, among other reasons because he considered it as leading to indifference with respect to the truth, the good, and God. He thus endeavored to reinterpret Montaignean skepticism—with the help of the new branch of skepticism brought about by Descartes—in view of neutralizing its antireligious potential and construing a new argument for his antihumanist view of the Christian religion. This argument is that both what is true and what is false in skepticism (the practical inadequacy of hyperbolic doubt) can be explained and reconciled only through the doctrine of the Fall of Man. The two fragments below exhibit Pascal's strategy. On another front, Pascal fought for an experimental new science free from the authority of tradition. He made experiments designed to show, against the Aristotelians, that nature does not abhor a vacuum. We reprint below Pascal's preface to his *Treatise on the Vacuum* (written in 1651) in which he vindicates the role of reason against authority in scientific matters and outlines an experimental philosophy of science skeptical with regard to metaphysical truths.

FROM *PENSÉES**

Fragment La 131

The chief argument of the Pyrrhonians—I pass over the lesser ones—are that we have no certainty of the truth of these principles apart from faith and revelation, except in so far as we naturally perceive them in ourselves. Now this natural intuition is not a convincing proof of their truth; since, having no certainty, apart from faith, whether man was created by a good God, or by a wicked demon, or by chance, it is doubtful whether these principles given to us are true, or false or uncertain, according to our origin.

Again no person is certain, apart from faith, whether he is awake or sleeps, seeing that during sleep we believe that we are awake as firmly as we do when we are awake. As we often dream that we dream, heaping dream upon dream, may it not be that this half of our life, wherein we think ourselves awake, is itself only a dream on which the others are grafted, from which we wake at death, during which we have as few principles of truth and good as during natural sleep. These different thoughts which disturb us being perhaps only illusions like the flight of time and the vain fancies of our dreams? We believe that we see space, figure, and motion; we are aware of the passage of time, we measure it; and in fact we act as if we were awake. So that half of our life being passed in sleep, we have on our own admission no idea of truth, whatever we may imagine. As all our intuitions are then illusions, who knows whether the other half of our life, in which we think we are awake, is not another sleep a little different from the former, from which we awake when we suppose ourselves asleep? (. . . *And who doubts that, if we dreamt in company, and the dreams chanced to agree, which is common enough, and if we were always alone when awake, we should believe that matters were reversed?*)

These are the chief arguments on one side and the other. I omit minor ones, such as the Pyrrhonians' talk against the impressions of custom, education, manners, country, and the like. Though these influence the majority of common folk, who dogmatize only on shallow foundations, they are upset by the least breath of the skeptics. We have only to see their books if we are not sufficiently convinced of this, and we shall very quickly become so, perhaps too much.

I notice the only strong point of the dogmatists, namely that, speaking in good faith and sincerely, we cannot doubt natural principles.

Against this the Pyrrhonians set up in one word the uncertainty of our origin, which includes that of our nature. The dogmatists have been trying to answer this objection ever since the world began. . . .

So there is an open war among men, in which each must take a part, and side either with dogmatism or Pyrrhonism. For he who thinks to remain neutral is above

---

*We have adjusted Trotter's translation to Lafuma's edition, putting in italics the parts of the fragments that Pascal crossed over, and maintaining the same paragraphs of this edition. We have also replaced Pyrrhonians (pyrrhoniens) for skeptics.

all a Pyrrhonian. This neutrality is the essence of the sect; he who is against them is essentially for them. In this appear their advantage. They are not for themselves; they are neutral, indifferent, in suspense as to all things, even themselves being no exception.

What then shall man do in this state? Shall he doubt everything? Shall he doubt whether he is awake, whether he is being pinched, or whether he is being burned? Shall he doubt whether he doubts? Shall he doubt whether he exists?

We cannot go as far as that; and I lay it down as a fact that there never has been a real complete Pyrrhonian. Nature sustains our feeble reason, and prevents it raving to that extent.

Shall he then say, on the contrary, that he certainly possesses truth—he who when pressed ever so little, can show no title to it, and is forced to let go his hold?

What a chimera then is man! What a novelty! What a monster, what a chaos, what a contradiction, what a prodigy! Judge of all things, imbecile worm of the earth; depositary of truth, a sink of uncertainty and error; the pride and refuse of the universe!

Who will unravel this tangle? . . .

Nature confutes the Pyrrhonians *(and the Academics)*, and reason confutes the dogmatists. What then will you become, O men! who try to find out by your natural reason what is your true condition? You cannot avoid one of these sects, nor adhere to one of them.

Know then, proud man, what a paradox you are to yourself. Humble yourself, weak reason; be silent foolish nature; learn that man infinitely transcends man, and learn from your Master your true condition, of which you are ignorant. Hear God.

(Is it not clear as the daylight that man's condition is double?) For in fact, if man had never been corrupt, he would enjoy in his innocence both truth and happiness with assurance; and if man had always been corrupt, he would have no idea of truth or bliss. But, wretched as we are, and more so than if there were no greatness in our condition, we have an idea of happiness, and cannot reach it. We perceive an image of truth, and possess only a lie. Incapable of absolute ignorance and of certain knowledge, we have been manifestly in a degree of perfection from which we have unhappily fallen. . . .

It is, however, an astonishing thing that the mystery furthest removed from our knowledge, namely that of the transmission of sin, should be a fact without which we can have no knowledge of ourselves. For it is beyond doubt that there is nothing which more shocks our reason than to say that the sin of the first man has rendered guilty those, who, being so removed from this source, seem incapable of participation in it. This transmission does not only seem to us impossible, it seems also very unjust.

For what is more contrary to the rules of our miserable justice than to damn eternally an infant incapable of will, for a sin wherein he seems to have so little a share, that it was committed six thousand years before he was in existence? Certainly nothing offends us more rudely than this doctrine, and yet, without this mystery, the most incomprehensible of all, we are incomprehensible to ourselves. The knot of our condition takes its twists and turns in this abyss, so that man is more inconceivable without this mystery than this mystery is inconceivable to man.

(Whence it seems that God, willing to render the difficulty of our existence unintelligible to ourselves, has concealed the knot so high, or, better speaking, so low, that we are quite incapable of reaching it; so that it is not by the proud exertions of our reason, but by the simple submissions of reason, that we can truly know ourselves.)

(These foundations, solidly established on the inviolable authority of religion, makes us know that there are two truths of faith equally certain; the one, that man, in the state of creation, or in that of grace, is raised above all nature, made like unto God and sharing in His divinity; the other, that, in the state of corruption and sin, he is fallen from this state and made like unto the beasts. These two propositions are equally sound and certain.

Scripture manifestly declares this to us, when it says in some places: My delights were with the sons of men, Proverbs 8:31; and in other places, I will pour out my spirit upon all flesh, Joel 2:28. Ye are gods, Psalms 82:6; and in other places, All flesh is grass, Isaiah 11:6. Man is like the beasts that perish, Psalms 49:12. I said in my heart concerning the state of the sons of men, Ecclesiastes 3:18.

Whence it clearly seems that man by grace is made like unto God, and a partaker in His divinity, and that without grace he is like unto the brute beasts.)

Fragment La 835

The prophecies, the very miracles and proofs of our religion, are not of such a nature that they can be said to be absolutely convincing. But they are also of such a kind that it cannot be said that it is unreasonable to believe them. Thus there is both evidence and obscurity to enlighten some and confuse others. But the evidence is such that it surpasses, or at least equals, the evidence to the contrary; so that it is not reason which can determine men not to follow it, and thus it can only be lust or malice of heart. And by this means there is sufficient evidence to condemn, and insufficient to convince; so that it appears in those who follow it, that it is grace, and not reason, which makes them follow it; and in those who shun it, that it is lust, not reason, which makes them shun it.

FROM *PREFACE TO THE TREATISE ON THE VACUUM*

The respect that is borne to antiquity being today at such a point regarding matters in which it ought to carry less weight that all its [antiquity's] thoughts are made oracular, and even its obscurities are made into mysteries; that novelties cannot be advanced without danger, and that the text of an author suffices to demolish the strength of arguments. . . .

It is not that my intention is to correct one vice by another, and to render no esteem to the ancients because others have rendered too much to them.

I do not claim to banish their authority in order to uphold that of reasoning alone, even though others wish to establish their sole authority to the detriment of that of Reasoning. . . .

In order to make this important distinction carefully, it is necessary to appreciate that the former depend solely on memory and are purely historical, only having as their object that of knowing what authors have written; the latter depend solely on reasoning, and are completely dogmatic, having as their object that of searching for and finding hidden truths. . . .

In matters in which one seeks only to know what authors have written, as in history, geography, jurisprudence, language, and especially in theology, and finally in all those areas which have as a basis either a simple fact, or a divine or human institution, one necessarily has to have recourse to their books, since all that one can know about them [these subjects] is contained therein: from which it is evident that one can have complete knowledge about them, and that it is not possible to add anything more to this.

If it is a question of knowing who was the first king of the French; where the geographers place the first meridian; what words are used in a dead language, and in all questions of this kind, what other means than books can guide us? And who could add anything new to what they teach us, since we only wish to know what they contain?

It is authority alone which can enlighten us about these matters. But it is in theology where this authority has the most strength, because there it is inseparable from the truth, and we only know it through her: so that in order to attain complete certainty concerning the matters that are most incomprehensible to reason, it suffices to show them in the sacred books (just as to point out the uncertainty of the most plausible matters, it is only necessary to show that these are not included therein) because its principles are above both nature and reason, and because man's mind being too weak to reach them by its own efforts, it cannot attain these lofty clear comprehensions unless it is carried thence by an all-powerful and supernatural force.

It is not the same with regard to subjects that fall under the senses or under reasoning; authority is useless here; reason alone is able to know them. They have their distinct rights: the former had all the advantages a little while ago; here the latter reigns in its turn. But as subjects of this kind are suited to the mind's capacity, it [the mind] finds a complete freedom to extend itself here: its inexhaustible fruitfulness continually produces, and its inventions can be entirely without limit and without interruption. . . .

Thus it is that geometry, arithmetic, music, physics, medicine, architecture, and all of the sciences which are subject to experience and reasoning, should be augmented in order to become perfect. The ancients merely found them roughly outlined by those who had preceded them; and we will leave them to those who will come after us in a more completed state than we received them.

Since their perfection depends on time and effort, it is evident that although our effort and time may have accomplished less than their labors did, distinct from ours, nevertheless both joined together should have more effect than each separately.

The clarification of this difference ought to make us pity the blindness of those who offer only authority as proof in questions of physics, instead of reasoning or experiments, and make us horrified at the maliciousness of others who use only reasoning in theology instead of the authority of Scripture and of the [Church] Fathers. It is necessary to restore the courage of those timid people who do not dare to discover anything in physics, and to confound the insolence of those rash persons who produce novelties in theology. However, the misfortune of our age is such that we see many new views in theology unknown in all of antiquity, held with obstinacy and received with applause; while those that are produced in physics, although few in number seem to have to be convicted of falsehood as soon as they shock the accepted views ever so little: as if the respect that is held for the ancient philosophers were a duty, and that which is borne for the most ancient of the Church Fathers were only a matter of propriety! I leave it to judicious persons to note the importance of this abuse which applied to other subjects, since the new inventions are infallibly errors in the [theological] subjects which are profaned with impunity; and they are absolutely necessary for the perfection of so many incomparably lower subjects that nevertheless we dare not deal with.

Let us divide our credulity and our distrust more justly; and let us limit that respect that we have for the ancients. As reason gives rise to it, she also ought to measure it; and let us consider that, if they [the ancients] had remained in that cautious state of not daring to add anything to the knowledge that they received, and [if] those of their time had created the same difficulty about receiving novelties that were offered to them, they themselves and their posterity would have been deprived of the fruits of their inventions.

Since they only made use of that which had been left to them as a means for achieving something new, and that this boldness had opened the road for them to great things, we should accept those that they had acquired for us in the same way, and following their example make them the means and not the end of our studies, and thus try to surpass them by imitating them.

For what is more unjust than to treat our ancestors with more reserve than they had for those who have preceded them, and to have that inviolable respect for them that they have only merited from us because they did not have a like one for those who had the same advantage over them!

Nature's secrets are hidden; although she is always active, we do not always discover her efforts: time reveals them from epoch to epoch, and although the same in herself all the time, she is not always equally known.

The experiments which give us an understanding of them [Nature's secrets] multiply continually; and, as they are the sole principles of physics, the consequences multiply proportionally.

It is in this way that we can today hold other views and new opinions without contempt and without ingratitude, since the basic knowledge that they have given to us has served as a stage for our own, and in these advantages we are indebted to them for the ascendancy that we have over them; before, having been raised up to a certain level to which they have carried us, the least effort makes us mount higher, and with less difficulty and less glory we find ourselves above them. It is thus that we are able to find out things that it was impossible for them to perceive. Our view is more extended, and, although they knew as well as we all that they were able to observe of nature, they nevertheless did not know it as well, and we see more than they did.

However it is strange in what way their views are venerated. It has been made a crime to contradict them, and an outrage to add to them, as if they have left no more truths to be known.

Does not this amount to treating man's reason unworthily, and to putting it on the same level as the instinct of animals, since the chief difference between them has been taken away, which consists in that the effects of reason augment without end, while those of instinct remain always in the same state? Beehives were as carefully measured a thousand years ago as today, and each of them constitutes as exactly a hexagon the first time as the last one. It is the same with all that animals produce by that occult motion. Nature instructs them to the degree that necessity impels them; but this fragile science is lost with the needs that give it to them. As they receive it without study, they have not the good fortune to conserve it; and every time that it is given to them, it is new to them, since Nature having only the goal of maintaining animals in an order of limited perfection. She inspires this necessary science, always the same, lest they will fall into decay, and She does not allow them to add to it, lest they go beyond the limits She has prescribed for them. It is not the same with man, who is created for infinity. He is ignorant at the beginning of his life, but he is continuously instructed in his progress: for he gains much, not only from his own experience, but also from that of his predecessors, because he always retains in his memory the knowledge that he has acquired, and that of the ancients is always present to him in the books that they have left. And since he guards this knowledge, he can thus easily add to it: so that men are today in somewhat the same state in which those ancients would be, if they had been able to grow old up into the present, while adding to the knowledge they had that which their study would have enabled them to acquire by virtue of so many centuries. Thus it is that by a special prerogative, not only each man advances from day to day in the sciences, but that all men together continually progress in them as the universe grows older, because the same thing happens in the succession of man as [happens] in the different ages of an individual person. So that the entire series of men, during the course of all the centuries, ought to be considered as one and the same man who endures all the time and who continually learns: from which we see how unjust it is to respect antiquity for its philosophers; for as old age is the period most remote from infancy, who does not see the old age of this universal man ought not to be sought for in the times nearest his birth, but in those which are the furthest from it? Those whom we call ancient were really new in all things, and actually constituted the infancy of mankind; and as we have joined to their knowledge the experiences of the centuries that have followed them, it is in us that this antiquity that we revere in the others can be found.

They ought to be admired for the results that they have obtained from the few principles that they had, and they ought to be forgiven for those in which they failed due more to the lack of the good fortune of experiments than to the force of reasoning. For are they not to be forgiven for the view that they had about the Milky Way, when, the weakness of their eyes not having received artificial help, they attributed that color to a very great density in that portion of the heavens that reflected the light more forcibly?

But would it not be unforgivable for us to keep the same view, now that helped by the advantages that the telescope gives us, we have discovered an infinity of small stars there, whose more abundant splendor has made us realize what is the real cause of that whiteness?

Did they not also have reason for saying that all the corruptible bodies were enclosed within the heavenly sphere of the moon's orbit, when during the course of so many centuries, they had still observed neither corruption nor generation outside of that space?

But should we not be sure of the opposite, when the whole world has visibly seen comets light up and disappear far beyond the limits of that sphere?

It is thus that, regarding the subject of the vacuum, they were right in saying that nature would not allow it, because all their experiments had always made them observe that she abhorred it and could not allow it.

But if the new experiments had been known to them, perhaps they would have found grounds for affirming what they had grounds for denying in that the vacuum had not yet appeared. Also in the judgment they made that nature would not allow any vacuum, they only heard about nature in the state in which they knew her, since, to speak generally, it would not suffice to have seen her constantly in a hundred instances, nor in a thousand, nor in any number, no matter how great it might be; since, if a single case remained to be examined, this alone would suffice to prevent the general definition, and if one sole instance was contrary, this alone. . . . For in all matters whose proof consists in experiments and not in demonstrations, no universal assertion can be made except by general enumeration of all the parts or all of the different cases. Thus it is that when we say that a diamond is the hardest of all bodies, we mean that all the bodies that we know of, and we neither can nor ought to include therein those that we do not know of; and when we say that gold is the heaviest of all bodies, we would be rash to include in this general proposition those which are not yet within our cognizance, although it is not impossible that they may exist in nature.

In the same way when the ancients asserted that nature would not allow a vacuum, they meant that she would not allow it in all of the instances they had seen, and they would not have been able, without rashness, to include therein, those of which they were not cognizant. Had they been aware of these, doubtless they would have drawn the same conclusion as we have and would have sanctioned them, by their approval, with that antiquity that some want nowadays to make the sole principle of the sciences.

So it is that, without contradicting them, we can assert the opposite of what they said, and, whatever strength finally that antiquity possesses, truth should always have more, even though just discovered, since it is always older than all the opinions that have been had about it, and that it would be not to know its nature to think that it has begun to exist at the time that it has begun to be known.

FURTHER READINGS

Carraud, Vincent. *Pascal et la philosophie*. Paris: Presses Universitaires de France, 1992.

Davidson, H. M. *The Origins of Certainty: Means and Meanings in Pascal's 'Pensées.'* Chicago: University of Chicago Press, 1979.

Maia Neto, José. R. *The Christianization of Pyrrhonism: Skepticism and Faith in Pascal, Kierkegaard and Shestov*. Dordrecht: Kluwer, 1995.

McKenna, Antony. *De Pascal à Voltaire: Le rôle des Pensées de Pascal dans l'histoire des idées entre 1670 et 1734*. 2 vols. Oxford: Voltaire Foundation at the Taylor Institute, 1990.

———. "Skepticism at Port-Royal: The Perversion of Pyrrhonian Doubt." In *The Return of Skepticism from Hobbes and Descartes to Bayle*, edited by Gianni Paganini, 249–65. Dordrecht: Kluwer, 2003.

Pascal, Blaise. *Pensées*. Translated by A. J. Krailsheimer. London: Penguin, 1966.

———. "Reply to Father Noel" and "Conversation with Sacy." In *Selections*, edited and translated by Richard H. Popkin, 49–55, 79–89. New York: Macmillan, 1989.

Popkin, Richard H. "The 'Incurable Scepticism' of Henry More, Blaise Pascal and Søren Kierkegaard." In *Scepticism from the Renaissance to the Enlightenment*, edited by Richard H. Popkin and Charles Schmitt, 169–84. Wiesbaden: O. Harrassowitz, 1987.

Wetsel, David. *Pascal and Disbelief*. Washington, DC: Catholic University of America Press, 1994.

Yhap, Jennifer. *The Rehabilitation of the Body as a Means of Knowing in Pascal's Philosophy of Experience*. Lewiston, NY: Edwin Mellen Press, 1991.

17

GLANVILL

Joseph Glanvill (1636–1680) is better known as the author of *Saducismus Triumphatus* (1681), in which he endeavors to prove the existence of witches and spirits, the denial of which he saw as a step toward complete materialism and atheism. However strange it may seem to today's reader, the fact is that his first book, *The Vanity of Dogmatizing* (1661), enlarged and republished in 1665 as *Scepsis Scientifica*, is a very detailed deployment of skeptical arguments against Aristotelian and dogmatic philosophy in general. (One of these arguments, against causal inferences, may have been a source of Hume's famous development of this kind of skepticism.) The attack upon metaphysical and certain knowledge, Glanvill believed, would help to legitimize the new experimental and hypothetical science practiced by the members of the Royal Society. We have selected excerpts that present Glanvill's later view (published in 1676) on skepticism, when he holds a position that anticipates his contemporary at Oxford, John Locke: an attack on Cartesian metaphysical doubt and certainty and a defense of a moral certainty sufficient for grounding experimental science and natural religion. This essay on skepticism and certainty also includes a discussion of the kinds of certainty of historical knowledge that also anticipates Locke's. The issue is a living one in France at the time due to the publication of Pascal's *Pensées* (1670) and Filleau de La Chaise's *Discours sur les Pensées de Pascal* (1672), which emphasizes the partially skeptical epistemic base of the historical proofs of Christianity given by Pascal. In the essay on "The Agreement of Reason and Religion," published in the same volume as "Of Skepticism and Certainty," Glanvill vindicates the use of reason in religious matters, distancing himself from the fideism professed by Renaissance and early seventeenth-century skeptics.

FROM *ESSAYS ON SEVERAL IMPORTANT SUBJECTS IN PHILOSOPHY AND RELIGION*

Essay II. Of Skepticism and Certainty (pp. 47–50)

Having said thus much of *skepticism*, and the *skeptics*, I shall enquire a little into the matter of *certainty*, a subject of both difficulty and importance.

It is taken either (1.) for a firm assent to any thing, of which there is no reason of doubt; and this may be called *indubitable* certainty; or (2.) for an absolute assurance, that things are as we conceive and affirm, and not possible to be otherwise, and this is *infallible* certainty.

In the first of these Descartes lays his foundations: I cannot doubt, but I *think*, though nothing should be as I conceive; and there I cannot suspect neither, but that I *my self, that think, am.* I am as sure that I have ideas, and conceptions of other things without me, as of God, heaven, earth, &c. Thus far that philosopher is safe, and our assent is full; and it is so in this likewise, that we can compound, or disjoin those images by affirming, and denying; and that we have a faculty of reasoning, and inferring one thing from another: so much as this we clearly perceive, and feel in our selves, what ever uncertainty there may be in other matters. To these we give a resolved and firm assent, and we have not the least reason of doubt here. Besides which principles we find others in our minds that are more general, and are used and supposed by us in all our affirmations and reasonings, to which we assent as fully, such are these: *every thing is, or is not; a thing cannot be and not be, in the same respects; nothing has no attributes; what we conceive to belong, or not to belong to any thing, we can affirm, or deny of it.*

These are the principles of all propositions, and ratiocinations whatsoever: and we assent to them fully, as soon as we understand their meaning, to which I add this great one more, *that our faculties are true, viz.* that what our understandings declare of things *clearly* and *distinctly perceived* by us, is truly so, and agreeing with the realities of things themselves. This is a principle that we believe firmly; but cannot prove, for all proof, and reasoning supposes it: and therefore I think Descartes is out of his method; when from the ideas he endeavors to prove that *God is*, and from his existence that our faculties are true; when as the truth of our faculties was presupposed to the proof of God's existence; yea, and to that of our own also. So that, that great man seems to argue in a circle. But to let that pass; this we constantly assent to without doubting, that our faculties do not always delude us, that they are not mere impostors and deceivers, but report things to us as they are, when they distinctly and clearly perceive them. And so this may be reckoned one of the prime certain principles, and the very foundation of certainty in the first sense of it.

These and such like principles result out of the nature of our minds; but,

2. There are other certainties arising from the evidence of sense; as, that there is matter, and motion in the world; that matter is extended divisible and impenetrable; that motion is direct, or oblique; that matter, and motion, are capable of great variety of modifications and changes. We learn that these, and many other such things are so, from sense, and we nothing doubt here; although the theory and speculative consideration of those matters be full of difficulty, and seeming contradiction. In these our assent is universal and indubitable; but in many particular cases, we are not assured of the report of our senses; yea, we dissent from, and correct their informations, when they are not in their due circumstances, of right disposition, medium, distance, and the like; and when they pronounce upon things which they

cannot judge of; on which account, though our senses, and the senses of mankind do represent the earth as quiescent; yet we cannot from thence have assurance that it does rest, since sense cannot judge of an even and regular motion, when it self is carried with the movement; so that though it should be true that the earth moves, yet to sense it would appear to rest, as now it does; as I have discoursed elsewhere. But when the senses are exercised about their right objects, and have the other circumstances that are requisite, we then assent without doubting. And this fullness of assent is all the certainty we have, or can pretend to; for after all, 'tis possible our senses may be so contrived, that things may not appear to us as they are; but we fear not this, and the bare possibility does not move us.

3. There are certainties arising from the testimony of others. This in ordinary cases is very doubtful, and fallacious, but again in some it is indubitable. As when the testimony is general, both as to time and place, uninterested, full, plain, and constant, in matters of sense and of easy knowledge; in such circumstances as these, the evidence of testimony is no more doubted, than the first principles of reason or sense. Thus we believe, without the least scruple about it, that there are such places as Rome, and Constantinople, and such countries of Italy and Greece, though we never saw them; and many other historical matters, which our selves never knew. The foundation of which assurance is this principle, that mankind cannot be supposed to combine to deceive, in things, wherein they can have no design or interest to do it. Though the thing have a remote possibility, yet no man in his wits can believe it ever was, or will be so; and therefore we assent to such testimonies with the same firmness, that we would do to the clearest demonstrations in the world.

The second sense of certainty is that, which I called certainty infallible; when we are assured that 'tis impossible things should be otherwise, than we conceive and affirm of them. This is a sort of certainty, that humanely we cannot attain unto, for it may not be absolutely impossible, but that our faculties may be so contrived, as always to deceive us in the things which we judge most certain and assured. This indeed we do not suspect, and we have no reason to do it; which shows that we are certain in the former sense. But we may not say 'tis utterly impossible; and consequently we cannot have the certainty of this latter sort; which perhaps is proper only to Him, who made all things what they are; and discerns their true natures by an infallible and most perfect knowledge.

The sum of which is, that though we are certain of many things, yet that certainty is no absolute infallibility; there still remains the possibility of our being mistaken in all matters of humane belief and inquiry. But this bare possibility (as I said) move us not, nor does it in the least weaken our assent to those things, that we clearly and distinctly perceive; but we believe with as much firmness of assurance the matters that our faculties do so report to us, as if there were no such possibility; and of greater certainty than this there is no need. It is enough for us, that we have such principles lodged in our minds, that we cannot but assent to; and we find nothing to give us occasion to doubt of the truth of them.

Essay V. The Agreement of Reason and Religion (pp. 20–21)

Now from the foregoing brief discourse [on what he means by "reason" and "religion"] I shall deduce some corollaries, that may be of use for the better understanding of the whole matter.

(1) *Reason is certain and infallible.* This follows from the state I gave of the nature and notion of reason in the beginning. It consists in first principles, and the conclusions that are raised from them, and the observations of sense. Now first principles are certain, or nothing can be so; for every possible conclusion must be drawn from those, or by their help; and every article of faith supposes them. And for the propositions that arise from those certain principles, they are certain likewise; for nothing can follow from truth, but truth in the longest series of deduction. If error creeps in, there is ill consequence in the case. And the sort of conclusions that arise from the observations of sense, if the sense be rightly circumstantiated, and the inference rightly made, are certain also. For if our senses in all their due circumstances deceive us, all is a delusion, and we are sure of nothing. But we know, that first principles are certain, and that our senses do not deceive us, because God, that bestowed them upon us, is True and Good; and we are as much assured, that whatever we duly conclude from either of them, is certain; because whatever is drawn from any principle, was virtually contained in it.

(2) I infer, *that reason is,* in a sense, *the word of God, viz.* That which he has written upon our minds and hearts; as Scripture is that which is written in a Book. The former is the Word, whereby he has declared his will to the church, and his peculiar people. Reason is that *Candle of the Lord,* of which Solomon speaks, *Prov.* 20:27, "that Light, whereby Christ hath enlightened every one that cometh into the world." . . .

(3) *The belief of our reason is an exercise of faith; and faith is an act of reason.* The former part is clear, from the last particular, and we believe our reasons, because we have them from God, who cannot mistake, and will not deceive. So that relying on them, in things clearly perceived, is trust in God's veracity and goodness, and that is an exercise of faith.

FURTHER READINGS

Carrithers, D. W. *Joseph Glanvill and Pyrrhonic Skepticism: A Study in the Revival of the Doctrines of Sextus Empiricus in Sixteenth and Seventeenth Century Europe.* New York: New York University Press, 1972.

Glanvill, Joseph, and Bernhard Fabian. *Collected Works of Joseph Glanvill.* 9 vols. Hildesheim: G. Olms, 1970–1985.

Popkin, Richard H. "Joseph Glanvill: A Precursor of Hume." *Journal of the History of Ideas* 14 (1953): 292–303.

———. "Joseph Glanvill's Continuation of the *New Atlantis*: Mitigated Skepticism and the Ideal of the Royal Society." *Actes du XIIe. Congrès International d'Histoire des Sciences.* Paris: Albert Blanchard, 1968, pp. 89–94.

Redgrove, H. S., and I. M. L. Redgrove. *Joseph Glanvill and Psychical Research in the Seventeenth Century*. London: William Rider & Son, 1921.

Talmor, Sascha. *Glanvill: The Uses and Abuses of Skepticism*. Oxford: Pergamon, 1981.

Van Leeuwen, Henry G. *The Problem of Certainty in English Thought 1630–1690*. The Hague: Martinus Nijhoff, 1963, pp. 71–89.

Wiley, Margaret L. *The Subtle Knot: Creative Scepticism in Seventeenth-Century England*. Cambridge, MA: Harvard University Press, 1952.

18

FOUCHER

S imon Foucher's (1644–1696) philosophic project was the rehabilitation and updating of Academic skepticism. The project was a reaction to Cartesian philosophy, in particular to Malebranche's views of representative ideas and vision in God. Foucher's attitude toward Descartes is not, however, wholly negative. He sees Descartes's method of doubt as an heir of the Academic tradition. The "laws of the Academics," given in the excerpt below from the *Apology for the Academics*, resemble Descartes's methodic rules presented in the *Discourse on the Method*. Foucher claims that Descartes goes wrong when he—and in his view, also Malebranche—attempts to know external material things which, according to Foucher's post-Cartesian version of Academic skepticism, cannot be grasped because of the veil of ideas. We have access only to ideas that are modifications of our minds, and therefore we cannot make any justified claim about things in themselves such as the claim that ideas represent external objects. Foucher considered Academic skepticism consistent with Christianity, arguing that Plato and Augustine were Academics. He took seriously Augustine's view that the Academics suspended judgment only strategically against the materialist philosophies of the Epicureans and Stoics, and argued that only after Christian revelation could a consistent antimaterialism be fully developed, a task he saw himself performing in the footsteps of Plato, Augustine, and Descartes but in opposition to Malebranche's endeavor. The excerpt from the *Critique of the Search for Truth* presents Foucher's perception of Malebranche's main sins against the rigorous philosophical method exhibited by the Academics and—to a certain extent— by Descartes. In criticizing Malebranche, Foucher raised several fundamental problems of epistemology that were taken up by Bayle, Berkeley, and Hume.

FROM *CRITIQUE [OF NICOLAS MALEBRANCHE'S]* *OF THE SEARCH FOR THE TRUTH*

Everyone easily takes up ultimate questions and delights in being involved with the most remote and extraordinary subjects, with almost scorn for beginnings. And this comes about only because they seek the approval of the vulgar who base their esteem on the appearance of the titles one chooses and on the elevated level or flashiness of the subject matters one undertakes to treat. Now, if the first principles had been well established, or in case they never were, if their establishment had been left to our century, I would pardon those who exempt themselves from discussing them because they intend to produce something new, even though they would still need to allude to these principles to show that their assertions are consequences of them.

It is, however, very true that these primary principles are still unknown, and that they are encumbered with nearly insurmountable difficulties, so far are we from finding the evidence necessary to establish true demonstrations. What is more, I am well enough persuaded of this truth. I remain readily in agreement that the principles on which we found our philosophy are very obscure, and wish that we had found principles more evident and incontestable than those we have exercised up to the present time. I freely admit that all things are problematic, to the extent that people who are accepted as accomplished in the sciences, when they have felt for a long time both the importance and the obscurity of first notions, recognize all the more the weakness and meagerness of the foundations of these great systems that are augmenting every day. Old men are even less affirmative than the young, and one will find hardly anyone who would find it difficult to use the well-known way of speaking: *I know one thing, that I know nothing (unun scio quod nihil scio).*

There, sir, is what one finds in most of the philosophers when one obliges them to explain first principles. But one could say that it is a forced confession and that if their minds consent to their words, it is in an abstract and metaphysical way that hardly affects them at all, as though this truth were too trifling and of too little consequence to merit any reflections. Or, rather, as though this truth were odious to them, they withdraw from it so fervently that it is not astonishing if they soon lose sight of it. Indeed, concerning ultimate questions, we do not hear them complaining anymore about the weakness of the human mind and the difficulty of finding something firm. All is clear to them, all is easy for them, and nothing is capable of unsettling their opinions. These are no longer men who doubt with sincerity. They are oracles who pronounce on all things with so much assurance that it seems that it would be a crime to suspect them of errors. Their first assertions draw forth others that are confirmed by entire volumes of similar propositions. But as these philosophers are not all of the same opinions because of the obscurity of the principles of which I speak, this permits them to propose all sorts of hypotheses according to their tastes and inclinations. From this is born the opposing sects that persuade their disciples to swear by the words of their master and to do their best to maintain the eternal discord that is the source of an infinity of supporting or of conflicting works. . . .

V. Supposition of ideas that represent what is outside us.

. . . The author [Malebranche] has very well remarked that our senses do not give us knowledge of things that are outside us.

Because objects outside us have nothing in themselves *like* what they produce in us, for matter cannot have ways of being that are *like* those of which the soul is capable.

But the same reasoning leads to the conclusion that we should no more judge of the objects that are outside us by the ideas we might have of them by the imagination or by pure intellection.

For if matter is not capable of having ways of being *like* those of the soul, it is necessary to recognize also that the soul cannot have ways of being *like* those that can be in matter.

One will say that the soul being in one way represents matter and being in another way does not represent matter. But this cannot be maintained in the system we are examining in which it is supposed that the soul is not capable of having any modification that is like the ways of being of matter. It follows from this evidently either that all our ideas represent material objects to us, or that we do not have any ideas that are capable of representing material objects to us. . . .

VII. Supposition that we know by the senses that there is extension outside us.

. . . Because all our sensations being nothing other than experiences of several ways of being of which our soul is capable, we know truly by the senses only what objects produce in us, from which it follows that if one admits that we know extension and figures by the senses as well as light and colors, one must conclude necessarily that this extension and these figures are no less in us than are that light and those colors.

And should one want to grant to extension the privilege that it is both in our soul and in external objects, whereas colors are only in our soul, this still would be to admit that the perception of extension that we would have by the senses would force us to recognize extension itself as a way of being of our soul, which would still destroy the system of Mr. Descartes. Besides supporting the view that the soul and matter can have the same way of being, this would be to advance something even more opposed to the principles of this philosopher than what one would like to avoid by this response.

FROM *DISSERTATION ON THE SEARCH FOR THE TRUTH, WITH AN APOLOGY FOR THE ACADEMICS, WHERE IT IS SHOWN THAT THEIR MANNER OF PHILOSOPHIZING IS THE MOST USEFUL TO RELIGION, AND THE MOST IN AGREEMENT WITH GOOD SENSE*

Part III—Where it is shown that the Academic way of philosophizing is the one which most agrees with good sense (*bons sens*).

Article 1—That the Laws of the Academics are of good sense. Explication of these Laws, with reply to some objections.

The first Law [accept only demonstration in philosophy] is so evident that it would be ridiculous and absurd to try to contest it, for it is manifest that if one does not have evidence in the sciences one does not know yet. Consequently, except if one acts out of opinion and prejudice—what the Academics and all those who follow

the good sense should not do—one must suspend judgment. In short, if the prejudices are not always accompanied by falsity, they are always accompanied by obscurity and no obscure knowledge gives us science.

One might say that sometimes one deceives oneself in taking as evident something which is not. But even in this case it is always necessary to recognize that one
must wait for the evidence before determining oneself. . . .

With respect to the second Law . . . one can easily see that if one fills one's mind
with useless questions and discussions, one cuts one's capacity, looses sight of the
principles, and finally finds oneself lost in an interminable chain of consequences.

It is therefore reasonable to say that *one should not raise questions which one
sees well that cannot be decided.* Note that we are talking about questions *which one
sees well that cannot be decided,* for it is not unreasonable to examine issues when
we are not sure if they can or can't be decided. One does not search for what one
knows that cannot be found, but we often search for that which we are not sure we
can find, so that it suffices to be in doubt in order to examine and search. For
example, it is clear that the decision about the consequences depends on that about
the principles. Given this, it is not prudent to try to decide the consequences before
deciding the difficulties present in the principles. One must therefore begin with the
principles, etc. Likewise, it is clear that if one lacks an infallible mark of truth . . .
one cannot be sure if one is not deceived. One must therefore try to have this mark
before engaging in judgments and reasonings which cannot be certain without this
mark. . . .

The third Law agrees as much as the others with good sense. Nothing but our
pride can prevail us from *recognizing that we do not know the things which we effec-
tively ignore.* We do not recognize that we deceive ourselves. We would willingly
pretend to be infallible. But true glory consists in surrendering oneself to truth, and
a sign of a well-formed spirit is to be no more condescending with oneself than with
others when one must judge seriously. One must elevate above oneself in order to
correct and perfect oneself. . . .

People who did not know more than you made you believe that you know a
number of things which in fact you ignore. This assurance and presumption with
which you judge everything precludes you from changing the ideas of your childhood. And because you see that the others do like you, you think that it is allowed
to prolong childhood into maturity. . . . One must therefore know that the character
of maturity is to be able to judge by oneself, and to reject the bad habits which we
have acquired under the guidance of our mothers and nursemaids. . . .

The fourth Law also agrees so much with common sense that it cannot be
doubted. It is evident that if we do not *distinguish the things which we know from
those which we do not know,* we will have only confusion in the mind. . . . It seems
that Descartes wanted to propose this law when he said that one must divide things
in many parcels (elements) in order to know some after others and to know that we
know such ones, for instance, and that we still must know such others. . . .

I will say nothing of the fifth Law except that it is so essential to philosophy that it is nothing but philosophy itself. For what is philosophy if not to *search for new knowledge*? The Laws which have just been related are but preparatory for this one.

Part IV: Where it is shown that the Academics' way of philosophizing leads to the knowledge of the main and most important truths.

Article 1: That we can receive the main truths from the views of the Academics.

To prove this it suffices to note that the Academics followed the views of Plato. Cicero made this claim and after him Saint Augustine as we have already remarked. This is also what Philo, leader of the fourth academy tried to show. . . . He denied that there were two distinct Academies and combated the error of those who made this distinction. What I do today is therefore not new, since these two illustrious Academics did the same thing. I demand a going back to the ancient Academy, and will not content myself to prove from authority that one can make this return. I will show it on the bases of general and common principles shared by all Academics. These principles lead to the recognition of the main truths which everybody agrees were recognized by Plato.

I am aware that I am going to reveal the secrets of the Academy, and that these truths are those which the Academics did not dare to reveal except to their friends and after having many times said *procul, o procul este prophani*: but I speak to Christians and to people who will not find paradoxes in the truths of the unity of God, the immortality of the soul, etc.

FURTHER READINGS

Armour, Leslie. "Simon Foucher, Knowledge and Idealism: Philo of Larissa and the Enigmas of a French 'Skeptic.'" In *Cartesian Views: Papers Presented to Richard A. Watson*, edited by Thomas M. Lennon, 97–115. Leiden: Brill, 2003.

Brown, Stuart. "Foucher's Critique and Leibniz's Defense of the 'New System.'" In *Leibniz: Reason and Experience*, edited by Stuart Brown, 96–104. Milton Keynes: Open University Press, 1983.

Lennon, Thomas. "Foucher, Huet, and the Downfall of Cartesianism." In Lennon, *Cartesian Views*, pp. 117–28.

Maia Neto, José R. "Foucher's Academic Cartesianism." In Lennon, *Cartesian Views*, pp. 71–95.

Popkin, Richard H. "L'Abbé Foucher et le problème des qualités premières." *Bulletin de la Société d' Etudes du XVIIe Siècle* 33 (1957): 633–47.

Scribano, Emanuela. "Foucher and the Dilemmas of Representation: A 'Modern' Problem?" In *The Return of Skepticism from Hobbes and Descartes to Bayle*, edited by Gianni Paganini, 197–212. Dordrecht: Kluwer, 2003.

Watson, Richard A. *The Downfall of Cartesianism 1673–1712: A Study of Epistemological Issues in Late 17th Century Cartesianism*. The Hague: Martinus Nijhoff, 1966.

19

HUET

Pierre-Daniel Huet (1630–1711) was an apologist for the Christian religion, a promoter of experimental science (he founded one of the first modern scientific societies, the Académie de Physique de Caen, modeled on the Royal Society of London), a philosopher, and an erudite (one of the greatest of his time) learned in Greek and Latin, expert on ancient and Judeo-Christian literature and history. Although he was at first—while still a student—seduced by Descartes's new philosophy, he eventually became its main critic at the time. We have selected excerpts from his two most philosophical works: the *Traité Philosophique de la Foiblesse de l'Esprit Humain* (published posthumously in 1723) and the *Censura Philosophiae Cartesianae* (1689). These two books were originally designed to form a single work with another one written at the same time: *Quaestiones Alnetanae de Concordia Rationis et Fidei* (1690). Huet's view is that human intellectual faculties cannot reach metaphysical certainty apart from faith. In the *Traité* he gives a number of arguments to prove this view. In the *Censura* he argued that Descartes—the main philosopher of the time—failed in his attempt to reach indubitable certainty. The weakness of reason and philosophy, and above all of the new one that pretended to succeed where the previous philosophies had failed, opens for Huet the way to show the strength of faith and Christian revelation whose truth he attempted to show, not by philosophical reason, but through an erudite philological and historical work, aimed at showing that Judeo-Christian revelation lies at the origin of all religions of the world. We have selected two of the proofs of the *Traité*, both dialectically derived from Cartesian views. The sections from the *Censura* show Huet's perception of Descartes's relation to ancient skepticism and his application of the Pyrrhonian mode of *diallelus* (circular reasoning) to Descartes's *cogito*.

FROM *AN ESSAY CONCERNING THE WEAKNESS OF HUMAN UNDERSTANDING*

Chapter 3: *The Second Proof: Man cannot know with perfect and entire certainty, that an external object answers exactly to the idea imprinted in him. (pp. 19–22, 25–28, 30–31, 33–36)*

But it must be showed from the nature of things, that man cannot know truth by reason, with perfect certainty. . . . Man cannot be certain [of the conformity of the external object with the judgment which our understanding forms of it], unless he is assured beforehand, that the species, or image, which proceeds from that external object, of what nature so ever it be, is the true image of that object. He must moreover be certain that this species, or image, is conveyed whole and entire to the instruments of senses, without having received any alteration by the interposition of things it meets by the way. Then he must know with certainty, that the instruments of the senses after they have been moved by this species or image, and advertised the brain of that motion, by means of the fibers of the body, were sure and faithful messengers, and made no alteration in the true state of the thing, of which they gave report. It is farther necessary to be assured, that when the brain excited by this advertisement, makes known to the soul joined to it, the advice it has received, gives in its report *bona fide*, without any alteration of the state of things. And lastly, man ought to know certainly, that the judgment which his soul forms upon this report of the brain, is just and sure. All these things are of such a nature, that what pains so ever the most subtle philosopher may take, he cannot allege any proof of the certainty of them. And on the contrary we have more reasons to doubt of the conformity of the image, or species, of the external object with that object. . . .

For first of all, who will venture to say, that the image, shadow, or species, which issues from the external body, which presents itself before us, is the true resemblance of it without any difference? . . .

But although I should grant that the image or species of the outward object, does absolutely resemble it, it will be nevertheless true by an infinity of experiences, that the medium this species passes through, which issues from the object, to come and move the organ of sense, is very variable, and subject to change. . . .

Let us suppose nevertheless, that the species . . . which flow incessantly from bodies, are received by our senses without any alteration, how many proofs have been brought by philosophers, to convince us of the deception of our senses? . . .

It must be acknowledged . . . that our senses do not perceive external objects, but only the impression of the species, or images, which proceed from the outside of things, and that this impression which comes from without does not produce the same effect in all men, but is different according to the different instruments of the senses; as sounds differ, according to the different thickness, and tension of the springs which occasion them. . . .

Let us go on in an easy manner, as we have begun; and suppose yet that the testimony of the senses is faithful . . . yet who will be answerable for the verdict of the senses when they report to the understanding the sensations which they had? Since for that purpose they make use of the fibers of the nerves, whose conformation being very different, as anatomists and physicians have observed, it follows that the reports they make to the understanding cannot be uniform. They use likewise the animal spirits, which are not in the same quantity, and whose motions are very different in all men. . . .

. . . Let us only add to what has been said that spirits sometimes are so agitated by sickness, sleep, wine, and other causes, and the fibers of the brain so violently shaken, that it receives divers impressions thereby; insomuch that the understanding sometimes thinks it has certain sensations, which the instruments of the senses never had.

Besides; the brain, which is the citadel of the soul, the laboratory of reason, the operator of perception, as is supposed; has it the same form and structure in all men? Do we not see it less in some, and greater in others? . . .

But if all these organs, which are so fallible, were of unquestionable fidelity, we should not for that reason be better instructed in the manner of the soul's perceiving the species, or images, imprinted in the brain, or in the manner whereby it judges of things it has perceived, or in that lastly whereby these species purely corporeal and material, can make themselves known to the soul, which is incorporeal and immaterial.

Since then we know not in what manner, that impression made in the brain can reach the soul, and since the soul in the mean time feels itself moved, and affected in some measure by the brain, which was affected itself by a corporeal motion, so as to conceive the external object in a certain measure, as for example, to conceive the sun to be like a luminous and shining dish, it will be uncertain whether this same figure be in the eye, or a figure different from it. . . .

The soul is likewise uncertain, whether the image which comes from the sun, be like that represented in the eye. Neither does it know, whether any image of the sun be represented in the eye, or whether it forms itself that idea on the traces imprinted in the brain before: as in those ideas man have in sleep, distraction, drunkenness, and which at the same time have no reality; and moreover as in the ideas we form ourselves, when awake, in our senses, and sober.

Besides, it has been sought even to this hour, by infinite disquisitions, and disputes, what the nature of our understanding is, the most noble faculty of the soul; in what part of our body it is placed, what its action is, whether it has no ideas, but by the ministry, and message of the senses, and whether nature did not imprint them in its first formation. That diversity of opinions also found among men, the difference of their ideas, and ways of conceiving things, which are the operations of the understanding, shows us clearly, how variable, uncertain, and unknown the nature of it is. Now all these disputes and questions about the understanding, cannot be decided but by the understanding itself, which being of a dubious nature, how shall a dubious thing be decided and determined by a thing which is dubious? Can the taste relish itself? The smelling smells itself? The sight sees itself?

. . . If [the understanding] be unknown to us, and we are ignorant of its operations, with what assurance can we make use of a thing unknown to us, for the perception of other things which are as much unknown? Or what credit can we give to things we perceive by means thereof?

Since the species, or images of external objects, that are the cause of the ideas which are formed in us are subject to so many alterations; since our bodily senses are so obtuse and dull; their organs so weak; the nature of human understanding so obscure, what knowledge can we promise ourselves of the conformity and agreement between the external object which presents itself to us, and the idea of that object imprinted in our soul?

Chapter 9: The Eighth Proof: Arguments against evidence. (pp. 54–55, 59–60)

All those who boast of being able to obtain the knowledge of truth, by means of a rule of truth or criterion, agree that besides this, it is necessary to have an evident and distinct perception of things, either by the senses, or reason, or some other way, whatever it may be; so that the understanding to comprehend any thing, has need of a distinct and evident idea of it. This is the language of all the dogmatists; wherein they don't perceive, that thereby they render the knowledge of truth still more difficult, and instead of one criterion, require two; namely the idea of a thing, and the evidence of that idea. But if we admit there is no criterion, as I have now proved [in chapter VIII], it follows that evidence which depends on criterion, will have no being. Add to this, that nothing is evident, but what appears so to him, true and false will be equally evident; for each of those who shall have contrary opinions, will allege evidence for proof of his opinion; and nothing is so evident as to appear so to all, and by consequence there is no evidence. . . .

It is agreed that the views of our understanding are formed by the impulse of the brain, and the motion of fiber and spirits. From hence it follows that the evidence of the images which are presented to my mind, (being nothing but a certain manner, or modification of those images) comes from the same cause, as the images themselves. If we grant this point, which cannot be contested, it must be likewise allowed that the brain may be moved, and the spirits and fibers agitated alike, as well by internal causes, as by outward objects. From whence we must conclude, that evidence may be found in things false, as well as true; and that the evidence of what is true bears no marks, whereby we can distinguish it from the evidence of what is false. And these marks can be had no where else, if it be as the defenders of evidence maintain, that what is evident is self-evident, and has no need of proofs from without.

Chapter 10: The Ninth Proof: Reason to doubt of all things, proposed by Descartes; namely that we are ignorant whether God has not made us of such a nature as to be always deceived. (pp. 63–64)

. . . [T]his doubting is of such importance, to hinder us from receiving any proposition as certain, while we make use of nothing but our reason, that Descartes has been so far from destroying it, that it cannot be destroyed, if reason does not borrow assistance from faith. For let any one be convinced that man is an animal so formed by nature, that what appears to him to be true, is false; all you shall propose against this opinion will appear to him to be false or true; if false, he will justly reject it; if true, believing himself to be so made he will still be obliged to reject it as false. Thus it will be easy for him to subvert all reasons that can be objected against his opinion: and we cannot invent one, which will not fall under this general law, that what appears to a man to be of most truth, is most false.

Chapter 15: From all this 'tis concluded we must doubt,
as the only way to avoid errors. (pp. 132–34)

Both as to the Academics, and Skeptics, what absurdities and ridiculous opinions can we reproach them with, since they maintain no opinions: truly they only merit the name of philosophers, if we stick to the true signification of that name. For philosophy being nothing else . . . but the study of wisdom and truth; and wisdom, as it is defined by the ancients, being the science of divine and human things, and causes depending on them, they who apply themselves to the study of wisdom, deserve the name of true philosophers; and they who have acquired the science of divine and human things, that is to say, wisdom, are truly wise. Now it is this science that dogmatists boasted they had obtained and even suffered themselves heretofore to be dignified by the name of sages. . . .

For as Aeschylus the poet very well observed, "to know by conjecture is different from knowing clearly." That knowledge properly belonged to the Academics, who not only confessed they actually knew nothing, but moreover that they could not know any thing of divine and human things, and did no more than consider them at a distance. Let the dogmatists usurp then the name of sages, as much as they please, since they think they may take liberty, and imagine they have attained that science, in which wisdom consists; the Academics and Skeptics will be content with the plain and modest title of philosophers, for loving and respecting that wisdom, which so far surpasses their capacity. In the meantime Lactantius in speaking of them rightly said, that those who in some measure knew themselves were wiser than such as thought themselves wise.

EXCERPTS OF "AN EXPOSITION OF DESCARTES'S VIEW ON DOUBT, AND THE ARGUMENT 'I AM THINKING, THEREFORE I AM'" FROM *AGAINST CARTESIAN PHILOSOPHY*

Descartes based the entire foundation of his philosophy on doubt. [I speak of a foundation in Vitrivius's sense of a place that is excavated in order for a solid substructure to be built there.] Nor does he require us to doubt lightly or inattentively, but in such a way that we would take all things for uncertain, and not just for uncertain but for completely false, not only whatever previously seemed uncertain or probable [*verisimilia*], but also what seemed completely certain to us. We are not even to except those principles that are said to be known in themselves and by the natural light, for example, that two and two makes four, the whole is greater than its part, things equal to the same thing are equal to each other—thus the theorems of the geometers that are based on these notions are also included by this rule. He declared that the bodies that we see and handle, the world at large that surround us, should be taken as figments of our mind [*animi*] and also that whether we ourselves exist should be regarded as uncertain. It is clear that this sweeping doubt so thoroughly and widely included all things that no certainty at all was left to the mind on which it might secure a footing. . . .

Thereupon anxiously seeking some scintilla of truth, he thought that he had found the following: even if he is always deceived, even if he is always asleep and dreaming, even if he is condemned by God to perpetual ignorance and error, it is nevertheless necessary that he exist because he is thinking about all these things. . . .

First of all, I say that Descartes begs the question. For the question is whether he exists, and rightly so, for he who wishes to doubt all things must doubt whether he exists, just as Democritus avowed that he had done. Then, to prove that he exists, he says: I am thinking, therefore I am. But what is that 'I'? if not some thing that exists. He asks whether he exists and assumes that he exists. He thus assumes as granted what is being questioned. What then is this 'I am thinking' [*Ego cogito*]? It is this: I am (a thing that is) thinking [*Ego sum cogitans*]. From this the following argument is produced: I am (a thing that is) thinking, therefore I am. This argument reduces to that of Chrysippus: if it is day, it is day; or, it is day, therefore it is day. If I exist, I exist; or, I am, therefore I am. I thereby assume that I am in order to prove that I am, and I argue in a vicious circle. . . .

What if we were to say that, even if it is given as true that he who thinks exists, it might yet also be true that he who thinks does not exist. For Descartes's view is that God can bring it about that contrary and contradictory propositions can be simultaneously true, from which it follows that he who thinks can both be and not be. Now, if it can be as true that he who thinks does not exist as that he does exist, let Descartes see whether he is able to produce anything of certainty with his argument that allows contraries to be produced. He will retort that it is contradictory for that which thinks not to exist while it thinks. And we shall say by parity of argument that it is contradictory for that which exists not to exist while it exists. Therefore, since Descartes has taught that it is possible for these things to occur simultaneously although they are contradictory, it is also possible for these to occur, namely, for someone to think and not to be. . . .

Therefore, when Descartes wrote in his [*Discourse on*] *The Method* that in beginning his philosophy, and in resolving to begin on the basis of doubt, he had not intended that it should be done in the fashion of the skeptics, "who doubt," he says, "for the sake of doubting, and seek nothing beyond uncertainty," but that he brought his doubts to a halt in the perfectly certain knowledge of this principle, 'I am thinking, therefore I am'—when he wrote this, I say, he began to go astray as soon as he departed from the skeptics. Both he and they saw that it was necessary to doubt. But he left off doubting just when it was most necessary to doubt, namely, at a principle that is no less uncertain than all the others that he subjected to doubt. They persist in doubting that same principle, which they saw as especially in need of doubt, doubting not at all just for the sake of doubting (which Descartes, would not have accused them of, if he had more diligently examined their reasons), but doubting because nothing seemed to them capable of being perceived with sufficient clarity or certainty. . . .

When Descartes tries to overturn the [skeptics'] doctrine, he greatly strengthens it with the argument that I have discussed, that we do not know whether we were created by God so as always to err. For since he had nothing to rebut this argument but the contradiction that if we had been created by God so as to always err, He would be a deceiver, and since I have shown that this does not comport with the rest of his doctrine, it is obvious that nothing more advantageous to the sect of skeptics and Academics could have been advanced. For the Cartesians, as well as Descartes himself, all concede that unless it is established that we were not made by God so as always to err, we cannot know whether the theorems of geometry are certain, or whether the visible world exists as it appears to exist, and, in short, that we have no rule of truth and are unable to distinguish dreams from real things, all of which is pure skepticism.

For when they say that Descartes only feigned doubt but that the skeptics really doubted, I agree with the latter but find the former unsupported by any argument. For by what mark can the feigned doubt of Descartes be distinguished from the real doubt of the skeptics? The skeptics philosophize in the same way as does Descartes: they each search after truth, they each avoid error, they each think that error is avoided through doubt, which they each therefore advocate. But when each of them is pressed by adversaries, Descartes, caught in an obvious contradiction and incon-sistency of views, abandons his previous doubt and, misusing its advantages to the benefit of his philosophy, he pretends to pretend, lest he be forced to expose the faults of sincere doubt—which ill befits philosophical candor. But the skeptics remain notably faithful to themselves. They defend their doubt through doubt and so do not relinquish their principles, since they are able to defend their cause with the same arts, the same pretense, and equal justification as are the Cartesians.

FURTHER READINGS

Guellouz, S., ed. *Pierre-Daniel Huet (1630–1721)*, Actes du Colloque de Caen (1993). Paris: Biblio 17, 1994.

Huet, Pierre-Daniel. *Mémoires*. Toulouse: Société de Littératures Classiques, 1993.

———. *Nouveaux mémoires pour servir à l'histoire du cartésianisme*. Rezé: Séquences, 1996.

Lennon, Thomas. "Foucher, Huet, and the Downfall of Cartesianism." In *Cartesian Views:*

Papers Presented to Richard A. Watson, edited by Thomas M. Lennon, 117–28. Leiden: Brill, 2003).

———. "Huet, Descartes, and the Objection of the Objections." In *Skepticism in Renaissance and Post-Renaissance Thought: New Interpretations*, edited by José R. Maia Neto and Richard H. Popkin, 123–42. Amherst, NY: Humanity Books, 2004.

———. "Huet, Malebranche and the Birth of Skepticism." In *The Return of Scepticism from Hobbes and Descartes to Bayle*, edited by Gianni Paganini, 149–65. Kluwer: Dordrecht, 2003.

———. "The Skepticism of Huet's *Traité philosophique de la foiblesse de l'esprit humain*." In *Scepticisme et Modernité*, edited by Marc André Bernier and Sébastien Charles, 65–75. Saint-Étienne: Publications de l'Université de Saint-Étienne, 2005.

Lux, David S. *Patronage and Royal Science in Seventeenth-Century France: The Académie de Physique in Caen*. Ithaca, NY: Cornell University Press, 1989.

Malbrail, German. "Descartes censuré par Huet." *Revue philosophique* 116 (1991): 311–28.

Popkin, Richard H. "Bishop Pierre-Daniel Huet's Remarks on Malebranche." In *Nicolas Malebranche: His Philosophical Critics and Successors*, edited by Stuart Brown, 10–21. Assen: Van Gorcum, 1991.

Popkin, Richard H., and José R. Maia Neto. "Bishop Pierre-Daniel Huet's Remarks on Pascal." *British Journal for the History of Philosophy* 3 (1995): 147–60.

Rapetti, Elena. *Percorsi anticartesiani nelle lettere a Pierre-Daniel Huet*. Firenze: Leo S. Olschiki, 2003.

———. *Pierre-Daniel Huet: Erudizione, filosofia, apologetica*. Milan: Vita e Pensiero, 1999.

Shelford, April. "Thinking Geometrically in Pierre-Daniel Huet's *Demonstratio Evangelica* (1679)." *Journal of the History of Ideas* 63 (2002): 599–617.

20

LOCKE

J ohn Locke (1632–1704) was directly and indirectly related to British and conti-
nental philosophers involved with skepticism. In England he was a friend of
Robert Boyle, author of *The Skeptical Chemist*, and a contemporary of Glanvill at
Oxford. In France he was in association with Gassendi's disciples and may have met
Huet. In the Netherlands he was quite close to Jean Le Clerc, who was often involved
in fighting off various forms of skepticism. Finally, through his secretary Pierre Coste,
Locke was in contact with Bayle. Locke's *Essay concerning Human Understanding*,
published in 1690, not only deals with epistemological issues related to skepticism but
also reacts to skeptical views of his time presented by Montaigne, Charron, Glanvill,
and, above all, Gassendi and Descartes. To cite one example, book 1, against innate
ideas, rehearses some ancient and modern skeptical tropes, such as Locke's arguments
pointing out the variety and conflict of habits and customs. Locke's argument resembles Sextus Empiricus's tenth trope and, in particular, Montaigne's, Charron's, and La
Mothe Le Vayer's extension and updating of this mode. The first excerpt below comes
from Locke's chapter on substance. Locke's arguments showing the problematic
nature of the concept from an empiricist point of view—we have experience only of
qualities and not of the substance that supports these qualities—are crucial in the
development of British empiricism and skepticism. The other selections are from book
4 in which Locke dwells on the many limitations and shortcomings of human knowledge. Of special interest for the subsequent history of skepticism is Locke's pragmatist and antimetaphysical reaction to Cartesian skepticism about the external world,
presented in chapter 9 of book 2.

FROM *AN ESSAY CONCERNING HUMAN UNDERSTANDING**

Book 2, chapter 23: Of Our Complex Ideas of Substances

1. The Mind being, as I have declared, furnished with a great number of the simple
Ideas, conveyed in by the *Senses*, as they are found in exterior things, or by *Reflection* on its own Operations, takes notice also, that a certain number of these simple

---

*Editorial notes were omitted.

Ideas go constantly together; which being presumed to belong to one thing, and Words being suited to common apprehensions, and made use of for quick dispatch, are called so united in one subject, by one name; which by inadvertency we are apt afterward to talk of and consider as one simple *Idea*, which indeed is a complication of many *Ideas* together; Because, as I have said, not imagining how these simple *Ideas* can subsist by themselves, we accustom our selves, to suppose some *Substratum*, wherein they do subsist, and from which they do result, which therefore we call *Substance*. 2. So that if any one will examine himself concerning his *Notion of pure Substance in general*, he will find he has no other *Idea* of it at all, but only a Supposition of he knows not what support of such Qualities, which are capable of producing simple *Ideas* in us; which Qualities are commonly called Accidents. If any one should be asked, what is the subject wherein Color or Weight inheres, he would have nothing to say, but the solid extended parts: And if he were demanded, what is it, that that Solidity and Extension inhere in, he would not be in a much better case, than the Indian before mentioned; who, saying the World was supported by a great Elephant, was asked, what the Elephant rested on; to which his answer was, a great Tortoise: But being again pressed to know what gave support to the broad-backed Tortoise, replied, something, he know not what. And thus here, as in all other cases, where we use Words without having clear and distinct *Ideas*, we talk like Children; who, being questioned, what such a thing is, which they know not, readily give this satisfactory answer, That it is *something*; which in truth signifies no more, when so used, either by Children or Men, but that they know not what; and that the thing they pretend to know, and talk of, is what they have no distinct *Idea* of at all, and so are perfectly ignorant of it, and in the dark. The *Idea* then we have, to which we give the general name Substance, being nothing, but the supposed, but unknown support of those Qualities, we find existing, which we imagine cannot subsist, *sine re substante*; without something to support them, we call that Support *Substantia*; which, according to the true import of the Word, is in plain *English*, *standing under*, or *upholding*.

3. An obscure and relative *Idea* of Substance in general being thus made, we come to have the *Ideas of particular sorts of Substances*, by collecting such Combinations of simple *Ideas*, as are by Experience and Observation of Men's Senses taken notice of to exist together, and are therefore supposed to flow from the particular internal Constitution, or unknown Essence of that Substance. Thus we come to have the *Ideas* of a Man, Horse, Gold Water, *etc.* of which Substances, whether any one has any other clear Idea, farther than of certain simple *Ideas* coexisting together, I appeal to every one's own Experience. 'Tis the ordinary Qualities, observable in Iron, or a Diamond, put together, that make the true complex *Idea* of those Substances, which a Smith, or a Jeweler, commonly knows better than a Philosopher; who, whatever substantial forms he may talk of, has no other *Idea* of those Substances, than what is framed by a collection of those simple *Ideas* which are to be found in them; only we must take notice, that our complex *Ideas* of Substances, besides all these simple *Ideas* they are made up of, have always the confused *Idea*

of something to which they belong, and in which they subsist: and therefore when we speak of any sort of Substance, we say it is a *thing* having such or such Qualities, as Body is a *thing* that is extended, figured, and capable of Motion; a Spirit a *thing* capable of thinking; and so Hardness, Friability, and Power to draw Iron, we say, are Qualities to be found in a Loadstone. These, and the like fashions of speaking intimate, that the Substance is supposed always something besides the Extension, Figure, Solidity, Motion, Thinking, or other observable *Ideas*, though we know not what it is. . . .

Book 4, chapter 2: Of the Degrees of Our Knowledge

1. All our knowledge consisting, as I have said, in the view the Mind has of its own *Ideas*, which is the utmost Light and greatest Certainty, we with our Faculties, and in our way of Knowledge are capable of, it may not be amiss, to consider a little the degrees of its Evidence. The different clearness of our Knowledge seems to me to lie in the different way of perception, the Mind has of the Agreement, or Disagreement of any of its *Ideas*. For if we will reflect on our own ways of Thinking, we shall find, that sometimes the Mind perceives the Agreement or Disagreement of two *ideas* immediately by themselves, without the intervention of any other: And this, I think, we may call *intuitive Knowledge*. For in this, the Mind is at no pains of proving or examining, but perceives the Truth, as the Eye doth light, only by being directed toward it. Thus the Mind perceives, that *White* is not *Black*, That a *Circle* is not a *Triangle*, That *Three* are more than *Two*, and equal to *One* and *Two*. Such kind of Truths, the Mind perceives at the first sight of the *Ideas* together, by bare *Intuition*, without the intervention of any other *Idea*; and this kind of Knowledge is the clearest, and most certain, that humane Frailty is capable of. This part of Knowledge is irresistible, and like the bright Sun-shine, forces it self immediately to be perceived, as soon as ever the Mind turns its view that way; and leaves no room for Hesitation, Doubt, or Examination, but the Mind is presently filled with the clear Light of it. 'Tis on this *Intuition*, that depends all the Certainty and Evidence of all our Knowledge, which Certainty every one finds to be so great, that he cannot imagine, and therefore not require a greater: For a Man cannot conceive himself capable of a greater Certainty, than to know that any *Idea* in his Mind is such, as he perceives it to be; and that two *Ideas* wherein he perceives a difference, are different, and not precisely the same. He that demands a greater Certainty than this, demands he knows not what, and shows only that he has a Mind to be a Skeptic, without being able to be so. Certainty depends so wholly on this Intuition, that in the next degree of *Knowledge*, which I call *Demonstrative*, this intuition is necessary in all the Connections of the intermediate *Ideas*, without which we cannot attain Knowledge and Certainty.

2. The next degree of Knowledge is, where the Mind perceives the Agreement or Disagreement of any *Ideas*, but not immediately. Though where-ever the Mind perceives the Agreement or Disagreement of any of its *Ideas*, there be certain Knowledge; Yet it does not always happen, that the Mind sees that Agreement or

Disagreement, which there is between them, even where it is discoverable; and in that case, remains in Ignorance, and at most, gets no farther than a probable conjecture. The Reason why the Mind cannot always perceive presently the Agreement or Disagreement of two *Ideas* is, because those *Ideas*, concerning whose Agreement or Disagreement the Enquiry is made, cannot by the Mind be so put together, as to show it. In this Case then, when the Mind cannot so bring its *Ideas* together, as by their immediate Comparison, and as it were Juxtaposition, or application one to another, to perceive their Agreement or Disagreement, it is fain, by the Intervention of other *Ideas* (one or more, as it happens) to discover the Agreement or Disagreement, which it searches; and this is that which we call *Reasoning*. Thus the Mind being willing to know the Agreement or Disagreement in bigness, between the three Angles of a Triangle, and two right ones, cannot by an immediate view and comparing them, do it: Because the three Angles of a Triangle cannot be brought at once, and be compared with any other one, or two Angles; to which the three Angles of a Triangle have an Equality; and finding those equal to two right ones, comes to know their Equality to two right ones.

3. Those intervening *Ideas*, which serve to show the Agreement of any two others, are called *Proofs*; and where the Agreement or Disagreement is by this means plainly and clearly perceived, it is called *Demonstration*, it being *shown* to the Understanding, and the Mind made see that it is so. A quickness in the Mind to find out these intermediate *Ideas*, (that shall discover the Agreement or Disagreement of any other), and to apply them right, is, I suppose, that which is called *Sagacity*.

4. *This Knowledge by intervening Proofs*, though it be certain, yet the evidence of it is *not* altogether *so clear* and bright, nor the assent so ready, *as in intuitive* Knowledge. For though in *Demonstration*, the Mind does at last perceive the Agreement or Disagreement of the *Ideas* it considers; yet 'tis not without pains and attention: There must be more than one transient view to find it. A steady application and pursuit is required to this Discovery: And there must be a Progression by steps and degrees, before the Mind can in this way arrive at Certainty, and come to perceive the Agreement or Repugnancy between two *Ideas* that need Proofs and the Use of Reason to show it. . . .

7. Now, *in every step Reason makes in demonstrative Knowledge, there is an intuitive Knowledge* of that Agreement or Disagreement, it seeks, with the next intermediate *Idea*, which it uses as a Proof: For if it were not so, that yet would need a Proof. Since without the Perception of such Agreement or Disagreement, there is no Knowledge produced: If it be perceived by it self, it is intuitive Knowledge: If it cannot be perceived by it self, there is need of some intervening *Idea*, as a common measure to show their Agreement or Disagreement. By which it is plain, that every step in Reasoning, that produces Knowledge, has intuitive Certainty; which when the Mind perceives, there is no more required, but to remember it to make the Agreement or Disagreement of the *Ideas*, concerning which we enquire, visible and certain. So that to make any thing a *Demonstration*, it is necessary to perceive the immediate Agreement of the intervening *Ideas*, whereby the Agreement or Dis-

agreement of the two *Ideas* under Examination (whereof the one is always the first, and the other the last in the Account) is found. This intuitive Perception of the Agreement or Disagreement of the intermediate *Ideas*, in each Step and progression of the *Demonstration*, must also be carried exactly in the Mind, and a Man must be sure that no part is left out; which because in long Deductions, and the use of many Proofs, the Memory does not always so readily and exactly retain: therefore it comes to pass, that this is more imperfect than intuitive Knowledge, and Men embrace often Falsehoods for Demonstrations. . . .

Book 4, chapter 3: Of the Extent of Human Knowledge

1. Knowledge, as has been said, lying in the Perception of the Agreement, or Disagreement, of any of our *Ideas*, it follows from hence, That,
    First, We can have *Knowledge* no farther than we have *Ideas*.
    2. *Secondly*, That we can have no Knowledge farther, than we can have Perception of that Agreement, or Disagreement: Which Perception being, 1. Either by Intuition, or the immediate comparing any two *Ideas*; or 2. By *Reason*, examining the Agreement, or Disagreement of two Ideas, by the Intervention of some others: Or, 3. By *Sensation*, perceiving the Existence of particular Things. Hence it also follows,
    3. *Thirdly*, That we cannot have an *intuitive Knowledge*, that shall extend it self to all our *Ideas*, and all that we would know about them; because we cannot examine and perceive all the Relations they have one to another by juxtaposition, or an immediate comparison one with another. Thus having the *Ideas* of an obtuse, and an acute angled Triangle, both drawn from equal Bases, and between Parallels, I can by intuitive Knowledge, perceive the one not to be the other; but cannot that way know, whether they be equal, or no; because their Agreement, or Disagreement in equality, can never be perceived by an immediate comparing them: The difference of Figure makes their parts incapable of an exact immediate application; and therefore there is need of some intervening Quantities to measure them by, which is Demonstration, or rational Knowledge.
    4. *Fourthly*, It follows also, from what is above observed, that our *rational Knowledge*, cannot reach to the whole extent of our *Ideas*. Because between two different *Ideas* we would examine, we cannot always find such *Mediums*, as we can connect one to another with an intuitive Knowledge, in all the parts of the Deduction; and where-ever that fails, we come short of Knowledge and Demonstration.
    5. *Fifthly, Sensitive Knowledge* reaching no farther than the Existence of Things actually present to our Senses, is yet much narrower than either of the former.
    6. From all which it is evident, that *the extent of our Knowledge* comes not only short of the reality of Things, but even of the extent of our own *Ideas*. Though our Knowledge be limited to our *Ideas*, and cannot exceed them either in extent, or perfection; and though these be very narrow bounds, in respect of the extent of All-being, and far short of what we may justly imagine to be in some even created understandings, not tied down to the dull and narrow Information, is to be received from some few, and not very acute ways of Perception, such as are our Senses; yet it

would be well with us, if our Knowledge were but as large as our *Ideas*, and there were not many Doubts and Enquiries concerning the *Ideas* we have, whereof we are not, nor I believe ever shall be in this World, resolved. Nevertheless, I do not question, but that Humane Knowledge, under the present Circumstances of our Beings and Constitutions may be carried much farther, than it hitherto has been, if Men would sincerely, and with freedom of Mind, employ all that Industry and Labor of Thought, in improving the means of covering Truth, which they do for the coloring or support of Falsehood, to maintain a System, Interest, or Party, they are once engaged in. But yet after all, I think I may, without injury to humane Perfection, be confident, that our Knowledge would never reach to all we might desire to know concerning those *Ideas* we have; nor be able to surmount all the Difficulties, and resolve all the Questions might arise concerning any of them. We have the *Ideas* of a *Square*, a *Circle*, and *Equality*; and yet, perhaps, shall never be able to find a Circle equal to a Square, and certainly know that is so. We have the *Ideas of Matter* and *Thinking*, but possibly shall never be able to know, whether any mere material Being thinks, or no; it being impossible for us, by the contemplation of our own Ideas, without revelation, to discover, whether Omnipotence has not given to some Systems of Matter fitly disposed, a power to perceive and think, or else joined and fixed to Matter so disposed, a thinking immaterial Substance: It being, in respect of our Notions, not much more remote from our Comprehension to conceive, that GOD can, if he pleases, superadd to Matter a Faculty of Thinking, than that he should superadd to it another Substance, with a Faculty of Thinking; since we know not wherein Thinking consists, nor to what sort of Substances the Almighty has been pleased to give that Power, which cannot be in any created Being, but merely by the good pleasure and Bounty of the Creator. For I see no contradiction in it, that the first eternal thinking Being should, if he pleased, give to certain Systems of created senseless matter, put together as he thinks fit, some degrees of sense, perception, and thought: Though, as I think, I have proved, *Lib.* 4. *c.* 10*th.* it is no less than a contradiction to suppose matter (which is evidently in its own nature void of sense and thought) should be that Eternal first thinking Being. . . .

Book 4, chapter 9: **Of Our Knowledge of the Existence of Other Things**

1. The knowledge of our own Being, we have by intuition. The Existence of God, Reason clearly makes known to us, as has been shown.

The *Knowledge of the Existence* of any other thing we can have only by *Sensation*: For there being no necessary connection of *real Existence*, with any *Idea* a Man has in his Memory, nor of any other Existence but that of GOD, with the Existence of any particular Man; no particular Man can know the *Existence* of any other Being, but only when by actual operating upon him, it makes it self perceived by him. For the having the *Idea* of any thing in our Mind, no more proves the Existence of that Thing, than the picture of a Man evidences his being in the World, or the Visions of a Dream make thereby a true History.

2. 'Tis therefore the actual receiving of *Ideas* from without, that give us notice of the *Existence* of other Things, and makes us know, that something does exist at that time without us, which causes that *Idea* in us, though perhaps we neither know nor consider how it does it: For it takes not from the certainty of our Senses, and the *Ideas* we receive by them, that we know not the manner wherein they are produced: *e.g.* whilst I write this, I have, by the paper affecting my Eyes, that *Idea* produced in my Mind, which whatever Object causes, I call *White*; by which I know, that that Quality or Accident (*i.e.* whose appearance before my Eyes, always causes that *Idea*) does really exist, and has a Being without me. And of this, the greatest assurance I can possibly have, and to which my Faculties can attain, is the Testimony of my Eyes, which are the proper and sole Judges of this thing, whose Testimony I have reason to rely on, as so certain, that I can no more doubt, whilst I write this, that I see White and Black, and that something really exists, that causes that Sensation in me, than that I write or move my Hand; which is a Certainty as great, as humane Nature is capable of, concerning the Existence of any thing, but a Man's self alone, and of GOD.

3. *The notice we have by our Senses, of the existing of Things without* us, though it be not altogether so certain, as our intuitive Knowledge, or the Deductions of our Reason, employed about the clear abstract *Ideas* of our own Minds; yet it is an assurance that *deserves the name of Knowledge.* If we persuade our selves, that our Faculties act and inform us right, concerning the existence of those Objects that affect them, it cannot pass for an ill-grounded confidence: For I think no body can, in earnest, be so skeptical, as to be uncertain of the Existence of those Things which he sees and feels. At least, he that can doubt so far, (whatever he may have with his own Thoughts) will never have any Controversy with me; since he can never be sure I say any thing contrary to his Opinion. As to my self, I think God has given me assurance enough of the Existence of Things without me: since by their different application, I can produce in my self both Pleasure and Pain, which is one great Concernment of my present state. This is certain, the confidence that our Faculties do not herein deceive us, is the greatest assurance we are capable of, concerning the Existence of material Beings. For we cannot act any thing, but by our Faculties; nor talk of Knowledge it self, but by the help of those Faculties, which are fitted to apprehend even what Knowledge is. But besides the assurance we have from our Senses themselves, that they do not err in the Information they give us, of the Existence of Things without us, when they are affected by them, we are farther confirmed in this assurance, by other concurrent Reasons.

4. *First,* 'Tis plain, those Perceptions are produced in us by exterior Causes affecting our Senses: Because *those that want the Organs of any Sense, never can have the* Ideas *belonging to that Sense* produced in their Minds. This is too evident to be doubted: and therefore we cannot but be assured, that they come in by the Organs of that Sense, and no other way. The Organs themselves, 'tis plain, do not produce them: for then the Eyes of a Man in the dark, would produce Colors, and his Nose smell Roses in the Winter: but we see no body gets the relish of a Pineapple, till he goes to the *Indies*, where it is, and tastes it.

5. *Secondly,* Because *sometimes I find, that I cannot avoid the having those* Ideas *produced in my Mind*. For though when my Eyes are shut, or Windows fast, I can at Pleasure re-call to my Mind the *Ideas* of *Light*, or the *Sun*, which former Sensations had lodged in my Memory; so I can at pleasure lay by that *Idea*, and take into my view that of the *smell* of a Rose, or *taste* of Sugar. But if I turn my Eyes at noon towards the Sun, I cannot avoid the *Ideas*, which the Light, or Sun, then produces in me. So that there is a manifest difference, between the *Ideas* laid up in my Memory; (over which, if they were there only, I should have constantly the same power to dispose of them, and lay them by at pleasure) and those which force themselves upon me, and I cannot avoid having. And therefore it must needs be some exterior cause, and the brisk acting of some Objects without me, whose efficacy I cannot resist, that produces those Ideas in my Mind, whether I will, or no. Besides, there is no body who does not perceive the difference in himself, between contemplating the Sun, as he has the *Idea* of it in his Memory, and actually looking upon it: Of which two, his perception is so distinct, that few of his Ideas are more distinguishable one from another. And therefore he hath certain knowledge, that they are not both Memory, or the Actions of his Mind, and Fancies only within him; but that actual seeing has a Cause without.

6. *Thirdly,* Add to this, that *many of those* Ideas *are produced in us with pain, which afterwards we remember without the least offence*. Thus the pain of Heat or Cold, when the Idea of it is revived in our Minds, gives us no disturbance; which, when felt, was very troublesome, and is again, when actually repeated: which is occasioned by the disorder the external Object causes in our Bodies, when applied to it: And we remember the pain of Hunger, Thirst, or the *Headache*, without any pain at all; which would either never disturb us, or else constantly do it, as often as we thought of it, were there nothing more but *Ideas* floating in our Minds, and appearances entertaining our Fancies, without the real Existence of Things affecting us from abroad. The same may be said of Pleasure, accompanying several actual Sensations: And though mathematical demonstrations depend not upon sense, yet the examining them by Diagrams, gives great credit to the Evidence of our Sight, and seems to give it a Certainty approaching to that of the Demonstration it self. For it would be very strange, that a Man should allow it for an undeniable Truth, that two Angles of a Diagram, should be bigger one than the other; and yet doubt of the Existence of those Lines and Angles, which by looking on, he makes use of to measure that by.

7. *Fourthly,* our *Senses,* in many cases bear *witness* to the Truth of each other's report, concerning the Existence of sensible Things without us. He that sees a *Fire,* may, if he doubt whether it be any thing more than a bare Fancy, feel it too; and be convinced, by putting his Hand in it. Which certainly could never be put into such exquisite pain, by a bare *Idea* or Phantom, unless that the pain be a fancy too: Which yet he cannot, when the Burn is well, by raising the *Idea* of it, bring upon himself again.

Thus I see, whilst I write this, I can change the Appearance of the Paper; and by designing the Letters, tell beforehand what new *Idea* it shall exhibit the very next moment, barely by drawing my Pen over it: which will neither appear (let me fancy as much as I will) if my Hand stands still; or though I move my Pen, if my Eyes be shut: Nor when those Characters are once made on the Paper, can I choose afterwards but see them as they are; that is, have the *Ideas* of such Letters as I have made. Whence it is manifest, that they are not barely the Sport and Play of my own Imagination, when I find, that the Characters, that were made at the pleasure of my own Thoughts, do not obey them; nor yet cease to be, whenever I shall fancy it, but continue to affect my Senses constantly and regularly, according to the Figures I made them. To which if we will add, that the sight of those shall, from another Man, draw such Sounds, as I beforehand design they shall stand for, there will be little reason left to doubt, that those Words, I write, do really exist without me, when they cause a long series of regular Sounds to affect my Ears, which could not be the effect of my Imagination, nor could my Memory retain them in that order.

8. But yet, if after all this, any one will be so skeptical, as to distrust his Senses, and to affirm, that all we see and hear, feel and taste, think and do, during our whole Being, is but the series and deluding appearances of a long Dream, whereof there is no reality; and therefore will question the Existence of all Things, or our Knowledge of any thing: I must desire him to consider, that if all be a Dream, then he does but dream, that he makes the Question; and so it is not much matter, that a waking Man should answer him. But yet, if he pleases, he may dream that I make him this answer, That *the certainty of* Things existing *in rerum Natura*, when we have *the testimony of our Senses* for it, is not only *as great* as our frame can attain to, but *as our Condition needs*. For our Faculties being suited not to the full extent of Being, nor to a perfect, clear, comprehensive Knowledge of things free from all doubt and scruple; but to the preservation of us, in whom they are; and accommodated to the use of Life: they serve to our purpose well enough, if they will but give us certain notice of those Things, which are convenient or inconvenient to us. For he that sees a Candle burning, and has experimented the force of its Flame, by putting his Finger in it, will little doubt, that this is something existing without him, which does him harm, and puts him to great pain: which is assurance enough, when no Man requires greater certainty to govern his Actions by, than what is as certain as his Actions themselves. And if our Dreamer pleases to try, whether the glowing heat of a glass Furnace, be barely a wandering Imagination in a drowsy Man's Fancy, by putting his Hand into it, he may perhaps be wakened into a certainty greater than he could wish, that it is something more than bare Imagination. So that this Evidence is as great, as we can desire, being as certain to us, as our Pleasure or Pain; *i.e.* Happiness or Misery; beyond which we have no concernment, either of Knowing or Being. Such an assurance of the Existence of Things without us, is sufficient to direct us in the attaining the Good and avoiding the Evil, which is caused by them, which is the important concernment we have of being made acquainted with them.

9. In fine then, when our Senses do actually convey into our Understandings any *Idea*, we cannot but be satisfied, that there does something at that time really exist without us, which does affect our Senses, and by them give notice of it self to our apprehensive Faculties, and actually produce that *Idea*, which we then perceive: and

we cannot so far distrust their Testimony, as to doubt, that such Collections of simple *Ideas*, as we have observed by our Senses to be united together, do really exist together. But *this Knowledge extends as far as the present Testimony of our Senses*, employed about particular Objects, that do then affect them, *and no farther*. For if I saw such a Collection of simple *Ideas*, as is wont to be called *Man*, existing together one minute since, and am now alone, I cannot be certain, that the same Man exists now, since there is no necessary connection of his Existence a minute since, with his Existence now: by a thousand ways he may cease to be, since I had the Testimony of my Senses for his Existence. And if I cannot be certain, that the Man I saw last to day, is now in Being, I can less be certain, that he is so, who has been longer removed from my Senses, and I have not seen since yesterday, or since the last year: and much less can I be certain of the Existence of Men, that I never saw. And therefore though it be highly probable, that Millions of Men do now exist, yet whilst I am alone writing this, I have not that Certainty of it, which we strictly call Knowledge; though the great likelihood of it put me past doubt, and it be reasonable for me to do several things upon the confidence, that there are Men (and Men also of my acquaintance, with whom I have to do) now in the World: But this is but probability, not Knowledge.

10. Whereby yet we may observe, how foolish and vain a thing it is, for a Man of narrow Knowledge, who having Reason given him to judge of the different evidence and probability of Things, and to be swayed accordingly; how *vain*, I say, it is *to expect Demonstration* and Certainty *in things not capable of it*; and refuse Assent to very rational Propositions, and act contrary to very plain and clear Truths, because they cannot be made out so evident, as to surmount every the least (I will not say Reason, but) pretense of doubting. He that in the ordinary Affairs of Life, would admit of nothing but direct plain Demonstration, would be sure of nothing, in this World, but of perishing quickly. The wholesomeness of his Meat or Drink would not give him reason to venture on it: And I would fain know, what 'tis he could do upon such grounds, as were capable of no Doubt, no Objection. . . .

12. What *Ideas* we have of Spirits, and how we come by them, I have already shown. But though we have those *Ideas* in our Minds, and know we have them there, the having the *Ideas* of Spirits does not make us know, that any such Things do exist without us, or *that there are any finite Spirits*, or any other spiritual Beings, but the Eternal GOD. We have ground from revelation, and several other Reasons, to believe with assurance, that there are such Creatures: but our Senses not being able to discover them, we want the means of knowing their particular Existences. For we can no more know, that there are finite Spirits really existing, by the *Idea* we have of such Beings in our Minds, than by the *Ideas* any one has of Fairies, or Centaurs, he can come to know, that Things answering those *Ideas*, do really exist.

And therefore concerning the Existence of finite Spirits, as well as several other Things, we must content our selves with the Evidence of Faith; but universal certain propositions concerning this matter are beyond our reach. For however true it may be, *v.g.* that all the intelligent Spirits that God ever created, do still exist; yet it can never make a part of our certain Knowledge. These and the like Propositions, we may assent to, as highly probable, but are not, I fear, in this state, capable of knowing. We are not then to put others upon demonstrating, nor our selves upon search of universal Certainty in all those matters, wherein we are not capable of any other Knowledge, but what our Senses give us in this or that particular.

FURTHER READINGS

Bolton, Martha B. "Locke and Pyrrhonism: The Doctrine of Primary and Secondary Qualities." In *The Skeptical Tradition*, edited by Myles Burnyeat, 353–75. Berkeley: University of California Press, 1983.

Ferreira, Jaime. "Locke's 'Constructive Skepticism'—A Reappraisal." *Journal of the History of Philosophy* 24 (1986): 211–22.

Lennon, Thomas. *The Battle of the Gods and Giants: The Legacies of Descartes and Gassendi*. Princeton, NJ: Princeton University Press, 1993.

Rogers, G. A. J. "John Locke and the Skeptics." In *The Return of Skepticism from Hobbes and Descartes to Bayle*, edited by Gianni Paganini, 37–53. Dordrecht: Kluwer, 2003.

———. "Boyle, Locke and Reason." *Journal of the History of Ideas* 27 (1966): 205–16.

Van Leeuwen, Henry G. *The Problem of Certainty in English Thought 1630–1690*. The Hague: Martinus Nijhoff, 1963, pp. 121–42.

Yolton, John. *Locke and the Compass of Human Understanding*. Cambridge: Cambridge University Press, 1970.

———. *Locke and the Way of Ideas*. Oxford: Oxford University Press, 1956.

21

BAYLE

Pierre Bayle's (1647–1706) *Historical and Critical Dictionary*, first published in 1697, is a unique work. One man working in Rotterdam in the 1690s was able to wander hither and yon through the world of man's intellectual and moral thought, from the beginning of written history to yesterday's newspapers, and could portray enough of it from A to Z to encompass all that his age had to offer, and to reveal so many of its failings in such sharp relief. The work is really a *Summa Sceptica* that deftly undermined all the foundations of the seventeenth-century intellectual world. Bayle employed the critical technique he learned at the Jesuit college in Toulouse to show the strength and the weakness of every human effort to make sense out of any aspect of human experience. Each theory in any area is inspected and examined and questioned, and in the course of this process it disintegrates into contradictions and paradoxes. We have selected some of the passages from the *Dictionary* that most brilliantly exhibit this process. They deal with some of the main issues related to skepticism for which Bayle is famous: the problem of evil, the attack on natural theology, and the exposition of the skepticism and idealism intrinsic in modern philosophy and in particular Cartesian philosophy. In order to give the reader a taste of Bayle's work, we present the remarks in the order of their appearance in the *Dictionary* and include Bayle's notes to these notes (for the remarks are extended footnotes to the various articles that make up the *Dictionary*).

FROM *HISTORICAL AND CRITICAL DICTIONARY: SELECTIONS**

"Manicheans," Remark D

. . . The most certain and the clearest ideas of order teach us that a Being who exists by himself, who is necessary, who is eternal, must be one, infinite, all-powerful, and endowed with every kind of perfection. Thus, by consulting these ideas, one finds that there is nothing more absurd than the hypothesis of two principles, eternal and independent of each other, one of which has no goodness and can stop the plans of the other. These are what I call the a priori arguments. They lead us necessarily to reject

---

*The editor's notes were omitted.

this hypothesis and to admit only one principle in all things. If this were all that was necessary to determine the goodness of a theory, the trial would be over, to the confusion of Zoroaster and all his followers. But every theory has need of two things in order to be considered a good one: first, its ideas must be distinct; and second, it must account for experience. It is necessary then to see if the phenomena of nature can be easily explained by the hypothesis of a single principle. When the Manicheans tell us that, since many things are observed in the world that are contrary to one another—cold and heat, white and black, light and darkness—therefore there necessarily are two principles, they argue pitifully. The opposition that exists among these entities, fortified as much as one likes by what are called variations, disorders, irregularities of nature, cannot make half an objection against the unity, simplicity, and immutability of God. All these matters are explained either by the various faculties that God has given to bodies, or by the laws of motion he has established, or by the concourse of intelligent occasional causes by which he has been pleased to regulate himself. . . . The heavens and the whole universe declare the glory, the power, and the unity of God. Man alone—this masterpiece of his Creation among the visible things—man alone, I say, furnishes some very great objections against the unity of God. Here is how:

Man is wicked and miserable. Everybody is aware of this from what goes on within himself, and from the commerce he is obliged to carry on with his neighbor. It suffices to have been alive for five or six years to be completely convinced of these two truths. Those who live long and who are much involved in worldly affairs know this still more clearly. Travel gives continual lessons of this. Monuments to human misery and wickedness are found everywhere—prisons, hospitals, gallows, and beggars. Here you see the ruins of a flourishing city; in other places you cannot even find the ruins. . . .

Properly speaking, history is nothing but the crimes and misfortunes of the human race. But let us observe that these two evils, the one moral and the other physical, do not encompass all history or all private experience. Both moral good and physical good are found everywhere, some examples of virtue, some examples of happiness; and this is what causes the difficulty. For if all mankind were wicked and miserable, there would be no need to have recourse to the hypothesis of two principles. It is the mixture of happiness and virtue with misery and vice that requires this hypothesis. It is in this that the strength of the sect of Zoroaster lies. . . .

To make people see how difficult it would be to refute this false system, and to make them conclude that it is necessary to have recourse to the light of revelation in order to destroy it, let us suppose here a dispute between Melissus and Zoroaster. They were both pagans and great philosophers. Melissus, who acknowledged only one principle, would say at the outset that his theory agrees admirably with the ideas of order. The necessary Being has no limits. He is therefore infinite and all-powerful, and thus he is one. And it would be both monstrous and inconsistent if he did not have goodness and did have the greatest of all vices—an essential malice. "I confess to you," Zoroaster would answer, "that your ideas are well connected; and I shall willingly acknowledge that in this respect your hypothesis surpasses mine. I will renounce an objection that I could employ, which is that infinity ought to comprehend all that is real, and malice is not less real than goodness.[1] Therefore the universe should require that there be wicked beings and good beings. And since supreme goodness and supreme malice cannot subsist in one subject, it is the case that in the nature of things there must be an essentially good being, and another essentially bad being. I renounce, I say, this objection. I allow you the advantage of being more conformable to the notion of order than I am. But by your hypothesis explain a little to me how it happens that man is wicked and so subject to pain and grief. I defy you to find in your principles the explanation of this phenomenon, as I can find it in mine. I then regain the advantage. You surpass me in the beauty of ideas and in a priori reasons, and I surpass you in the explanation of phenomena and in a posteriori reasons. And since the chief characteristic of a good system is its being capable of accounting for experience, and since the mere incapacity of accounting for it is a proof that a hypothesis is not good, however fine it appears to be in other respects, you must grant that I hit the nail on the head by admitting two principles and that you miss it by admitting only one."

Doubtless we are now at the main point of the whole affair. Here is the great chance for Melissus. . . . Let us continue to listen to Zoroaster.

"If man is the work of a single supremely good, supremely holy, supremely powerful principle, is it possible that he can be exposed to illnesses, to cold, to heat, to hunger, to thirst, to pain, to vexation? Is it possible he should have so many bad inclinations and commit so many crimes? Is it possible that the supreme holiness would produce so criminal a creature? Is it possible that the supreme goodness would produce so unhappy a creature? Would not the supreme power joined to an infinite goodness pour down blessings upon its work and defend it from everything that might annoy or trouble it?" If Melissus consults the ideas of order, he will answer that man was not wicked when God created him. He will say that man received a happy state from God, but not having followed the lights of his conscience, which according to the intention of his author would have conducted him along the virtuous path, he became wicked, and he deserved that the supremely just and supremely good God made him feel the effects of His wrath. Then it is not God who is the cause of moral evil; but he is the cause of physical evil, that is to say, the punishment of moral evil—punishment which, far from being incompatible with the supremely good principle, necessarily flows from one of God's attributes, I mean that of justice, which is no less essential to man than God's goodness. This answer, the most reasonable that Melissus could make, is basically fine and sound. But it can be combated by arguments which have something in them more specious and dazzling. For Zoroaster would not fail to set forth that, if man were the work of an infinitely good and holy principle, he would have been created not only with no actual evil but also without any inclination to evil, since that inclination is a defect that cannot have such a principle for a cause. It remains then to be said that, when man came from the hands of his creator, he had only the power of self-determination to

---

1. That is to say, malicious action. I add this note so that one cannot tell me that evil is only a privation.

evil, and that since he determined himself in that way, he is the sole cause of the crime that he committed and the moral evil that was introduced into the universe. But, (1) we have no distinct idea that could make us comprehend how a being not self-existent should, however, be the master of its own actions. Then Zoroaster will say that the free will given to man is not capable of giving him an actual determination since its being is continuously and totally supported by the action of God. (2) He will pose this question, "Did God foresee that man would make bad use of his free will?" If the answer is affirmative he will reply that it appears impossible to foresee what depends entirely on an undetermined cause. "But I will readily agree with you," he will say, "that God foresaw the sin of his creature; and I conclude from this that he would have prevented it; for the ideas of order will not allow that an infinitely good and holy cause that can prevent the introduction of moral evil does not stop it, especially when by permitting it he will find himself obliged to pour down pains and torments upon his own work. If God did not foresee the fall of man, he must at least have judged that it was possible; therefore, since he saw he would be obliged to abandon his paternal goodness if the fall ever did occur, only to make his children miserable by exercising upon them the role of a severe judge, he would have determined man to moral good as he has determined him to physical good. He would not have left in man's soul any power for carrying himself toward sin, just as he did not leave any power for carrying himself toward misery in so far as it was misery. This is where we are led by the clear and distinct ideas of order when we follow, step by step, what an infinitely good principle ought to do. For, if a goodness as limited as that of a human father necessarily requires that he prevent as much as possible the bad use which his children might make of the goods he gives them, much more will an infinite and all-powerful goodness prevent the bad effects of its gifts. Instead of giving them free will, it will determine its creatures to good; or if it gives them free will, it will always efficiently watch over them to prevent their falling into sin." I very well believe that Melissus would not be silenced at this point, but whatever he might answer would be immediately combated by reasons as plausible as his, and thus the dispute would never terminate.[2] . . .

A thousand great difficulties could be proposed to this philosopher; but as he would still find answers and after that demand that he be given a better hypothesis and claim that he had thoroughly refuted that of Melissus, he would never be led back to the truth. Human reason is too feeble for this. It is a principle of destruction and not of edification. It is only proper for raising doubts, and for turning things on all sides in order to make disputes endless; and I do not think I am mistaken if I say of natural revelation, that is to say, the light of reason, what the theologians say of the Mosaic Dispensation. They say that it was only fit for making man realize his own weakness and the necessity of a redeemer and a law of grace. It was a teacher— these are their terms—to lead us to Jesus Christ. Let us say almost the same thing about reason. It is only fit to make man aware of his own blindness and weakness,

---

2. All this is more fully discussed in the remarks of the article "Paulicians."

and the necessity for another revelation. That is the one of Scripture. It is there that we find the means to refute invincibly the hypothesis of the two principles and all the objections of Zoroaster. There we find the unity of God and his infinite perfections, the fall of the first man, and what follows from it. Let someone tell us with a great apparatus of arguments that it is not possible that moral evil should introduce itself into the world by the work of an infinitely good and holy principle, we will answer that this however is in fact the case, and therefore this is very possible. There is nothing more foolish than to argue against the facts. . . .

"Pyrrho," Remark B

([*Pyrrhonism*] *is rightly detested in the schools of theology.*) Pyrrhonism is dangerous in relation to this divine science, but it hardly seems so with regard to the natural sciences or to the state. It does not matter much if one says that the mind of man is too limited to discover anything concerning natural truths, concerning the causes producing heat, cold, the tides, and the like. It is enough for us that we employ ourselves in looking for probable hypotheses and collecting data. I am quite sure that there are very few good scientists of this century who are not convinced that nature is an impenetrable abyss and that its springs are known only to Him who made and directs them. Thus, all these philosophers are Academics and Pyrrhonists in this regard. Society has no reason to be afraid of skepticism; for skeptics do not deny that one should conform to the customs of one's country, practice one's moral duties, and act upon matters on the basis of probabilities without waiting for certainty. They could suspend judgment on the question of whether such and such an obligation is naturally and absolutely legitimate; but they did not suspend judgment on the question of whether it ought to be fulfilled on such and such occasions. It is therefore only religion that has anything to fear from Pyrrhonism. Religion ought to be based on certainty. Its aim, its effects, its usages collapse as soon as the firm conviction of its truths is erased from the mind. But this should not be a cause of uneasiness. There never were, and there never will be more than a small number of people who can be fooled by the arguments of the skeptics. The grace of God in the faithful, the force of education in other men, and, even if you wish, ignorance[3] and the natural inclination to reach decisions, all these constitute an impenetrable shield against the arrows of the Pyrrhonists although this sect thinks it is more formidable today than it was in former times. We shall now see what this strange claim is based on.

About two months ago a very able man told me much about a discussion he had attended. Two *abbés*, of whom one knew only his duties and obligations and the other was a good philosopher, got into a fairly heated debate that almost became a

---

3. It is a saying of Simonides that "those people are not clever enough to be deceived by a man like me." Balzac said the same thing about the girls of his village. Agesilaus complained about having to deal with opponents who did not understand enough about war, so that his stratagems were useless; he could not deceive troops who were inexperienced.

full-fledged quarrel. The first had said rather bluntly that he could pardon the pagan philosophers for having drifted into the uncertainty of opinions but that he could not understand how there were still any miserable Pyrrhonists after the arrival of the light of the Gospel. "You are wrong," said the other, "to reason this way. Were Arcesilaus to return to this world, and were he to combat our theologians, he would be a thousand times more formidable than he was against the dogmatists of ancient Greece. Christian theology would furnish him with unanswerable arguments." All those present were much surprised to hear this, and begged the *abbé* to explain himself further, having no doubts that he had advanced a paradox that would only lead to his own confusion. Here is the answer he gave, addressing himself to the first *abbé*: "I will not make use of the advantages the new philosophy has given the Pyrrhonists. One hardly knew the name of Sextus Empiricus in our schools. The methods he had proposed so subtly for bringing about suspense of judgment were not less known than the *Terra Australis*, when Gassendi[4] gave us an abridgement of it, which opened our eyes. Cartesianism put the final touches to this, and now no good philosopher any longer doubts that the skeptics were right to maintain that the qualities of bodies that strike our senses are only appearances. Every one of us can justly say, 'I feel heat in the presence of fire,' but not, 'I know that fire is, in itself, such as it appears to me.' This is the way the ancient Pyrrhonists spoke. Today the new philosophy speaks more positively. Heat, smells, colors, and the like, are not in the objects of our senses. They are modifications of my soul. I know that bodies are not at all as they appear to me. They would have wished to exempt extension and motion, but they could not. For if the objects of our senses appear colored, hot, cold, odoriferous, and yet they are not so, why can they not appear extended and shaped, in rest and in motion, though they are not so?[5] Still further, sense objects cannot be the cause of my sensations. I could therefore feel heat and cold, see colors and shapes, extension and motion, even though there were no bodies in the universe. I have therefore no good proof of the existence of bodies.[6] The only proof that could be given me of this would be based on the contention that God would be deceiving me if he imprinted in my mind the ideas that I have of bodies without there actually being any.[7] But this proof is very weak; it proves too much. Ever since the beginning of the world, all mankind, except perhaps one out of two hundred millions, has firmly believed that bodies are colored, and this is an error. I ask, does God deceive mankind with regard to colors? If he deceives them about this, what prevents him from so doing with regard to extension? This second deception would not be less innocent, nor less compatible with the nature of a supremely perfect being than the

---

4. In his work, *De fini logicae*, chap. 3, pp. 72ff., in his *Opera* (1658 ed.), vol. I.

5. The Abbé Foucher proposed this objection in his *Critique de la recherche de la vérité*. Father Malebranche made no reply to it. He realized how strong it was. See footnote 6, following.

6. Father Malebranche, in *Eclaircissement sur la recherché de la vérité*, shows that "it is extremely difficult to prove that there are bodies and that faith alone can convince us that bodies actually exist."

7. Cf. chap. 28 of Arnaud's *Traité des vrayes et des fausses idées*, where he refutes the above-mentioned *Eclaircissement* of Father Malebranche, by reasons all based on this principle.

first deception is. If he does not deceive mankind with regard to colors, this is no doubt because he does not irresistibly force them to say, 'These colors exist outside of my mind,' but only, 'It seems to me that there are colors there.' The same thing could be said with regard to extension. God does not irresistibly force you to say, 'There is some,' but only to judge that you are aware of it and that it seems to you that there is some. A Cartesian has no more difficulty in suspending judgment on the existence of extension than a peasant has in forbearing affirming that the sun shines, that snow is white, and so on. That is why, if we deceive ourselves in affirming the existence of extension, God would not be the cause, since you grant that he is not the cause of the peasant's errors. These are the advantages that the new philosophers would give to the Pyrrhonists and which I will not use here."

Right afterwards, the philosophical *abbé* declared to the other that if one had any hopes of victory over the skeptics, one would have to prove to them first of all that truth is certainly recognizable by certain marks. These are commonly called the criterion of truth (*criterium veritatis*). You could rightly maintain to him that self-evidence (*l'évidence*) is the sure characteristic of truth; for if self-evidence were not, nothing else could be. "So be it," he will say to you. "It is right here that I have been waiting for you. I will make you see that some things you reject as false are as evident as can be. (1) It is evident that things which are not different from a third thing are not different from each other. This is the foundation of all of our reasonings, and it is on this that we base all our syllogisms. And nevertheless, the revelation of the mystery of the Trinity assures us that this axiom is false. Invent as many distinctions as you please, you will never be able to show that this maxim of logic is not denied by this great mystery. (2) It is evident that there is no difference between an individual, a nature, and a person. However, this same mystery has convinced us that persons can be multiplied without the individuals and the natures ceasing to be unique. . . . (4) It is evident that a human body cannot be in several places at the same time and that its head cannot be penetrated with all the rest of its parts into an indivisible point. And nevertheless, the mystery of the Eucharist teaches us that these two things happen every day.[8] From whence it follows that neither you nor I can be certain whether we are distinct from other men, or whether we are at this moment in the seraglio at Constantinople, in Canada, in Japan, and in every city of the world, under different conditions in each place. Since God does nothing in vain, would he create many men when one, created in various places and possessing different qualities according to the places, would suffice? By this doctrine we lose the truths that we found in numbers, for we no longer know how much two and three are. We do not know what constitutes unity or diversity. If we judge that John and Peter are two men, it is only because we see them in different places and because one does not have all the properties of the other. But the basis for this distinction is

---

8. Note that it is an *abbé* who is speaking. I am obliged to add this, in the second edition, because several Protestants have been shocked to see the mystery of the Trinity and that of the Incarnation put on the same level as the dogma of the real presence and that of transubstantiation.

destroyed by the Eucharist. Perhaps there is only one creature in the whole universe, produced many times in several places and with a diversity of qualities. We make great rules of arithmetic as if there were many distinct things.[9] All is illusory. Not only do we not know if there are two bodies; we do not even know if there is a body and a spirit. For if matter is penetrable, it is clear that extension is only an accident of bodies, and thus that body, according to its essence, is an unextended substance. It can then have all the attributes that we conceive of as belonging to spirit—understanding, will, passions, sensations. Therefore, there is no longer any standard for discerning if a substance is spiritual by nature or if it is corporeal. (5) It is evident that the modes of a substance cannot subsist without that which they modify. Nevertheless, we know by the mystery of transubstantiation that this is false. This confuses all our ideas. There is no longer any means of defining substance; for if the accidents can subsist without any subject, then substance in its turn can subsist dependent on another substance in the way accidents do. Mind could exist in the way bodies do, just as in the Eucharist matter exists in the way minds do. The latter could be impenetrable, just as matter becomes penetrable in the mystery. Now, if in passing from the darkness of paganism to the light of the Gospel, we have learned the falsity of so many self-evident notions and so many certain definitions, what will it be like when we pass from the obscurity of this life to the glory of paradise? Is it not very obvious that we will learn the falsity of thousands of things that now seem incontestable? Let us profit from the temerity with which those who lived before the Gospel tidings affirmed to us as true certain self-evident doctrines whose falsity has been revealed to us by the mysteries of our theology.

"Let us turn to ethics. (1) It is evident that we ought to prevent evil if we can and that we sin if we allow it when we can prevent it. However, our theology shows us that this is false. It teaches us that God does nothing unworthy of his perfections when he permits all the disorders in the world which he could easily have prevented. (2) It is evident that a creature who does not exist cannot be an accomplice in an evil action. (3) And that it is unjust to punish him as an accomplice of that action. Nevertheless, our doctrine of original sin shows us the falsity of these evident truths. (4) It is evident that we ought to prefer what is righteous to what is profitable; and that the more holy a being is, the less it is allowed to prefer what is profitable to what is righteous. Nevertheless, our theologians tell us that God, having to choose between a world perfectly regulated, adorned with every virtue, and a world like ours, where sin and disorder predominate, preferred ours to the other as suiting better the interest of his glory. You are going to tell me that the duties of the creator should not be measured by our standards. But, if you do this, you fall into the nets of your adversaries. This is where they want you. Their major aim is to prove that the absolute nature of things is unknown to us and that we can know them only relatively. We do not know, they say, if sugar is sweet in itself. We know only that it appears sweet when it is placed on our tongues. We do

---

9. Note that if a body may be produced in several places, every other being—spirit, place, accident, etc.—may be multiplied in the same manner; and thus there will not be a multitude of beings, but all will be reduced to one sole created being.

not know if a certain action is righteous in itself and by its nature. We only believe that with regard to such a person, with respect to certain circumstances, it has the appearance of righteousness. But it is something else in other respects and other relations. Behold then what you are exposed to when you say that the ideas we have of justice and righteousness admit of exceptions and are relative. Consider also that the more you elevate the power or right of God not to act according to our ideas, the more you destroy the one means you have left for proving the existence of bodies, namely, that God does not deceive us, and that he would if there were no corporeal world. To show a whole people a sight or spectacle that does not exist outside their minds would be a deception. You might wish to answer that one should distinguish two cases. If a king did it, it would be a deception; but if God does it, it is not; for the obligations of a king and of God are quite different. Besides this, if the exceptions you make to the principles of morality are based on the infinite incomprehensibility of God, then I can never be sure of anything. For I can never be able to comprehend the whole extent of the rights and privileges of God. And now I conclude. If there were a mark or characteristic by which truth could certainly be known, this would be self-evidence. Now, self-evidence is not such a mark since it is compatible with falsities. Therefore, etc."

The *abbé* to whom this long disclosure was directed could hardly forbear interrupting it. He listened to it with pain; and when he saw that no one else was speaking, he flew into a rage against the Pyrrhonists and did not spare the other *abbé* for mentioning the difficulties that he drew from the systems of theology. He was answered modestly that one knew very well that these difficulties were sophisms and trivialities, but that it would be good if those who were so haughty to the skeptics were aware of what the state of things is. "You believed up to now," he was told, "that a Pyrrhonist could not puzzle you. Answer me, therefore; you are forty-five years old; you do not doubt this. And, if you are sure of anything, it is that you are the same person to whom the abbey of —— was given two years ago. I will show you that you have no good reason at all to be certain of this. I shall argue from the principles of our theology. Your soul has been created. God must therefore renew its existence every moment, for the preservation of creatures is a continual creation. How do you know that this very morning God did not allow that soul, which he continually created from the first moments of your life until now, to fall back into nothingness. How do you know that he has not created another soul with modifications like the ones yours had?[10] This new soul is the one that you have at the moment. Show me what is wrong with my argument and let those present judge the merits of my case." A learned theologian who was present spoke up and acknowledged that once creation was supposed, it was just as easy for God to create a new soul at every moment as it was to reproduce the same soul; but that nevertheless, the ideas of his wisdom, and still more the light that we draw from his Word, are able to give us a legitimate certainty that we have the identical soul today that we had yesterday, the day before that, and so on. He concluded that it was wrong to waste time disputing

---

10. That is, with the memories he would have reproduced had he continued to create the soul of the *abbé*.

with the Pyrrhonists or to imagine that their sophisms can be easily eluded by the mere force of reason; that it was necessary above all to make them feel the infirmity of reason so that this feeling might lead them to have recourse to a better guide, which is faith. This is the subject of the following remark.

"Pyrrho," Remark C

. . . When one is able to comprehend well all the tropes set forth by Sextus Empiricus for suspending judgment, one realizes that this logic is the greatest effort of subtlety that the human mind has been able to accomplish. But, at the same time, one sees that this subtlety is in no way satisfactory. It confounds itself; for if it were solid, it would prove that it is certain that we ought to be in doubt. There would then be some certitude; there would then be a criterion or sure rule of truth. Now this ruins that system, but do not fear that it will come to this, the reasons for doubting being themselves doubtful. We must then doubt if it is necessary to doubt. How great a chaos, and how great a torment for the human mind! It seems therefore that this unfortunate state is the most proper one of all for convincing us that our reason is a path that leads us astray since, when it displays itself with the greatest subtlety, it plunges us into such an abyss. The natural conclusion of this ought to be to renounce this guide and to implore the cause of all things to give us a better one. This is a great step toward the Christian religion; for it requires that we look to God for knowledge of what we ought to believe and what we ought to do, and that we enslave our understanding to the obeisance of faith. . . .

"Zeno of Elea," Remark G

. . . *The modes of suspending judgment employed against the existence of extension.*
   Add to this that all the means of suspending judgment that overthrow the reality of corporeal qualities also overthrow the reality of extension. Since the same bodies are sweet to some men and bitter to others, one is right in inferring that they are neither sweet nor bitter in themselves and absolutely speaking. The "new" philosophers, although they are not skeptics, have so well understood the bases of suspension of judgment with regard to sounds, smells, heat, cold, hardness, softness, heaviness and lightness, tastes, colors, and the like, that they teach that all these qualities are perceptions of our soul and that they do not exist at all in the objects of our senses. Why should we not say the same thing about extension? If an entity that has no color appears to us, however, with a determinate color with respect to its species, shape, and location, why could not an entity that had no extension be visible to us under an appearance of a determinate, shaped, and located extension of a certain type? And notice carefully that the same body appears to us to be small or large, round or square, according to the place from which it is viewed; and let us have no doubts that a body that seems very small to us appears very large to a fly. It is not then by their own real or absolute extension that bodies present themselves to

our minds. We can therefore conclude that they are not extended in themselves. Would you dare to reason in this way today, "Since certain bodies appear sweet to one man, sour to another, bitter to a third, and so on, I ought to affirm that in general they are savory, though I do not know what savor belongs to them absolutely and in themselves"? All the "new" philosophers would hoot at you. Why then would you dare to say, "Since certain bodies appear large to one animal, medium to another, and very small to a third, I ought to affirm that in general they are extended, though I do not know their absolute extension?" . . .

"Zeno of Elea," Remark H (The proofs that reason furnishes us
of the existence of matter are not evident enough to furnish
a good demonstration on this point.)

There are two philosophical axioms that teach us: the one, that nature does nothing in vain; and the other, that it is useless to do by several methods what may be done by fewer means with the same ease. By these two axioms the Cartesians I am speaking of can maintain that no bodies exist; for whether they exist or not, God is equally able to communicate to us all the thoughts that we have. It is no proof at all that there are bodies to say that our senses assure us of this with the utmost evidence. They deceive us with regard to all of the corporeal qualities, the magnitude, size, and motion of bodies not excepted;[11] and when we believe them about these latter qualities, we are also convinced that there exist outside our souls a great many colors, tastes, and other entities that we call hardness, fluidity, cold, heat, and the like. However it is not true that anything like these exists outside our minds. Why then should we trust our senses with regard to extension? It can very easily be reduced to appearance, just like colors. . . . Thirdly, it is useful to know that a Father of the Oratory, as illustrious for his piety as for his philosophical knowledge, maintained that faith alone can truly convince us of the existence of bodies. Neither the Sorbonne, nor any other tribunal, gave him the least trouble on that account. The Italian inquisitors did not disturb Fardella, who maintained the same thing in a printed work. This ought to show my readers that they must not find it strange that I sometimes point out that, concerning the most mysterious matters in the Gospel, reason gets us nowhere, and thus we ought to be completely satisfied with the light of faith. . . .

Third Clarification

II. *The nature of the Pyrrhonists.* Now, of all the philosophers who ought not to be permitted to dispute about the mysteries of Christianity until they have accepted Revelation as the criterion, there are none as unworthy of being heard as the followers of Pyrrhonism; for they are people who profess to acknowledge no certain sign that distinguishes the true from the false; so that if, by chance, they came across the truth,

---

11. See Malebranche.

they could never be sure that it was the truth. They are not satisfied with opposing the testimony of the senses, the maxims of morality, the rules of logic, and the axioms of metaphysics; they also try to overthrow the demonstrations of the geometers, and all that the mathematicians can produce of the most evident character. If they stopped at the ten modes or tropes for suspending judgment, and if they had limited themselves to employing them against natural science, they could still be dealt with. But they go much further; they have a kind of weapon that they call the *diallelos*,[12] which they wield at the first instant it is needed. After this is done, it is impossible to withstand them on any subject whatsoever. It is a labyrinth in which the thread of Ariadne cannot be of any help. They lose themselves in their own subtleties; and they are overjoyed at this, since this serves to show more clearly the universality of their hypothesis, that all is uncertain, not even excepting the arguments that attack uncertainty. Their method leads people so far that those who have really seen the consequences of it are forced to admit that they do not know if anything exists.[13]

Theologians should not be ashamed to admit that they cannot enter a contest with such antagonists, and that they do not want to expose the Gospel truths to such an attack. The bark of Jesus Christ is not made for sailing on this stormy sea, but for taking shelter from this tempest in the haven of faith. It has pleased the Father, the Son, and the Holy Ghost, Christians ought to say, to lead us by the path of faith, and not by the path of knowledge or disputation. They are our teachers and our directors. We cannot lose our way with such guides. And reason itself commands us to prefer them to its direction. . . .

IV. A true believer, a Christian, who knows the spirit of his religion well, does not expect to see it conform to the aphorisms of the Lyceum, or to be capable of refuting, merely by the strength of reason, the difficulties of reason. He is well aware that natural things are not proportional to supernatural ones, and that if a philosopher were asked to put on a level basis and in a perfect harmony the Gospel mysteries and the Aristotelian axioms, one would be requesting of him what the nature of things will not permit. One must necessarily choose between philosophy and the Gospel. If you do not want to believe anything but what is evident and in conformity with the common notions, choose philosophy and leave Christianity. If you are willing to believe the incomprehensible mysteries of religion, choose Christianity and leave philosophy. For to have together self-evidence and incomprehensibility is something that cannot be. The combination of these two items is hardly more impossible than the combination of the properties of a square and a circle. A choice must necessarily be made. If the advantages of a round table do not satisfy you, have a square one made; and do not pretend that the same table could furnish you with the advantages of both a round table and a square one. Once again, a true Christian, well versed in the characteristics of supernatural truths and firm on the principles that are peculiar

---

12. See Sextus Empiricus, *Pyrrhon. Hypotyp. Lib*. I, chap. XV [I.164–174] and *Lib*. II, chap. IV [II.18–21].

13. See Sextus Empiricus, in *Adversus Mathematicos* VII.65ff, says of Gorgias of Leontini; and see above, article "Zeno of Elea," remark E.

to the Gospel, will only laugh at the subtleties of the philosophers, and especially those of the Pyrrhonists. Faith will place him above the regions where the tempests of disputation reign. He will stand on a peak, from which he will hear below him the thunder of arguments and distinctions; and he will not be disturbed at all by this—a peak, which will be for him the real Olympus of the poets and the real temple of the sages, from which he will see in perfect tranquility the weaknesses of reason and the meanderings of mortals who only follow that guide. Every Christian who allows himself to be disconcerted by the objections of the unbelievers, and to be scandalized by them, has one foot in the same grave as they do.

V. . . . Nothing is more necessary than faith, and nothing is more important than to make people aware of the price of this theological virtue. Now, what is there that is more suitable for making us aware of this than meditating on the attitude that distinguishes it from the other acts of the understanding? Its essence consists in binding us to the revealed truths by a strong conviction, and in binding us to these solely by the motive of God's authority. Those who believe in the immortality of the soul on the basis of philosophical reasons are orthodox but so far they have no share in the faith of which we are speaking. They only have a share in it insofar as they believe this doctrine because God has revealed it to us, and they submit humbly to the voice of God everything that philosophy presents to them that is most plausible for convincing them of the mortality of the soul. Thus, the merit of faith becomes greater in proportion as the revealed truth that is its object surpasses all the powers of our mind; for, as the incomprehensibility of this object increases by the greater number of maxims of the natural light that oppose it, we have to sacrifice to God's authority a stronger reluctance of reason; and consequently we show ourselves more submissive to God, and we give him greater signs of our respect than if the item were only moderately difficult to believe. Why was it, I ask you, that the faith of the Father of the faithful [Abraham] was of so great a degree? Is it not because it was he "who against hope believed in hope" (Romans 4:18)? There would not have been very much merit in hoping, on the basis of God's promise, for something that was very probable naturally. The merit therefore consisted in this, that the hope of this promise was opposed by all kinds of appearances. Let us say also that the highest degree of faith is that which embraces on divine testimony truths that are the most opposed to reason.

This view has been set forth in a ridiculous light, coming from the pen of a master. "The devil take me if I believed anything," the Maréchal d'Hocquincourt is made to say, "but since that time I could bear to be crucified for religion. It is not that I see more reason in it than I did before; on the contrary, I see less than ever. But I know not what to say to you, for I would submit to be crucified without knowing why or wherefore." "So much the better, my Lord," replied the father, twanging it very devoutly through the nose, "so much the better; these are not human impulses but are inspired by heaven. Away with reason; this is the true religion, away with reason. What an extraordinary grace, my Lord, has heaven bestowed upon you! 'Be ye as little children.' Children are still in their state of innocence; and why? Because they are not endowed with reason. 'Blessed are the poor in spirit.' They commit no sin, and for this reason, because they are not endowed with reason. 'No reason; I know not why nor wherefore.' Beautiful words! They ought to be written in gold letters. 'It is not that I see more reason in it than I did before; on the contrary, I see less than ever.' This is really altogether divine to those who delight in celestial things. 'Away with reason.' What an extraordinary grace, my Lord, has heaven bestowed upon you."[14] If one gives this passage a more serious and modest air, it will become reasonable.

FURTHER READINGS

Bracken, Henry. "Bayle's Attack on Natural Theology: The Case of Christian Pyrrhonism." In *Skepticism and Irreligion in the Seventeenth and Eighteenth Centuries*, edited by Richard H. Popkin and A. Vanderjagt, 254–66. Leiden: Brill, 1993.

———. "Bayle Not a Sceptic?" *Journal of the History of Ideas* 25 (1964): 169–80.

Brahami, Frédéric. *Le travail du scepticisme: Montaigne, Bayle, Hume*. Paris: Presses Universitaires de France, 2001.

Brush, Craig. *Montaigne and Bayle: Variations on the Theme of Skepticism*. The Hague: Martinus Nijhoff, 1966.

Labrousse, Elizabeth. *Pierre Bayle*. 2 vols. The Hague: Martinus Nijhoff, 1963–1964.

Lennon, Thomas. *Reading Bayle*. Toronto: University of Toronto Press, 1999.

———. "Bayle's Anticipation of Popper." *Journal of the History of Ideas* 58 (1997): 695–705.

Maia Neto, José R. "Bayle's Academic Skepticism." In *Everything Connects: In Conference with Richard H. Popkin*, edited by James E. Force and David S. Katz, 264–75. Leiden: Brill, 1999.

Mori, Gianluca. *Bayle philosophe*. Paris: Honoré Champion, 1999.

———. "Pierre Bayle on Skepticism and 'Common Notions.'" In *The Return of Skepticism from Hobbes and Descartes to Bayle*, edited by Gianni Paganini, 383–413. Dordrecht: Kluwer, 2003.

———. "Scepticisme ancien et moderne chez Bayle." *Libertinage et philosophie* 7 (2003): 271–90.

Paganini, Gianni. *Analisi della fede e critica della ragione nella filosofia di Pierre Bayle*. Florence: La Nuova Italia, 1980.

Popkin, Richard H. "Pierre Bayle's Place in 17th Century Skepticism." In *Pierre Bayle, le philosophe de Rotterdam*, edited by Paul Dibon, 1–19. Amsterdam: Elsevier, 1959.

Sandberg, Karl C. *At the Crossroads of Faith and Reason: An Essay on Pierre Bayle*. Tucson: University of Arizona Press, 1966.

Whelan, Ruth. *The Anatomy of Superstition: A Study of the Historical Theory and Practice of Pierre Bayle*. Oxford: Voltaire Foundation at the Taylor Institute, 1989.

———. "The Wisdom of Simonides: Bayle and La Mothe Le Vayer." In Popkin and Vanderjagt, *Scepticism and Irreligion in the Seventeenth and Eighteenth Centuries*, 230–53.

---

14. "Conversation between Maréchal d'Hocquincourt and Father Canaye," in *Oeuvres mêlées de St. Evremond*, vol. IV.

22

LEIBNIZ

G ottfried Wilhelm von Leibniz (1646–1716) was interested in and engaged with the main skeptical issues of his time. He planned to give a point-by-point reply to Sextus's *Outlines of Pyrrhonism*, book 1, which he actually did up to the five modes (*PH* 1.177). He corresponded extensively with the three French skeptics of the late seventeenth century: Huet, Bayle, and Foucher. He praised—and partially agreed with—Huet's skeptical *Censura philosophiae cartesianae*. He strived with Bayle over the problem of evil, a discussion that led to the publication of his *Essais de Théodicée* in 1710. And he corresponded for a long time with Simon Foucher, whose project was to revive Academic skepticism. We have selected extracts of two letters from Leibniz to Foucher, the first from 1675, the second written nine years later, in 1686. Both exhibit Leibniz's reactions to Foucher's Academic skepticism. In the first he argues that necessary and eternal truths have objective validity and so cannot be doubted, but that Foucher is right in doubting the existence of external material bodies. Leibniz rejects Descartes's proof of the existence of a material world and Descartes's arguments against the dream and the deceiver skeptical doubts. In the second letter, Leibniz disputes Foucher's rejection of suppositions in philosophical inquiries (see Foucher's Academic laws in this volume) and proposes a solution to the problem of the existence of the external material world. This is one of the first statements of Leibniz's famous doctrine of preestablished harmony, which became known to the public nine years later, in 1696, with the publication of his "Système nouveau de la nature et de la communication des substances" in the *Journal des Savants*. The letters were selected by Stuart Brown.

EXTRACT FROM A LETTER WRITTEN IN 1675 TO FOUCHER

I agree with you that it is important once and for all to examine all our presuppositions in order to establish something sound. For I hold that it is only when we can prove everything we assert that we understand perfectly the thing being considered. . . . As I see it, your purpose is to examine those truths which affirm that there is something outside of us. You seem to be most fair in this, for thus you will grant us all hypothetical truths which affirm, not that something does exist outside of us, but only what would happen if anything existed there. So we at once save arithmetic, geometry, and a large number of propositions in metaphysics, physics, and morals, whose convenient expression depends on arbitrarily chosen definitions, and whose truth depends on those axioms which I am wont to call identical; such, for example, as that two contradictories cannot exist and that at any given time a thing is as it is; that it is, for example, equal to itself, as great as itself, similar to itself, etc.

But, although you do not enter explicitly into an examination of hypothetical propositions, I am still of the opinion that this should be done and that we should admit none without having entirely demonstrated and resolved it into identities.

It is the truth which deal with what is in fact outside of us which are the primary subject of your investigations. Now in the first place, we cannot deny that the very truth of hypothetical propositions themselves is something outside of us and independent of us. For all hypothetical propositions assert what would be or would not be, if something or its contrary were posited; consequently, they assume two things at the same time which agree with each other, or the possibility or impossibility, necessity or indifference, of something. But this possibility, impossibility, or necessity (for the necessity of one thing is the impossibility of its contrary) is not a chimera which we create, since all that we do consists in recognizing them, in spite of ourselves and in a constant manner. So, of all the things which actually are, the possibility or impossibility of being is itself the first. But this possibility and this necessity form or compose what are called the essences or natures and the truths which are usually called eternal. And we are right in calling them this, for there is nothing so eternal as what is necessary. Thus the nature of the circle with its properties is something which exists and is eternal, that is, there is some constant cause outside of us which makes everyone who thinks carefully about a circle discover the same thing, not merely in the sense that their thoughts agree with each other, for this could be attributed solely to the nature of the human mind, but also in the sense that phenomena or experiences confirm them when some appearance of a circle strikes our senses. These phenomena necessarily have some cause outside of us.

But, although the existence of necessities comes before all others in itself and in the order of nature, I nevertheless agree that it is not first in the order of our knowledge. For you see that, in order to prove its existence, I have taken for granted that we think and that we have sensations. So there are two absolute general truths; truths, that is, which tell of the actual existence of things. One is that we think; the other, that there is a great variety in our thoughts. From the former it follows that we are; from the latter, that there is something other than us, that is to say, something other than that which thinks, which is the cause of the variety of our experiences. Now one of these truths is just as incontestable and as independent as the other, and, having stressed only the former in the order of his meditations, Descartes failed to attain the perfection to which he had aspired. If he had followed with exactness what I call a *filum meditandi*, I believe that he would really have achieved the *first philosophy*. . . .

But I return to these truths which are primary with respect to ourselves, and first to those which assert that there is something outside of us; namely, that we think and that there is a great variety in our thoughts. This variety cannot come from that which thinks, since one thing by itself cannot be the cause of the changes occurring in it. For everything remains in the state in which it is, unless there is something which changes it. And since it has not been determined by itself to undergo certain changes rather than others, we cannot begin to attribute any variety to it without saying something which admittedly has no reason, which is absurd. Even if we tried to say that our thoughts have no beginning, we should be obliged to assert that each of us has existed from all eternity; yet we should not escape the difficulty, for we should always have to admit that there is no reason for this variety which would have existed from all eternity in our thoughts, since there is nothing in us which determines us to one variety rather than to another. Thus there is some cause outside of us for the variety of our thoughts. And since we agree that there are some subordinate causes of this variety which themselves still need a cause, we have established particular beings or substances to whom we ascribe some action, that is, from whose change we think that some change follows in us. So we make great strides toward fabricating what we call matter and body.

But at this point you are right in stopping us for a while and renewing the criticisms of the ancient Academy. For at bottom all our experiences assure us of only two things: first, that there is a connection among our appearances which provides the means to predict future appearances successfully; and, second, that this connection must have a constant cause. But it does not follow strictly from this that matter or bodies exist but only that there is something which give us appearances in a good sequence. For if some invisible power were to take pleasure in giving us dreams that are well tied into our preceding life and in conformity with each other, could we distinguish them from reality before we had awakened? Now, what prevents the course of our life from being one long well-ordered dream, about which we could be undeceived in a moment? Nor do I see that such a power would be imperfect just on this ground, as Descartes asserts, to say nothing of the fact that its imperfection is not involved in the present question. For it might be a kind of subordinate power, or a demon who for some unknown reason could interfere with our affairs and who would have at least as much power over us as that caliph had over the man whom he caused to be carried, drunk, into his palace, and let taste of the paradise of Mohammed after he was awakened; after which he was once more made drunk and returned in that condition to the place where he had been found. When this man came to himself, he naturally interpreted this experience, which seemed inconsistent with the course of his life, as a vision, and spread among the people maxims and revelations which he had believed he had learned in his pretended paradise; this was precisely what the caliph wished. Since reality has thus passed for a vision, what is to prevent a vision from passing for reality? The more consistency we see in what happens to us, it is true, the more our belief is confirmed that what appears to us is reality. But it is also true that, the more closely we examine our appearances, the better ordered we find them, as microscopes and other means of observation have shown. The permanent consistency gives us great assurance, but, after all, it will be only moral until somebody discovers a priori the origin of the world which we see and pursues the question of why things are as they appear back to its foundations in essence. For when this is done, he will have demonstrated that what appears to us is reality and that it is impossible for us ever to be deceived in it. But I believe that this would very nearly approach the beatific vision and that it is difficult to aspire to this in our state. Yet we do learn therefrom how confused the knowledge which we commonly have of the body and matter must be, since we believe we are certain that they exist, but eventually find that we could be mistaken. This confirms Mr. Descartes's excellent thought concerning the proof of the difference between body and soul, since one can doubt the one without being able to question the other. For even if there were only appearances or dreams, we should be nonetheless certain of the existence of that which thinks, as Descartes has very well said. I may add that one could still demonstrate the existence of God by ways different from those of Descartes but, I believe, leading further. For we have no need to assume a being who guarantees us against being deceived, since it lies in our power to undeceive ourselves about many things, at least about the most important ones.

I wish, Sir, that your meditations on this matter may have all the success you desire; but, to accomplish this, it is well to proceed in order and to establish your propositions. This is the way to gain ground and make sure progress. I believe you would oblige the public also by conveying it, from time to time, selections from the Academy and especially from Plato, for I know there are things in them more beautiful and substantial than is usually thought.

EXTRACT FROM A LETTER WRITTEN IN 1686 TO FOUCHER

The Philosophy of the Academics, which is the knowledge of the weaknesses of our reason, is good for the foundations, and since we are always at the foundations in matters of religion, it is certainly suitable for the better subjection of reason to authority. You have shown this very well in one of your discourses [*Dissertation sur la recherche de la vérité, contenant l'apologie des académiciens*, pt. 1, art. 4]. But in matters of the human sciences we must try to advance and even if the only way to do so was by establishing many things on a few suppositions, that is still of use: at least we should know that all that remained to reach a full demonstration was to prove these few suppositions, and in the meantime we should have some hypothetical truths and escape from the confusion of disputes. This is the method of the Geometers. For example, Archimedes supposes only these few things: that the straight line is the shortest, that of two lines of which each is everywhere concave on the same side, the line included is shorter that the including line, and on that basis he completes his demonstration with vigor. . . .

Hence, if for example we supposed the principle of contradiction as well as that in every true proposition the notion of the predicate is included in that of the subject, and several other axioms of this nature, and if from these we could prove many things as demonstratively as the Geometers, would you not find this result of consequence? But we would have to begin this method one day if we were to begin to finish the disputes. It would always be a means of gaining territory.

It is certain, even, that some truths must be supposed, unless all hope of making demonstrations is given up, for proofs could not go to infinity. We must not ask for the impossible, otherwise we would be witnessing that we were not seriously searching for the truth. Hence, I will continue to suppose boldly that two contradictories could not be true, and that what implies a contradiction could not be, and consequently that necessary propositions (that is those of which the opposite implies a contradiction) have not been set up by free decree. Otherwise we are misusing words. Nothing more clear could be produced for proving these things. You yourself suppose them in writing and reasoning, or else at any moment you could defend quite the opposite of what you say. Let this do for the second supposition. . . .

I feel that you are also right . . . to doubt that bodies can act on minds and vice versa. On this matter I have an amusing opinion, which appears to me necessary and is very different from that of the author [Malebranche] of the *Recherche*. I believe that every individual substance expresses the entire universe in its manner and that its following state is a consequence (though often free) of its previous state, as if there were only God and it in the world; but since all substances are a continual production of the sovereign Being, and express the same universe or the same phenomena, they agree with each other exactly, and that makes us say that the one acts on the other, because the one expresses more distinctly than the other the cause or reason of the changes, rather in the way we attribute motion to the vessel rather than to the whole of the sea, and with reason. I also draw this consequence, that if bodies are substances, they could not consist of extension alone. But that changes nothing in our explanations of particular phenomena of nature which should always be explained mathematically and mechanically, provided that we understand that the principles of mechanics do not depend on extension alone. Hence I am neither for the common Hypothesis of the real influence of one created substance on the other, nor for the Hypothesis of occasional causes, as if God produced thoughts in the soul on the occasion of motions of the body, and so changed the course the soul would otherwise have taken by a totally useless kind of perpetual miracle; but I maintain a concomitance or agreement of what happens in the different substances, since God created the soul in the first place so that everything happens to it or arises from its own being without it having to accommodate itself to the body thereafter, no more than the body has to accommodate itself to the soul. Each following its own laws, the one freely, the other without choice, agree with each other in the same phenomena.

FURTHER READINGS

Brown, Stuart. "Foucher's Critique and Leibniz's Defense of the 'New System.'" In *Leibniz: Reason and Experience*, edited by Stuart Brown, 96–104. Milton Keynes: Open University Press, 1983.

———. "The Leibniz-Foucher Alliance and Its Philosophical Basis." In *Leibniz and His Correspondence*, edited by Paul Lodge. Cambridge: Cambridge University Press, 2004.

———. "Leibniz as Platonist and Academic Skeptic." *Skepsis* 9 (1998): 111–38.

Leibniz, G. W. *Die Philosophischen Schriften*. 7 vols. Edited by C. J. Gerhardt. Berlin: Weidmann, 1875–1899.

———. *Discourse on Metaphysics and Related Writings*. 2nd ed. Edited and translated by Martin Niall and Stuart Brown. Dordrecht: D. Reidel, 1969.

———. *Theodicy: Essays on the Goodness of God, the Freedom of Man and the Origin of Evil*. Edited by Austin Farrer and translated by E. M. Huggard. London: 1951.

Olaso, Ezequiel. "Leibniz and Skepticism." In *Scepticism from the Renaissance to the Enlightenment*, edited by Richard H. Popkin and Charles Schmitt, 133–67. Wiesbaden: O. Harrassowitz, 1987.

———. "Skepticism and the Infinite." In *L'infinito in Leibniz: problemi e terminologia*, edited by Antonio Lamarra, 95–118. Roma: Edizioni dell'Anteneo, 1990.

Popkin, Richard H. "Leibniz and the French Skeptics." *Revue Internationale de Philosophie* 76–77 (1966): 228–48.

23

CROUSAZ

Jean-Pierre Crousaz (1663–1750) was an enthusiastic defender of science. He published a *Logic* in 1712 and in 1733 a 776-folio-page (2,530 pages in the recent Fayard edition) attack on skepticism. In this monstrous volume Crousaz begins by defining and explaining the causes of Pyrrhonism (section from where the following excerpt was extracted). Then he gives a detailed point-by-point reply to Sextus Empiricus (he exams the three books of *Outlines of Pyrrhonism* and—more briefly and superficially—the books of *Adversus Mathematicos*). In the sequence he attacks the main target of his book—Pierre Bayle—replying to nearly all metaphysical paradoxes raised by Bayle in the *Dictionary* and other works: the problem of evil, the difficulties of the great metaphysical systems (Aristotelian, Cartesian, Malebranchean), the paradoxes concerning extension and movement, the problem of the soul of beasts, etc. Finally, he gives a point-by-point reply to Pierre-Daniel Huet's *Traité philosophique de la foiblesse de l'esprit humain*. The violence of Crousaz's antiskepticism is clear in the passages below, selected by Flávio Loque, which also show the main grounds for his aversion to this philosophy, namely his belief that it is an untenable—and thus a hypocritical and vicious—position, that it is contrary to the improvement of sciences, and that it leads either to straightforward atheism or to religious enthusiasm, which for Crousaz is almost as pernicious as atheism itself.

FROM *EXAMEN DU PYRRHONISME ANCIEN ET MODERNE*

III. To best prepare my reader for understanding my difficulty [in defining Pyrrhonism], let us imagine that we are transported to some land where no one has yet heard of Pyrrhonism, and where this way of philosophizing and disputation has not yet arisen in the minds of the people who live there. Imagine that I am in some corner of the Indies in conversation with a judicious philosopher who is curious to know about the state of sciences in Europe. . . .

. . . I tell him about the *chemists* who have discovered how nature works by imitating it. I speak of the mathematicians who measure and calculate everything, and who have learned how to evaluate and exactly measure the forces of every natural agent. Finally, I tell him about some extremely hardworking and intelligent scholars . . . who work to assure themselves of diverse facts, but who also proceed with great caution. When they collect a large enough number of separate truths, the time will perhaps come when they can draw enough of them together to form a system better than mere chance.

Is this what we have come to and where we remain fixed? No, I will say to him. Many people deviate from this method in two very opposed ways. Some still build systems that they defend with all imaginable heat. But others believe that . . . it is impossible for the human mind ever to compose anything that is accurate and certain. . . .

What! . . . am I . . . to believe that in your land there are men of letters whom you count as philosophers who have reputation and disciples, and who doubt that 2 + 2 = 4, that 6 is an even number, that the whole is larger than its parts, that two sides of a triangle are larger than the third, etc. You might as well tell me that they doubt that they have eyes or a mouth, whether or not they live, sleep, eat, or walk on the earth. . . .

. . . I do not know what takes place in the minds of others, and I do not know for certain that there are people who doubt that 2 + 2 = 4. I simply report what I have heard, which is that there are people who profess to push doubt that far. . . .

VI. I should add that the most extreme and most opinionated Pyrrhonians are not continually occupied with their incertitude. That state, which so surprises you, they take up and then abandon, turn by turn. Ordinarily, they think and live very much as everyone else, and they doubt only to the extent that people provide them with the occasion to do so, and then only to the extent that people solicit and force them. . . .

. . . The pleasure of contradicting, perplexing, and of supporting paradoxes becomes more and more seductive to them from moment to moment. This pleasure grows to the extent that they experience it. But if you abandon the dispute, then they return to their natural feelings, and they act and think like everyone else. . . .

Such a man persuades himself that what he knows, and knows for certain, is reduced to virtually nothing. This thought pleases him. Not only does he find that this puts him on a level with those who pass for being the most knowledgeable, but also he finds himself above most of them, that is, above all those who think they know what they do not know. When someone is always vain and lazy, hates to work, and cannot without suffering witness the reputations of others, it gives him pleasure to think that these men have acquired only a tiny bit of knowledge. He also feels pleasure in persuading himself that they will not acquire any more knowledge than they already have. Now if a true man of knowledge wishes to take the trouble, he can disturb the pleasure of this presumptuous man who contradicts the modest scholar. The scholar asks if there appears to be any truth of which one can be assured. If the doubter proposes one, the scholar will draw from it some consequences so necessarily tied to it that he will avow that no one could refuse to recognize the connection. If the scholar is asked on what ground he ascribes the truth to a number of certain propositions, he says that it is because the characteristic of certitude that is found in the one will be found also in the others. With that, the doubter will find himself exposed to the mortification of being instructed and of having to follow step by step men who are wiser than he is. But at this point a man of the temperament of which I speak and who astonishes you so much prefers to revoke the bit of knowledge he first proposed. And after having first avowed that one knows or could know something in general, although very little, then when the scholar goes into detail, the doubter alters the meaning of the words in his avowal. He then treats as uncertain everything he is asked about, his vanity and the spirit of disputation having led him to this extremity. . . .

XV. I will agree if one considers Pyrrhonism a pernicious error, fatal and shameful to humankind. I will also agree if one says that Pyrrhonism encompasses everything that is dangerous in all other [sects], I will agree. And when I publish these views, I believe that no one will find my words too strong, and that no one will accuse me of exaggeration. People have made laws, and those who have made them have understood or have believed that they understood what is best for the utility of humankind. People have observed these laws because they believe that it is better to observe them than to neglect them. But none of this would have been done if everyone had been a Pyrrhonian, or if they had conformed their thoughts to Pyrrhonism. Why make laws that could be *unjust* or perhaps *useless* or *pernicious*? Why observe them when it is no more certain that they will lead to good than that they will lead to evil? . . . A man who is uncertain whether he does good or evil, whether his life is happy or unhappy, or of the difference between a person who is good and one who deceives and does evil deeds, what should he think of those who do not reflect at all, when all reflection results only in new uncertainties, and because of that, in new anxieties? . . . Why prefer duty to interest when I have no certainty concerning duty, when perhaps this interest to which I have abandoned myself will do me injury? But I ignore these thoughts. On the contrary, I feel that this interest will give me present pleasure, and it appears to me that it will lead to several more pleasures. Why will a man take the trouble to read, meditate, make conjectures, or seek to justify himself by experience? Why scrupulously take account of all circumstances? Why look for causes and draw consequences, if, by all his care, he learns nothing? Will one say: It is true that one is assured of nothing, but if one is deprived of this satisfaction, one at least has the pleasure of combating opposed sentiments, and of showing those who think they know something that they flatter themselves and are far from being what they think they are. Thus what supports the labor of a Pyrrhonian is solely the pleasure of contradicting. But if this does not discourage him, he does all he can to discourage others. From all this it follows that in Pyrrhonism one finds the effacement of the sciences and good morals and behavior. . . .

There is, however, one occasion on which I permit myself to press the advantage of a Pyrrhonian. This is when he says to me, as in fact he does, that reason appears to him incapable of leading to any certitude, and that in particular and above all, that reason has no application in matters of religion nor to what religion presents to us and makes us see, and that the lights with which reason claims to provide us clarification are so uncertain that religion is overturned from top to bottom. But then, even given this, he goes on to say that his faith is not shaken, that he holds firmly to Revelation, and that he mocks all the contradictions that reason opposes to Revelation. In this case . . . I ask him to tell me by what means he has come to prove such an unshakable faith . . . he must acquaint me with some of his reasoning. Because he, who doubts always because he never finds strong enough proofs, has now abandoned these means, and he has ceased to doubt on a certain subject, and he now is fully assured without proofs. But when a man accepts some reasoning, it is necessary that he has found in that reasoning the character of certitude, that indubitable mark of certainty, and I would make him notice this mark equally in a great number of subjects. If he tells me that he believes without having been guided by any proof, I would ask again by what traits he distinguishes his proofless persuasion from that of so many fanatics who are not in agreement among themselves, who believe in dreams and who support the assurance of their belief only with reference to the all-powerful force of Divine Emanation.

FURTHER READINGS

Crousaz, Jean-Pierre de. *La Logique ou système de réflexions qui peuvent contribuer à la netteté et l'étendue de nos connaissances.* Seconde édition revue, corrigée et augmentée. 3 vols. Amsterdam: L'Honoré et Chatelien, 1720.

Häseler, Jens. "Formey et Crousaz, ou comment fallait-il combattre le scepticisme?" In *The Return of Skepticism from Hobbes and Descartes to Bayle*, edited by Gianni Paganini, 449–62. Dordrecht: Kluwer, 2003.

Laursen, John Christian. "Crousaz." In *Grundriss der Geschichte der Philosophie, 18 Jhr*, edited by Friedrich Ueberweg. Band 2/1-2. Forthcoming.

———. "Skeptics, Unconvincing Anti-Skepticism, and Politics." In *Scepticisme et modernité*, edited by Marc André Bernier and Sébastien Charles, 167–88. Saint-Étienne: Publications de la Université de Saint-Étienne, 2005.

24

BERKELEY

G eorge Berkeley (1685–1753) was an Irish philosopher and clergyman who con-
travened materialism by holding that material bodies are merely phenomenal.
Berkeley arrived at immaterialism radicalizing and pointing out inconsistencies in
Locke's empiricism, building on Malebranche's denial of causes among created substances, and reflecting on Foucher's denial of the primary and secondary qualities distinction (a position he read in note B of the article "Pyrrho" of Bayle's *Dictionary*,
included in this anthology). In the section of the First Dialogue between Hylas and Philonous reproduced below, we see Berkeley's use of skeptical arguments to undermine the
standard realist position of the time and his reversal of the force of skeptical arguments
by using his principle that to be is to be perceived: that reality is what we perceive.
Despite the self-proclaimed explicit antiskeptical direction of his philosophy, Berkeley's
immaterialism was first received as a still more radical form of modern skepticism.

FROM *THREE DIALOGUES BETWEEN HYLAS AND PHILONOUS*

PHILONOUS. That there is no such thing as what philosophers call *material substance*, I am seriously persuaded: but if I were made to see anything absurd or skeptical in this, I should then have the same reason to renounce this, that I imagine I
have now to reject the contrary opinion.

HYLAS. What! can anything be more fantastical, more repugnant to common
sense, or a more manifest piece of skepticism, than to believe there is no such thing
as *matter*?

PHILONOUS. Softly, good Hylas. What if it should prove, that you, who hold there
is, are by virtue of that opinion a greater *skeptic*, and maintain more paradoxes and
repugnancies to common sense, than I who believe no such thing?

HYLAS. You may as soon persuade me, the part is greater than the whole, as that,
in order to avoid absurdity and skepticism, I should ever be obliged to give up my
opinion in this point.

PHILONOUS. Well then, are you content to admit that opinion for true, which upon
examination shall appear most agreeable to common sense, and remote from skepticism?

HYLAS. With all my heart. Since you are for raising disputes about the plainest
things in Nature, I am content for once to hear what you have to say.

PHILONOUS. Pray, Hylas, what do you mean by a *skeptic*?

HYLAS. I mean what all men mean, one that doubts of everything.

PHILONOUS. He then who entertains no doubt concerning some particular point, with regard to that point cannot be thought a *skeptic*.

HYLAS. I agree with you.

PHILONOUS. Whether doth doubting consist in embracing the affirmative or negative side of a question?

HYLAS. In neither; for whoever understands English, cannot but know that *doubting* signifies a suspense between both.

PHILONOUS. He then that denieth any point, can no more be said to doubt of it, than he who affirmeth it with the same degree of assurance.

HYLAS. True.

PHILONOUS. And consequently, for such his denial is no more to be esteemed a *skeptic* than the other.

HYLAS. I acknowledge it.

PHILONOUS. How cometh it to pass then, Hylas, that you pronounce me a *skeptic*, because I deny what you affirm, to wit, the existence of matter? Since, for ought you can tell, I am as peremptory in my denial, as you in your affirmation.

HYLAS. Hold, Philonous, I have been a little out in my definition; but every false step a man makes in discourse is not to be insisted on. I said indeed, that a *skeptic* was one who doubted of everything; but I should have added, or who denies the reality and truth of things.

PHILONOUS. What things? Do you mean the principles and theorems of sciences? But these you know are universal intellectual notions, and consequently independent of matter; the denial therefore of this doth not imply the denying them.

HYLAS. I grant it. But are there no other things? What think you of distrusting the senses, of denying the real existence of sensible things, or pretending to know nothing of them. Is not this sufficient to denominate a man a *skeptic*?

PHILONOUS. Shall we therefore examine which of us it is that denies the reality of sensible things, or professes the greatest ignorance of them; since, if I take you rightly, he is to be esteemed the greatest *skeptic*?

HYLAS. That is what I desire.

PHILONOUS. What mean you by sensible things?

HYLAS. Those things which are perceived by the senses. Can you imagine that I mean anything else?

PHILONOUS. Pardon me, Hylas, if I am desirous clearly to apprehend your notions, since this may much shorten our inquiry. Suffer me then to ask you this farther question. Are those things only perceived by the senses which are perceived immediately? Or may those things properly be said to be *sensible*, which are perceived mediately, or not without the intervention of others?

HYLAS. I do not sufficiently understand you.

PHILONOUS. In reading a book, what I immediately perceive are the letters, but mediately, or by means of these, are suggested to my mind the notions of God, virtue, truth, &c. Now, that the letters are truly sensible things, or perceived by sense, there is no doubt: but I would know whether you take the things suggested by them to be so too.

HYLAS. No certainly, it were absurd to think *God* or *Virtue* sensible things, though they may be signified and suggested to the mind by sensible marks, with which they have an arbitrary connection.

PHILONOUS. It seems then, that by *sensible things* you mean those only which can be perceived immediately by sense.

HYLAS. Right.

PHILONOUS. Doth it not follow from this, that though I see one part of the sky red, and another blue, and that my reason doth thence evidently conclude there must be some cause of that diversity of colours, yet that cause cannot be said to be a sensible thing, or perceived by the sense of seeing?

HYLAS. It doth.

PHILONOUS. In like manner, though I hear a variety of sounds, yet I cannot be said to hear the causes of those sounds.

HYLAS. You cannot.

PHILONOUS. And when by my touch I perceive a thing to be hot and heavy, I cannot say with any truth or propriety, that I feel the cause of its heat or weight.

HYLAS. To prevent any more questions of this kind, I tell you once for all, that by *sensible things* I mean those only which are perceived by sense, and that in truth the senses perceive nothing which they do not perceive immediately: for they make no inferences. The deducing therefore of causes or occasions from effects and appearances, which alone are perceived by sense, entirely relates to reason.

PHILONOUS. This point then is agreed between us, that *sensible things are those only which are immediately perceived by sense.* You will farther inform me, whether we immediately perceive by sight any thing beside light, and colours, and figures: or by hearing, any thing but sounds: by the palate, any thing beside tastes: by the smell, beside odours: or by the touch, more than tangible qualities.

HYLAS. We do not.

PHILONOUS. It seems therefore, that if you take away all sensible qualities, there remains nothing sensible.

HYLAS. I grant it.

PHILONOUS. Sensible things therefore are nothing else but so many sensible qualities, or combinations of sensible qualities.

HYLAS. Nothing else.

PHILONOUS. Heat then is a sensible thing.

HYLAS. Certainly.

PHILONOUS. Doth the reality of sensible things consist in being perceived? or, is it something distinct from their being perceived, and that bears no relation to the mind?

HYLAS. To *exist* is one thing, and to be *perceived* is another.

PHILONOUS. I speak with regard to sensible things only: and of these I ask, whether by their real existence you mean a subsistence exterior to the mind, and distinct from their being perceived?

HYLAS. I mean a real absolute being, distinct from, and without any relation to their being perceived.

PHILONOUS. Heat therefore, if it be allowed a real being, must exist without the mind.

HYLAS. It must.

PHILONOUS. Tell me, Hylas, is this real existence equally compatible to all degrees of heat which we perceive: or is there any reason why we should attribute it to some, and deny it others? And if there be, pray let me know that reason.

HYLAS. Whatever degree of heat we perceive by sense, we may be sure the same exists in the object that occasions it.

PHILONOUS. What, the greatest as well as the least?

HYLAS. I tell you, the reason is plainly the same in respect of both: they are both perceived by sense; nay, the greater degree of heat is more sensibly perceived; and consequently, if there is any difference, we are more certain of its real existence than we can be of the reality of a lesser degree.

PHILONOUS. But is not the most vehement and intense degree of heat a very great pain?

HYLAS. No one can deny it.

PHILONOUS. And is any unperceiving thing capable of pain or pleasure?

HYLAS. No certainly.

PHILONOUS. Is your material substance a senseless being, or a being endowed with sense and perception?

HYLAS. It is senseless, without doubt.

PHILONOUS. It cannot therefore be the subject of pain.

HYLAS. By no means.

PHILONOUS. Nor consequently of the greatest heat perceived by sense, since you acknowledge this to be no small pain.

HYLAS. I grant it.

PHILONOUS. What shall we say then of our external object; is it a material substance, or no?

HYLAS. It is a material substance with the sensible qualities inhering in it.

PHILONOUS. How then can a great heat exist in it, since you own it cannot in a material substance? I desire you would clear this point.

HYLAS. Hold, Philonous, I fear I was out in yielding intense heat to be a pain. It should seem rather, that pain is something distinct from heat, and the consequence or effect of it.

PHILONOUS. Upon putting your hand near the fire, do you perceive one simple uniform sensation, or two distinct sensations?

HYLAS. But one simple sensation.

PHILONOUS. Is not the heat immediately perceived?

HYLAS. It is.

PHILONOUS. And the pain?

HYLAS. True.

PHILONOUS. Seeing therefore they are both immediately perceived at the same time, and the fire affects you only with one simple, or uncompounded idea, it follows that this same simple idea is both the intense heat immediately perceived, and the pain; and consequently, that the intense heat immediately perceived is nothing distinct from a particular sort of pain.

HYLAS. It seems so.

PHILONOUS. Again, try in your thoughts, Hylas, if you can conceive a vehement sensation to be without pain, or pleasure.

HYLAS. I cannot.

PHILONOUS. Or can you frame to yourself an idea of sensible pain or pleasure in general, abstracted from every particular idea of heat, cold, tastes, smells? &c.

HYLAS. I do not find that I can.

PHILONOUS. Doth it not therefore follow, that sensible pain is nothing distinct from those sensations or ideas, in an intense degree?

HYLAS. It is undeniable; and to speak the truth, I begin to suspect a very great heat cannot exist but in a mind perceiving it?

PHILONOUS. What! are you then in that *skeptical* state of suspense, between affirming and denying?

HYLAS. I think I may be positive in the point. A very violent and painful heat cannot exist without the mind.

PHILONOUS. It hath not therefore, according to you, any real being.

HYLAS. I own it.

FURTHER READINGS

Bracken, Henry M. *Berkeley*. London: Macmillan, 1974.

———. *The Early Reception of Berkeley's Immaterialism: 1710–1733*. Revised edition. The Hague: Martinus Nijhoff, 1965.

Burnyeat, Myles F. "Idealism and Greek Philosophy: What Descartes Saw and Berkeley Missed." *Philosophical Review* 91, no. 1 (1982): 3–40.

Charles, Sébastien. *Berkeley au Siècle des Lumières: Immatérialisme et Scepticisme au XVIIIe Siècle*. Paris: Vrin, 2003.

Popkin, Richard H. "Berkeley and Pyrrhonism." *Review of Metaphysics* 5 (1951): 227–31. Reprinted in *The High Road to Pyrrhonism*, edited by Richard A. Watson and James E. Force, 297–318. San Diego: Austin Hill, 1980.

———. "Berkeley in the History of Skepticism." In *Skepticism in the Enlightenment*, edited by Richard H. Popkin, Ezequiel de Olaso, and Giorgio Tonelli, 173–86. Dordrecht: Kluwer, 1997.

25

RAMSAY

ndrew Michael Ramsay (1686–1743) was a skeptic in his early intellectual life. After studying with some Protestant mystics in Holland, he was converted to Catholicism by the French mystic François de Fénelon (1651–1743) at Cambrai in 1709 or 1710. He later became the leader of the Scottish Freemasons. In his major work, *The Philosophical Principles of Natural and Revealed Religion*, he sought an answer to Pyrrhonism, using both standard philosophical materials and spiritual ones. One of the main goals of the work is to give a philosophically grounded Christian answer to the philosophies that developed after Descartes, first and foremost Spinoza's—whose geometrical form employed in the *Ethics* was adopted by Ramsay—but also—in the part of the book from which we extracted the passage reprinted in this anthology—the idealist philosophies of Malebranche and Berkeley, which Ramsay considered as leading to Spinozism and atheism. Ramsay, who was the mentor of David Hume early in his career, argues in the extract below that there can be no demonstration of the existence of an external material world since this is a matter of fact. However, he offers a "proof" of this existence beyond any reasonable doubt.

FROM *THE PHILOSOPHICAL PRINCIPLES OF NATURAL AND REVEALED RELIGION UNFOLDED IN A GEOMETRICAL ORDER*

Book III: Of the Properties of Finite Beings, *Scholium* of Proposition XXXVII: There may, is, and must be in nature, a third substance besides God and finite spirits, called body or matter.

It may seem strange, that in this chain of truths, the proof of the existence of matter is placed as the thirty-seventh proposition: but in the order of just reasoning, all the others must be demonstrated [before] this can be proved. I grant indeed that all this series of reasonings by which we evince the existence of matter is only a proof and not a demonstration. I have remarked from the beginning that demonstration belongs only to necessary, eternal, and immutable truths. Thus we can demonstrate the existence of a God, because it is eternal, immutable, and necessary: but the existence of matter being contingent, mutable, and temporary, it can only be proved; that is, we have all reasons to believe it, none to deny it, and the negation of it reduces to absurdities equally impious and fanatical. Now this is all the proof that can be demanded by reasonable minds, for a matter of fact.

All the use that can be made of the Berkeleyan and Malebranchian reasonings against the existence and activity of bodies, is to confute Materialism, to show that we have a greater certainty of the existence of spirit, than of that of matter, to prove, that, absolutely speaking, we might have the most vivid ideas and sensations of matter, [though] there were no bodies at all; and therefore it is certain, uncontestable, and demonstrated, that a being whose existence is only contingent and possible, cannot be the necessary, eternal, and self-existent substance. Materialism therefore is a poor, weak system without any shadow of reason; whereas Idealism requires a great strength, and vivacity of imagination, a wonderful subtlety of genius, a complication of the most abstract ideas; but at the same time it is not solid; since it is founded upon false consequences drawn from true principles; its fundamental maxim is indemonstrable, and its natural consequences lead us to look upon God as the author of sin, and the immediate, deliberate, voluntary cause of all moral and physical evil. Materialism affirms that there is a necessary relation of cause and effect where it sees none; it confounds identity with union; it supposes that the self-same substance may have contradictory, and incompatible attributes. Idealism denies that there can be a real activity in second causes, because we cannot conceive the manner of their operation; it measures the absolute possibility of things by its own capacity; it denies modifying power in the creatures, for the same reason that Spinoza denies creating power in the God-head.

Both these systems are equally indemonstrable and incapable of solid proofs: but Idealism is far more dangerous than Materialism. The Materialists can only impose upon weak, superficial, wanton imaginations that pretend openly to degrade human nature, and flatter all the passions: but the Idealists have a devout and serious air, an apparent zeal for the rights of the deity, a specious pretense of seeing all things in God, and God in all things, which allures at first virtuous minds; but it hurries them at last into the darkest Atheism, when they reason consequentially, and are not startled at the necessary consequences of the principles laid down. Thus the Malebranchian enthusiasm, and the Berkeleyan fiction end inevitably in Spinozian blasphemy, contrary to the pious intention of their inventors, and thus these three sprouts of the Cartesian philosophy have corrupted, debauched, and perverted some of the greatest and finest Genii of the last age. Wherefore it was with reason that some learned men of all nations contemporary with Descartes declaimed against his system as dangerous, [though] they were unjust to attack his designs as pernicious.

Cor. I.

Hence it is absolutely false that the existence of matter is neither probable, nor possible.

Cor. II.

Hence it is pure Fanaticism to maintain that we can be sure of the existence of matter only by revelation.

Thus we have demonstrated the properties, differences and existence of material and immaterial substances. . . .

FURTHER READINGS

Baldi, Marialuisa. *Verisimili, non vero: filosofia e politica in Andrew Michael Ramsay*. Milan: Franco Angeli, 2002.

Henderson, George. D. *Chevalier Ramsay*. Edinburgh: Thomas Nelson & Sons, 1952.

Popkin, Richard H. "David Hume and the Pyrrhonian Controversy." *Review of Metaphysics* 6 (1952): 65–81. Reprinted in *The High Road to Pyrrhonism*, edited by Richard A. Watson and James E. Force, 133–47. San Diego, CA: Austin Hill, 1980.

26

HUME

D avid Hume (1711–1776) is the most important and influential modern skeptic. He awoke Kant from his dogmatic slumber (see selection of Kant in this volume), was one of the philosophical sources of Kierkegaard's religious views, and may be considered the father of Anglo-American analytic philosophy. Hume developed new and important skeptical arguments. The main one is that our inferences from cause to effect in matters of fact have no rational ground. Although the ancient Pyrrhonians had skeptical tropes dealing with causality, Hume's argument is original and much more influential, although he might have been influenced by Joseph Glanvill, who developed a similar kind of argument in his *Skepsis Scientifica* (1665). Hume was also influenced by previous early modern skeptics. Some interesting philosophical affinities with Montaigne have been pointed out by scholars. He mentions Huet in his *Dialogues concerning Natural Religion*, sympathizes with a version of Academic skepticism that has some common features with the Academic skepticism Simon Foucher aimed to rehabilitate, and was directly influenced by Bayle in a large number of philosophical issues such as his criticism of natural theology, skepticism about reason, and his skepticism about the existence of an external material world, to cite only the main ones. We have selected key sections of the first book of Hume's major work, *A Treatise of Human Nature*, containing Hume's most skeptical texts that carry skepticism into an unanswerable and unbelievable state. We conclude this chapter on Hume with Philo's concluding remarks in the *Dialogue concerning Natural Religion*.

FROM *A TREATISE OF HUMAN NATURE**

1.3.8. . . . Thus all probable reasoning is nothing but a species of sensation. It is not solely in poetry and music, we must follow our taste and sentiment, but likewise in philosophy. When I am convinced of any principle, it is only an idea, which strikes more strongly upon me. When I give the preference to one set of arguments above another, I do nothing but decide from my feeling concerning the superiority of their influence. Objects have no discoverable connection together; nor is it from any other

---

*Editorial notes were omitted.

principle but custom operating upon the imagination, that we can draw any inference from the appearance of one to the existence of another. . . .

1.3.15. According to the precedent doctrine, there are no objects, which by the mere survey, without consulting experience, we can determine to be the causes of any other; and no objects, which we can certainly determine in the same manner not to be the causes. Any thing may produce any thing. Creation, annihilation, motion, reason, volition; all these may arise from one another, or from any other object we can imagine. Nor will this appear strange, if we compare two principles explained above, *that the constant conjunction of objects determines their causation,* and *that properly speaking, no objects are contrary to each other, but existence and nonexistence.* Where objects are not contrary, nothing hinders them from having that constant conjunction, on which the relation of cause and effect totally depends. . . .

1.4.1. In all demonstrative sciences the rules are certain and infallible; but when we apply them, our fallible and uncertain faculties are very apt to depart from them, and fall into error. We must, therefore, in every reasoning form a new judgment, as a check or control on our first judgment or belief; and must enlarge our view to comprehend a kind of history of all the instances, wherein our understanding has deceived us, compared with those, wherein its testimony was just and true. Our reason must be considered as a kind of cause, of which truth is the natural effect; but such-a-one as by the irruption of other causes, and by the inconstancy of our mental powers, may frequently be prevented. By this means all knowledge degenerates into probability; and this probability is greater or less, according to our experience of the veracity or deceitfulness of our understanding, and according to the simplicity or intricacy of the question.

There is no Algebraist nor Mathematician so expert in his science, as to place entire confidence in any truth immediately upon his discovery of it, or regard it as any thing, but a mere probability. Every time he runs over his proofs, his confidence increases; but still more by the approbation of his friends; and is raised to its utmost perfection by the universal assent and applauses of the learned world. Now it is evident, that this gradual increase of assurance is nothing but the addition of new probabilities, and is derived from the constant union of causes and effects, according to past experience and observation.

In accounts of any length or importance, Merchants seldom trust to the infallible certainty of numbers for their security; but by the artificial structure of the accounts, produce a probability beyond what is derived from the skill and experience of the accountant. For that is plainly of itself some degree of probability; though uncertain and variable, according to the degrees of his experience and length of the account. Now as none will maintain, that our assurance in a long numeration exceeds probability, I may safely affirm, that there scarce is any proposition concerning numbers, of which we can have a fuller security. For it is easily possible, by gradually diminishing the numbers, to reduce the longest series of addition to the most simple question, which can be formed, to an addition of two single numbers; and upon this supposition we shall find it impracticable to show the precise limits of knowledge and of probability, or discover that particular number, at which the one ends and the other begins. But knowledge and probability are of such contrary and disagreeing natures, that they cannot well run insensibly into each other, and that because they will not divide, but must be either entirely present, or entirely absent. Besides, if any single addition were certain, every one would be so, and consequently the whole or total sum; unless the whole can be different from all its parts. I had almost said, that this was certain; but I reflect, that it must reduce *itself*, as well as every other reasoning, and from knowledge degenerate into probability.

Since therefore all knowledge resolves itself into probability, and becomes at last of the same nature with that evidence, which we employ in common life, we must now examine this latter species of reasoning, and see on what foundation it stands.

In every judgment, which we can form concerning probability, as well as concerning knowledge, we ought always to correct the first judgment, derived from the nature of the object, by another judgment, derived from the nature of the understanding. It is certain a man of solid sense and long experience ought to have, and usually has, a greater assurance in his opinions, than one that is foolish and ignorant, and that our sentiments have different degrees of authority, even with ourselves, in proportion to the degrees of our reason and experience. In the man of the best sense and longest experience, this authority is never entire; since even such-a-one must be conscious of many errors in the past, and must still dread the like for the future. Here then arises a new species of probability to correct and regulate the first, and fix its just standard and proportion. As demonstration is subject to the control of probability, so is probability liable to a new correction by a reflex act of the mind, wherein the nature of our understanding, and our reasoning from the first probability become our objects.

Having thus found in every probability, beside the original uncertainty inherent in the subject, a new uncertainty derived from the weakness of that faculty, which judges, and having adjusted these two together, we are obliged by our reason to add a new doubt derived from the possibility of error in the estimation we make of the truth and fidelity of our faculties. This is a doubt, which immediately occurs to us, and of which, if we would closely pursue our reason, we cannot avoid giving a decision. But this decision, though it should be favorable to our preceding judgment, being founded only on probability, must weaken still further our first evidence, and must itself be weakened by a fourth doubt of the same kind, and so on *in infinitum*; till at last there remain nothing of the original probability, however great we may suppose it to have been, and however small the diminution by every new uncertainty. No finite object can subsist under a decrease repeated *in infinitum*; and even the vastest quantity, which can enter into human imagination, must in this manner be reduced to nothing. Let our first belief be never so strong, it must infallibly perish by passing through so many new examinations, of which each diminishes somewhat of its force and vigor. When I reflect on the natural fallibility of my judgment, I have less confidence in my opinions, than when I only consider the objects concerning which I reason; and when I proceed still farther, to turn the scrutiny against every successive estimation I make of my faculties, all the rules of logic require a continual diminution, and at last a total extinction of belief and evidence.

Should it here be asked me, whether I sincerely assent to this argument, which I seem to take such pains to inculcate, and whether I be really one of those skeptics, who hold, that all is uncertain, and that our judgment is not in *any* thing possessed of *any* measures of truth and falsehood; I should reply, that this question is entirely superfluous, and that neither I, nor any other person was ever sincerely and constantly of that opinion. Nature, by an absolute and uncontrollable necessity has determined us to judge as well as to breathe and feel; nor can we any more forbear viewing certain objects in a stronger and fuller light, upon account of their customary connection with a present impression, than we can hinder ourselves from thinking as long as we are awake, or seeing the surrounding bodies, when we turn our eyes towards them in broad sunshine. Whoever has taken the pains to refute the cavils of this total skepticism, has really disputed without an antagonist, and endeavored by arguments to establish a faculty, which nature has antecedently implanted in the mind, and rendered unavoidable.

My intention then in displaying so carefully the arguments of that fantastic sect, is only to make the reader sensible of the truth of my hypothesis, *that all our reasonings concerning causes and effects are derived from nothing but custom; and that belief is more properly an act of the sensitive, than of the cogitative part of our natures*. I have here proved, that the very same principles, which make us form a decision upon any subject, and correct that decision by the consideration of our genius and capacity, and of the situation of our mind, when we examined that subject; I say, I have proved, that these same principles, when carried farther and applied to every new reflex judgment, must, by continually diminishing the original evidence, at last reduce it to nothing, and utterly subvert all belief and opinion. If belief, therefore, were a simple act of the thought, without any peculiar manner of conception, or the addition of a force and vivacity, it must infallibly destroy itself, and in every case terminate in a total suspense of judgment. But as experience will sufficiently convince any one, who thinks it worth while to try, that though he can find no error in the foregoing arguments, yet he still continues to believe, and think, and reason as usual, he may safely conclude, that his reasoning and belief is some sensation or peculiar manner of conception, which it is impossible for mere ideas and reflections to destroy.

But here, perhaps, it may be demanded, how it happens even upon my hypothesis, that these arguments above-explained produce not a total suspense of judgment, and after what manner the mind ever retains a degree of assurance in any subject? For as these new probabilities, which by their repetition perpetually diminish the original evidence, are founded on the very same principles, whether of thought or sensation, as the primary judgment, it may seem unavoidable, that in either case they must equally subvert, and by the opposition, either of contrary thoughts or sensations, reduce the mind to a total uncertainty. I suppose, there is some question proposed to me, and that after revolving over the impressions of my memory and senses, and carrying my thoughts from them to such objects, as are commonly conjoined with them, I feel a stronger and more forcible conception of the one side, than on the other. This strong conception forms my first decision. I suppose, that afterwards I examine my judgment itself, and observing from experience, that it is sometimes just and sometimes erroneous, I consider it as regulated by contrary principles or causes, of which some lead to truth and some to error; and in balancing these contrary causes, I diminish by a new probability the assurance of my first decision. This new probability is liable to the same diminution as the foregoing, and so on, *in infinitum*. It is therefore demanded, *how it happens, that even after all we retain a degree of belief, which is sufficient for our purpose, either in philosophy or common life.*

I answer, that after the first and second decision; as the action of the mind becomes forced and unnatural, and the ideas faint and obscure; though the principles of judgment, and the balancing of opposite causes be the same as at the very beginning; yet their influence on the imagination, and the vigor they add to, or diminish from the thought, is by no means equal. Where the mind reaches not its objects with easiness and facility, the same principles have not the same effect as in a more natural conception of the ideas; nor does the imagination feel a sensation, which holds any proportion with that which arises from its common judgment and opinions. The attention is on the stretch: The posture of the mind is uneasy; and the spirits being diverted from their natural course, are not governed in their movements by the same laws, at least not to the same degree, as when they flow in their usual channel.

If we desire similar instances, it will not be very difficult to find them. The present subject of metaphysics will supply us abundantly. The same argument, which would have been esteemed convincing in a reasoning concerning history or politics, has little or no influence in these abstruser subjects, even though it be perfectly comprehended; and that because there is required a study and an effort of thought, in order to its being comprehended: And this effort of thought disturbs the operation of our sentiments, on which the belief depends. The case is the same in other subjects. The straining of the imagination always hinders the regular flowing of the passions and sentiments. A tragic poet, that would represent his heroes as very ingenious and witty in their misfortunes, would never touch the passions. As the emotions of the soul prevent any subtle reasoning and reflection, so these latter actions of the mind are equally prejudicial to the former. The mind, as well as the body, seems to be endowed with a certain precise degree of force and activity, which it never employs in one action, but at the expense of all the rest. This is more evidently true, where the actions are of quite different natures; since in that case the force of the mind is not only diverted, but even the disposition changed, so as to render us incapable of a sudden transition from one action to the other, and still more of performing both at once. No wonder, then, the conviction, which arises from a subtle reasoning, diminishes in proportion to the efforts, which the imagination makes to enter into the reasoning, and to conceive it in all its parts. Belief, being a lively conception, can never be entire, where it is not founded on something natural and easy.

This I take to be the true state of the question and cannot approve of that expeditious way, which some take with the skeptics, to reject at once all their arguments without inquiry or examination. If the skeptical reasonings be strong, say they, it is a proof, that reason may have some force and authority: if weak, they can never be sufficient to invalidate all the conclusions of our understanding. This argument is not just; because the skeptical reasonings, were it possible for them to exist, and were they not destroyed by their subtlety, would be successively both strong and weak, according to the successive dispositions of the mind. Reason first appears in possession of the throne, prescribing laws, and imposing maxims, with an absolute sway and authority. Her enemy, therefore, is obliged to take shelter under her protection, and by making use of rational arguments to prove the fallaciousness and imbecility of reason, produces, in a manner, a patent under her hand and seal. This patent has at first an authority, proportioned to the present and immediate authority of reason, from which it is derived. But as it is supposed to be contradictory to reason, it gradually diminishes the force of that governing power, and its own at the same time; till at last they both vanish away into nothing, by a regular and just diminution. The skeptical and dogmatic reason are of the same kind, though contrary in their operation and tendency; so that where the latter is strong, it has an enemy of equal force in the former to encounter; and as their forces were at first equal, they still continue so, as long as either of them subsists; nor does one of them lose any force in the contest, without taking as much from its antagonist. It is happy, therefore, that nature breaks the force of all skeptical arguments in time, and keeps them from having any considerable influence on the understanding. Were we to trust entirely to their self-destruction, that can never take place, until they have first subverted all conviction, and have totally destroyed human reason.

2.4.2. Thus the skeptic still continues to reason and believe, even though he asserts, that he cannot defend his reason by reason; and by the same rule he must assent to the principle concerning the existence of body, though he cannot pretend by any arguments of philosophy to maintain its veracity. Nature has not left this to his choice, and has doubtless esteemed it an affair of too great importance to be trusted to our uncertain reasonings and speculations. We may well ask, *What causes induce us to believe in the existence of body?* But it is in vain to ask, *Whether there be body or not?* That is a point, which we must take for granted in all our reasonings. . . .

1.4.7. . . . For with what confidence can I venture upon such bold enterprises [to proceed in the accurate anatomy of human nature in books 2 and 3 of the *Treatise*], when beside those numberless infirmities peculiar to myself, I find so many which are common to human nature? Can I be sure, that in leaving all established opinions I am following truth; and by what criterion shall I distinguish her, even if fortune should at last guide me on her foot-steps? After the most accurate and exact of my reasonings, I can give no reason why I should assent to it; and feel nothing but a *strong* propensity to consider objects *strongly* in that view, under which they appear to me. Experience is a principle, which instructs me in the several conjunctions of objects for the past. Habit is another principle, which determines me to expect the same for the future; and both of them conspiring to operate upon the imagination, make me form certain ideas in a more intense and lively manner, than others, which are not attended with the same advantages. Without this quality, by which the mind enlivens some ideas beyond others (which seemingly is so trivial, and so little founded on reason) we could never assent to any argument, nor carry our view beyond those few objects, which are present to our senses. Nay, even to these objects we could never attribute any existence, but what was dependent on the senses; and must comprehend them entirely in that succession of perceptions, which constitutes our self or person. Nay farther, even with relation to that succession, we could only admit of those perceptions, which are immediately present to our consciousness, nor could those lively images, with which the memory presents us be ever received as true pictures of past perceptions. The memory, sense, and understanding are, therefore, all of them founded on the imagination, or the vivacity of our ideas.

No wonder a principle so inconstant and fallacious should lead us into errors, when implicitly followed (as it must be) in all its variations. It is this principle, which makes us reason from causes and effects; and it is the same principle, which convinces us of the continued existence of external objects, when absent from the senses. But though these two operations be equally natural and necessary in the human mind, yet in some circumstances they are directly contrary, nor is it possible for us to reason justly and regularly from causes and effects, and at the same time believe the continued existence of matter. How then shall we adjust those principles together? Which of them shall we prefer? Or in case we prefer neither of them, but successively assent to both, as is usual among philosophers, with what confidence can we afterwards usurp that glorious title, when we thus knowingly embrace a manifest contradiction?

This contradiction would be more excusable, were it compensated by any degree of solidity and satisfaction in the other parts of our reasoning. But the case is quite contrary. When we trace up the human understanding to its first principle, we find it to lead us into such sentiments, as seem to turn into ridicule all our past pains and industry, and to discourage us from future enquiries. Nothing is more curiously enquired after by the mind of man, than the causes of every phenomenon; nor are we content with knowing the immediate causes, but push on our enquiries, until we arrive at the original and ultimate principle. We would not willingly stop before we are acquainted with that energy in the cause, by which it operates on its effect; that tie, which connects them together; and that efficacious quality, on which the tie depends. This is our aim in all our studies and reflections: And how must we be disappointed, when we learn, that this connection, tie, or energy lies merely in ourselves, and is nothing but that determination of the mind, which is acquired by custom, and causes us to make a transition from an object to its usual attendant, and from the impression of one to the lively idea of the other? Such a discovery not only cuts off all hope of ever attaining satisfaction, but even prevents our very wishes; since it appears, that when we say we desire to know the ultimate and operating principle, as something which resides in the external object, we either contradict ourselves or talk without a meaning.

This deficiency in our ideas is not, indeed, perceived in common life, nor are we sensible, that in the most usual conjunctions of cause and effect we are as ignorant of the ultimate principle which binds them together, as in the most unusual and extraordinary. But this proceeds merely from an illusion of the imagination; and the question is, how far we ought to yield to these illusions. This question is very difficult and reduces us to a very dangerous dilemma, whichever way we answer it. For if we assent to every trivial suggestion of the fancy; beside that these suggestions are often contrary to each other; they lead us into such errors, absurdities, and obscurities, that we must at last become ashamed of our credulity. Nothing is more dangerous to reason, than the flights of the imagination, and nothing has been the occasion of more mistakes among philosophers. Men of bright fancies may in this respect be compared to those angels, whom the scripture represents as covering their eyes with their wings. This has already appeared in so many instances, that we may spare ourselves the trouble of enlarging upon it any farther.

But on the other hand, if the consideration of these instances makes us take a resolution to reject all the trivial suggestions of the fancy, and adhere to the understanding, that is, to the general and more established properties of the imagination; even this resolution, if steadily executed, would be dangerous and attended with the most fatal consequences. For I have already shown, that the understanding, when it acts alone, and according to its most general principles, entirely subverts itself, and leaves not the lowest degree of evidence in any proposition, either in philosophy or common life. We save ourselves from this total skepticism only by means of that singular and seemingly trivial property of the fancy, by which we enter with difficulty into remote views of things, and are not able to accompany them with so sensible an impression, as we do those which are more easy and natural. Shall we, then, establish it for a general maxim, that no refined or elaborate reasoning is ever to be received? Consider well the consequences of such a principle. By this means you cut off entirely all science and philosophy: You proceed upon one singular quality of the imagination, and by a parity of reason must embrace all of them: And you expressly contradict yourself; since this maxim must be built on the preceding reasoning, which will be allowed to be sufficiently refined and metaphysical. What party, then, shall we choose among these difficulties? If we embrace this principle, and condemn all refined reasoning, we run into the most manifest absurdities. If we reject it in favor of these reasonings, we subvert entirely the human understanding. We have, therefore, no choice left but betwixt a false reason and none at all. For my part, I know not what ought to be done in the present case. I can only observe what is commonly done; which is, that this difficulty is seldom or never thought of; and even where it has once been present to the mind, is quickly forgot, and leaves but a small impression behind it. Very refined reflections have little or no influence upon us; and yet we do not, and cannot establish it for a rule, that they ought not to have any influence; which implies a manifest contradiction.

But what have I here said, that reflections very refined and metaphysical have little or no influence upon us? This opinion I can scarce forbear retracting, and condemning from my present feeling and experience. The *intense* view of these manifold contradictions and imperfections in human reason has so wrought upon me, and heated my brain, that I am ready to reject all belief and reasoning, and can look upon no opinion even as more probable or likely than another. Where am I, or what? From what causes do I derive my existence, and to what condition shall I return? Whose favor shall I court, and whose anger must I dread? What beings surround me? And on whom have I any influence, or who have any influence on me? I am confounded with all these questions, and begin to fancy myself in the most deplorable condition imaginable, environed with the deepest darkness and utterly deprived of the use of every member and faculty.

Most fortunately it happens, that since reason is incapable of dispelling these clouds, nature herself suffices to that purpose, and cures me of this philosophical melancholy and delirium, either by relaxing this bent of mind, or by some avocation and lively impression of my sense, which obliterate all these chimeras. I dine, I play a game of backgammon, I converse, and am merry with my friends; and when after three or four hours' amusement, I would return to these speculations, they appear so cold, and strained, and ridiculous, that I cannot find in my heart to enter into them any farther.

Here then I find myself absolutely and necessarily determined to live, and talk, and act like other people in the common affairs of life. But notwithstanding that my natural propensity, and the course of my animal spirits and passions reduce me to this indolent belief in the general maxims of the world, I still feel such remains of my former disposition, that I am ready to throw all my books and papers into the fire and resolve never more to renounce the pleasures of life for the sake of reasoning and philosophy. For those are my sentiments in that splenetic humor, which governs me at present. I may, nay I must yield to the current of nature, in submitting to my senses and understanding; and in this blind submission I show most perfectly my skeptical disposition and principles. But does it follow, that I must strive against the current of nature, which leads me to indolence and pleasure; that I must seclude myself, in some measure, from the commerce and society of men, which is so agreeable; and that I must torture my brain with subtleties and sophistries, at the very time that I cannot satisfy myself concerning the reasonableness of so painful an application, nor have any tolerable prospect of arriving by its means at truth and certainty. Under what obligation do I lie of making such an abuse of time? And to what end can I serve either for the service of mankind, or for my own private interest? No: If I must be a fool, as all those who reason or believe any thing *certainly* are, my follies shall at least be natural and agreeable. Where I strive against my inclination, I shall have a good reason for my resistance; and will no more be led a wandering into such dreary solitudes, and rough passages, as I have hitherto met with.

These are the sentiments of my spleen and indolence; and indeed I must confess, that philosophy has nothing to oppose to them and expects a victory more from the returns of a serious good-humored disposition, than from the force of reason and conviction. In all the incidents of life we ought still to preserve our skepticism. If we believe, that fire warms or water refreshes, it is only because it costs us too much pains to think otherwise. Nay if we are philosophers, it ought only to be upon skeptical principles, and from an inclination, which we feel to the employing ourselves after that manner. Where reason is lively, and mixes itself with some propensity, it ought to be assented to. Where it does not, it never can have any title to operate upon us.

At the time, therefore, that I am tired with amusement and company, and have indulged a *reverie* in my chamber, or in a solitary walk by a riverside, I feel my mind all collected within itself, and am naturally *inclined* to carry my view into all those subjects about which I have met with so many disputes in the course of my reading and conversation. I cannot forbear having a curiosity to be acquainted with the principles of moral good and evil, the nature and foundation of government, and the cause of those several passions and inclinations, which actuate and govern me. I am uneasy to think I approve of one object, and disapprove of another; call one thing beautiful, and another deformed; decide concerning truth and falsehood, reason and folly, without knowing upon what principles I proceed. I am concerned for the condition of the learned world, which lies under such a deplorable ignorance in all these particulars. I feel an ambition to arise in me of contributing to the instruction of mankind, and of acquiring a name by my inventions and discoveries. These sentiments spring up naturally in my present disposition; and should I endeavor to banish them by attaching myself to any other business or diversion, I *feel* I should be a loser in point of pleasure; and this is the origin of my philosophy.

But even suppose this curiosity and ambition should not transport me into speculations without the sphere of common life, it would necessarily happen, that from my very weakness I must be led into such enquiries. It is certain, that superstition is much more bold in its systems and hypotheses than philosophy; and while the latter contents itself with assigning new causes and principles to the phenomena, which appear in the visible world, the former opens a world of its own, and presents us with scenes, and beings, and objects, which are altogether new. Since therefore it is almost impossible for the mind of man to rest, like those of beasts, in that narrow circle of objects, which are the subject of daily conversation and action, we ought only to deliberate concerning the choice of our guide, and ought to prefer that which is safest and most agreeable. And in this respect I make bold to recommend philosophy and shall not scruple to give it the preference to superstition of every kind or denomination. For as superstition arises naturally and easily from the popular opinions of mankind, it seizes more strongly on the mind and is often able to disturb us in the conduct of our lives and actions. Philosophy on the contrary, if just, can present us only with mild and moderate sentiments; and if false and extravagant, its opinions are merely the objects of a cold and general speculation, and seldom go so far as to interrupt the course of our natural propensities. The Cynics are an extraordinary instance of philosophers, who from reasonings purely philosophical ran into as great extravagancies of conduct as any *Monk* or *Dervish* that ever was in the world. Generally speaking, the errors in religion are dangerous; those in philosophy only ridiculous.

I am sensible, that these two cases of the strength and weakness of the mind will not comprehend all mankind, and that there are in *England*, in particular, many honest gentlemen, who being always employed in their domestic affairs, or amusing themselves in common recreations, have carried their thoughts very little beyond those objects, which are every day exposed to their senses. And indeed, of such as these I pretend not to make philosophers, nor do I expect them either to be associates in these researches or auditors of these discoveries. They do well to keep themselves in their present situation; and instead of refining them into philosophers, I wish we could communicate to our founder of systems a share of this gross earthy mixture as an ingredient, which they commonly stand much in need of, and which would serve to temper those fiery particles, of which they are composed. While a warm imagination is allowed to enter into philosophy, and hypotheses embraced merely for being specious and agreeable, we can never have any steady principles, nor any sentiments, which will suit with common practice and experience. But were these hypotheses once removed, we might hope to establish a system or set of opinions, which if not true (for that, perhaps, is too much to be hoped for) might at least be satisfactory to the human mind, and might stand the test of the most critical examination. Nor should we despair of attaining this end, because of the many chimerical systems, which have successively arisen and decayed away among men, would we consider the shortness of that period, wherein these questions have been the subjects of enquiry and reasoning. Two thousand years with such long interruptions, and under such mighty discouragements are a small space of time to give any tolerable perfection to the sciences; and perhaps we are still too early an age of the world to discover any principles, which will bear the examination of the latest posterity. For my part, my only hope is, that I may contribute a little to the advancement of knowledge, by giving in some particulars a different turn to the speculations of philosophers, and pointing out to them more distinctly those subjects, where alone they can expect assurance and conviction. Human Nature is the only science of man; and yet has been hitherto the most neglected. It will be sufficient for me, if I can bring it a little more into fashion; and the hope of this serves to compose my temper from that spleen, and invigorate it from that indolence, which sometimes prevail upon me. If the reader finds himself in the same easy disposition, let him follow me in my future speculations. If not, let him follow his inclination, and wait the returns of application and good humor. The conduct of a man, who studies philosophy in this careless manner, is more truly skeptical than that of one, who feeling in himself an inclination to it, is yet so overwhelmed with doubts and scruples, as totally to reject it. A true skeptic will be diffident of his philosophical doubts, as well as of his philosophical conviction; and will never refuse any innocent satisfaction, which offers itself, upon account of either of them.

Nor is it only proper we should in general indulge our inclination in the most elaborate philosophical researches, notwithstanding our skeptical principles, but also that we should yield to that propensity, which inclines us to be positive and certain in *particular points*, according to the light, in which we survey them in any *par-*

ticular instant. It is easier to forbear all examination and enquiry, than to check ourselves in so natural a propensity, and guard against that assurance, which always
arises from an exact and full survey of an object. On such an occasion we are apt not
only to forget our skepticism, but even our modesty too; and make use of such terms
as these, *it is evident, it is certain, it is undeniable*; which a due deference to the
public ought, perhaps, to prevent. I may have fallen into this fault after the example
of others; but I here enter a *caveat* against any objections, which may be offered on
that head; and declare that such expressions were extorted from me by the present
view of the object, and imply no dogmatic spirit, nor conceited idea of my own judgment, which are sentiments that I am sensible can become no body, and a skeptic
still less than any other.

FROM *DIALOGUES CONCERNING NATURAL RELIGION*

It seems evident that the dispute between the skeptics and dogmatists is entirely
verbal, or, at least, regards only the degrees of doubt and assurance which we ought
to indulge with regard to all reasoning: and such disputes are commonly, at the
bottom, verbal and admit not of any precise determination. No philosophical dogmatist denies that there are difficulties both with regard to the senses and to all science, and that these difficulties are, in a regular, logical method, absolutely insolv-
able. No skeptic denies that we lie under an absolute necessity, notwithstanding
these difficulties, of thinking, and believing, and reasoning, with regard to all kinds
of subject, and even of frequently assenting with confidence and security. The only
difference, then, between these sects, if they merit that name, is that the skeptic,
from habit, caprice, or inclination, insists most on the difficulties; the dogmatist, for
like reasons, on the necessity.

[Philo's concluding speech]
    If the whole of natural theology, as some people seem to maintain, resolves
itself into one simple, though somewhat ambiguous, at least undefined, proposition,
*That the cause or causes of order in the universe probably bear some remote
analogy to human intelligence*: If this proposition be not capable of extension, vari-
ation, or more particular explication: If it affords no inference that affects human
life, or can be the source of any action or forbearance: And if the analogy, imperfect
as it is, can be carried no further than to the human intelligence, and cannot be trans-
ferred, with any appearance of probability, to the other qualities of the mind: If this
really be the case, what can the most inquisitive, contemplative, and religious man
do more than give a plain, philosophical assent to the proposition, as often as it
occurs, and believe that the arguments on which it is established exceed the objections which lie against it? Some astonishment, indeed, will naturally arise from the
greatness of the object: Some melancholy from its obscurity: Some contempt of
human reason that it can give no solution more satisfactory with regard to so extra-

ordinary and magnificent a question. But believe me, *Cleanthes*, the most natural sentiment which a well-disposed mind will feel on this occasion is a longing desire and expectation that heaven would be pleased to dissipate, at least alleviate, this profound ignorance by affording some more particular revelation to mankind, and making discoveries of the nature, attributes, and operations of the divine object of our faith. A person, seasoned with a just sense of the imperfections of natural reason, will fly to revealed truth with the greatest avidity: While the haughty dogmatist, persuaded that he can erect a complete system of theology by the mere help of philosophy, disdains any further aid and rejects this adventitious instructor. To be a philosophical skeptic is, in a man of letters, the first and most essential step towards being a sound, believing *Christian*—a proposition which I would willingly recommend to the attention of *Pamphilus*; and I hope *Cleanthes* will forgive me for interposing so far in the education and instruction of his pupil.

FURTHER READINGS

Brahami, Frédéric. *Le travail du scepticisme: Montaigne, Bayle, Hume*. Paris: Presses Universitaires de France, 2001.

Fogelin, Robert J. *Hume's Skepticism in the* Treatise of Human Nature. London: Routledge, 1985.

Groarke, Leo, and Graham Solomon. "Some Sources for Hume's Account of Cause." *Journal of the History of Ideas* 52 (1991): 645–63.

Laursen, John Christian. *The Politics of Skepticism in the Ancients, Montaigne, Hume and Kant*. Leiden: J. Brill, 1992.

Maia Neto, José R. "Academic Skepticism in Early Modern Philosophy." *Journal of the History of Ideas* 58, no. 2 (1997): 199–220.

———. "Hume and Pascal: Pyrrhonism vs Nature." *Hume Studies* 17, no. 1 (1991): 41–49.

Norton, David F. *David Hume: Common-Sense Moralist, Skeptical Metaphysician*. Princeton, NJ: Princeton University Press, 1982.

Paganini, Gianni. "Hume, Bayle et les *Dialogues concerning natural religion*." In *Pierre Bayle dans la République des Lettres: Philosophie, Religion, Critique*, edited by Antony McKenna and Gianni Paganini, 527–67. Paris: Honoré Champion, 2004.

Popkin, Richard H. "David Hume: His Pyrrhonism and His Critique of Pyrrhonism." *Philosophical Quarterly* 1 (1951): 385–407.

———. "Joseph Glanvill: A Precursor of David Hume." *Journal of the History of Ideas* 14 (1953): 292–303. Reprinted in *The High Road to Pyrrhonism*, edited by Richard A. Watson and James E. Force, 181–95. San Diego, CA: Austin Hill, 1980.

———. "Sources of Knowledge of Sextus Empiricus in Hume's Time." *Journal of the History of Ideas* 54 (1993): 137–41.

Smith, Norman Kemp. *The Philosophy of David Hume: A Critical Study of Its Origins and Central Doctrines*. London: Macmillan, 1941.

Stroud, Barry. *Hume*. London: Routledge, 1977.

Wright, John P. *The Skeptical Realism of David Hume*. Minneapolis: University of Minnesota Press, 1983.

27

VOLTAIRE

François-Marie Arouet (known as Voltaire, 1694–1778) was a leading and most largely known figure of the French Enlightenment. He spent some time in England, where he was influenced by British empirical philosophy from Bacon to Newton and Locke. Like other French Enlightenment philosophers such as Diderot, Voltaire combined the skeptical side of Locke's views with Gassendi's *via media* between skepticism and dogmatism. He accepted Locke's view that there is no scientific knowledge that cannot possibly be false and that we can have no knowledge of the real nature of substances, material or spiritual. Along with this kind of skepticism, Voltaire—like Diderot—developed positive views about knowing enough scientifically to understand the physical world and to improve human life. In the selection below from the article "Soul" of the *Philosophical Dictionary*, Voltaire attacks Aristotelian and above all Cartesian dogmatism about knowledge of the soul. He points out philosophical *diaphonia* on the subject and employs Gassendian and Lockean empiricist skeptical arguments about the possibility of knowing the nature of the soul. The article makes clear that Voltaire's skepticism is not limited to knowledge of spiritual substances. Following Gassendi and Locke, Voltaire holds that the nature or essence of any existing thing lies beyond the scope of human knowledge. The article also exemplifies Voltaire's religious skepticism. He attempts to show that Judeo-Christianity does not exhibit, nor give any support to, philosophical speculations about the nature of the soul. Besides Gassendi, another French philosopher closely related to the skeptical tradition who Voltaire greatly admired is Bayle. Bayle's *Historical and Critical Dictionary* is Voltaire's main model for his *Philosophical Dictionary*.

"SOUL" FROM THE *PHILOSOPHICAL DICTIONARY*

Âme • Soul

It would be a fine thing to see our soul. *Know thyself* is an excellent precept, but it remains for God alone to put it into practice: who but he alone can know his own essence?

We call soul that which animates. Since our intelligence is limited, we know hardly anything more about the subject. Three-fourths of mankind go no further and don't worry about this thinking being; the other fourth look for it; no one has found it or will find it.

Poor pedant, you see a plant that vegetates, and you say *vegetation*, or even *vegetative soul*. You notice that bodies have and produce motion, and you say *force*; you see your hunting dog learn his craft from you, and you exclaim *instinct, sensitive soul*; you have complex ideas, and you say *spirit*.

But, please, what do you understand by these words? This flower vegetates, but is there any real being called *vegetation*? This body pushes another, but does it possess within itself a distinct being called *force*? This dog brings you a partridge, but is there a being called *instinct*? Wouldn't you laugh at a logician (had he been teacher to Alexander) who told you: "All animals live, therefore there is in them a being, a substantial form, which is life"?

If a tulip could talk and were to tell you: "My vegetation and I are two beings evidently joined together," wouldn't you laugh at the tulip?

Let's see first of all what you know and what you are sure of: that you walk with your feet, that you digest with your stomach, that you feel with your whole body, and that you think with your head. Let's see if your reason could have given you enough insight by itself to conclude, without supernatural aid, that you have a soul. . . .

What, then, do you call your soul? What notion do you have of it? You cannot by yourself, without revelation, admit of anything more within you than a power of feeling, of thinking, unknown to you. . . .

Here is this soul of thought, which has the ascendancy over the animal soul on a thousand occasions. The thinking soul commands its hands to take, and they take. But it does not tell its heart to beat, its blood to flow, its chyle to form; all this is done without it. Here are two souls deeply enmeshed, and hardly master in their own house.

Now, this animal soul certainly does not exist; it is nothing more than the movement of our organs. Take care, O man! Your feeble reason may have no more proof that the other soul exists. You cannot know it except through faith. You are born, you live, you act, you think, you wake, you sleep, without knowing how. . . .

Let's look at the fine systems about souls your philosophy has fabricated.

One says that the soul of man is part of the substance of God himself; another, that it is part of the great whole; a third, that it is created from all eternity; a fourth, that it is made, and not created; others assert that God makes souls as they are needed, and that they arrive at the moment of copulation. . . .

Nor have there been fewer systems about the manner in which this soul will feel when it has left the body it feels with; how it will hear without ears, smell without a nose, and touch without hands; . . . by what contrivance a soul, whose leg was cut off in Europe and which lost an arm in America, will recover this leg and this arm, which will have passed into the blood of some other animal after being transformed into vegetables. . . .

What is quite remarkable is that the laws of God's people don't say one word about the spirituality and immortality of the soul: nothing in the Decalogue, nothing in Leviticus, or in Deuteronomy.

It is quite certain, it is beyond doubt, that Moses nowhere offers the Jews rewards and punishments in another life. . . .

He told them before he died, in his Deuteronomy:

"When you beget children and children's children, and have grown old in the land, if you act corruptly, you will soon utterly perish from the land; and you will be left few in number among the nations where the Lord will drive you."

"I the Lord your God am a jealous God, visiting the iniquity of the fathers upon the children to the third and fourth generation."

"Honor your father and your mother, that your days may be prolonged."

"You shall eat and be full."

"If you serve other gods and worship them, you will perish quickly. . . ."

It is evident that in all these promises and all these treats there is nothing but the temporal, and that we don't find a word about the immortality of the soul or the future life. . . .

It appears that it was not until after the founding of Alexandria that the Jews split into three sects: The Pharisees, the Sadducees, and the Essenes. The historian Josephus, who was a Pharisee, informs us in book XIII of his *Antiquities* that the Pharisees believed in metempsychosis; the Sadducees believed that the soul perishes with the body; the Essenes, Josephus continues, held that souls were immortal. According to them, souls descended into bodies in aerial form from the highest region of the air; they were carried back there by a violent attraction, and after death those which had belonged to good men dwelt beyond the Ocean, in a country where there was neither heat nor cold, neither wind nor rain. The souls of the wicked passed into the opposite kind of climate. This was the theology of the Jews.

He who alone was to instruct all men, came and condemned these three sects; without him we should never have known anything about our soul, since the philosophers never had a settled idea of it, while Moses, the world's only true lawgiver before our own, Moses, who spoke with God face to face, left men in profound ignorance on this great matter. It is, then, only for seventeen hundred years that we have been certain of the existence and immortality of the soul.

Cicero had nothing but doubts; his grandson and granddaughter might have learned the truth from the first Galileans who came to Rome.

But before that time, and since then, in all the rest of the world where the apostles did not penetrate, everyone must have said to his soul: "What are you? Where do you come from? What are you doing? Whither do you go? You are I know not what; you think and feel, and were you to feel and think for a hundred thousand million years, you would never know any more about it by your own intelligence, without the assistance of a God."

O man! God has given you understanding to conduct yourself well, and not to penetrate into the essence of the things he has created.

This is what Locke thought, and before Locke, Gassendi, and before Gassendi, a multitude of sages; but we have bachelors of arts who know everything those great men didn't know.

Cruel enemies of reason have dared to rise up against these truths acknowledged by all the sages. They have carried bad faith and impudence so far as to charge the authors of this Dictionary with affirming that the soul is matter. You know perfectly well that at the bottom of page 64, there are these very words against Epicurus, Democritus, and Lucretius: "My friend, how does an atom think? Acknowledge that you know nothing about it." Obviously, then, you are slanderers.

FURTHER READINGS

Haag, Éliane M. "Diderot et Voltaire lecteurs de Montaigne: du jugement suspendu à la raison libre." *Revue de Métaphysique et de Morale* 3 (1997): 365–83.

Mason, Haydn. "Voltaire devant Bayle." In *Pierre Bayle dans la République des Lettres: Philosophie, religion, critique*, edited by Antony McKenna and Gianni Paganini, 443–56. Paris: Honoré Champion, 2004.

Popkin, Richard H. "New Views on the Role of Scepticism in the Enlightenment." *Modern Language Quarterly* 53 (1992): 279–97. Reprinted in *Scepticism in the Enlightenment*, edited by Richard H. Popkin, Ezequiel de Olaso, and Giorgio Tonelli, 157–72. Dordrecht: Kluwer, 1997.

Tonelli, Giorgio. "The Weakness of Reason in the Age of Enlightenment." *Diderot Studies* 14 (1971): 217–44. Reprinted in Popkin, Olaso, and Tonelli, *Scepticism in the Enlightenment*, pp. 35–50.

28

DIDEROT

D enis Diderot (1713–1784) is most known for the *Encyclopedia of the Sciences, Arts and Crafts*, a collective work to which he contributed the majority of articles, including the one on skepticism partially included in this anthology. There are two articles in the *Encyclopedia* on skepticism/Pyrrhonism. The article "Skepticism," the shorter one, examines the issue whether there are real differences between Pyrrhonism and the New Academy, basically citing Sextus's view that there are but concluding that they are insignificant. The other article, "Pyrrhonian or Skeptic Philosophy," from which we have extracted what follows, is much longer. The article contains a history of skepticism from antiquity to Bayle. Diderot follows the schema and the historical data given by Jacob Brucker's (1686–1770) *Historia critica philosophiae*. However, Diderot's philosophical evaluation of the skeptical philosophers is his own. We have italicized the parts of the article that were censored by the publisher of the *Encyclopedia*, Le Breton, and which are given in footnotes in the edition of Diderot's works by John Lough and Jacques Proust. As the article "Skeptic or Pyrrhonian" of the *Encyclopedia* included in this anthology and the bibliographical elements indicated below attest, Diderot's own philosophical views were quite influenced by skepticism.

FROM *ENCYCLOPÉDIE* IN *OEUVRES COMPLETES**

PYRRHONIAN or SKEPTIC Philosophy (History of Philosophy). The Greeks were fatigued by the great number of disputes concerning the true and the false, good and bad, beautiful and ugly, when there arose among them a sect that in a short time acquired many proselytes. This was the Pyrrhonian or skeptic sect. Other schools have a received system of avowed principles for proving everything and doubting nothing. The Pyrrhonians follow a totally opposite method. They maintain that nothing is either demonstrated or demonstrable; that "real science" or "true knowledge" is only an empty phrase; that those who claim to have such knowledge are

---

*Translated by Richard A. Watson, except for the censored passages of the article, published in footnotes in the French critical edition and which we reproduce here in italics, translated by Nelly S. Hoyt and Thomas Cassirer.

either ignorant, vain, or liars; that all things about which a philosopher could examine are, however his efforts, hidden under the thickest darkness; that the more one studies the less one knows; and that we are condemned to float eternally in a sea of uncertainties and mere opinions without ever finding a fixed point on which we could stand, depart from, and return to. Therefore the skeptics conclude that it is ridiculous to give definitions; that nothing is certain; that a wise man will suspend his judgment about everything; that he will never be lured by the chimera of truth; that he regulates his life on the basis of probabilities, thus showing by his circumspection that even if the nature of things is no more clear to him than it is to the most determined dogmatists, at least he knows better than they do the feebleness of human reason. . . .

When the skeptic establishes distinctions between things good and bad, just and unjust, he is conforming to common usage, whereas the dogmatist believes that he is conforming to evidence and reason.

The skeptic is without passion relative to certain things, and is very moderate in his passion relative to other things. Everything is a matter of convention for him. He knows that what is good for him at a given time is at the same time bad for someone else, and in the following moment will be bad for him; that what is esteemed as honest or dishonest in Athens or Rome is elsewhere deemed indifferent. Whatever he sees or hears, and whatever anyone does, he remains unmoved and everything appears to him equally good, bad, or indifferent.

But if goodness and badness are nothing in themselves, then there remains no rules or principles either for manners and morals or for life.

Virtue is a habit, and one does not know what is only a habit either in itself nor by its effects.

For the skeptic, the words 'arts' and 'sciences' are void of sense. Even so, he asserts these paradoxes only to detach himself from things; to drive away the troubles of his soul; to reduce what surrounds him to its appropriate value; to fear, to desire, admire, praise, and blame nothing; to be happy; and to make the dogmatist sense his poverty and his rashness.

Thus one can see that doubt has conducted the skeptic to the same conclusion that the Stoic reaches by necessity.

These skeptical philosophers have rendered a very important service to philosophy by discovering the real sources of errors, and by marking the limits of our understanding.

Given the results of their school, one should be very circumspect in making pronouncements about those things one believes one understands the best.

The skeptical doctrine indicates those things concerning which we are in darkness and that we will never know.

It tends to make men tolerant of others, and temperate concerning all impetuosity of the passions.

The conclusion from all this is that in the use of reason, there is a kind of sobriety from which one cannot part without harm.

It was not possible for a sect that shakes all principles, that says that vice and virtue are words void of ideas, and that nothing in itself is true or false, good or bad, right or wrong, just or unjust, honest or dishonest, to make any great progress among any people on earth. However finely the skeptic protests that he has one way of making judgments in the School and another in society, it is certain that his doctrines tend to degrade all that is most sacred among men. Our opinions have too immediate an influence on our actions for one to be able to treat skepticism with indifference. This philosophy promptly came to a stop in Athens, and it made little progress in Rome. . . . From time to time, however, some skeptics appeared.

Claude Ptolemy was called a skeptic. It is certain that he made little enough of reason and the light of understanding. Corneille Celse had too varied and superficial an erudition to be dogmatic. We will say nothing of Sextus Empiricus: Who does not know his *Hypotyposes*? Sextus Empiricus was an African. He wrote at the beginning of the third century. He had Saturninus as a disciple, and Théodore Tripolite as a follower. The skeptic Uranus appeared under the reign of Justinian.

Skepticism languished then until 1562, when the Portuguese François Sanchez published *De multium nobili & prima universali scientia quod nihil scitur*. This was Sanchez's clever way of attacking Aristotelianism without compromising himself. Sanchez did this by criticizing all the errors that reigned in his time. Jérôme Hirnhaym extended the attack to all human knowledge as shown by the title of his work *De Tvpho generis humani, sive scientiarum humanarum inani ac ventoso humore, difficultate, labilitate, falsitate, jacantia, presumptione, incommodis & periculis tractatus brevis, in quos etiam vera sapienta a falsa discernitur, & simplicitas mundo contempta extollitur, idiotis in solatium, doctis in cautelam conscriptus*. Hirnhaym was a Canon of the Prémontré Order, and Abbé of Strahow in Bohemia. This pious skeptic pushed doubt as far as it could go. For him, no axiom of philosophy is infallible. He opposed theology to philosophy, revelation to reason, creation to the axiom *ex nihilo nihil fit*, the Eucharist to the axiom that it is impossible for the same body to be in several places at the same time, and the Trinity to the axiom that one plus one make two, and two plus one make three. According to him, the apostles who lived with Jesus Christ, who saw, heard, and touched him, and with whom they had eaten, are sure of these facts only by faith, and not by witness of their senses that were capable of deceiving them. He related everything to the infallibility of the Church. An honest man can perceive only the proposition that the Church is infallible, and could never acquire evidence that he refuses to such propositions as that it is impossible for something to be and not be at the same time, the whole is greater than a part, and others that he opposed in good faith.

The Pyrrhonian François La Mothe Le Vayer was born in Paris in 1586 and is the French Plutarch. He read and reflected very much. He is a skeptic in his *Horatius Tuberon* and a cynic in his *Hexameron rustique*. Free in his writings and severe in his morals, he is an example to counter those who hasten to judge of men's actions by their discourse.

Pierre-Daniel Huet followed in the steps of La Mothe Le Vayer, and is a very strong scourge against reason.

Huet was born in Caen in 1630. He was one of the most learned that we have: literature, philosophy, mathematics, astronomy, poetry, Hebraic languages, Greek, Latin, erudition—he was nearly equally familiar with all branches of knowledge. He had close relations with most of the great men of his century: Petau, Labbe, Cossart, Bochart, Vavasseur, and Rapin. He had an early inclination toward skepticism because he took as a measure of the extent of the human mind the force of his own mind that he often found inadequate to the difficulties of the questions. In this he was unjust to very few men, and he concluded that we are not destined to know the truth. From day to day this secret presumption fortified itself within him, and he perhaps knew that he was a skeptic only at the moment when he wrote his work on the weakness of the human understanding. One arrives at Pyrrhonism by two opposed ways, either because one does not know enough or because one knows too much. Huet followed the second way, which is not the most common.

Since the time of Huet, theologians seem to have been conspiring to discredit the use of reason. Do they not realize how difficult most of the questions are that pertain to the experience of God, the immortality of the soul, the need of ritual, the truth of the Christian religion? Do they desire a belief that is blind or one that is enlightened? If it is the former, let them admit it in good faith. If it is the latter, let them convince us, by all kinds of measures, of the feebleness of our mind. The way they are going about it, they will produce more skeptics than Christians. Is it not an astonishing paradox that it is precisely those men who are supposed to acquaint us with the most profound and most thorny questions, who also preach that our reason is weak. Should they succeed in convincing us that the instrument nature gave us stands in no relation to the weight we have to move, what conclusion could we draw from this. If God exists, would it not be simpler to do nothing and entrust oneself to his goodness; surely He would not punish us for having been ignorant of something that, according to his own ministers, we could not possibly know? What folly it is to claim that one can set up the authority of tradition against that of reason, as if the authenticity of tradition did not have to be examined in the light of reason. And what guarantee will I have that I did not commit an error, once my confidence in natural reason was destroyed?

But among the followers of Pyrrhonism, we have forgotten Michel de Montaigne, the author of essays that will be read as long as there are men who love truth, strength, and simplicity. Montaigne's work is the touchstone of a good soul. Whoever is displeased in reading Montaigne has some flaw in his heart or understanding. There is nearly no question that Montaigne has not examined for and against, always in the same persuasive manner. The contradictions in his work are faithful images of the contradictions in the human understanding. He follows without artifice the chain of his ideas. It is of little importance to him where he begins, how he goes, or where he ends. What he says is what strikes him at the moment. He is neither more restrained nor more loose in his writing than he is in his thinking or dreaming. It is impossible for a man who thinks or dreams to be entirely unrestrained. It is only a subtle appearance that one stops and begins again without a cause. There is a necessary connection between any two thoughts, even the most disparate. This liaison is either in sensation, in words, in memory, either within or outside a man. It is a rule to which even madmen are subject even in their greatest disorders of reason. If we have the complete history of all that has passed within them, we will see that everything there is drawn together as much as in the most wise and sensible man. Although nothing is so varied as the suite of objects that present themselves to Montaigne, and although they seem to be introduced by hazard, they are all related in one way or another. And although it is a great distance from the subject of public coaches to the oration the Mexicans addressed to Europeans when they first set foot in the new world, nevertheless one travels from Bordeaux to Cusco without interruption, although in truth by way of rather long detours. Once we are underway, the road shows itself under all sorts of faces, now good, then depraved, compassionate, vain, incredulous, superstitious. After having written forcefully against the truth of miracles, Montaigne presents a defense of the soothsayers. But whatever he says, he interests and instructs. But neither ancient nor modern skepticism has a more formidable champion than Bayle.

Bayle was born in 1647. Nature gave him imagination, power, subtlety, and memory, and education contributed to the emergence of these natural qualities. He learned Greek and Latin. He early applied himself almost without relief to all sorts of reading and studies. His favorite authors were Plutarch and Montaigne. From them he acquired the germ of Pyrrhonism that later developed in him in such a surprising way. He was occupied with its dialectic before he was twenty. When he was still young he made the acquaintance of an ecclesiastic who, profiting from the uncertainties in which Bayle was immersed, preached to him the necessity of depending upon some authority to decide for us, and he convinced Bayle to abjure publicly the religion he had received from his parents *and made him expose his parents to shame and grief by abjuring [having him abjure] publicly the religion he had received from them [of his parents].* He had barely taken this step when the spirit of proselytizing took possession of him. Bayle, who raged against the converters, became one, and the fact that his brothers, parents, and friends were not inspired by the sentiments he had adopted did not decrease his ardor. But his brother, a man who was not without merit and who was a reformed minister, led him back to the cult of his family. Catholicism offered nothing with which he could afflict himself, nor Protestantism anything to make him glory in his return. It did not take Bayle long to realize the vanity of most religious systems, and he attacked them all under the pretext of defending the one he had embraced. His time in France had exposed him to persecutions, so he returned to Geneva. There he followed his first abjuration with a second: He quit Aristotelianism for Cartesianism, but with as little attachment to the doctrines of the one as to those of the other because subsequently he opposed the sentiments of all the philosophers and attacked them all equally. We cannot suppress our regret for the time he lost to the two educations he successively undertook. His time as professor of philosophy at Sedan was no better employed. It was in these circumstances that Poiret published his work on God, the soul, and evil. Bayle proposed some difficulties to the author, who responded, and this controversy poisoned the lives of them both. Bayle said Poiret was crazy and Poiret called Bayle an atheist. But one is crazy and not an atheist without difficulties. Poiret loved Bourignon. Bayle said Bourignon had the bad brain of a disturbed woman. Poiret said that Bayle was a secret follower of Spinozism. Poiret suspected that Bayle had excited the severity of the magistrates against him, and he avenged himself with an accusation that compromised his adversary in their eyes in a much more dangerous way. Poiret had perhaps been imprisoned, but Bayle had been burned. Descartes's principle that the essence of the body is extension engaged them in another dispute. In 1681, that comet famous by its size appeared, and perhaps even more by Bayle's thoughts in his work on the occasion of this phenomenon and on the popular terrors that accompanied it. Bayle asked most important questions concerning miracles, the nature of God, and superstition. *The philosophic freedom evident in this book pleased sensible people considerably and displeased the theologians all the more.* He followed this with an examination of the history of Calvinism published by *the verbose liar* Mainbourg, who even praised Bayle's work. The Great Condé disclaimed reading it, but everyone else devoured it and the government had it burned. In 1684, Bayle commenced publishing his *Republique des Lettres*. This work required him to read all sorts of works, to study in depth the most disparate matters, and to discuss questions of mathematics, philosophy, physics, theology, jurisprudence, and history. What an arena for a Pyrrhonian! Then the theosophist Malebranche appeared on the scene. Among the great number of opinions particular to him, he advanced the view that all sensual pleasure is good. Arnauld saw in this maxim the overturning of morality, and he attacked it. Bayle intervened in this quarrel, explained the terms, and absolved Malebranche of Arnauld's accusation. *The latter was a vain and opinionated man. Since he was the head of a faction, and besides exceedingly quarrelsome by nature, he felt it incumbent upon him to attack Bayle, to indulge in verbiage and to muddle a clear subject. In this he succeeded very well. During this period members of the Reformed Church were subjected to unheard-of persecutions. France was being returned to Catholicism at the price of her ruin; the extirpation of heresy was being achieved by violating the most sacred laws of humanity and by dishonoring religion. This is what Bayle demonstrated in a little pamphlet on what Catholic France really was.* Bayle had already done this in some other writings on principles favorable to tolerance, where he carefully explicates this important subject in his *Commentaire philosophique.* This work, *Bayle's best and most useful,* was published by parties, and at first he pleased all parties equally. Then he displeased the Catholics and continued to please the Reformers; then he displeased both of them equally and conserved the constant approbation only of the philosophers. *That is because they are the only truly tolerant men. We cannot recommend this work sufficiently*; it is a masterwork of eloquence. . . . The disputes in which Bayle had entered began to calm down. He occupied himself with them night and day, and published the first volume in 1697. Everyone knows of his intellect, talents, and dialectic, of the immensity of his erudition and his decided penchant for Pyrrhonism. In effect, what are the questions of politics, literature, criticism, ancient and modern philosophy, theology, history, logic, and morals he does not examine pro and con? It is there that one sees him as being similar to Homer's Jupiter who arranges the clouds. In the midst of the clouds one wanders confused and in despair. Everything Sextus Empiricus and Huet say against reason, one in his *Hypotyposes*, the other in his *Treatise of the weakness of the human understanding*, is not worth any article chosen from Bayle's *Dictionary*. One learns very well there to ignore what one thought he knew. The works given account of here are not the only ones this surprising man wrote. He lived, however, only fifty years and died in January 1706. *Do you wish to know what to think of him? Take into account that there was, is, and will be only men of a certain kind, who have, do, and will speak badly of him. From this you can conclude that it is not truth but some particular bias which makes them speak. In this world there are only three courses one can pursue: one can express one's real thoughts, one can disavow one's real thoughts, one can remain silent. The last course is undoubtedly the safest and the least honest. At the time of his death Bayle was writing a criticism of some proofs of God's existence. According to some people, this augurs ill for his salvation. Those people have not taken into account the fact that, in the eyes of the Supreme Being who is universally good and just, it is neither truth nor falsehood which renders us guilty or innocent, but the way in which we remain true to ourselves.*

He will not reward us for having been witty, nor will He punish us for having been dullards. Our behavior depends on our will, our reasoning on our abilities. We are free to do good and avoid evil, but we are not free to know truth and to escape error. To err is a misfortune but not a crime. Our bad deeds will damn us, the ideas we perceive will not save us. I am more confident of the salvation of a man who preaches a lie in which he believes with all his heart, than I am of the salvation of someone who preaches a gospel in which he does not believe. The former may be a right-thinking man; the latter is clearly wicked. Certain opinions may well arouse dissensions in one's own society. But since Bayle wrote in a country where freedom of the press is tolerated he cannot be accused of this. Moreover, when certain truths may not be stated openly, this can only be due to poor legislation, which mistakenly links the political and the religious system. Wherever civil authority supports religion or uses religion as a prop, the progress of reason will be slow and there will be persecution, which is useless and ineffective, because men's minds can never be successfully put in fetters. Whenever this occurs there is at best limited toleration, which is scarcely less distressing than no toleration at all. Tolerance must be universal; universality alone can produce the two main advantages, enlightenment and tranquility. A truth, whatever it may be, even if harmful for the present, will necessarily become useful in the future. A lie, whatever it may be, even if advantageous at present, will necessarily become harmful in time. To hold otherwise is to be unable to distinguish between truth and falsehood. As the Persians said, and as the skeptics repeat after them, doubt is the first step toward science or truth. Whoever does not question will be sure of nothing; whoever does not doubt, will discover nothing and whoever discovers nothing is blind and will remain blind. Dissensions among men are caused by ignorance and lies: ignorance, which confuses everything and is opposed to everything, and lies, which can never be so firmly established in men's minds that they are not suspect, open to challenge, and contested. Only in truth can man find tranquility. Why is it that questions of metaphysics have always caused divisions among men? It is because they are obscure and untrue. Why is it that principles of natural morality, instead of creating dissensions among men have always brought them closer together? It is because they are clear, obvious, and true. If I had the proof of some great truth, a truth so self-evident that no man of good will could refuse to believe it, I would proclaim it immediately, no matter how troublesome it might be for my time and my country. I am persuaded that no good can be achieved in this world that does not cause trouble, and truth is the greatest good. Sooner or later man will taste its sweetest fruit.

Bayle had few equals in the art of reasoning, and perhaps none superior. No one knew more subtly how to seize the weakness of a system, no one could so well utilize his advantages. He was formidable in giving proofs, and also in making objections. Endowed with a wicked and prolific imagination, at the same time he gave a proof he also amused, portrayed, and seduced. Although he heaped doubt upon doubt, he always proceeded in order, his arguments like a polyp that divides into many other living polyps that were engendered one from another. Whatever thesis he undertook to prove, everything—history, erudition, philosophy—came to his aid. If the truth was on his side, no one could resist him. If he argued for a lie, he wrote with all the appearances of truth. Impartial or not, he always appeared impartial, and one never saw the author, only the subject matter.

. . . *In order to mitigate his skeptical passages, he always introduced them under the pretext of confirming Revelation while on the other hand, when the occasion presented itself, he knew full well how to undermine Revelation. He would alternately vindicate reason against authority and authority against reason, convinced that men would not give up their rights and freedom in favor of a yoke which would irk them and which they would want to shake off. He knew too much either to believe or to doubt everything.* It has been said of Bayle's writings, *quamdiu vigebunt, lis erit*, and we finish our history on that note.

It follows from the preceding that the first skeptics rose against reason only to mortify the pride of the dogmatists, and that among modern skeptics, some have set out to depreciate philosophy in order to give authority to Revelation, and others have attacked philosophy directly to destroy the basis on which it is established. And among both ancient and modern skeptics there are some who have doubted in good faith because they have perceived only reasons for uncertainty concerning most questions.

On our part, we conclude that everything in nature is interconnected, and that properly speaking there is nothing of which man has perfect, absolute, complete knowledge, not even of the most evident axioms, because that would require that he had knowledge of everything.

Because everything is connected with everything else, it is necessary that in all discussions one will arrive at something unknown. Thus when one arrives at this unknown, one will have to conclude with respect to it either ignorance, obscurity, or uncertainty concerning the preceding point, and of the point preceding it, and thus all the way back to the most evident principle.

Thus one should subject oneself to a kind of sobriety in the use of reason, or resolve to drift in uncertainty. The moment comes when one's light, which had always been increasing, begins to grow dim and then one must stop all discussions.

When I have conducted someone from consequence to consequence to an evident proposition, I will cease to dispute. I will no longer listen to those who deny the existence of bodies, the rules of logic, the witness of the senses, the distinctions between true and false, good and bad, pleasure and pain, vice and virtue, decent and indecent, just and unjust, honest and dishonest. I will turn my back on those who seek to turn me away from a simple question to embark on dissertations on the nature of matter, understanding, substance, thought, and other subjects that have no boundaries or bottom.

A man who is undivided and true will not have two philosophies, one for the study and the other for society. He will not speculate about principles when he is forced to forget these speculations in practice.

What shall I say to one who claims that although he sees, touches, hears, and perceives, he nevertheless never perceives anything but his own sensations, that it could be the case that everything is organized as it now appears to him without there being anything outside him, and that perhaps he is the only being who exists? I will recognize instantly the absurdity and the profundity of this paradox, and will guard myself well from losing my time destroying in someone an opinion that he does not have and to which I have nothing to oppose that is more clear than what he denies. To confute him I would have to go outside nature to reason from some point outside him and me, and this is impossible. This sophist lacks even that decency in conversation that consists in objecting only to those things about which he can himself provide some solid ground. Why should I waste my breath disputing a doubt you do not have? Is my time of so little value in your eyes? And is your time worth so little to you? Are there not many truths to look for or to clarify? Let us occupy ourselves with something more important, if we have only these present frivolities, take a nap to aid our digestion.

FURTHER READINGS

Bourdin, Jean-Claude. "Matérialisme et skepticisme chez Diderot: Diderot, philosophie, matérialisme." *Recherches sur Diderot et sur l'Encyclopédie* 26 (1999): 85–97.

Brucker, Jacob. *Historia critica philosophiae.* 6 vols. Hildesheim: Olms, 1975. Facsimile reproduction of the Leipzig 1742–1767 edition.

Chouillet, Jacques. "Le personnage sceptique dans les premières oeuvres de Diderot." *Dix-Huitième Siècle* 1 (1969): 195–211.

Diderot, Denis. "La Promenade du sceptique." In *Oeuvres*. 5 vols. Edition établie par Laurent Versini. Paris: Robert Laffont, 1994, 1:65–132.

Haag, Éliane M. "Diderot et Voltaire lecteurs de Montaigne: du jugement suspendu à la raison libre." *Revue de Métaphisique et de Morale* 3 (1997): 365–83.

Lom, Petr. *The Limits of Doubt: The Moral and Political Implications of Skepticism*. Albany: State University of New York Press, 2001, pp. 59–73.

Schwartz, Jerome. *Diderot and Montaigne: The "Essais" and the Shaping of Diderot's Humanism*. Geneva: Droz, 1966.

29

ROUSSEAU

J ean-Jacques Rousseau (1712–1778), the famous moral and political philosopher, is not usually associated with the skeptical trend in modern philosophy. However, in a section of his book on education—*Émile* (written between 1758 and 1759 and published in 1762)—he gives the speech to a fictional Catholic priest who assumes the role of Émile's teacher on religious matters. He says he does not want to teach—let alone preach—anything to the young boy, and what he does instead is a personal moving confession of his religious (Christian) views. He begins describing a painful skeptical personal crisis and, in a way following Descartes's trajectory in the *Meditations*, but from a sensualist (Lockean) starting point, moves from doubt and rejection of all philosophical systems to a kind of deistic natural theology based on his philosophy of natural feeling. The confessional style of a philosopher deluded by the philosophical schools that led him to skepticism and who overcomes the crisis by construing his own philosophy resembles the form chosen by Bishop Pierre-Daniel Huet in his *Traité Philosophique* published in Amsterdam in 1723. The skeptical bishop's *Traité* may well have been Rousseau's formal model for his "Creed of a Savoyard Priest," although in what concerns content, Huet's work is much more skeptical than Rousseau's and Rousseau's quite more irreligious than Huet's.

FROM *ÉMILE OR EDUCATION*

My child, do not look to me for learned speeches or profound arguments. I am no great philosopher, nor do I desire to be one. I have, however, a certain amount of common-sense and a constant devotion to truth. I have no wish to argue with you nor even to convince you; it is enough for me to show you, in all simplicity of heart, what I really think. Consult your own heart while I speak; that is all I ask. If I am mistaken, I am honestly mistaken, and therefore my error will not be counted to me as a crime; if you, too, are honestly mistaken, there is no great harm done. If I am right, we are both endowed with reason, we have both the same motive for listening to the voice of reason. Why should not you think as I do?

By birth I was a peasant and poor; to till the ground was my portion; but my parents thought it a finer thing that I should learn to get my living as a priest and they found means to send me to college. I am quite sure that neither my parents nor I had any idea of seeking after what was good, useful, or true; we only sought what was wanted to get me ordained. I learned what was taught me, I said what I was told to say, I promised all that was required, and I became a priest. But I soon discovered that when I promised not to be a man, I had promised more than I could perform.

Conscience, they tell us, is the creature of prejudice, but I know from experience that conscience persists in following the order of nature in spite of all the laws of man. In vain is this or that forbidden; remorse makes her voice heard but feebly when what we do is permitted by well-ordered nature, and still more when we are doing her bidding. My good youth, nature has not yet appealed to your senses; may you long remain in this happy state when her voice is the voice of innocence. Remember that to anticipate her teaching is to offend more deeply against her than to resist her teaching; you must first learn to resist, that you may know when to yield without wrong-doing.

From my youth up I had reverenced the married state as the first and most sacred institution of nature. Having renounced the right to marry, I was resolved not to profane the sanctity of marriage; for in spite of my education and reading I had always led a simple and regular life, and my mind had preserved the innocence of its natural instincts; these instincts had not been obscured by worldly wisdom, while my poverty kept me remote from the temptations dictated by the sophistry of vice.

This very resolution proved my ruin. My respect for marriage led to the discovery of my misconduct. The scandal must be expiated; I was arrested, suspended, and dismissed; I was the victim of my scruples rather than of my incontinence, and I had reason to believe, from the reproaches which accompanied my disgrace, that one can often escape punishment by being guilty of a worse fault.

A thoughtful mind soon learns from such experiences. I found my former ideas of justice, honesty, and every duty of man overturned by these painful events, and day by day I was losing my hold on one or another of the opinions I had accepted. What was left was not enough to form a body of ideas which could stand alone, and I felt that the evidence on which my principles rested was being weakened; at last I knew not what to think, and I came to the same conclusion as yourself, but with this difference: My lack of faith was the slow growth of manhood, attained with great difficulty, and all the harder to uproot.

I was in that state of doubt and uncertainty which Descartes considers essential to the search for truth. It is a state which cannot continue, it is disquieting and painful; only vicious tendencies and an idle heart can keep us in that state. My heart was not so corrupt as to delight in it, and there is nothing which so maintains the habit of thinking as being better pleased with oneself than with one's lot.

I pondered, therefore, on the sad fate of mortals, adrift upon this sea of human opinions, without compass or rudder, and abandoned to their stormy passions with no guide but an inexperienced pilot who does not know whence he comes or whither he is going. I said to myself, "I love truth, I seek her, and cannot find her. Show me truth and I will hold her fast; why does she hide her face from the eager heart that would fain worship her?"

Although I have often experienced worse sufferings, I have never led a life so uniformly distressing as this period of unrest and anxiety, when I wandered incessantly from one doubt to another, gaining nothing from my prolonged meditations but uncertainty, darkness, and contradiction with regard to the source of my being and the rule of my duties.

I cannot understand how any one can be a skeptic sincerely and on principle. Either such philosophers do not exist or they are the most miserable of men. Doubt with regard to what we ought to know is a condition too violent for the human mind; it cannot long be endured; in spite of itself the mind decides one way or another, and it prefers to be deceived rather than to believe nothing.

My perplexity was increased by the fact that I had been brought up in a church which decides everything and permits no doubts, so that having rejected one article of faith I was forced to reject the rest; as I could not accept absurd decisions, I was deprived of those which were not absurd. When I was told to believe everything, I could believe nothing, and I knew not where to stop.

I consulted the philosophers, I searched their books and examined their various theories; I found them all alike proud, assertive, dogmatic, professing, even in their so-called skepticism, to know everything, proving nothing, scoffing at each other. This last trait, which was common to all of them, struck me as the only point in which they were right. Braggarts in attack, they are weaklings in defense. Weigh their arguments, they are all destructive; count their voices, every one speaks for himself; they are only agreed in arguing with each other. I could find no way out of my uncertainty by listening to them.

I suppose this prodigious diversity of opinion is caused, in the first place, by the weakness of the human intellect; and, in the second, by pride. We have no means of measuring this vast machine, we are unable to calculate its workings; we know neither its guiding principles nor its final purpose; we do not know ourselves, we know neither our nature nor the spirit that moves us; we scarcely know whether man is one or many; we are surrounded by impenetrable mysteries. These mysteries are beyond the region of sense, we think we can penetrate them by the light of reason, but we fall back on our imagination. Through this imagined world each forces a way for himself which he holds to be right; none can tell whether his path will lead him to the goal. Yet we long to know and understand it all. The one thing we do not know is the limit of the knowable. We prefer to trust to chance and to believe what is not true, rather than to own that not one of us can see what really is. A fragment of some vast whole whose bounds are beyond our gaze, a fragment abandoned by its Creator to our foolish quarrels, we are vain enough to want to determine the nature of that whole and our own relations with regard to it.

If the philosophers were in a position to declare the truth, which of them would care to do so? Every one of them knows that his own system rests on no surer foundations than the rest, but he maintains it because it is his own. There is not one of them who, if he chanced to discover the difference between truth and falsehood, would not prefer his own lie to the truth which another had discovered. Where is the philosopher who would not deceive the whole world for his own glory? If he can rise above the crowd, if he can excel his rivals, what more does he want? Among believers he is an atheist; among atheists he would be a believer.

The first thing I learned from these considerations was to restrict my inquiries to what directly concerned myself, to rest in profound ignorance of everything else, and not even to trouble myself to doubt anything beyond what I required to know.

I also realized that the philosophers, far from ridding me of my vain doubts, only multiplied the doubts that tormented me and failed to remove any one of them. So I chose another guide and said, "Let me follow the Inner Light; it will not lead me so far astray as others have done, or if it does it will be my own fault, and I shall not go so far wrong if I follow my own illusions as if I trusted to their deceits."

I then went over in my mind the various opinions which I had held in the course of my life, and I saw that although no one of them was plain enough to gain immediate belief, some were more probable than others, and my inward consent was given or withheld in proportion to this improbability. Having discovered this, I made an unprejudiced comparison of all these different ideas, and I perceived that the first and most general of them was also the simplest and the most reasonable, and that it would have been accepted by every one if only it had been last instead of first. Imagine all your philosophers, ancient and modern, having exhausted their strange systems of force, chance, fate, necessity, atoms, a living world, animated matter, and every variety of materialism. Then comes the illustrious Clarke who gives light to the world and proclaims the Being of beings and the Giver of things. What universal admiration, what unanimous applause would have greeted this new system—a system so great, so illuminating, and so simple. Other systems are full of absurdities; this system seems to me to contain fewer things which are beyond the understanding of the human mind. I said to myself, "Every system has its insoluble problems, for the finite mind of man is too small to deal with them; these difficulties are therefore no final arguments, against any system. But what a difference there is between the direct evidence on which these systems are based! Should we not prefer that theory which alone explains all the facts, when it is no more difficult than the rest?"

Bearing thus within my heart the love of truth as my only philosophy, and as my only method a clear and simple rule which dispensed with the need for vain and subtle arguments, I returned with the help of this rule to the examination of such knowledge as concerned myself; I was resolved to admit as self-evident all that I could not honestly refuse to believe, and to admit as true all that seemed to follow directly from this; all the rest I determined to leave undecided, neither accepting nor rejecting it, nor yet troubling myself to clear up difficulties which did not lead to any practical ends.

But who am I? What right have I to decide? What is it that determines my judgments? If they are inevitable, if they are the results of the impressions I receive, I am wasting my strength in such inquiries; they would be made or not without any interference of mine. I must therefore first turn my eyes upon myself to acquaint myself with the instrument I desire to use, and to discover how far it is reliable.

I exist, and I have senses through which I receive impressions. This is the first truth that strikes me and I am forced to accept it. Have I any independent knowledge of my existence, or am I only aware of it through my sensations? This is my first difficulty, and so far I cannot solve it. For I continually experience sensations, either directly or indirectly through memory, so how can I know if the feeling of *self* is something beyond these sensations or if it can exist independently of them?

My sensations take place in myself, for they make me aware of my own existence; but their cause is outside me, for they affect me whether I have any reason for them or not, and they are produced or destroyed independently of me. So I clearly perceive that my sensation, which is within me, and its cause or its object, which is outside me, are different things.

Thus, not only do I exist, but other entities exist also, that is to say, the objects of my sensations; and even if these objects are merely ideas, still these ideas are not me.

But everything outside myself, everything which acts upon my senses, I call matter, and all the particles of matter which I suppose to be united into separate entities I call bodies. Thus all the disputes of the idealists and the realists have no meaning for me. Their distinctions between the appearance and the reality of bodies are wholly fanciful.

I am now as convinced of the existence of the universe as of my own. I next consider the objects of my sensations, and I find that I have the power of comparing them, so I perceive that I am endowed with an active force of which I was not previously aware. . . .

Being now, so to speak, sure of myself, I begin to look at things outside myself. . . .

The first causes of motion are not to be found in matter; matter receives and transmits motion, but does not produce it. . . . In a word, no motion which is not caused by another motion can take place, except by a spontaneous, voluntary action; inanimate bodies have no action but motion, and there is no real action without will. This is my first principle. I believe, therefore, that there is a will which sets the universe in motion and gives life to nature. This is my first dogma, or the first article of my creed. . . .

I believe . . . that the world is governed by a wise and powerful will; I see it or rather I feel it, and it is a great thing to know this. But has this same world always existed, or has it been created? Is there one source of all things? Are there two or many? What is their nature? I know not; and what concern is it of mine? When these things become of importance to me I will try to learn them; till then I abjure these idle speculations, which may trouble my peace, but cannot affect my conduct nor be comprehended by my reason.

FURTHER READINGS

Olaso, Ezequiel de. "The Two Scepticisms of the Savoyard Vicar." In *The Skeptical Mode in Modern Philosophy*, edited by Richard A. Watson and James E. Force, 43–59. Dor-

drecht: Kluwer, 1988. Reprinted in *Scepticism and the Enlightenment*, edited by Richard H. Popkin, Ezequiel de Olaso, and Georgio Tonelli, 131–46. Dordrecht: Kluwer, 1997.
Zanin, Seguey. "L'entremise du scepticisme: Jean-Jacques Rousseau et la composition du *Discours sur les sciences et les arts*." In *Scepticisme & Modernité*, edited by Marc André Bernier and Sébastien Charles, 155–66. Saint-Étienne: Publications de l'Université de Saint-Étienne, 2005.

30

KANT

I mmanuel Kant (1724–1804) is one of the major and most influential philoso-phers of the Western tradition. His critical philosophy (Kant calls it "transcen-dental"), which asks for the necessary conditions for any true claim, was directly inspired by and reactive to skeptical attack on dogmatism, in particular to Hume's skeptical refutation of metaphysics. Skepticism was a current issue in Germany at Kant's time and, as Manfred Kuehn has established, Kant's critical philosophy was first received as a new form of skepticism. Kant's disciple Carl Reinhold (1758–1823) was the first to present Kant's philosophy as the only possible refuta-tion of skepticism, a view that is largely accepted to this day. We have included in this anthology the beginning of Kant's preface to the first edition of his *Critique of Pure Reason* and most of his preface to the *Prolegomena to Any Future Metaphysics*. These texts show how crucial Hume's skepticism was for Kant's development of his critical philosophy. "I freely admit," Kant avows, "that the remembrance of *David Hume* was the very thing that many years ago first interrupted my dogmatic slumber and gave a completely different direction to my researches in the field of speculative philosophy." However, as John Christian Laursen claims, skepticism is not merely instrumental in Kant's critical philosophy. He incorporated the modern skeptics' central view (see, for instance, the selection of Bayle—whose work Kant knew well—included in this volume) of the inaccessibility of the things in themselves to human knowledge.

FROM *CRITIQUE OF PURE REASON*

At first, her [metaphysics] government, under the administration of the *dogmatists*, was an absolute *despotism*. But, as the legislative continue to show traces of the ancient barbaric rule, her empire gradually broke up, and intestine wars introduced the reign of *anarchy*; while the *skeptics*, like nomadic tribes, who hate a permanent habitation and settled mode of living, attacked from time to time those who had orga-nized themselves into civil communities. But their number was, very happily, small; and thus they could not entirely put a stop to the exertions of those who persisted in raising new edifices, although on no settled or uniform plan. In recent times the hope dawned upon us of seeing those disputes settled, and the legitimacy of her claims established by a kind of *physiology* of the human understanding—that of the celebrated Locke. But it was found that—although it was affirmed that this so-called queen could not refer her descent to any higher source than that of common experience, a circumstance which necessarily brought suspicion on her claims—as this *genealogy* was incorrect, she persisted in the advancement of her claims to sovereignty. Thus metaphysics necessarily fell back into the antiquated and rotten constitution of *dogmatism*, and again became obnoxious to the contempt from which efforts had been made to save it. At present, as all methods, according to the general persuasion, have been tried in vain, there reigns naught but weariness and complete *indifferentism*—the mother of chaos and night in the scientific world, but at the same time the source of, or at least the prelude to, the re-creation and reinstallation of a science, when it has fallen into confusion, obscurity, and disuse from ill-directed effort.

FROM *PROLEGOMENA TO ANY FUTURE METAPHYSICS**

These prolegomena are not for the use of apprentices, but of future teachers, and indeed are not to help them to organize the presentation of an already existing science, but to discover this science itself for the first time.

There are scholars for whom the history of philosophy (ancient as well as modern) is itself their philosophy; the present prolegomena have not been written for them. They must wait until those who endeavor to draw from the wellsprings of reason itself have finished their business, and then it will be their turn to bring news of these events to the world. Failing that, in their opinion nothing can be said that has not already been said before; and in fact this opinion can stand for all time as an infallible prediction, for since the human understanding has wandered over countless subjects in various ways through many centuries, it can hardly fail that for anything new something old should be found that has some similarity with it.

My intention is to convince all of those who find it worthwhile to occupy themselves with metaphysics that it is unavoidably necessary to suspend their work for the present, to consider all that has happened until now as if it had not happened, and before all else to pose the question: "whether such a thing as metaphysics is even possible at all."

If metaphysics is a science, why is it that it cannot, as other sciences, attain universal and lasting acclaim? If it is not, how does it happen that, under the pretense of a science it incessantly shows off, and strings along the human understanding with hopes that never dim but are never fulfilled? Whether, therefore, we demonstrate our knowledge or our ignorance, for once we must arrive at something certain concerning the nature of this self-proclaimed science; for things cannot possibly remain on their present footing. It seems almost laughable that, while every other science makes con-

---

*The editor's notes were omitted.

tinuous progress, metaphysics, which desires to be wisdom itself, and which everyone consults as an oracle, perpetually turns round on the same spot without coming a step further. Furthermore, it has lost a great many of its adherents, and one does not find that those who feel strong enough to shine in other sciences wish to risk their reputations in this one, where anyone, usually ignorant in all other things, lays claim to a decisive opinion, since in this region there are in fact still no reliable weights and measures with which to distinguish profundity from shallow babble.

It is, after all, not completely unheard of after long cultivation of a science, that in considering with wonder how much progress has been made someone should finally allow the question to arise: whether and how such a science is possible at all. For human reason is so keen on building that more than once it has erected a tower, and has afterwards torn it down again in order to see how well constituted its foundation may have been. It is never too late to grow reasonable and wise; but if the insight comes late, it is always harder to bring it into play.

To ask whether a science might in fact be possible assumes a doubt about its actuality. Such a doubt, though, offends everyone whose entire belongings may perhaps consist in this supposed jewel; hence he who allows this doubt to develop had better prepare for opposition from all sides. Some, with their metaphysical compendia in hand, will look down on him with scorn, in proud consciousness of their ancient, and hence ostensibly legitimate, possession; others, who nowhere see anything that is not similar to something they have seen somewhere else before, will not understand him; and for a time everything will remain as if nothing at all had happened that might yield fear or hope of an impending change.

Nevertheless I venture to predict that the reader of these prolegomena who thinks for himself will not only come to doubt his previous science, but subsequently will be fully convinced that there can be no such science unless the requirements expressed here, on which its possibility rests, are met, and, as this has never yet been done, that there is as yet no metaphysics at all. Since, however, the demand for it can never be exhausted, [Kant's note omitted here] because the interest of human reason in general is much too intimately interwoven with it, the reader will admit that a complete reform or rather a rebirth of metaphysics, according to a plan completely unknown before now, is inevitably approaching, however much it may be resisted in the meantime.

Since the Essays of *Locke* and *Leibniz*, or rather since the rise of metaphysics as far as the history of it reaches, no event has occurred that could have been more decisive with respect to the fate of this science than the attack made upon it by *David Hume*. He brought no light to this kind of knowledge, but he certainly struck a spark from which a light could well have been kindled, if it had hit some welcoming tinder whose glow was carefully kept going and made to grow.

Hume started mainly from a single but important concept in metaphysics, namely, that of the *connection of cause and effect* (and of course also its derivative concepts, of force and action, etc.), and called upon reason, which pretends to have generated this concept in her womb, to give him an account of by what right she thinks: that something could be so constituted that, if it is posited, something else necessarily must thereby be posited as well; for that is what the concept of cause says. He indisputably proved that it is wholly impossible for reason to think such a connection *a priori* and from concepts, because this connection contains necessity; and it is simply not to be seen how it could be, that because something is, something else necessarily must also be, and therefore how the concept of such a connection could be introduced *a priori*. From this he concluded that reason completely and fully deceives herself with this concept, falsely taking it for her own child, when it is really nothing but a bastard of the imagination, which, impregnated by experience, and having brought certain representations under the law of association, passes off the resulting subjective necessity (i.e., habit) for an objective necessity (from insight). From which he concluded that reason has no power at all to think such connections, not even merely in general, because its concepts would then be bare fictions, and all of its cognitions allegedly established *a priori* would be nothing but falsely marked ordinary experiences; which is so much as to say that there is no metaphysics at all, and cannot be any. [Kant's note omitted here]

As premature and erroneous as his conclusion was, nevertheless it was at least founded on inquiry, and this inquiry was of sufficient value, that the best minds of his time might have come together to solve (more happily if possible) the problem in the sense in which he presented it, from which a complete reform of the science must soon have arisen.

But fate, ever ill-disposed toward metaphysics, would have it that Hume was understood by no one. One cannot, without feeling a certain pain, behold how utterly and completely his opponents, *Reid, Oswald, Beattie*, and finally *Priestley*, missed the point of his problem, and misjudged his hints for improvement—constantly taking for granted just what he doubted, and, conversely, proving with vehemence and, more often than not, with great insolence exactly what it had never entered his mind to doubt—so that everything remained in its old condition, as if nothing had happened. The question was not, whether the concept of cause is right, useful, and, with respect to all cognition of nature, indispensable, for this *Hume* had never put in doubt; it was rather whether it is thought through reason *a priori*, and in this way has an inner truth independent of all experience, and therefore also a much more widely extended use which is not limited merely to the objects of experience: regarding this *Hume* awaited enlightenment. The discussion was only about the origin of this concept, not about its indispensability in use; if the former were only discovered, the conditions of its use and the sphere in which it can be valid would already be given.

In order to do justice to the problem, however, the opponents of this celebrated man would have had to penetrate very deeply into the nature of reason so far as it is occupied solely with pure thought, something that did not suit them. They therefore found a more expedient means to be obstinate without any insight, namely, the appeal to ordinary common sense. It is in fact a great gift from heaven to possess right (or, as it has recently been called, plain) common sense. But it must be proven through deeds, by the considered and reasonable things one thinks and says, and not by appealing to it as an oracle when one knows of nothing clever to advance in one's defense. To appeal to ordinary common sense when insight and science run short, and not before, is one of the subtle discoveries of recent times, whereby the dullest windbag can confidently take on the most profound thinker and hold his own with him. So long as a small residue of insight remains, however, one would do well to avoid resorting to this emergency help. And seen in the light of day, this appeal is nothing other than a call to the judgment of the multitude; applause at which the philosopher blushes, but at which the popular wag becomes triumphant and defiant. I should think, however, that *Hume* could lay just as much claim to sound common sense as *Beattie*, and on top of this to something that the latter certainly did not possess, namely, a critical reason, which keeps ordinary common sense in check, so that it doesn't lose itself in speculations, or, if these are the sole topic of discussion, doesn't want to decide anything, since it doesn't understand the justification for its own principles; for only so will it remain sound common sense. Hammer and chisel are perfectly fine for working raw lumber, but for copperplate one must use an etching needle. Likewise, sound common sense and speculative understanding are both useful, but each in its own way; the one, when it is a matter of judgments that find their immediate application in experience, the other, however, when judgments are to be made in a universal mode, out of mere concepts, as in metaphysics, where what calls itself (but often *per antiphrasin*) sound common sense has no judgment whatsoever.

I freely admit that the remembrance of *David Hume* was the very thing that many years ago first interrupted my dogmatic slumber and gave a completely different direction to my researches in the field of speculative philosophy. I was very far from listening to him with respect to his conclusions, which arose solely because he did not completely set out his problem, but only touched on a part of it, which, without the whole being taken into account, can provide no enlightenment. If we begin from a well-grounded though undeveloped thought that another bequeaths us, then we can well hope, by continued reflection, to take it further than could the sagacious man whom one has to thank for the first spark of this light.

So I tried first whether *Hume's* objection might not be presented in a general manner, and I soon found that the concept of the connection of cause and effect is far from being the only concept through which the understanding thinks connections of things *a priori*; rather, metaphysics consists wholly of such concepts. I sought to ascertain their number, and as I had successfully attained this in the way I wished, namely from a single principle, I proceeded to the deduction of these concepts from which I henceforth became assured that they were not, as Hume had feared, derived from experience, but had arisen from the pure understanding. This deduction, which appeared impossible to my sagacious predecessor, and which had never even occurred to anyone but him, even though everyone confidently made use of these concepts without asking what their objective validity is based on—this deduction, I say, was the most difficult thing that could ever be undertaken on behalf of metaphysics; and the worst thing about it is that metaphysics, as much of it as might be present anywhere at all, could not give me the slightest help with this, because this very deduction must first settle the possibility of metaphysics. As I had now succeeded in the solution of the Humean problem not only in a single case but with respect to the entire faculty of pure reason, I could therefore take sure, if still always slow, steps toward finally determining, completely and according to universal principles, the entire extent of pure reason with regard to its boundaries as well as its contents, which was indeed the very thing that metaphysics requires in order to build its system according to a sure plan.

FURTHER READINGS

Kuehn, Manfred. "Skepticism: Philosophical Disease or Cure?" In *The Skeptical Tradition around 1800: Skepticism in Philosophy, Science, and Society*, edited by Johan van der Zande and Richard H. Popkin, 81–100. Dordrecht: Kluwer, 1998.

Laursen, John Christian. *The Politics of Skepticism in the Ancients, Montaigne, Hume and Kant*. Leiden: J. Brill, 1992.

———. "Kant in the History of Skepticism." In *John Locke und Immanuel Kant: Historische Rezeption und gegenwärtiger Relevanz*, edited by Martyn P. Thompson, 254–68. Berlin: Duncker & Humblot, 1991.

Laursen, J. C., and R. H. Popkin. "Sources of Knowledge of Sextus Empiricus in Kant's Time: A French Translation of Sextus Empiricus from the Prussian Academy, 1779." *British Journal for the History of Philosophy* 6, no. 2 (1998): 261–68.

Makkreel, Rudolf A. "Kant's Responses to Skepticism." In Van der Zande and Popkin, *The Skeptical Tradition around 1800*, pp. 101–109.

Stroud, Barry. *The Significance of Philosophical Skepticism*. Oxford: Oxford University Press, 1984.

Tonelli, Giorgio. "Kant and the Ancient Skeptics." In *Skepticism in the Enlightenment*, edited by Richard H. Popkin, Ezequiel de Olaso, and Giorgio Tonelli, 69–98. Dordrecht: Kluwer, 1997.

Washburn, Michael C. "Dogmatism, Skepticism, Criticism: The Dialectic of Kant's Silent Decade." *Journal of the History of Philosophy* 13 (1975): 167–76.

31

SCHULZE

K ant's critical philosophy soon led to skeptical reactions in Germany by Solomon Maimon (1754–1800), Ernst Platner (1744–1818), and Gottlob Ernst Schulze (1761–1833). Schulze addressed anonymously (under the pseudonym of the ancient Pyrrhonian, Aenesidemus) Kant's disciple Carl Reinhold, targeting the pretension that Kant had given the definitive answer to skepticism. Schulze's Aenesidemus is not, however, the ancient Pyrrhonian. The skepticism he purports to defend against Kant's critical philosophy is the idealist skepticism developed from Descartes through Foucher, Bayle, and Berkeley to Hume. Schulze questions whether Kant's critical philosophy has solved the problem of justifying the existence of a material world external to the mind. He offers an internal criticism of Kant's alleged refutation of idealism, basically arguing that the assumption of things in themselves and of their supposedly causal action on the mind is inconsistent with the main tenets of the critical philosophy. Schulze's attack on Kant caused some impact in Germany and probably played a role in the development of German Idealism. Fichte took Schulze's defense of skepticism very seriously, and one of Hegel's first publications was an attack on another book by Schulze in which he developed further his idealist skepticism.

**FROM *AENESIDEMUS ODER UBER DIE FUNDAMENTE
DER VON DEM HERRN PROF. REINHOLD IN JENA GELIEFERTEN
ELEMENTAR-PHILOSOPHIE; NEBST EINER VERTHEIDIGUNG DES
SKEPTICISMUS GEGEN DIE ANMAASUNGEN DER VERNUNFT*
(AENESIDEMUS, OR ON THE FOUNDATIONS OF THE ELEMENTARY
PHILOSOPHY PROPOUNDED IN JENA BY PROF. REINHOLD,
INCLUDING A DEFENSE OF SKEPTICISM AGAINST
THE PRETENSIONS OF THE CRITIQUE OF PURE REASON)**

If we compare the conclusions of the critique of reason with its premises we can easily detect the contradiction that holds between them. According to the transcendental deduction of the pure concepts of the understanding presented by the critique of reason, the categories *causality* and *reality* can be applied only to empirical intuitions, only to something which has been perceived in time. Beyond this application, these categories have no sense or meaning. The object beyond our representations (the thing in itself) which, according to the critique of reason, furnishes the material of our intuitions through the influx on our sensibility, is neither an intuition nor a sensible representation in itself but something of a *realiter* different and independent from both. Therefore one cannot apply to this object, according to the very results of the critique of reason, either the concept of cause or the concept of reality, and if the transcendental deduction of the categories presented by the critique of reason is correct, then one of the foundational principles of the critique of reason is false and wrong, namely, that all knowledge begins with the action of objects on our mind (Gemüt).

. . . The mind (Gemüt), which can also be thought of as the sole ground of all our knowledge and reason, finds in the idea of the subject of the internal sense an absolute subject which it can use to raise the knowledge of experience to an absolute level. If the critique of reason wanted to fortify itself it should have explained that— and why—the mind (Gemüt) cannot be considered as the source of all the components of our knowledge. But the critique of pure reason not only has not done so but has even claimed that it has demonstrated with certainty that the thought of an object outside the empirical experience is a thought only from the formal point of view, a thought deprived of any reality and relation to something real. It takes as the basis of its speculations the proposition that all knowledge begins with the action of objective objects on the mind (Gemüt) and then later contests the truth and even the reality of this proposition. Indeed, since the critique of reason pretends to have demonstrated that the things which exist *realiter*—according to what they can be in themselves—are totally unknown to us, and that to discern them lies beyond all our capacities, all human knowledge is explained as something about which we cannot know if it is minimally something more than an empty appearance. Our knowledge is real—as the critique of reason itself admits—only to the extent that the representations have a connection with something exterior to them. But if the things themselves are totally unknown to us, so their connections to our representations, and even the possibility of such a connection, will necessarily be completely unknown to us. Whoever admits the former must necessarily admit the latter if he wants to think coherently. For of that which is completely—and in all its properties and attributes—unknown to me I cannot know if it exists, if it has some relation to me, and if it can produce anything at all. Therefore, to the extent that the critique of reason denies the reality and possibility of any knowledge of the thing in itself and, besides, explains the principle of causality (whose applicability to the things in themselves is the only way to demonstrate that our representations have causes external to them) as a principle which has to do only with the subjective connections of our empirical intuitions in the understanding—and is not an objective law of the things themselves—to this extent the critique of reason also denies the possibility of the knowledge of the connection between our representations and something exterior to them, and therefore, according to the critique of reason, the acceptance of a reality in some of our representations is a mere illusion. . . .

Berkeley denied the existence of things in space objectively and totally independent of our representations for the reason that it would be simply inconceivable to these things to produce an effect [representations] totally contrary to their nature. . . . One would expect that the refutation of [Berkeley's] idealism, which has been announced so noisily, would attempt to demonstrate the real and objective existence of corporeal things and to deny his main axiom. However, this axiom is neither mentioned nor attacked in the refutation of idealism given by the critique of reason. For first, according to the critique of reason, the existence of the things in themselves, absolutely independent of our representations, must be completely unknown to us, so that we know nothing about them and can know the things in themselves only through the phenomena that we possess of them and, as such, they are something only subjective. [Schulze's note omitted] But this is what Berkeley's idealism in a certain sense claims with respect to the material world—or it is something that at least he never denied, since, according to him, only representations of the corporeal things occur in us. Second, the critique of reason claims, in order to refute idealism, that the empirical awareness of our existence in time appears itself associated to the awareness of a relation between our existence and something existing outside us, and that in order to possess an awareness of the internal experience and of the determination of our self in time, it is necessary to have an immediate awareness of persisting things outside us. But again, idealism never claimed that perceptions of mutations could occur without being thought in relation to a persisting thing or that one could have the perception of the empirical determinations of our own existence without these perceptions being referred to a persisting existence of external objects. Idealism does admit that we have representations of objects in space and that we must have the perception of these objects as persisting things. Idealism can thus also admit—ignoring their specific thesis—that the awareness of external objects persisting in space is indispensable for the awareness of our own empirically determined existence and that the latter cannot happen without the former. However, it derives the awareness of persisting objects in space not from a supposedly real causation of external finite things on us, but from the determined way in which divinity acts on our mind (Gemüt) causing representations in it.

Third, idealism requires that the objective and real existence of material objects outside us be demonstrated. Whoever pretends to have refuted idealism must have unequivocally explained the existence of such objects. But the critique of reason claims, in its refutation of idealism, that we have an awareness of our existence in time and that this awareness is likewise associated with an awareness of a relation of our existence with something persisting outside us. But Berkeley never pretended to have demonstrated such a thing, and the awareness of a relation of our empirical existence with persisting things outside us in space is far from being an objective existence of real things external to us. In its refutation of idealism, the critique of reason therefore affirms that which idealism never denied, and denies that which idealism has never affirmed. [Schulze's note omitted]

FURTHER READINGS

Engstler, Achim. "Commentary: Reading Schulze's *Aenesidemus*." In *The Skeptical Tradition around 1800: Skepticism in Philosophy, Science, and Society*, edited by Johan Van der Zande and Richard H. Popkin, 159–72. Dordrecht: Kluwer, 1998.

Grundmann, Thomas. "Polemic and Dogmatism: The Two Faces of Skepticism in Aenesidemus-Schulze." In Van der Zande and Popkin, *The Skeptical Tradition around 1800*, pp. 133–41.

Hegel, Georg W. F. "Verhältnis des Skeptizismus zur Philosophie." *Kritisches Journal der Philosophie* 2 (1802): 1–74.

Radrizzani, Ives. "Le scepticisme à l'époque kantienne: Maimon contre Schulze." *Archives de philosophie* 54, no. 4 (1991): 553–70.

Schulze, Gottlob Ernst. *Kritik der Theoretischen Philosophie*. Hamburg: C. E. Bohn, 1801.

Stamm, Marcelo. "Skepticism and Methodological Monism: Aenesidemus-Schulze versus Arcesilaus-Erhard." In Van der Zande and Popkin, *The Skeptical Tradition around 1800*, pp. 143–58.

32

STÄUDLIN

Carl Friedrich Stäudlin (1761–1826), a German historian of philosophy and theology, was a friend of Kant. He wrote a detailed and well-informed (given the available scholarship at the time) history of skepticism. It is the first covering the whole history of skepticism, from the roots of the school among the pre-Socratic philosophers to Hume, Kant, and early skeptical reactions to Kant's philosophy in Germany (Schulze and Platner). In the introduction, from which we selected the text below, Stäudlin depicts grades of philosophical skepticism and points out the psychological roots of practical doubt. He portrays dismal effects of skepticism on university students of the time, who were becoming dubious of everything, including the value of life itself. Stäudlin also indicates practical benefits of skepticism, which he took partially from Hume. Skepticism combats the arrogance of dogmatists and leads to the proper delimitation of the objects that are adequate to human understanding. We thank Rogério Lopes for transcribing parts of Stäudlin's introduction and the Staatsbibliotek zu Berlin (STABI) for allowing the transcription.

FROM *GESCHICHTE UND GEIST DER SKEPTICISMUS, VORZÜGLICH IN RÜCKSICHT AUF MORAL UND RELIGION* (HISTORY AND SPIRIT OF SKEPTICISM, ESPECIALLY WITH RESPECT TO RELIGION AND MORALS)

1. What Is Skepticism and What Are Its Different Types?

. . . The Pyrrhonists did not deny or contest the correlation of our perceptions with things as such; they doubted it. Perhaps no one will doubt that this or that object appears to us, Sextus says, but the question is, is it constituted as it appears? [Stäudlin's note omitted] Thus it was a question, something that was being searched out, that is, in the skeptical sense of the word, it was doubted [Stäudlin's note omitted] that objects were really constituted as they appeared. The Pyrrhonists also doubted if in general these appearances corresponded to objects external to us. Assuming that they actually did, they raised the new doubt whether these objects appeared to us in their true nature. They compared the different impressions of the same objects on different people under different circumstances. From this, one can conclude with probability that the Pyrrhonists knew how to differentiate between objects as they are constituted in themselves and as they are constituted in their appearance. How far the Pyrrhonists took skepticism can be seen from another detail in the above-mentioned passage from Sextus. He expresses indeed the doubt, with the skeptical word *isoos*, that everybody admits to appearances. We are thus again led to the conclusion that ancient skepticism was not a system but an art. [Stäudlin's note omitted]

The definitions of skepticism that we have listed and considered so far lead to the conclusion that, when one considers skepticism a way of thinking or a system, then one can and must differentiate among various types, because nothing that the afore-mentioned writers call skepticism is entirely unworthy of being called this name. The best way of thinking of these types may well be to see them as gradations of the ideal of skepticism in general. The ideal is unattainable by any human soul; but if it could be realized, one could neither take away more or less of anything from it, since it is something empty, something negative, nor add more or less of anything to it. Thus the first and lowest grade of skepticism would be an admission of appearances—facts of consciousness which irresistibly call for approval or action, but which declares all else doubtful. A second grade would be an admission of subjective truth and doubt of all objective truth, that objects may be perceived through the senses or reason. But since subjective truth exists neither purely in the agreement of our thoughts among themselves, nor in the agreement of our perceptions with the facts in our conscious-ness, nor in both, it is obvious that there can be other gradations within this grade depending upon how much subjective truth one would admit to. A third grade of skepticism would be a dogmatic denial of any correlation between our perceptions and the true constitution of objects outside of us, and based on this rejection doubts about objective truth are founded. This grade, too, can have other gradations within it, which depend on whether all correlation of perceptions with objects, or only part of it, is denied, again depending on whether, for example, one denies the bodies only the *qualitates secundarias* or also the *primarias*—whether one denies knowledge of deity in itself and according to its being, or also in its relationship with ourselves. A fourth grade of skepticism does not concern the denial of the possibility of objective truth for us, but only the reality of the recognized objective truth, in such a way that one can hope that one day philosophy may perhaps be able to define what the objects are in themselves. Thus one can differentiate between hopeless and hopeful skepti-cism. This type borders, on the one hand, on the original complete skepticism of the ancients and, on the other hand, on dogmatism.

The ancient skeptics saw themselves as in search of truth, admitting the hope that perhaps one day it may be found—Whereas they differentiated themselves, insofar as they did not simply deny that anything of objective truth had already been discovered, and they did not limit their doubts to objective truth alone. For this reason, this type borders on dogmatism, but additionally, also because it is based on the belief—which would be the precept of any careful dogmatist—that one has to search for objective truth as if nothing had been discovered and one has to withhold one's judgment until the investigation is completed. In just such a way one could think through still other grades of skepticism in closer or wider distance from the ideal. If one wanted obstinately to insist that there was only one certain way of thinking that deserved the name of skepticism, one would contradict the nature of the thing and, although not making it impossible, would render a history of skepticism so meager and uninteresting that it would not be worth the effort. The skeptical way of thinking is by its very nature volatile and uncertain, and these characteristics are so pronounced that even the genuine skeptical philosopher who sets out on certain and fast principles will in the end feel inclined to make his principles the subject of his doubts . . .

II. THE SOURCES AND ORIGIN OF SKEPTICISM

. . . Most often doubt begins with religion, that is to say the religion in which one was brought up. Much here depends on the constitution of the positive religion and the instruction received during one's youth. [Stäudlin's note omitted] Those who were born into and brought up in a very superstitious religion, who received abstract, incomprehensible religious instruction in which at least the dogma was not accompanied by moral teaching, are far more prone to fall into this condition than others when they reach a time when they can think a little for themselves. They start with doubt about the positive religion into which they were born and extend this doubt gradually to revelation as such. Then they go over to the religion of reason until this finally becomes doubtful, too. Not only individuals but whole races and nations go through this process of human thinking. Raynal said once, Catholicism moves incessantly toward Protestantism, Protestantism toward Socinianism, Socinianism toward deism, deism toward skepticism.

During my years at university I met several thinking youths who followed this path. The period of doubt did not have the same effect on all of them, and did not flow from the same source. One with a particular talent for mathematics ended in despair and misery: hypochondria, ill health, and an inclination to parody which combined with wild skepticism. Religion was the first subject that preoccupied all of his lively feeling in all its strength. He became a fanatical pietist. A comedy by Molière which mocked skepticism engaged him, because he thought the criticism unjustified. With his tendency to doubt he listened to metaphysical lectures—his inclination grew even stronger. He made the destiny of man the main subject of his own investigation and sank deeper and deeper into uncertainty. He read Tetens and Kant, and sank ever deeper. He is no longer with us—I do not want to stir the memory among those of my friends who knew him through a detailed description of his life and destiny which I have before me in a very interesting correspondence. Of several others, I have essays on their experience while in this condition. . . .

III. THE CONSEQUENCES AND EFFECTS OF SKEPTICISM

. . . Skepticism often corrupts science and can be a real poison for it. When science has become too presumptuous, too refined, when practical culture cannot keep up with it, skepticism can grow on it like a poisonous plant. On the other hand, it can also be very beneficial for science. When pedantic dogmatism rests on presumptuous assertions, skepticism can awaken it from its slumber—when science is stagnant, when one holds it for perfected where there is only a beginning, when one builds without firm foundations, when curiosity sleeps, then skepticism can stimulate new expansion in science, lead us back to the basis for human knowledge and show its limitations. That skepticism has sometimes had these effects will be shown in its history.

Its most beautiful fruit is modesty, a modest dogmatism and a constant urge to advance knowledge. Few people are made for such skepticism who can limit themselves to subjective conviction. We have in us an urge to accept something as objective and even to transform the subjective into something objective. [Stäudlin's note omitted] We find even in our most common ideas and judgments traces that reveal the impressions of external objects, which could not have come from ourselves. [Stäudlin's note omitted]. . . . This drive to be dogmatic which is in our nature should, it seems, not be destroyed, but be restrained, if we want to attain our goal. Skepticism is a good means to achieve this restraint. It can limit pedantic arrogance that contradicts with insults and is a constant know-it-all, which consciousness of high intelligence and knowledgeable so easily leads to. It moderates us in showing us that the few advantages that distinguish us from the masses are negligible compared to the puzzle and confusion of our nature. There is a certain doubt, a certain prudence and modesty, that should accompany even the most decided dogmatist in all his investigations. A similar fruit of skepticism is when it teaches the dogmatist to limit his investigations to such objects as are suitable for limited human understanding and do not exceed his horizon. Man likes to lose himself in the furthest regions of the excessive when he wants to philosophize. He finds the objects which lie near him and which he is accustomed to trust unworthy of closer examination, and he pleases himself in the investigation of that which is extraordinary and is way above his head. The more the objects of his philosophizing are removed from the accustomed objects of general human understanding, the more superior he feels. He strives for the knowledge of objects without having measured the knowledge that he possesses; he flies too high and does not consider that his feathers may be burned by the sun. A small dose of skepticism can show us the limits of our understanding, within which he may exercise it with happy success. [Stäudlin's note omitted] Hume's skepticism has given us Kant's dogmatism, which is the most modest, prudent, and most favorable for human tranquility and virtue until now. One has, in fact, only to go back to the preposterous presumptions and claims of the proud dogmatists to find that the critical philosophy will lead again to skepticism.

FURTHER READINGS

Blackwell, Constance W. T. "Skepticism as a Sect, Skepticism as a Philosophical Stance: Johann Jakob Brucker versus Carl Friedrich Stäudlin." In *The Skeptical Tradition around 1800: Skepticism in Philosophy, Science, and Society*, edited by Johan van der Zande and Richard H. Popkin, 343–63. Dordrecht: Kluwer, 1998.

Laursen, John C. "Skepticism and the History of Moral Philosophy: The Case of Carl Friedrich Stäudlin." In Van der Zande and Popkin, *The Skeptical Tradition around 1800*, pp. 365–78.

Popkin, Richard H. "Some Thoughts about Stäudlin's 'History and Spirit of Skepticism.'" In Van der Zande and Popkin, *The Skeptical Tradition around 1800*, pp. 339–42.

Schneider, Ulrich J. "Commentary: Stäudlin and the Historiography of Philosophy." In Van der Zande and Popkin, *The Skeptical Tradition around 1800*, pp. 379–84.

33

HEGEL

Georg Wilhelm Friedrich Hegel (1770–1831) was interested in skepticism early in his philosophical career. One of his first publications was a criticism of the modern idealist skepticism held by Schulze (see chapter 31), which he contrasted with the genuine skepticism held by the ancient Pyrrhonians. Skepticism also plays a central role in Hegel's major early book, the *Phenomenology of Spirit*, where Hellenistic skepticism figures as the moment when the Spirit or Mind makes effective its own freedom and autonomy from any external finite thing. In Hegel's later works, skepticism is discussed from a historical point of view in the *Lectures on the History of Philosophy* and from a logical or epistemological viewpoint in the *Encyclopaedia of the Philosophical Sciences*. We include here sections 202–206 from Hegel's *Phenomenology*, which deal with skepticism, and a short—but dense—text from Hegel's *Encyclopaedia*, which exhibits the main features of Hegel's view of skepticism: the distinction between the modern spurious skepticism (Berkeley's and Schulze's idealism) and the ancient genuine skepticism (which he interprets as the self-assurance of the Spirit), his view that in its genuine form skepticism is identical with the dialectical modus operandi of reason, which is the driving force of the mind, and, consequently, that skepticism constitutes an essential part of philosophy itself.

FROM *PHENOMENOLOGY OF SPIRIT*

202. *Skepticism* is the realization of that of which Stoicism was only the Notion, and is the actual experience of what the freedom of thought is. This is *in itself* the negative and must exhibit itself as such. With the reflection of self-consciousness into the simple thought of itself, the independent existence or permanent determinateness that stood over against that reflection has, as a matter of fact, fallen outside of the infinitude of thought. In Skepticism, now, the wholly unessential and non-independent character of this 'other' becomes explicit *for consciousness*; the [abstract] thought becomes the concrete thinking which annihilates the being of the world in all its manifold determinateness, and the negativity of free self-consciousness comes to know itself in the many and varied forms of life as a real negativity.

It is clear that just as Stoicism corresponds to the *Notion* of the *independent* consciousness which appeared as the lord and bondsman relationship, so Skepticism corresponds to its realization as a negative attitude towards otherness, to desire and work. But although desire and work were unable to effect the negation for self-consciousness, this polemical bearing towards the manifold independence of things will, on the other hand, be successful, because it turns against them as a free self-consciousness that is already complete in its own self; more specifically, because it is *thinking*, or is in its own self infinite, and in this infinitude the independent things in their differences from one another are for it only vanishing magnitudes. The differences, which in the pure thinking of self-consciousness are only the abstraction of differences, here become the *entirety* of the differences, and the whole of differentiated being becomes a difference of self-consciousness.

203. Thus the foregoing has defined the nature of the activity of skepticism as such, and the way in which it operates. It exhibits the *dialectical movement* which Sense-certainty, Perception, and the Understanding each is; as also the unessential character of what, in the relationship of lord and bondsman, and for abstract thinking itself, is held to be a determinate element. That relationship at the same time embraces a *specific mode* in which ethical laws, too, are present as sovereign commands. The determinations in abstract thinking, however, are scientific Notions in which [formal] contentless thinking spreads itself, attaching the Notion in fact in a merely external way to the being constituting its content, and which for it is independent, and holding as valid only *determinate* Notions, even though these are only pure abstractions.

204. Dialectic as a negative movement, just as it immediately *is*, at first appears to consciousness as something which has it at its mercy, and which does not have its source in consciousness itself. As Skepticism, on the other hand, it is a moment of self-consciousness, to which it does not *happen* that its truth and reality vanish without its knowing how, but which, in the certainty of its freedom, makes this 'other' which claims to be real, vanish. What Skepticism causes to vanish is not only objective reality as such, but its own relationship to it, in which the 'other' is held to be objective and is established as such, and hence, too, its *perceiving*, along with firmly securing what it is in danger of losing, viz. *sophistry*, and the truth it has itself determined and established. Through this self-conscious negation it procures for its own self the certainty of its freedom, generates the experience of that freedom, and thereby raises it to truth. What vanishes is the determinate element, or the moment of difference, which, whatever its mode of being and whatever its source, sets itself up as something fixed and immutable. It contains no permanent element, and must vanish before thought, because the 'different' is just this, not to be in possession of itself, but to have its essential being only in an other. Thinking, however, is the insight into this nature of the 'different,' it is the negative essence, as simple.

205. The skeptical self-consciousness thus experiences in the flux of all that would stand secure before it its own freedom as given and preserved by itself. It is aware of this stoical indifference of a thinking which thinks itself, the unchanging and genuine certainty of itself. This self-certainty does not issue from something

alien, whose complex development was deposited within it, a result which would leave behind it the process of its coming to be. On the contrary, consciousness itself is the *absolute dialectical unrest*, this medley of sensuous and intellectual representations whose differences coincide, and whose identity is equally again dissolved, for it is itself determinateness as contrasted with the non-identical. But it is just in this process that this consciousness, instead of being self-identical, is in fact nothing but a purely casual, confused medley, the dizziness of a perpetually self-engendered disorder. It is itself aware of this; for itself maintains and creates this restless confusion. Hence it also admits to it, it owns to being a wholly contingent, single, and separate consciousness—a consciousness which is *empirical*, which takes its guidance from what has no reality for it, which obeys what is for it not an essential being, which does those things and brings to realization what it knows has no truth for it. But equally, while it takes itself in this way to be a single and separate, contingent and, in fact, animal life, and a *lost* self-consciousness, it also, on the contrary, converts itself again into a consciousness that is universal and self-identical; for it is the negativity of all singularity and all difference. From this self-identity, or within its own self, it falls back again into the former contingency and confusion, for this same spontaneous negativity has to do solely with what is single and separate, and occupies itself with what is contingent. This consciousness is therefore the unconscious, thoughtless rambling which passes back and forth from the one extreme of self-identical self-consciousness to the other extreme of the contingent consciousness that is both bewildered and bewildering. It does not itself bring these two thoughts of itself together. At one time it recognizes that its freedom lies in rising above all the confusion and contingency of existence, and at another time equally admits to a relapse into occupying itself with what is unessential. It lets the unessential content in its thinking vanish; but just in doing so it is the consciousness of something unessential. It pronounces an absolute vanishing, but the pronouncement *is*, and this consciousness is the vanishing that is pronounced. It affirms the nullity of seeing, hearing, etc., yet it is itself seeing, hearing, etc. It affirms the nullity of ethical principles, and lets its conduct be governed by these very principles. Its deeds and its words always belie one another and equally it has itself the doubly contradictory consciousness of unchangeableness and sameness, and of utter contingency and non-identity with itself. But it keeps the poles of this its self-contradiction apart, and adopts the same attitude to it as it does in its purely negative activity in general. Point out likeness or identity to it, and it will point out unlikeness or non-identity; and, when it is now confronted with what it has just asserted, it turns round and points out likeness or identity. Its talk is in fact like the squabbling of self-willed children, one of whom says A if the other says B, and in turn says B if the other says A, and who by contradicting *themselves* buy for themselves the pleasure of continually contradicting *one another*.

206. In Skepticism, consciousness truly experiences itself as internally contradictory. From this experience emerges a *new form* of consciousness which brings together the two thoughts which Skepticism holds apart. Skepticism's lack of

thought about itself must vanish, because it is in fact *one* consciousness which contains within itself these two modes. This new form is, therefore, one which *knows* that it is the dual consciousness of itself, as self-liberating, unchangeable, and self-identical, and as self-bewildering and self-perverting, and it is the awareness of this self-contradictory nature of itself.

In Stoicism, self-consciousness is the simple freedom of itself. In Skepticism, this freedom becomes a reality, negates the other side of determinate existence, but really duplicates itself, and now knows itself to be a duality. Consequently, the duplication which formerly was divided between two individuals, the lord and the bondsman, is now lodged in one. The duplication of self-consciousness within itself, which is essential in the Notion of Spirit, is thus here before us, but not yet in its unity: the *Unhappy Consciousness* is the consciousness of self as a dual-natured, merely contradictory being.

FROM *THE ENCYCLOPAEDIA LOGIC*

(1) The dialectical, taken separately in its own by the understanding, constitutes *skepticism*, especially when it is exhibited in scientific concepts. Skepticism contains the mere negation that results from the dialectic. (2) Dialectic is usually considered as an external art, which arbitrarily produces a confusion and a mere *semblance* of *contradictions* in determinate concepts, in such a way it is this semblance, and not these determinations, that is supposed to be null and void, whereas on the contrary what is understandable would be true. Dialectic is often no more than a subjective seesaw of arguments that sway back and forth, where basic import is lacking and the [resulting] nakedness is covered by the astuteness that gives birth to such argumentations—According to its proper determinacy, however, the dialectic is the genuine nature that properly belongs to the determinations of the understanding, to things, and to the finite in general. Reflection is initially the transcending of the isolated determinacy and a relating of it, whereby it is posited in relationship but is nevertheless maintained in its isolated validity. The dialectic, on the contrary, is the *immanent* transcending, in which the one-sidedness and restrictedness of the determinations of the understanding displays itself as what it is, i.e., as their negation. That is what everything finite is: its own sublation. Hence, the dialectical constitutes the moving soul of scientific progression, and it is the principle through which alone *immanent coherence and necessity* enter into the content of science, just as all genuine, nonexternal elevation above the finite is to be found in this principle.

Addition 2

Skepticism should not be regarded merely as a doctrine of doubt; rather, it is completely certain about its central point, i.e., the nullity of everything finite. The person who simply doubts still has the hope that his doubt can be resolved, and that one or other of the determinate [views] between which he wavers back and forth will turn out to be a firm and genuine one. Skepticism proper, on the contrary, is complete despair about everything that the understanding holds to be firm, and the disposition that results is imperturbability and inward repose. This is the high ancient skepticism, as we find it presented specifically in Sextus Empiricus, and as it was developed in the later Roman period as a complement to the dogmatic systems of the Stoics and the Epicureans. This ancient high skepticism must not be confused with the modern one . . . which partly preceded the Critical Philosophy and partly grew out of it. This consists simply in denying that anything true and certain can be said about the supersensible, and in designating, on the contrary, the sensible and what is present in immediate sense-experience as what we have to hold onto.

Even nowadays, of course, skepticism is often regarded as an irresistible foe of any positive knowledge, and hence of philosophy too, so far as the latter deals with positive cognition. In response to this it needs to be remarked that in fact it is only the finite and abstract thinking of the understanding that has anything to fear from skepticism, and that cannot resist it; philosophy, on the other hand, contains the skeptical as a moment within itself—specifically as the dialectical moment. But then philosophy does not stop at the merely negative result of the dialectic, as is the case with skepticism. The latter mistakes its results, insofar as it holds fast to it as mere, i.e., abstract, negation. When the dialectic has the negative as its result, then, precisely as a result, this negative is at the same time the positive, for it contains what it resulted from sublated within itself, and it cannot be without it. This, however, is the basic determination of the third form of the Logical, namely, the *speculative* or positively rational [moment].

FURTHER READINGS

Forster, Michael N. *Hegel and Skepticism*. Cambridge, MA: Harvard University Press, 1989.
Hegel, G. W. F. *Lectures on the History of Philosophy*. 3 vols. Translated by E. J. Haldane. Lincoln: University of Nebraska Press, 1995.
———. "Verhältnis des Skeptizismus zur Philosophie." *Kritisches Journal der Philosophie* 2 (1802): 1–74.
Verneaux, R. "L'essence du scepticisme selon Hegel." *Histoire de la philosophie et métaphysique: Recherches de philosophie* I. Paris: Desclée de Brower, 1955.

34

KIERKEGAARD

Søren Kierkegaard (1813–1855) was probably the greatest Christian philosopher of modern times. He struggled against the subordination of religious faith to rational philosophy and natural theology, in particular the Hegelian type quite in vogue in Denmark at the time. His attack upon philosophical systems—Hegel's in particular—which he saw as contrary to the genuine expression of the individual, is one of the roots of the Existentialist movement of the first half of the nineteenth century. We have selected passages from three works of Kierkegaard. The first selection is the preface to *Fear and Trembling*, published under the pseudonym Johannes de Silentius. This is the main work in which Kierkegaard introduces his famous concept of the "leap of faith" by "poetically" describing Abraham's willingness to sacrifice Isaac. The other two selections are from the two philosophical works published under the pseudonym Johannes Climacus, the first from *Philosophical Fragments* and the second from *Concluding Unscientific Postscript* (to the *Philosophical Fragments*). The preface to *Fear and Trembling* criticizes modern (Hegelian) doubt by contrasting it with the living authentic Socratic and ancient skeptical doubt (a view on skepticism also held by Hegel—see chapter 33). The passages from Climacus's works show Kierkegaard's opposition to the speculative (philosophical) and historical approaches to Christian faith and explain Kierkegaard's interest in ancient doubt. The philosophical explanation of the authentic, existential, ancient doubt helps Kierkegaard to clarify his view of genuine faith.

FROM *FEAR AND TREMBLING**

Not only in the business world but also in the world of ideas, our age stages *ein wirklicher Ausverkauf* [a real sale]. Everything can be had at such a bargain price that it becomes a question whether there is finally anyone who will make a bid. Every speculative monitor who conscientiously signals the important trends in modern philosophy, every assistant professor, tutor, and student, every rural outsider and tenant incumbent in philosophy is unwilling to stop with doubting everything but goes further. Perhaps it would be premature and untimely to ask them where they really are

---

*Editorial notes were omitted.

going, but in all politeness and modesty it can probably be taken for granted that they have doubted everything, since otherwise it certainly would be odd to speak of their having gone further. They have all made this preliminary movement and presumably so easily that they find it unnecessary to say a word about how, for not even the person who in apprehension and concern sought a little enlightenment found any, not one suggestive hint or one little dietetic prescription with respect to how a person is to act in carrying out this enormous task. "But did not Descartes do it?" Descartes, venerable, humble, honest thinker, whose writings no one can read without being profoundly affected—he did what he said and said what he did. Alas! Alas! Alas! That is a great rarity in our day! As Descartes himself so frequently said, he did not doubt with respect to faith: "Memores tamen, ut jam dictum est, huic lumini naturali tamdiu tantum esse credendum, quamdiu nihil contrarium a Deo ipso revelatur. ... Præter cætera autem, memoriæ nostræ pro summa regula est infigendum, ea quæ nobis a Deo revelata sunt, ut omnium certissima esse credenda; et quamvis forte lumen rationis, quam maxime clarum et evidens, aliud quid nobis suggerere videretur, soli tamen auctoritati divinæ potius quam proprio nostro judicio fidem esse adhibendam [but we must keep in mind what has been said, that we must trust to this natural light only so long as nothing contrary to it is revealed by God Himself. ... Above all we should impress on our memory as an infallible rule that what God has revealed to us is incomparably more certain than anything else; and that we ought to submit to the Divine authority rather than to our own judgment even though the light of reason may seem to us to suggest, with the utmost clearness and evidence, something opposite]." *Principles of Philosophy*, I, para. 28 and para. 76. He did not shout "Fire! Fire!" and make it obligatory for everyone to doubt, for Descartes was a quiet and solitary thinker, not a shouting street watchman; he modestly let it be known that his method had significance only for him and was partly the result of his earlier warped knowledge. ... [Thus my design is not here to teach the Method which everyone should follow in order to promote the good conduct of his Reason, but only to show in what manner I have endeavored to conduct my own. ... But so soon as I had achieved the entire course of study at the close of which one is usually received into the ranks of the learned, I entirely changed my opinion. For I found myself embarrassed with so many doubts and errors that it seemed to me that the effort to instruct myself had no effect other than the increasing discovery of my own ignorance]." *Dissertation on Method*, pp. 2 and 3.

What those ancient Greeks, who after all did know a little about philosophy, assumed to be a task for a whole lifetime, because proficiency in doubting is not acquired in days and weeks, what the old veteran disputant attained, he who had maintained the equilibrium of doubt throughout all the specious arguments, who had intrepidly denied the certainty of the senses and the certainty of thought, who, uncompromising, had defied the anxiety of self-love and the insinuations of fellow feeling—with that everyone begins in our age.

In our age, everyone is unwilling to stop with faith but goes further. It perhaps would be rash to ask where they are going, whereas it is a sign of urbanity and culture for me to assume that everyone has faith, since otherwise it certainly would be odd to speak of going further. It was different in those ancient days. Faith was then a task for a whole lifetime, because it was assumed that proficiency in believing is not acquired either in days or in weeks. When the tried and tested oldster approached his end, had fought the good fight and kept the faith, his heart was still young enough not to have forgotten the anxiety and trembling that disciplined the youth, that the adult learned to control, but that no man outgrows—except to the extent that he succeeds in going further as early as possible. The point attained by those venerable personages is in our age the point where everyone begins in order to go further.

The present author is by no means a philosopher. He has not understood the system, whether there is one, whether it is completed; it is already enough for his weak head to ponder what a prodigious head everyone must have these days when everyone has such a prodigious idea. Even if someone were able to transpose the whole content of faith into conceptual form, it does not follow that he has comprehended faith, comprehended how he entered into it or how it entered into him. The present author is by no means a philosopher. He is *poetice et eleganter* [in a poetic and refined way] a supplementary clerk who neither writes the system nor gives *promises* of the system, who neither exhausts himself on the system nor binds himself to the system. He writes because to him it is a luxury that is all the more pleasant and apparent the fewer there are who buy and read what he writes. He easily envisions his fate in an age that has crossed out passion in order to serve science, in an age when an author who desires readers must be careful to write in such a way that his book can be conveniently skimmed during the after-dinner nap, must be careful to look and act like that polite gardener's handyman in *Adresseavisen* [The Advertiser] who with hat in hand and good references from his most recent employer recommends himself to the esteemed public. He foresees his fate of being totally ignored; he has a terrible foreboding that the zealous critic will call him on the carpet many times. He dreads the even more terrible fate that some enterprising abstracter, a gobbler of paragraphs (who, in order to save science, is always willing to do to the writing of others what Trop magnanimously did with [his] *The Destruction of the Human Race* in order to "save good taste"), will cut him up into paragraphs and do so with the same inflexibility as the man who, in order to serve the science of punctuation, divided his discourse by counting out the words, fifty words to a period and thirty-five to a semicolon.—I throw myself down in deepest submission before every systematic ransacker: "This is not the system; it has not the least thing to do with the system. I invoke everything good for the system and for the Danish shareholders in this omnibus, for it will hardly become a tower. I wish them all, each and every one, success and good fortune."

Respectfully,
Johannes de Silentio

FROM *PHILOSOPHICAL FRAGMENTS**

Immediate sensation and immediate cognition cannot deceive. This alone indicates that the historical cannot become the object of sense perception or of immediate cognition, because the historical has in itself that very illusiveness that is the illusiveness of coming into existence. In relation to the immediate, coming into existence is an illusiveness whereby that which is most firm is made dubious. For example, when the perceiver sees a star, the star becomes dubious for him the moment he seeks to become aware that it has come into existence. It is just as if reflection removed the star from his senses. It is clear, then, that the organ for the historical must be formed in likeness to this, must have within itself the corresponding something by which in its certitude it continually annuls the incertitude that corresponds to the uncertainty of coming into existence—a double uncertainty: the nothingness of non-being and the annihilated possibility, which is also the annihilation of every other possibility. This is precisely the nature of belief [*Tro*], for continually present as the nullified in the certitude of belief is the incertitude that in every way corresponds to the uncertainty of coming into existence. Thus, belief believes what it does not see; it does not believe that the star exits, for that it sees, but it believes that the star has come into existence. The same is true of an event. The occurrence can be known immediately but not that it has occurred, not even that it is in the process of occurring, even though it is taking place, as they say, right in front of one's nose. The illusiveness of the occurrence is that it has occurred, and therein lies the transition from nothing, from non-being, and from the multiple possible "how." Immediate sense perception and cognition do not have any intimation of the unsureness with which belief approaches its object, but neither do they have the certitude that extricates itself from the incertitude.

Immediate sensation and cognition cannot deceive. It is important to understand this in order to understand doubt and in order through it to assign belief its place. However strange it may seem, this thought underlies Greek skepticism. Yet it is not so difficult to understand this or to understand how this casts light on belief, provided one is not utterly confused by the Hegelian doubt about everything, against which there is really no need to preach, for what the Hegelians say about it is of such a nature that it seems rather to favor a modest doubt as to whether there really is anything to their having doubted something. Greek skepticism was a withdrawing skepticism *epoche* [suspension of judgment]; they doubt not by virtue of knowledge but by virtue of will (deny assent—*metriopatheia* [moderate feeling]). This implies that doubt can be terminated only in freedom, by an act of will, something every Greek skeptic would understand, inasmuch as he understood himself, but he would not terminate his skepticism precisely because he *willed* to doubt. We must leave that up to him, but we must not lay at his door the stupid opinion that one doubts by way of necessity, as well as the even more stupid opinion that, if that were the case, doubt could be terminated. The Greek skeptic did not deny the correctness of sensation and

---

*Editorial notes were omitted.

of immediate cognition, but, said he, error has an utterly different basis—it comes from the conclusion I draw. If I can only avoid drawing conclusions, I shall never be deceived. If, for example, sensation shows me in the distance a round object that close at hand is seen to be square or shows me a stick that looks broken in the water although it is straight when taken out, sensation has not deceived me, but I am deceived only when I conclude something about that stick and that object. This is why the skeptic keeps himself continually *in suspenso*, and this state was what he *willed*. As for calling Greek skepticism . . . [philosophy zetetic, aporetic, skeptic], these predicates do not express what is distinctive in Greek skepticism, which unfailingly used cognition only to preserve the cast of mind, which was the main consideration, and therefore it would not even declare its negative cognitive results . . . [positively] lest it be trapped in having drawn a conclusion. The cast of mind was to them the primary issue. . . . [The skeptics say that the end in view is a mind suspended, which brings with it tranquility like its shadow]. (*Diogenes Laertius*, IX, para. 107.)*

In contrast, it is now readily apparent that belief is not a knowledge but an act of freedom, an expression of will. It believes the coming into existence and has annulled in itself the incertitude that corresponds to the nothingness of that which is not. It believes the "thus and so" of that which has come into existence and has annulled in itself the possible "how" of that which has come into existence, and without denying the possibility of another "thus and so," the "thus and so" of that which has come into existence is nevertheless most certain for belief.

Insofar as that which by belief becomes the historical, and as the historical becomes the object of belief (the one corresponds to the other), does exist immediately and is apprehended immediately, it does not deceive. The contemporary does, then, use his eyes etc., but he must pay attention to the conclusion. He cannot know immediately and directly that it has come into existence, but neither can he know with necessity that it has come into existence, for the first mark of coming into existence is specifically a break in continuity. At the moment belief believes that it has come into existence, that it has occurred, it makes dubious what occurred and what has come into existence in the coming into existence and its "thus and so" in the possible how of coming into existence. The conclusion of belief is no conclusion [*Slutning*] but a resolution [*Beslutning*], and thus doubt is excluded. It might seem to be an inference from effect to cause when belief concludes: this exists, *ergo* it came into existence. But this is not entirely true, and even if it were, one must remember that the cognitive inference is from cause to effect or rather from ground to consequent (Jacobi). This is not entirely true, because I cannot immediately sense or know that what I immediately sense or know is an effect, for immediately it simply is. That it is an effect is something I believe, because in order to predicate that it is an effect, I

---

*Both Plato and Aristotle emphasize that immediate sensation and cognition cannot deceive. Later, Descartes says, just as the Greek skeptics did, that error comes from the will, which is in too great a hurry to draw conclusions. This casts light on belief also. When belief resolves to believe, it runs the risk that it was an error, but nevertheless it wills to believe. One never believes in any other way; if one wants to avoid risk, then one wants to know with certainty that one can swim before going into water.

must already have made it dubious in the uncertainty of coming into existence. But if belief decides on this, then the doubt is terminated; in that very moment the balance and neutrality of doubt are terminated—not by knowledge but by will. Thus, while making an approach, belief is the most disputable (for doubt's uncertainty, strong and invincible in making duplicitous—*dis-putare* [double-reckon]—has run aground in it) and is the least. Disputable by virtue of its new quality. Belief is the opposite of doubt. Belief and doubt are not two kinds of knowledge that can be defined in continuity with each other, for neither of them is a cognitive act, and they are opposite passions. Belief is a sense for coming into existence, and doubt is a protest against any conclusion that wants to go beyond immediate sensation and immediate knowledge. The doubter, for example, does not deny his own existence, but he draws no conclusions, for he does not want to be deceived. Insofar as he uses dialectic in continually making the opposite equally probable, he does not erect his skepticism on dialectical arguments, which are nothing more than outer fortifications, human accommodations; therefore he has no results, not even negative ones (for this would mean the acknowledgment of knowledge), but by the power of the will he decides to restrain himself and hold himself back . . . [ephectic philosophy]) from any conclusion.

Instead of having the immediacy of sensation and cognition (which, however, cannot apprehend the historical), the person who is not contemporary with the historical has the report of contemporaries, to which he relates in the same manner as the contemporaries to the immediacy. Even if what is said in the report has also undergone change, he cannot treat it in such a way that he does not personally assent to it and render it historical unless he transforms it into the unhistorical for himself. The immediacy of the report, that is, that the report is there, is the immediate present, but the historical character of the present is that it has come into existence, and the historical character of the past is that it was a present by having come into existence. As soon as someone who comes later believes the past (not the truth of it, for that is a matter of cognition, which involves essence and not being, but believes that it was something present by having come into existence), then the uncertainty of coming into existence is there, and this uncertainty of coming into existence (the nothingness of that which is not—the possible "how" of the actual **thus and so**) must be the same for him as for the contemporary; his mind must be *in suspenso* just as the contemporary's. Then he no longer faces immediacy, or any necessity of coming into existence, but only the "thus and so" of *coming into existence*. The one who comes later does indeed believe by virtue of the contemporary's declaration, but only in the same sense as the contemporary believes by virtue of immediate sensation and cognition, but the contemporary cannot believe by virtue of that, and thus the one who comes later cannot believe by virtue of the report.

Thus at no moment does the past become necessary, no more than it was necessary when it came into existence or appeared necessary to the contemporary who believed it—that is, believed that it had come into existence. Belief and coming into existence correspond to each other and involve the annulled qualifications of being, the past and the future, and the present only insofar as it is regarded under the annulled qualification of being as that which has come into existence. Necessity, however, pertains to essence and in such a way that the qualification of essence specifically excludes coming into existence. The possibility from which emerged the possible that became the actual always accompanies that which came into existence and remains with the past though centuries lie between. As soon as one who comes later repeats that it has come into existence (which he does by believing it), he repeats its possibility, regardless of whether there may or may not be more specific conceptions of this possibility.

FROM *CONCLUDING UNSCIENTIFIC POSTSCRIPT*

When subjectivity is the truth, the conceptual determination of the truth must include an expression for the antithesis to objectivity, a memento of the fork in the road where the way swings off; this expression will at the same time serve as an indication of the tension of the subjective inwardness. Here is such a definition of truth: *An objective uncertainty held fast in an appropriation-process of the most passionate inwardness is the truth*, the highest truth attainable for an existing individual. At the point where the way swings off (and where this cannot be specified objectively, since it is a matter of subjectivity), there objective knowledge is placed in abeyance. Thus the subject merely has, objectively, the uncertainty; but it is this which precisely increases the tension of that infinite passion which constitutes his inwardness. The truth is precisely the venture which chooses an objective uncertainty with the passion of the infinite. I contemplate the order of nature in the hope of finding God, and I see omnipotence and wisdom; but I also see much else that disturbs my mind and excites anxiety. The sum of all this is an objective uncertainty. But it is for this very reason that the inwardness becomes as intense as it is, for it embraces this objective uncertainty with the entire passion of the infinite. In the case of a mathematical proposition the objectivity is given, but for this reason the truth of such a proposition is also an indifferent truth.

But the above definition of truth is an equivalent expression for faith. Without risk there is no faith. Faith is precisely the contradiction between the infinite passion of the Individual's inwardness and the objective uncertainty. If I am capable of grasping God objectively, I do not believe, but precisely because I cannot do this I must believe. If I wish to preserve myself in faith I must constantly be intent upon holding fast the objective uncertainty, so as to remain out upon the deep, over seventy thousand fathoms of water, still preserving my faith.

In the principle that subjectivity, inwardness, is the truth, there is comprehended the Socratic wisdom, whose everlasting merit it was to have become aware of the essential significance of existence, of the fact that the knower is an existing individual. For this reason Socrates was in the truth by virtue of his ignorance, in the highest sense in which this was possible within paganism. To attain to an understanding of this, to comprehend that the misfortune of speculative philosophy is again and again to have forgotten that the knower is an existing individual, is in our objective age difficult enough. But to have made an advance upon Socrates without even having understood what he understood, is at any rate not "Socratic." . . .

Let us now start from this point, and as was attempted in the *Fragments*, seek a determination of thought which will really carry us further. I have nothing here to do with the question of whether this proposed thought-determination is true or not, since I am merely experimenting; but it must at any rate be clearly manifest that the Socratic thought is understood within the new proposal, so that at least I do not come out behind Socrates.

When subjectivity, inwardness, is the truth, the truth becomes objectively a paradox; and the fact that the truth is objectively a paradox shows in its turn that subjectivity is the truth. For the objective situation is repellent; and the expression for the objective repulsion constitutes the tension and the measure of the corresponding inwardness. The paradoxical character of the truth is its objective uncertainty; this uncertainty is an expression for the passionate inwardness, and this passion is precisely the truth. So far the Socratic principle. The eternal and essential truth, the truth which has an essential relationship to an existing individual because it pertains essentially to existence (all other knowledge being from the Socratic point of view accidental, its scope and degree a matter of indifference), is a paradox. But the eternal essential truth is by no means in itself a paradox; but it becomes paradoxical by virtue of its relationship to an existing individual. The Socratic ignorance gives expression to the objective uncertainty attaching to the truth, while his inwardness in existing is the truth. To anticipate here what will be developed later, let me make the following remark. The Socratic ignorance is an analogue to the category of the absurd, only that there is still less of objective certainty in the absurd, and in the repellent effect that the absurd exercises. It is certain only that it is absurd, and precisely on that account incites to an infinitely greater tension in the corresponding inwardness. The Socratic inwardness in existing is an analogue to faith; only that the inwardness of faith, corresponding as it does, not to the repulsion of the Socratic ignorance, but to the repulsion exerted by the absurd is infinitely more profound.

Socratically the eternal essential truth is by no means in its own nature paradoxical, but only in its relationship to an existing individual. This finds expression in another Socratic proposition, namely, that all knowledge is recollection. This proposition is not for Socrates a cue to the speculative enterprise, and hence he does not follow it up; essentially it becomes a Platonic principle. Here the way swings off; Socrates concentrates essentially upon accentuating existence, while Plato forgets this and loses himself in speculation. Socrates' infinite merit is to have been an *existing* thinker, not a speculative philosopher who forgets what it means to exist. For Socrates therefore the principle that all knowledge is recollection has at the moment of his leave-taking and as the constantly rejected possibility of engaging in speculation, the following two-fold significance: (1) that the knower is essentially *integer*, and that with respect to the knowledge of the eternal truth he is confronted with no other difficulty than the circumstance that he exists; which difficulty, how-ever, is so essential and decisive for him that it means that existing, the process of transformation to inwardness in and by existing, is the truth; (2) that existence in time does not have any decisive significance, because the possibility of taking one-self back into eternity through recollection is always there, though this possibility is constantly nullified by utilizing the time, not for speculation, but for the transfor-mation to inwardness in existing. [Kierkegaard's note omitted]

The infinite merit of the Socratic position was precisely to accentuate the fact that the knower is an existing individual, and that the task of existing is his essential task. Making an advance upon Socrates by failing to understand this, is quite a mediocre achievement. This Socratic principle we must therefore bear in mind, and then inquire whether the formula may not be so altered as really to make an advance beyond the Socratic position.

Subjectivity, inwardness, has been posited as the truth; can any expression for the truth be found which has a still higher degree of inwardness? Aye, there is such an expression, provided the principle that subjectivity or inwardness is the truth begins by positing the opposite principle: that subjectivity is untruth. Let us not at this point succumb to such haste as to fail in making the necessary distinctions. Speculative philosophy also says that subjectivity is untruth, but says it in order to stimulate a movement in precisely the opposite direction, namely, in the direction of the principle that objectivity is the truth. Speculative philosophy determines subjec-tivity negatively as tending toward objectivity. This second determination of ours, however, places a hindrance in its own way while proposing to begin, which has the effect of making the inwardness far more intensive. Socratically speaking, subjec-tivity is untruth if it refuses to understand that subjectivity is truth, but, for example, desires to become objective. Here, on the other hand, subjectivity in beginning upon the task of becoming the truth through a subjectifying process, is in the difficulty that it is already untruth. Thus, the labor of the task is thrust backward, backward, that is, in inwardness. So far is it from being the case that the way tends in the direction of objectivity, that the beginning merely lies still deeper in subjectivity.

But the subject cannot be untruth eternally, or eternally be presupposed as having been untruth; it must have been brought to this condition in time, or here become untruth in time. The Socratic paradox consisted in the fact that the eternal was related to an existing individual, but now existence has stamped itself upon the existing indi-vidual a second time. There has taken place so essential an alteration in him that he cannot now possibly take himself back into the eternal by way of recollection. To do this is to speculate; to be able to do this, but to reject the possibility by apprehending the task of life as a realization of inwardness in existing, is the Socratic position. But now the difficulty is that what followed Socrates on his way as a rejected possibility, has become an impossibility. If engaging in speculation was a dubious merit even from the point of view of the Socratic, it is now neither more nor less than confusion.

The paradox emerges when the eternal truth and existence are placed in juxta-position with one another; each time the stamp of existence is brought to bear, the paradox becomes more clearly evident. Viewed Socratically the knower was simply an existing individual, but now the existing individual bears the stamp of having been essentially altered by existence.

Let us now call the untruth of the individual *Sin*. Viewed eternally he cannot be sin, nor can he be eternally presupposed as having been in sin. By coming into existence therefore (for the beginning was that subjectivity is untruth), he becomes a sinner. He is not born as a sinner in the sense that he is presupposed as being a sinner before he is born, but he is born in sin and as a sinner. This we might call *Original Sin*. But if existence has in this manner acquired a power over him, he is prevented from taking himself back into the eternal by way of recollection. If it was paradoxical to posit the eternal truth in relationship to an existing individual, it is now absolutely paradoxical to posit it in relationship to such an individual as we have here defined. But the more difficult it is made for him to take himself out of existence by way of recollection, the more profound is the inwardness that his existence may have in existence; and when it is made impossible for him, when he is held so fast in existence that the back door of recollection is forever closed to him, then his inwardness will be the most profound possible. But let us never forget that the Socratic merit was to stress the fact that the knower is an existing individual; for the more difficult the matter becomes, the greater the temptation to go the easy road of speculation, away from fearful dangers and crucial decisions, to the winning of renown and honors and property, and so forth. If even Socrates understood the dubiety of taking himself speculatively out of existence back into the eternal, although no other difficulty confronted the existing individual except that he existed, that existing was his essential task, now it is impossible. Forward he must, backward he cannot go.

Subjectivity is the truth. By virtue of the relationship subsisting between eternal truth and the existing individual, the paradox came into being. Let us now go further, let us suppose that the eternal essential truth is itself a paradox. How does the paradox come into being? By putting the eternal essential truth into juxtaposition with the existence. Hence when we posit such a conjunction within the truth itself, the truth becomes a paradox. The eternal truth has come into being in time: this is the paradox. If in accordance with the determinations just posited, the subject is prevented by sin from taking himself back into the eternal, now he need not trouble himself about this; for now the eternal essential truth is not behind him but in front of him, through its being in existence or having existed, so that if the individual does not existentially and in existence lay hold of the truth, he will never lay hold of it.

Existence can never be more sharply accentuated than by means of these determinations. The evasion by which speculative philosophy attempts to recollect itself out of existence has been made impossible. With reference to this, there is nothing for speculation to do except to arrive at an understanding of this impossibility; every speculative attempt which insists on being speculative show *eo ipso* that it has not understood it. The individual may thrust all this away from him, and take refuge in speculation; but it is impossible first to accept it, and then to revoke it by means of speculation, since it is definitely calculated to prevent speculation.

When the eternal truth is related to an existing individual it becomes a paradox. The paradox repels in the inwardness of the existing individual, through the objective uncertainty and the corresponding Socratic ignorance. But since the paradox is not in the first instance itself paradoxical (but only in its relationship to the existing individual), it does not repel with a sufficient intensive inwardness. For without risk there is no faith, and the greater the risk the greater the faith; the more objective security the less inwardness (for inwardness is precisely subjectivity), and the less objective security the more profound the possible inwardness. When the paradox is paradoxical in itself, it repels the individual by virtue of its absurdity, and the corresponding passion of inwardness is faith. But subjectivity, inwardness, is the truth; for otherwise we have forgotten what the merit of the Socratic position is. But there can be no stronger expression for inwardness than when the retreat out of existence into the eternal by way of recollection is impossible; and when, with truth confronting the individual as a paradox, gripped in the anguish and pain of sin, facing the tremendous risk of the objective insecurity, the individual believes. But without risk no faith, not even the Socratic form of faith, much less the form of which we here speak.

When Socrates believed that there was a God, he held fast to the objective uncertainty with the whole passion of his inwardness, and it is precisely in this contradiction and in this risk, that faith is rooted. Now it is otherwise. Instead of the objective uncertainty, there is here a certainty, namely, that objectively it is absurd; and this absurdity, held fast in the passion of inwardness, is faith. The Socratic ignorance is as a witty jest in comparison with the earnestness of facing the absurd; and the Socratic existential inwardness is as Greek light-mindedness in comparison with the grave strenuosity of faith.

What now is the absurd? The absurd is—that the eternal truth has come into being in time, that God has come into being, has been born, has grown up, and so forth, precisely like any other individual human being, quite indistinguishable from other individuals. For every assumption of immediate recognizability is pre-Socratic paganism, and from the Jewish point of view, idolatry; and every determination of what really makes an advance beyond the Socratic must essentially bear the stamp of having a relationship to God's having come into being; for faith *sensu strictissimo*, as was developed in the *Fragments*, refers to becoming. When Socrates believed that there was a God, he saw very well that where the way swings off there is also an objective way of approximation, for example by the contemplation of nature and human history, and so forth. His merit was precisely to shun this way, where the quantitative siren song enchants the mind and deceives the existing individual.

In relation to the absurd, the objective approximation-process is like the comedy, *Misunderstanding upon Misunderstanding*, which is generally played by *Privatdocents* and speculative philosophers. The absurd is precisely by its objective repulsion the measure of the intensity of faith in inwardness. Suppose a man who wishes to acquire faith; let the comedy begin. He wishes to have faith, but he wishes also to safeguard himself by means of an objective inquiry and its approximation-process. What happens? With the help of the approximation-process the absurd becomes something different; it becomes probable, it becomes increasingly probable, it becomes extremely and emphatically probable. Now he is ready to believe it, and he ventures to claim for himself that he does not believe as shoemakers and tailors and simple folk believe, but only after long deliberation. Now he is ready to believe it; and lo, now it has become precisely impossible to believe it. Anything that is almost probable, or probable, or extremely and emphatically probable, is something he can almost know, or as good as know, or extremely and emphatically almost *know*—but it is impossible to *believe*. For the absurd is the object of faith, and the only object that can be believed.

FURTHER READINGS

Evans, C. Stephen. *Kierkegaard's Fragments and Postscript: The Religious Philosophy of Johannes Climacus*. Atlantic Highlands, NJ: Humanities Press, 1983.

Grimsley, Ronald. *Sören Kierkegaard and French Literature*. Cardiff: University of Wales Press, 1966.

Maia Neto, José. R. *The Christianization of Pyrrhonism: Skepticism and Faith in Pascal, Kierkegaard and Shestov*. Dordrecht: Kluwer, 1995.

Popkin, Richard H. "The 'Incurable Scepticism' of Henry More, Blaise Pascal and Søren Kierkegaard." In *Scepticism from the Renaissance to the Enlightenment*, edited by Richard H. Popkin and Charles Schmitt, 169–84. Wiesbaden: O. Harrassowitz, 1987.

———. "Hume and Kierkegaard." *Journal of Religion* 31 (1951): 274–81.

———. "Kierkegaard and Skepticism." *Algemeen Nederlands Tijdschrift voor Wijsbegeerte en Psychologie* 51 (1959): 123–41.

35

NIETZSCHE

Friedrich Nietzsche (1844–1900) was one of the greatest German philosophers. His philosophy of "the will to power"—which has been quite differently interpreted—has been one of the main sources of the contemporary movement in philosophy often called postmodernism. His place in the history of skepticism is not limited to this influence. Nietzsche knew well and discussed both ancient and modern skepticism, and not only Cartesian skepticism but also the skepticism exhibited by Pascal and the French skeptics often associated with early modern libertine and free thought (Montaigne, Charron, La Mothe Le Vayer, and Bayle). The texts below were selected by Rogério Lopes. They were extracted from works of the different phases of Nietzsche's thought. They show that Nietzsche's early understanding of skepticism is closely related to the debate about the "end of metaphysics" after Kant's critical philosophy and Schopenhauer's reaction to Kant. They also bring to light the skepticism related to Nietzsche's critical assessment of Christianity (skepticism about values). Last, but not least, they show Nietzsche's strong support and development of the notion of intellectual integrity—which lies at the basis of his view of the superman. Nietzsche recognizes, in his later work, that intellectual integrity is characteristic—and exclusive—of the ancient skeptics: "Zarathustra is a skeptic," says Nietzsche. The texts were extracted from the Web site http://turn.to/nietzsche.

SCHOPENHAUER AS EDUCATOR, SECTION 3

This was the first danger in whose shadow Schopenhauer grew up: isolation. The second was despair of the truth. This danger attends every thinker who sets out from the Kantian philosophy, provided he is a vigorous and whole man in suffering and desire and not a mere clattering thought—and calculating-machine. Now we all know very well the shameful implications of this presupposition; it seems to me, indeed, that Kant has had a living and life-transforming influence on only a very few men. One can read everywhere, I know, that since this quiet scholar produced his work a revolution has taken place in every domain of the spirit; but I cannot believe it. For I cannot see it in those men who would themselves have to be revolutionized before a revolution could take place in any whole domain whatever. If Kant ever should begin to exercise any wide influence we shall be aware of it in the form of a gnawing and disintegrating skepticism and relativism; and only in the most active and noble spirits who have never been able to exist in a state of doubt would there appear instead that undermining and despair of all truth such as Heinrich von Kleist for example experiences as the effect of the Kantian philosophy.

HUMAN, ALL-TOO-HUMAN 21, 225, 226, AND 630

21. *Presumed triumph of skepticism.* Let us accept for the moment the skeptical starting point: assuming there were no other, metaphysical world and that we could not use any metaphysical explanations of the only world known to us, how would we then look upon men and things? One can imagine this; it is useful to do so, even if one were to reject the question of whether Kant and Schopenhauer proved anything metaphysical scientifically. For according to historical probability, it is quite likely that men at some time will become *skeptical* about this whole subject. So one must ask the question: how will human society take shape under the influence of such an attitude? Perhaps the *scientific proof* of any metaphysical world is itself so *difficult* that mankind can no longer keep from distrusting it. And if one is distrustful of metaphysics, then we have, generally speaking, the same consequences as if metaphysics had been directly refuted and one were no longer *permitted* to believe in it. The historical question about mankind's unmetaphysical views remains the same in either case. . . .

225. *The free spirit a relative concept.* A man is called a free spirit if he thinks otherwise than would be expected, based on his origin, environment, class, and position, or based on prevailing contemporary views. He is the exception: bound spirits are the rule; the latter reproach him that his free principles have their origin either in a need to be noticed, or else may even lead one to suspect him of free actions, that is, actions that are irreconcilable with bound morality. Sometimes it is also said that certain free principles derive from perverseness and eccentricity; but this is only the voice of malice, which does not, itself, believe what it says, but only wants to hurt: for the free spirit generally has proof of his greater kindness and sharp intellect written so legibly on his face that bound spirits understand it well enough. But the two other derivations of free-thinking are meant honestly; and many free spirits do indeed come into being in one or the other of these ways: But the tenets they arrive at thereby could still be more true and reliable than the tenets of bound spirits. In the knowledge of truth, what matters *is having* it, not what made one seek it, or how one found it. If the free spirits are right, the bound spirits are wrong, whether or not the former came to truth out of immorality and the others have kept clinging to untruth out of morality. Incidentally, it is not part of the nature of the free spirit that his views are more correct, but rather that he has released himself from tradition, be it successfully or unsuccessfully. Usually, however, he has truth, or at least the spirit of the search for truth, on his side: he demands reasons, while others demand faith.

226. *Origin of faith.* The bound spirit assumes a position, not for reasons, but out

of habit; he is a Christian, for example, not because he had insight into the various religions and chose among them; he is an Englishman not because he decided for England; but rather, Christianity and England were givens, and he accepted them without having reasons, as someone who was born in wine country becomes a wine drinker. Later, when he was a Christian and an Englishman, he may also have devised some reasons in favor of his habit; even if these reasons are overthrown, he, in his whole position, is not. Ask a bound spirit for his reasons against bigamy, for example, and you will learn whether his holy zeal for monogamy is based on reasons or on habit. The habit of intellectual principles without reasons is called faith. . . .

630. Conviction is the belief that in some point of knowledge one possesses absolute truth. Such a belief presumes, then, that absolute truths exist; likewise, that the perfect methods for arriving at them have been found; finally, that every man who has convictions makes use of these perfect methods. All three assertions prove at once that the man of convictions is not the man of scientific thinking; he stands before us still in the age of theoretical innocence, a child, however grown up he might be otherwise. But throughout thousands of years, people have lived in such childlike assumptions, and from out of them mankind's mightiest sources of power have flowed. The countless people who sacrificed themselves for their convictions thought they were doing it for absolute truth. All of them were wrong: probably no man has ever sacrificed himself for truth; at least, the dogmatic expression of his belief will have been unscientific or half-scientific. But actually one wanted to be right because one thought he had to be right. To let his belief be torn from him meant perhaps to put his eternal happiness in question. With a matter of this extreme importance, the "will" was all too audibly the intellect's prompter. Every believer of every persuasion assumed he could not be refuted; if the counterarguments proved very strong, he could still always malign reason in general and perhaps even raise as a banner of extreme fanaticism the "credo quia absurdum est." It is not the struggle of opinions that has made history so violent, but rather the struggle of belief in opinions, that is, the struggle of convictions.

THE GAY SCIENCE 1.2, 3.122, AND 5.347

1.2. *The intellectual* conscience—I keep having the same experience and keep resisting it every time. I do not want to believe it although it is palpable: *the great majority of people lack an intellectual conscience*. Indeed, it has often seemed to me as if anyone calling for an intellectual conscience were as lonely in the most densely populated cities as if he were in a desert. Everybody looks at you with strange eyes and goes right on handling his scales, calling this good and that evil. Nobody even blushes when you intimate that their weights are underweight; nor do people feel outraged; they merely laugh at your doubts. I mean: *the great majority of people* does not consider it contemptible to believe this or that and to live accordingly, without first having given themselves an account of the final and most certain reasons pro and con, and without even troubling themselves about such reasons afterward: the most gifted men and the noblest women still belong to this "great majority." But what is goodheartedness, refinement, or genius to me, when the person who has these virtues tolerates slack feelings in his faith and judgments and when he does not account *the desire for certainty* as his inmost craving and deepest distress—as that which separates the higher human beings from the lower. . . .

3.122. *The Element of Moral Skepticism in Christianity.* Christianity also has made a great contribution to enlightenment, and has taught moral skepticism—in a very impressive and effective manner, accusing and embittering, but with untiring patience and subtlety; it annihilated in every individual the belief in his virtues: it made the great virtuous ones, of whom antiquity had no lack, vanish for ever from the earth, those popular men, who, in the belief in their perfection, walked about with the dignity of a hero of the bullfight. When, trained in this Christian school of skepticism, we now read the moral books of the ancients, for example those of Seneca and Epictetus, we feel a pleasurable superiority, and are full of secret insight and penetration—it seems to us as if a child tallied before an old man, or a pretty, gushing girl before La Rochefoucauld; we know better what virtue is? After all, however, we have applied the same skepticism to all religious states and processes, such as sin, repentance, grace, sanctification, etc., and have allowed the worm to burrow so well, that we have now the same feeling of subtle superiority and insight even in reading all Christian books; we know also the religious feelings better! And it is time to know them well and describe them well, for the pious ones of the old belief die out also; let us save their likeness and type, at least for the sake of knowledge.

5.347. *Believers and their need to believe.* How much one needs a faith in order to flourish, how much that is "firm" and that one does not wish to be shaken because one *clings* to it, that is a measure of the degree of one's strength (or, to put the point more clearly, of one's weakness). Christianity, it seems to me, is still needed by most people in old Europe even today; therefore it still finds believers. For this is how man is: An article of faith could be refuted before him a thousand times—if he needed it, he would consider it "true" again and again, in accordance with that famous "proof of strength" of which the Bible speaks. Metaphysics is still needed by some; but so is that impetuous *demand for certainty* that today discharges itself among large numbers of people in a scientific-positivistic form. The demand that one *wants* by all means that something should be firm (while on account of the ardor of this demand one is easier and more negligent about the demonstration of this certainty)—this, too, is still the demand for a support, a prop, in short, that *instinct of weakness* which, to be sure, does not create religious, metaphysical systems, and convictions of all kinds but—conserves them. . . . Faith is always coveted most and needed most urgently where will is lacking; for will, as the affect of command, is the decisive sign of sovereignty and strength. In other words, the less one knows how to command, the more urgently one covets someone who commands, who commands severely—a god, prince, class, physician, father confessor, dogma, or party conscience. From this one might perhaps gather that the two world religions, Buddhism and Christianity, may have owed their origin and above all their sudden spread to a tremendous collapse and *disease of the will*. And that is what actually happened: both religions encountered a situation in which the will had become diseased, giving rise to a demand that had become utterly desperate for some "thou shalt." Both religions taught fanaticism in ages in which the will had become exhausted, and thus they offered innumerable people some support, a new possibility of willing, some delight in willing. For fanaticism is the only "strength of the will" that even the weak and insecure can be brought to attain, being a sort of hypnotism of the whole system of the senses and the intellect for the benefit of an excessive nourishment (hypertrophy) of a single point of view and feeling that henceforth becomes dominant— which the Christian calls his *faith*. Once a human being reaches the fundamental conviction that he *must* be commanded, he becomes "a believer." Conversely, one could conceive of such a pleasure and power of self-determination, such a *freedom* of the will that the spirit would take leave of all faith and every wish for certainty, being practiced in maintaining himself on insubstantial ropes and possibilities and dancing even near abysses. Such a spirit would be the *free spirit* par excellence.

BEYOND GOOD AND EVIL 1.5 AND 2.54

1.5. What provokes one to look at all philosophers half suspiciously, half mockingly, is not that one discovers again and again how innocent they are—how often and how easily they make mistakes and go astray; in short, their childishness and childlikeness— but that they are not honest enough in their work, although they make a lot of virtuous noise when the problem of truthfulness is touched even remotely. They all pose as if they had discovered and reached their real opinions through the self-development cold, pure, divinely unconcerned dialectic (as opposed to the mystics of every rank, who are more honest and doltish—and talk of "inspiration"); while at bottom it is an assumption, a hunch, indeed a kind of "inspiration"—most often a desire of the heart that has been filtered and made abstract—that they defend with reasons they have sought after the fact. They are all advocates who resent that name, and for the most part even wily spokesmen for their prejudices which they baptize "truths"—and very far from having the courage of the conscience that admits this, precisely this, to itself; very far from having the good taste of the courage which also lets this be known, whether to warn an enemy or friend, or, from exuberance, to mock itself. . . .

2.54. What, at bottom, is the whole of modern philosophy doing? Since Descartes—and indeed rather in spite of him than on the basis of his precedent—all philosophers have been making an *attentat* on the ancient soul concept under the cloak of a critique of the subject-and-predicate concept—that is to say, an *attentat* on the fundamental presupposition of Christian doctrine. Modern philosophy, as an epistemological skepticism, is, covertly or openly, *anti-Christian*: although, to speak to more refined ears, by no means anti-religious. For in the past one believed in 'the soul' as one believed in grammar and the grammatical subject: one said 'I' is the condition, 'think' is the predicate, and conditioned-thinking is an activity to which a subject *must* be thought of as cause. Then one tried with admirable artfulness and tenacity to fathom whether one could not get out of this net—whether the reverse was not perhaps true: 'think' the condition, 'I' conditioned; 'I' thus being only a synthesis *produced* by thinking. Kant wanted fundamentally to prove that, starting from the subject, the subject could not be proved—nor could the object: the possibility of an apparent existence of the subject, that is to say of 'the soul,' may not always have been remote from him, that idea which, as the philosophy of the Vedanta, has exerted immense influence on earth before.

THE ANTICHRIST 12 AND 54

12. I put aside a few skeptics, the types of decency in the history of philosophy: the rest haven't the slightest conception of intellectual integrity. They behave like women, all these great enthusiasts and prodigies—they regard "beautiful feelings" as arguments, the "heaving breast" as the bellows of divine inspiration, conviction as the *criterion* of truth. In the end, with "German" innocence, Kant tried to give a scientific flavor to this form of corruption, this dearth of intellectual conscience, by calling it "practical reason." He deliberately invented a variety of reasons for use on occasions when it was desirable not to trouble with reason—that is, when morality, when the sublime command "thou shalt," was heard. When one recalls the fact that, among all peoples, the philosopher is no more than a development from the old type of priest, this inheritance from the priest, this *fraud upon self*, ceases to be remarkable. When a man feels that he has a divine mission, say to lift up, to save, or to liberate mankind—when a man feels the divine spark in his heart and believes that he is the mouthpiece of supernatural imperatives—when such a mission inflames him, it is only natural that he should stand beyond all merely reasonable standards of judgment. He feels that he is *himself* sanctified by this mission, that he is himself a type of a higher order! . . . What has a priest to do with philosophy! He stands far above it!—And hitherto the priest has *ruled*!—He has determined the meaning of "true" and "not true"!

54. Do not let yourself be deceived: great intellects are skeptical. Zarathustra is a skeptic. The strength, the *freedom* which proceed from intellectual power, from a superabundance of intellectual power, *manifest* themselves as skepticism. Men of fixed convictions do not count when it comes to determining what is fundamental in values and lack of values. Men of convictions are prisoners. They do not see far enough, they do not see what is *below* them: whereas a man who would talk to any purpose about value and non-value must be able to see five hundred convictions *beneath* him—and *behind* him. . . . A mind that aspires to great things, and that *wills* the means thereto, is necessarily skeptical. Freedom from any sort of conviction *belongs* to strength, and to an independent point of view. . . . That grand passion which is at once the foundation and the power of a skeptic's existence, and is both more enlightened and more despotic than he is himself, drafts the whole of his intel-

lect into its service; it makes him unscrupulous; it gives him courage to employ unholy means; under certain circumstances it does not *begrudge* him even convictions. Conviction as a means: one may achieve a good deal by means of a conviction. A grand passion makes use of and uses up convictions; it does not yield to them—it knows itself to be sovereign. On the contrary, the need of faith, of some thing unconditioned by yea or nay, of Carlylism, if I may be allowed the word, is a need of *weakness*. The man of faith, the "believer" of any sort, is necessarily a dependent man—such a man cannot posit *himself* as a goal, nor can he find goals within himself. The "believer" does not belong to himself; he can only be a means to an end; he must be *used up*; he needs some one to use him up. His instinct gives the highest honors to an ethic of self-effacement; he is prompted to embrace it by everything: his prudence, his experience, his vanity. Every sort of faith is in itself an evidence of self-effacement, of self-estrangement. . . . When one reflects how necessary it is to the great majority that there be regulations to restrain them from without and hold them fast, and to what extent control, or, in a higher sense, *slavery*, is the one and only condition which makes for the well-being of the weak-willed man, and especially woman, then one at once understands conviction and "faith." To the man with convictions they are his backbone. To *avoid* seeing many things, to be impartial about nothing, to be a party man through and through, to estimate all values strictly and infallibly—these are conditions necessary to the existence of such a man. But by the same token they are *antagonists* of the truthful man—of the truth. . . . The believer is not free to answer the question, "true" or "not true" according to the dictates of his own conscience: integrity on *this* point would work his instant downfall. The pathological limitations of his vision turn the man of convictions into a fanatic—Savonarola, Luther, Rousseau, Robespierre, Saint-Simon—these types stand in opposition to the strong, *emancipated* spirit. But the grandiose attitudes of these *sick* intellects, these intellectual epileptics, are of influence upon the great masses—fanatics are picturesque, and mankind prefers observing poses to listening to *reasons*. . . .

FURTHER READINGS

Bett, Richard. "Nietzsche on the Skeptics and Nietzsche as Skeptic." *Archiv für Geschichte der Philosophie* 82 (2000): 62–86.

Hull, Robert. "Skepticism, Enigma and Integrity: Horizons of Affirmation in Nietzsche's Philosophy." *Man and World* 23 (1990): 375–91.

Lom, Petr. *The Limits of Doubt: The Moral and Political Implications of Skepticism*. Albany: State University of New York Press, 2001, pp. 17–29.

Magnus, Bernd. "Nietzsche's Mitigated Skepticism." *Nietzsche-Studien* 9 (1980): 260–67.

Mosser, Kurt. "Should the Skeptic Live His Skepticism? Nietzsche and Classical Skepticism." *Manuscrito* 21 (1998): 47–84.

Poellner, Peter. *Nietzsche and Metaphysics*. Oxford: Clarendon Press, 1995.

Richter, Raoul. *Der Skeptizismus in der Philosophie*. 2 vols. Leipzig: Dürr'sche Buchhandlung, 1904, 1908.

36

JAMES

W illiam James (1842–1910) was one of the founders of American pragmatism. He exhibits a skeptical epistemology to the extent that he rejects both the empiricist and the rationalist (he calls "absolutist") foundations of knowledge. He rejects the conception of truth, targeted by the skeptics, of correspondence between beliefs and things, holding that truth depends on the consequences of beliefs. In his famous conference "The Will to Believe," partially reproduced below, he breaks with skepticism in that he rejects—for certain kinds of beliefs—the skeptical rationalist principle of intellectual integrity that judgment must be suspended in the lack of sufficient rational warrant. James argues that this principle cannot hold for the class of religious and moral beliefs that are crucial in one's society. Crucial beliefs are living and forceful ones, about which the members of the society in which these beliefs are held cannot remain indifferent. As James points out in this conference in a section not reproduced below, his position on belief and skepticism is similar to that of Pascal's, who was skeptical about the metaphysical arguments that purported to prove the existence of God and the immortality of the soul and offered pragmatic ones such as the wager as alternative to traditional proofs.

FROM "THE WILL TO BELIEVE"

IV

. . . The thesis I defend is, briefly stated, this: Our passional nature not only lawfully may, but must, decide an option between propositions, whenever it is a genuine option that cannot by its nature be decided on intellectual grounds; for to say, under such circumstances, "Do not decide, but leave the question open," is itself a passional decision,—just like deciding yes or no,—and is attended with the same risk of losing the truth. The thesis thus abstractly expressed will, I trust, soon become quite clear. But I must first indulge in a bit more of preliminary work.

V

It will be observed that for the purposes of this discussion we are on 'dogmatic' ground,—ground, I mean, which leaves systematic philosophical skepticism altogether out of account. The postulate that there is truth, and that it is the destiny of our minds to attain it, we are deliberately resolving to make, though the skeptic will not make it. We part company with him, therefore, absolutely, at this point. But the faith that truth exists, and that our minds can find it, may be held in two ways. We may talk of the *empiricist* way and of the *absolutist* way of believing in truth. The absolutists in this matter say that we not only can attain to knowing truth, but we can *know when* we have attained to knowing it; while the empiricists think that although we may attain it, we cannot infallibly know when. To *know* is one thing, and to know for certain *that* we know is another. One may hold to the first being possible without the second; hence the empiricists and the absolutists, although neither of them is a skeptic in the usual philosophic sense of the term, show very different degrees of dogmatism in their lives.

If we look at the history of opinions, we see that the empiricist tendency has largely prevailed in science, while in philosophy the absolutist tendency has had everything its own way. The characteristic sort of happiness, indeed, which philosophies yield has mainly consisted in the conviction felt by each successive school or system that by it bottom-certitude had been attained. "Other philosophies are collections of opinions, mostly false; *my* philosophy gives standing-ground forever,"— who does not recognize in this the key-note of every system worthy of the name? A system, to be a system at all, must come as a *closed* system, reversible in this or that detail, perchance, but in its essential features never!

Scholastic orthodoxy, to which one must always go when one wishes to find perfectly clear statement, has beautifully elaborated this absolutist conviction in a doctrine which it calls that of 'objective evidence.' If, for example, I am unable to doubt that I now exist before you, that two is less than three, or that if all men are mortal then I am mortal too, it is because these things illumine my intellect irresistibly. The final ground of this objective evidence possessed by certain propositions is the *adæquatio intellectûs nostri cum rê.* The certitude it brings involves an *aptitudinem ad extorquendum certum assensum* on the part of the truth envisaged, and on the side of the subject a *quietem in cognitione,* when once the object is mentally received, that leaves no possibility of doubt behind; and in the whole transaction nothing operates but the *entitas ipsa* of the object and the *entitas ipsa* of the mind. We slouchy modern thinkers dislike to talk in Latin,—indeed, we dislike to talk in set terms at all; but at bottom our own state of mind is very much like this whenever we uncritically abandon ourselves: You believe in objective evidence, and I do. Of some things we feel that we are certain: we know, and we know that we do know. There is something that gives a click inside of us, a bell that strikes twelve, when the hands of our mental clock have swept the dial and meet over the meridian hour. The greatest empiricists among us are only empiricists on reflection: when left to their instincts, they dogmatize like infallible popes. When the Cliffords tell us how sinful it is to be Christians on such 'insufficient evidence,' insufficiency is really the last thing they have in mind. For them the evidence is absolutely sufficient, only it makes the other way. They believe so completely in an anti-christian order of the universe that there is no living option: Christianity is a dead hypothesis from the start.

VI

But now, since we are all such absolutists by instinct, what in our quality of students of philosophy ought we to do about the fact? Shall we espouse and indorse it? Or shall we treat it as a weakness of our nature from which we must free ourselves, if we can?

I sincerely believe that the latter course is the only one we can follow as reflective men. Objective evidence and certitude are doubtless very fine ideals to play with, but where on this moonlit and dream-visited planet are they found? I am, therefore, myself a complete empiricist so far as my theory of human knowledge goes. I live, to be sure, by the practical faith that we must go on experiencing and thinking over our experience, for only thus can our opinions grow more true; but to hold any one of them—I absolutely do not care which—as if it never could be reinterpretable or corrigible, I believe to be a tremendously mistaken attitude, and I think that the whole history of philosophy will bear me out. There is but one indefectibly certain truth, and that is the truth that pyrrhonistic skepticism itself leaves standing,—the truth that the present phenomenon of consciousness exists. That, however, is the bare starting-point of knowledge, the mere admission of a stuff to be philosophized about. The various philosophies are but so many attempts at expressing what this stuff really is. And if we repair to our libraries what disagreement do we discover! Where is a certainly true answer found? Apart from abstract propositions of comparison (such as two and two are the same as four), propositions which tell us nothing by themselves about concrete reality, we find no proposition ever regarded by any one as evidently certain that has not either been called a falsehood, or at least had its truth sincerely questioned by some one else. The transcending of the axioms of geometry, not in play but in earnest, by certain of our contemporaries (as Zöllner and Charles H. Hinton), and the rejection of the whole Aristotelian logic by the Hegelians, are striking instances in point.

No concrete test of what is really true has ever been agreed upon. Some make the criterion external to the moment of perception, putting it either in revelation, the *consensus gentium*, the instincts of the heart, or the systematized experience of the race. Others make the perceptive moment its own test,—Descartes, for instance, with his clear and distinct ideas guaranteed by the veracity of God; Reid with his 'common-sense'; and Kant with his forms of synthetic judgment *a priori*. The inconceivability of the opposite; the capacity to be verified by sense; the possession of complete organic unity or self-relation, realized when a thing is its own other,—are standards which, in turn, have been used. The much lauded objective evidence is never triumphantly there; it is a mere aspiration or *Grenzbegriff*, marking the infinitely remote ideal of our thinking life. To claim that certain truths now possess it, is simply to say that when you think them true and they *are* true, then their evidence is objective, otherwise it is not. But practically one's conviction that the evidence one goes by is of the real objective brand, is only one more subjective opinion added to the lot. For what a contradictory array of opinions have objective evidence and absolute certitude been claimed! The world is rational through and through,—its existence is an ultimate brute fact; there is a personal God,—a personal God is inconceivable; there is an extra-mental physical world immediately known,—the mind can only know its own ideas; a moral imperative exists,—obligation is only the resultant of desires; a permanent spiritual principle is in every one,—there are only shifting states of mind; there is an endless chain of causes,—there is an absolute first cause; an eternal necessity,—a freedom; a purpose,—no purpose; a primal One,—a primal Many; a universal continuity,—an essential discontinuity in things; an infinity,—no infinity. There is this,—there is that; there is indeed nothing which some one has not thought absolutely true, while his neighbor deemed it absolutely false; and not an absolutist among them seems ever to have considered that the trouble may all the time be essential, and that the intellect, even with truth directly in its grasp, may have no infallible signal for knowing whether it be truth or no. When, indeed, one remembers that the most striking practical application to life of the doctrine of objective certitude has been the conscientious labors of the Holy Office of the Inquisition, one feels less tempted than ever to lend the doctrine a respectful ear.

But please observe, now, that when as empiricists we give up the doctrine of objective certitude, we do not thereby give up the quest or hope of truth itself. We still pin our faith on its existence, and still believe that we gain an ever better position towards it by systematically continuing to roll up experiences and think. Our great difference from the scholastic lies in the way we face. The strength of his system lies in the principles, the origin, the *terminus a quo* of his thought; for us the strength is in the outcome, the upshot, the *terminus ad quem*. Not where it comes from but what it leads to is to decide. It matters not to an empiricist from what quarter an hypothesis may come to him: he may have acquired it by fair means or by foul; passion may have whispered or accident suggested it; but if the total drift of thinking continues to confirm it, that is what he means by its being true.

FURTHER READINGS

Goodman, Russell. *Pragmatism: Critical Concepts in Philosophy*. 4 vols. London: Routledge, 2005.

———, ed. *Wittgenstein and William James*. Cambridge: Cambridge University Press, 2002.

Meyers, R. G. "Meaning and Metaphysics in James." *Philosophy and Phenomenology Research* 31 (1971): 369–80.

O'Connell, Robert J. *William James on the Courage to Believe*. New York: Fordham University Press, 1984.

37

SANTAYANA

George Santayana (1863–1951) was born in Madrid, Spain. He taught philosophy at Harvard University from 1889 to 1912. His most famous work is *Skepticism and Animal Faith*, which he published in 1923. Santayana holds that from a strictly epistemological view, no theory or belief—including the Cartesian *cogito*—is immune from doubt. However, suspension of judgment is impossible because nature impels human beings to believe, a phenomenon that he calls "animal faith." The excerpt below exhibits Santayana's almost lyrical presentation of the joys of the skeptical point of view.

FROM *SKEPTICISM AND ANIMAL FAITH:*
INTRODUCTION TO A SYSTEM OF PHILOSOPHY

Chapter II—Dogma and Doubt

Custom does not breed understanding, but takes its place, teaching people to make their way contentedly through the world without knowing what the world is, nor what they think of it, nor what they are. When their attention is attracted to some remarkable thing, say to the rainbow, this thing is not analyzed nor examined from various points of view, but all the casual resources of the fancy are called forth in conceiving it, and this total reaction of the mind precipitates a dogma; the rainbow is taken for an omen of fair weather, or for a trace left in the sky by the passage of some beautiful and elusive goddess. Such a dogma, far from being an interpenetration or identification of thought with the truth of the object, is a fresh and additional object in itself. The original passive perception remains unchanged; the thing remains unfathomed; and as its diffuse influence has by chance bred one dogma today, it may breed a different dogma tomorrow. We have therefore, as we progress in our acquaintance with the world, an always greater confusion. Besides the original fantastic inadequacy of our perceptions, we have now rival clarifications of them, and a new uncertainty as to whether these dogmas are relevant to the original object, or are themselves really clear, or if so, which of them is true.

A prosperous dogmatism is indeed not impossible. We may have such determinate minds that the suggestions of experience always issue there in the same

311

dogmas; and these orthodox dogmas, perpetually revived by the stimulus of things, may become our dominant or even our sole apprehension of them. We shall really have moved to another level of mental discourse; we shall be living on ideas. In the gardens of Seville I once heard, coming through the tangle of palms and orange trees, the treble voice of a pupil in the theological seminary, crying to his playmate: "You booby! of course angels have a more perfect nature than men." With his black and red cassock that child had put on dialectic; he was playing the game of dogma and dreaming in words, and was insensible to the scent of violets that filled the air. How long would that last? Hardly, I suspect, until the next spring; and the troubled awakening which puberty would presently bring to that little dogmatist, sooner or later overtakes all elder dogmatists in the press of the world. The more perfect the dogmatism, the more insecure. A great high topsail that can never be reefed nor furled is the first carried away by the gale.

To me the opinions of mankind, taken without any contrary prejudice (since I have no rival opinions to propose) but simply contrasted with the course of nature, seem surprising fictions; and the marvel is how they can be maintained. What strange religions, what ferocious moralities, what slavish fashions, what sham! I can explain it all only by saying to myself that intelligence is naturally forthright; it forges ahead; it piles fiction on fiction; and the fact that the dogmatic structure, for the time being, stands and grows, passes for a proof of its rightness. Right indeed it is in one sense, as vegetation is right; it is vital; it has plasticity and warmth, and a certain indirect correspondence with its soil and climate. Many obviously fabulous dogmas, like those of religion, might for ever dominate the most active minds, except for one circumstance. In the jungle one tree strangles another, and luxuriance itself is murderous. So is luxuriance in the human mind. What kills spontaneous fictions, what recalls the impassioned fancy from its improvisation, is the angry voice of some contrary fancy. Nature, silently making fools of us all our lives, never would bring us to our senses; but the maddest assertions of the mind may do so, when they challenge one another. Criticism arises out of the conflict of dogmas.

May I escape this predicament and criticize without a dogmatic criterion? Hardly; for though the criticism may be expressed hypothetically, as for instance in saying that if any child knew his own father he would be a wise child, yet the point on which doubt is thrown is a point of fact, and that there are fathers and children is assumed dogmatically. If not, however obscure the essential relation between fathers and children might be ideally, no one could be wise or foolish in assigning it in any particular instance, since no such terms would exist in nature at all. Skepticism is a suspicion of error about facts, and to suspect error about facts is to share the enterprise of knowledge, in which facts are presupposed and error is possible. The skeptic thinks himself shrewd, and often is so; his intellect, like the intellect he criticizes, may have some inkling of the true hang and connection of things; he may have pierced to a truth of nature behind current illusions. Since his criticism may thus be true and his doubt well grounded, they are certainly assertions; and if he is sincerely a skeptic, they are assertions which he is ready to maintain stoutly. Skepticism is accordingly a form of belief. Dogma cannot be abandoned; it can only be revised in view of some more elementary dogma which it has not yet occurred to the skeptic to doubt; and he may be right in every point of his criticism, except in fancying that his criticism is radical and that he is altogether a skeptic.

This vital compulsion to posit and to believe something, even in the act of doubting, would nevertheless be ignominious, if the beliefs which life and intelligence forced upon me were always false. I should then be obliged to honor the skeptic for his heroic though hopeless effort to eschew belief, and I should despise the dogmatist for his willing subservience to illusion. The sequel will show, I trust, that this is not the case; that intelligence is by nature veridical, and that its ambition to reach the truth is sane and capable of satisfaction, even if each of its efforts actually fails. To convince me of this fact, however, I must first justify my faith in many subsidiary beliefs concerning animal economy and the human mind and the world they flourish in.

That skepticism should intervene in philosophy at all is an accident of human history, due to much unhappy experience of perplexity and error. If all had gone well, assertions would be made spontaneously in dogmatic innocence, and the very notion of a *right* to make them would seem as gratuitous as in fact it is; because all the realms of being lie open to a spirit plastic enough to conceive them, and those that have ears to hear, may hear. Nevertheless, in the confused state of human speculation this embarrassment obtrudes itself automatically, and a philosopher today would be ridiculous and negligible who had not strained his dogmas through the utmost rigors of skepticism, and who did not approach every opinion, whatever his own ultimate faith, with the courtesy and smile of the skeptic.

The brute necessity of believing something so long as life lasts does not justify any belief in particular; nor does it assure me that not to live would not for this very reason, be far safer and saner. To be dead and have no opinions would certainly not be to discover the truth; but if all opinions are necessarily false, it would at least be not to sin against intellectual honor. Let me then push skepticism as far as I logically can, and endeavor to clear my mind of illusion, even at the price of intellectual suicide.

Chapter VI—Ultimate Skepticism

. . . The animal mind treats its data as facts, or as signs of facts, but the animal mind is full of the rashest presumptions, positing, time, change, a particular station in the midst of events yielding a particular perspective of those events, and the flux of all nature precipitating that experience at that place. None of these posited objects is a datum in which a skeptic could rest. Indeed, existence or fact, in the sense which I give to these words, cannot be a datum at all, because existence involves external relations and actual (not merely specious) flux: whereas, however complex a datum may be, with no matter what perspectives opening within it, it must be embraced in a single stroke of apperception, and nothing outside it can belong to it at all. The datum is a pure image; it is essentially illusory and unsubstantial, however thunderous its sound or keen its edge, or however normal and significant its presence may be. When the mystic asserts enthusiastically the existence of his immediate, ideal, unutterable object, Absolute Being, he is peculiarly unfortunate in his faith: it would be impossible to choose an image less relevant to the agencies that actually bring that image before him. The burden and glow of existence which he is conscious of come entirely from himself; his object is eminently empty, impotent, nonexistent; but the heat and labor of his own soul suffuse that emptiness with light, and the very hum of change within him, accelerated almost beyond endurance and quite beyond discrimination, sounds that piercing note.

The last step in skepticism is now before me. It will lead me to deny existence to any datum, whatever it may be; and as the datum, by hypothesis, is the whole of what solicits my attention at any moment, I shall deny the existence of everything, and abolish that category of thought altogether. If I could not do this, I should be a tyro in skepticism. Belief in the existence of anything, including myself, is something radically incapable of proof, and resting, like all belief, on some irrational persuasion or prompting of life. Certainly, as a matter of fact, when I deny existence I exist; but doubtless many of the other facts I have been denying, because I found no evidence for them, were true also. To bring me evidence of their existence is no duty imposed on facts, nor a habit of theirs: I must employ private detectives. The point is, in this task of criticism, to discard every belief that is a belief merely—, and the belief in existence, in the nature of the case, can be a belief only. The datum is an idea, a description; I may contemplate it without belief; but when I assert that such a thing exists I am hypostatizing this datum, placing it in presumptive relations which are not internal to it, and worshipping it as an idol or thing. Neither its existence nor mine nor that of my belief can be given in any datum. These things are incidents involved in that order of nature which I have thrown over; they are no part of what remains before me.

Assurance of existence expresses animal watchfulness: it posits, within me and round me, hidden and imminent events. The skeptic can easily cast a doubt on the remoter objects of this belief; and nothing but a certain obduracy and want of agility prevents him from doubting present existence itself. For what could present existence mean, if the imminent events for which animal sense is watching failed altogether, failed at the very roots, so to speak, of the tree of intuition, and let nothing but its branches flowering in vacuum? Expectation is admittedly the most hazardous of beliefs: yet what is watchfulness but expectation? Memory is notoriously full of illusion; yet what would experience of the present be if the veracity of primary memory were denied, and if I no longer believed that anything had just happened, or that I had ever been in the state from which I suppose myself to have passed into this my present condition.

It will not do for the skeptic to take refuge in the confused notion that expectation *possesses* the future, or memory the past. As a matter of fact, expectation is like hunger; it opens its mouth, and something probably drops into it, more or less, very often, the sort of thing, it expected; but sometimes a surprise comes, and sometimes nothing. Life involves expectation, but does not prevent death: and expectation is never so thoroughly stultified as when it is not undeceived, but cancelled. The open mouth does not then so much as close upon nothing. It is buried open. Nor is memory in a better case. As the whole world might collapse and cease at any moment, nullifying all expectation, so it might at any moment have sprung out of nothing: for it is thoroughly contingent, and might have begun today, with this degree of complexity and illusive memory, as well as long ago, with whatever energy or momentum it was first endowed with. The backward perspective of time is perhaps really an inverted expectation; but for the momentum of life forward, we might not be able to space the elements active in the present so as to assign to them a longer or a shorter history; for we should not attempt to discriminate amongst these elements such as we could still count on in the immediate future, and such as we might safely ignore: so that our conception of the past implies, perhaps, a distinction between the living and the dead. This distinction is itself practical, and looks to the future. In the absolute present all is specious; and to pure intuition the living are as ghostly as the dead, and the dead as present as the living.

In the sense of existence there is accordingly something more than the obvious character of that which is alleged to exist. What is this complement? It cannot be a feature in the datum, since the datum by definition is the whole of what is found. Nor can it be, in my sense at least of the word existence, the intrinsic constitution or specific being of this object, since existence comports external relations, variable, contingent, and not discoverable in a given being when taken alone: for there is nothing that may not lose its existence, or the existence of which might not be conceivably denied. The complement added to the datum when it is alleged to exist seems, then, to be added by *me*; it is the finding, the occurrence, the assault, the impact of that being here and now; it is the experience of it. But what can experience be, if I take away from it the whole of what is experienced? And what meaning can I give to such words as impact, assault, occurrence, or finding, when I have banished and denied my body, my past, my residual present being, and everything except the datum which I find? The sense of existence evidently belongs to the intoxication, to the *Rausch*, of existence itself; it is the strain of life within me, prior to all intuition, that in its precipitation and terror, passing as it continually must from one untenable condition to another, stretches my attention absurdly over what is not given, over the lost and the unattained, the before and after which are wrapped in darkness, and confuses my breathless apprehension of the clear presence of all I can ever truly behold.

Indeed, so much am I a creature of movement, and of the ceaseless metabolism of matter, that I should never catch even these glimpses of the light, if there were not rhythms, pauses, repetitions, and nodes in my physical progress, to absorb and reflect it here and there: as the traveler, hurried in a cloud of smoke and dust through tunnel after tunnel in the Italian Riviera, catches and loses momentary visions of blue sea and sky, which he would like to arrest, but cannot; yet if he had not been rushed and whistled along these particular tunnels, even those snatches in the form in which they come to him, would have been denied him. So it is the rush of life that at its open moments, floods me with intuitions, partial and confused, but still revelations; the landscape is wrapped in the smoke of my little engine, and turned into a tantalizing incident of my hot journey. What appears (which is an ideal object and not an event) is thus confused with the event of its appearance; the picture is identified with the kindling or distraction of my attention falling by chance upon it; and the strain of my material existence, battling with material accidents, turns the ideal object too into a temporal fact, and makes it seem substantial. But this fugitive existence which I egotistically attach to it, as if its fate was that of my glimpses of it, is no part of its true being, as even my intuition discerns it; it is a practical dignity or potency attributed to it by the irrelevant momentum of my animal life. Animals, being by nature hounded and hungry creatures, spy out and take alarm at any datum of sense or fancy, supposing that there is something substantial there, something that will count and work in the world. The notion of a moving world is brought implicitly with them; they fetch it out of the depths of their vegetating psyche, which is a small dark cosmos, silently revolving within. By being noticed, and treated as a signal for I know not what material opportunity or danger, the given image is taken up into the business world, and puts on the garment of existence. Remove this frame, strip off all suggestion of a time when this image was not yet present, or a time when it shall be past, and the very notion of existence is removed. The datum ceases to be an appearance, in the proper and pregnant sense of this word, since it ceases to imply any substance that appears or any mind to which it appears. It is an appearance only in the sense that its nature is wholly manifest, that it is a specific being, which may be mentioned, thought of, seen or defined, if any one has the wit to do so. But its own nature says nothing of any hidden circumstances that shall bring it to light, or any adventitious mind that shall discover it. It lies simply in its own category. If a color, it is just this color; if a pain, just this pain. Its appearance is not an event: its presence is not an experience; for there is no surrounding world in which it can arise, and no watchful spirit to appropriate it. The skeptic has here withdrawn into the intuition of a surface form, without roots, without origin or environment, without a seat or a locus; a little universe, an immaterial absolute theme, rejoicing merely in its own quality. This theme, being out of all adventitious relations and not in the least threatened with not being the theme it is, has not the contingency nor the fortunes proper to an existence; it is simply that which it inherently, logically, and unchangeably is.

Existence, then, not being included in any immediate datum, is a fact always open to doubt. I call it a fact notwithstanding, because in talking about the skeptic I am positing his existence. If he has any intuition, however little the theme of that intuition may have to do with any actual world, certainly I who think of his intuition, or he himself thinking of it afterwards, see that this intuition of his must have been an event, and his existence at that time a fact; but like all facts and events, this one can be known only by an affirmation which posits it, which may be suspended or reversed, and which is subject to error. Hence all this business of intuition may perfectly well be doubted by the skeptic: the existence of his own doubt (however confidently I may assert it for him) is not given to him then: all that is given is some ambiguity or contradiction in images; and if afterwards he is sure that he has doubted, the sole cogent evidence which that fact can claim lies in the psychological impossibility that, so long as he believes he has doubted, he should not believe it. But he may be wrong in harboring this belief, and he may rescind it. For all an ultimate skepticism can see, therefore, there may be no facts at all, and perhaps nothing has ever existed.

Skepticism may thus be carried to the point of denying change and memory, and the reality of all facts. Such a skeptical dogma would certainly be false, because this dogma itself would have to be entertained, and that event would be a fact and an existence: and the skeptic in framing that dogma discourses, vacillates, and lives in the act of contrasting one assertion with another—all of which is to exist with a vengeance. Yet this false dogma that nothing exists is tenable intuitively and, while it prevails, is irrefutable. There are certain motives (to be discussed later) which render ultimate skepticism precious to a spiritual mind, as a sanctuary from grosser illusions. For the wayward skeptic, who regards it as no truer than any other view, it also has some utility: it accustoms him to discard the dogma which an introspective critic might be tempted to think self-evident, namely, that he himself lives and thinks. That he does so is true; but to establish that truth he must appeal to animal faith. If he is too proud for that, and simply stares at the datum, the last thing he will see is himself.

Chapter XIX—Belief in Substance

. . . Skepticism, if it could be sincere, would be the best of philosophies. But I suspect that other skeptics, as well as I, always believe in substance, and that their denial of it is sheer sophistry and the weaving of verbal arguments in which their most familiar and massive convictions are ignored.

It might seem ignominious to believe something on compulsion, because I can't help believing it; when reason awakes in a man it asks for reasons for everything. Yet this demand is unreasonable: there cannot be a reason for everything. It is mere automatic habit in the philosopher to make this demand, as it is in the common man not to make it. When once I have admitted the facts of nature, and taken for granted the character of animal life, and the incarnation of spirit in this animal life, then indeed many excellent reasons for the belief in substance will appear; and not only reasons for using the category of substance, and positing substance or some vague ambient sort, but reasons for believing in a substance rather elaborately defined and scientifically describable in many of its habits and properties. But I am not yet ready for that. Lest that investigation, when undertaken, should ignore its foundations or be impatient of its limits, I must insist here that trust in knowledge, and belief in anything to know, are merely instinctive and, in a manner, pathological. . . .

FURTHER READINGS

Schilpp, Paul A., ed. *The Philosophy of George Santayana*. Evanston and Chicago: North-western University Press, 1940. Second edition: La Salle, IL: Open Court, 1971.
Sprigge, Timothy L. S. *Santayana*. London: Routledge, 1999.

38

SHESTOV

Lev Shestov (1866–1938) was a Russian philosopher exiled in France after the Bolshevik revolution. He reacted to the arrival, in particular through Kant and neo-Kantianism, of Western Enlightenment in Russia. He strongly attacked all kinds of philosophical rationalism ("Athens"), which he saw as contrary to Judeo-Christianity ("Jerusalem"). He was a friend and bitter critic of Edmund Husserl, and a pioneer in using the label "existential philosophy" and presenting Kierkegaard as the forerunner of the movement. He was influential in the French existentialist movement, particularly in relation to Albert Camus. We have selected an excerpt from Shestov's interpretation of Dostoevsky's *Notes from the Underground*. In this piece, as in most of his other writings, Shestov presents a kind of nonepistemologically based skepticism, indeed a radical irrationalism contrary to the Academic skeptical principle of intellectual integrity (that assent ought to be given only to what cannot be rationally doubted). Shestov radically dissociates practice from reason (in opposition to Kantianism), vindicating the "right" of the former to reject the latter.

FROM "THE CONQUEST OF THE SELF-EVIDENT; DOSTOEVSKY'S PHILOSOPHY," IN *IN JOB'S BALANCES: ON THE SOURCES OF THE ETERNAL TRUTHS*

Matter and energy are indestructible, but Socrates and Giordano Bruno are destructible, says reason. And all bow down to the dictum without a word; no one dares even hazard the question: Why has reason decreed this law? Why is it so paternally occupied in safeguarding matter and energy when it has forgotten all about Socrates and Giordano Bruno? Still less do they think of asking another question . . . : whence does it derive the strength needful to accomplish this decision? And to accomplish it so perfectly that in no single instance since the beginning of the world has a single atom disappeared completely; that not only no gram of energy—not a fraction of a gram has vanished into space? This is a miracle indeed, the more so because ultimately reason has not actual existence either. Try to find it, to point it out; you cannot. It accomplishes miracles like the most real of beings; but it has no existence. And all of us, who are used to questioning everything, admit this miracle quite easily; for science, created by reason, pays us a good price; out of worthless "facts," it creates "experience," through which we become masters of nature. Reason has taken man up into an exceeding high mountain and shown him all the kingdoms of the world, and has said unto him: All these things will I give thee if thou wilt fall down and worship me. And man has worshipped, and obtained the promised reward (though, to be sure, no fully).

Since that day the worship of reason has been regarded as man's first duty. And any other relationship to reason seems to us unthinkable, in some sense impossible. Regarding God there is a commandment: "Thou shalt love the Lord thy God with all thy heart and with all thy soul." Reason does without commandments, men will love it of themselves, unbidden. The theory of knowledge simply sings the praises of reason, but no one has the audacity to question it, and still less dare doubt its sovereign power. The miracle of the transformation of facts into "experience" has conquered all minds; all admit that reason is judge and is itself subject to no other jurisdiction.

Dostoievsky, thanks to his second sight, soon saw that the experience from which men derive their science is a theory and not a reality. And no success, no conquest, no miracle even, can justify theory. He put the question: has "omnitude," common consciousness (from which self-evidence springs) any right to the high prerogatives which it has arrogated to itself? In other words: has reason any right to judge autonomously, rendering account to none; or are we only dealing with an usurpation of rights sanctified by centuries of possession?

Dostoievsky looks on the case between the living individual on the one hand, and common consciousness on the other, not so much as one of facts as of rights. "Omnitude" has usurped the power. We must wrest it away; and if we are to accomplish this, the first step is to cease to believe in the legitimacy of the usurpation, and to tell ourselves that its strength lies only in our belief in its strength. "Natural laws" and their inimitability, truths and the self-evidence thereof, are perhaps only magic, auto-suggestion, or influences from outside which hypnotize us as a goose is hypnotized if we trace round her a circle of chalk. The goose will not be able to get out of the circle, as though it were a wall that surrounded her, instead of merely a line. If the goose knew how to reason and express her thoughts in words, she would create a theory of knowledge, and hold forth on self-evidence, holding the line of chalk to be the limit of possible experience. But if this is the case, our warfare against the principles of scientific knowledge must be waged not with arguments but with other weapons. Arguments served only as long as we admitted the truth of the premises from which they follow, but if we do not admit them we must seek something else.

"'Twice two is four,' gentlemen, is not life, it is the beginning of death—at any rate, man has always been afraid of this 'twice two is four,' and I am still afraid of it now. It is true that man thinks of nothing else but the search for this 'twice two is four'; he will cross oceans, risk his life in order to find it, but as for discovering what it really is when he has found it—that frightens him, I promise you. But in my opinion 'twice two is four' is simply an impertinence—'Twice two is four' is a lout; he plants himself across our path, arms akimbo, and spits on the ground. I admit that 'twice two is four' is an excellent thing, but if we are to praise all that is praiseworthy, I will tell you that 'twice two is five' is also a charming thing."

You are not accustomed to such arguments against philosophical theories; perhaps you are even incensed that when discussing the theory of knowledge I should quote these passages from Dostoievsky. You would be right, these arguments would really be out of place, if Dostoievsky had not raised the question of right and usurpation. But that is the point. "Twice two is four," and reason and all its proofs simply will not admit discussion of the question of rights. They cannot, for if they once admit it they are lost. They refuse to be judged, they wish to be both judge and lawgiver, and whosoever would refuse them this right, him they will anathematize and excommunicate from the ecumenical human church. With this all possibility of discussion ceases, and a desperate and mortal struggle begins.

The underground man is outlawed in reason's name. Laws, as we know, protect only matter, energy, and principles. There is nothing keeping guard over Socrates, Giordano Bruno, or any man great or small. And then a man, a miserable, humiliated, pitiable man, dares to rise up in defense of himself and his so-called rights. And behold, the glance of this miserable little functionary is deeper and more piercing than that of the famous scholars. Generally speaking, the philosopher fights against materialism and feels proud indeed if he succeeds in collecting a few more or less cogent arguments with which to confront his opponent. But Dostoievsky . . . does not even deign to argue with the materialists; he knows that materialism is powerless in itself, that it only borrows strength from idealism, from ideas, i.e., from reason which admits nothing else above itself. But how can the tyrant be overthrown? What methods can one invent? Do not forget that it is impossible to argue with reason. All arguments are rational arguments, which exist only to sustain the pretensions of reason. There is only one weapon: mockery, invective, a categorical "no" to all the demands of reason. . . .

The underground man has no clear and definite object. He longs, ardently, passionately, madly, but he does not know, and he will never know, what it is for which he longs. Now he declares that he will never give up the pleasure of putting out his tongue, now he says that he has no particular wish to mock. At one moment he will say that the underworld amply suffices for him, he wants nothing more; the next he will consign it to the devil. Suddenly he launches into this wild tirade.

"So, long live the underworld! I did indeed say that I envy the normal man with the last drop of my bile; but when I see him as he is, I have no wish to be in his place (though all the while I shall go envying him). No, no! when all is said and done, underground is better! There one can at least . . . Ah! but I am lying again. I am lying because I know quite clearly myself, as well as I know that "twice two is four," that it is not underground that is worth so much, but some quite different place which I ardently desire, but shall never find. To the devil to the underground!"

What happens to the mind of the underground man has no resemblance at all to thinking, not even to seeking. He does not think, he excites himself desperately, throws himself about, knocks his head against the wall. He inflames himself the whole time, dashing up to unknown heights of fury, to fling himself into God knows what abysses of despair. He has no control of himself; a force far greater than himself has him completely under its sway.

"If only I myself believed a single word of what I have written here! I swear to you, gentlemen, that I do not believe a word, a single word of what I have put down here. That is to say, perhaps I believe it, but at the same time I feel and suspect, I do not know why, that I am lying like a trooper."

He to whom the Angel of Death has given the mysterious gift, does not and cannot any longer possess the certainty which accompanies our ordinary judgments and confers a beautiful solidity on the truths of our common consciousness. Henceforth he must live without certainty and without conviction. He will have to give his mind over into strange keeping, become inert matter, clay of which the potter must shape what he will. This is the only thing of which the underground man can be absolutely certain. He sees that neither the works of reason nor any human work can save him. He has passed under review, with what carefulness, with what superhuman effort, everything that man can accomplish by the use of his reason, all the glass palaces, and ant-heaps; for they were built on the principle of death, on "twice two is four." And the more he feels this, the more violently there wells up from the depth of his soul that more than rational, unknown, that primal chaos, which most of all horrifies our ordinary consciousness. That is why, in his "theory of knowledge," Dostoievsky renounces all certainty, and opposes to it as his supreme goal—uncertainty. That is why he simply puts out his tongue at evidence, why he lauds caprice, unconditional, unforeseen, always irrational, and makes mock of all the human virtues.

FURTHER READINGS

Camus, Albert. *The Myth of Sisyphus and Other Essays*. Translated by Justin O'Brien. New York: Vintage Books, 1955.

Curtis, James. "Shestov's Use of Nietzsche in His Interpretation of Tolstoy and Dostoievsky." *Literature and Language* 27 (1974): 289–302.

Desilets, André. *Léon Chestov: Des paradoxes de la philosophie*. Québec: Editions du Beffroi, 1984.

Dostoevsky, Fiodor. "Notes from the Underground." In *Existentialism from Dostoevsky to Sartre*, Walter Kaufmann, 52–82. Cleveland and New York: Meridian, 1956.

Maia Neto, José. R. *The Christianization of Pyrrhonism: Skepticism and Faith in Pascal, Kierkegaard and Shestov*. Dordrecht: Kluwer, 1995.

Patterson, David. "Shestov, Kierkegaard, and the Origins of Nothingness: Reflections of the Fall." *American Benedictine Review* 39 (1988): 15–30.

Shein, Louis L. "The Philosophy of Infinite Possibility: An Examination of Lev Shestov's *Weltanschauung*." *Ultimate Reality Meaning* 2 (1979): 59–68.

Shestov, Lev. *Athens and Jerusalem*. Translated with an introduction by Bernard Martin. New York: Ohio University Press, 1966.

Struve, Nikita, ed. *Léon Chestov: Un philosophe pas comme les autres?* Paris: Institut d'Etudes Slaves, 1996.

39

WITTGENSTEIN

Ludwig Wittgenstein (1889–1951) was one of the greatest and most influential (next to no other except perhaps Heidegger) twentieth-century philosophers. He played a central role in the linguistic turn in contemporary philosophy. Wittgenstein's philosophy of language opposes the so-called Cartesian kind of skepticism that challenges the possibility of rationally justifying the existence of a world external to the mind. He does so in particular in his later works *Philosophical Investigations* and *On Certainty*. In the first, he sets out what is known as the private language argument, basically that Cartesian skepticism presupposes that there is a private language whereas language is public. In *On Certainty*, Wittgenstein attempts to show that the public nature of language renders universal doubt impossible. In order to meaningfully doubt something one must take something else for granted. However, if Wittgenstein's later philosophy inaugurated the linguistic type of answer to modern "Cartesian" skepticism, his views have also been seen as leading to, or agreeing with, other forms of skepticism. The view that meaning and truth are dependent on language games that are social and mutable is one of the major sources of contemporary relativism and postmodern skepticism. At the other extreme of the skeptical tradition, Wittgenstein's attack on philosophical theorizing (exhibited both in *Philosophical Investigations* and the *Tractatus*) and his therapeutic conception of philosophy have been assimilated to ancient Pyrrhonian skepticism. (See, for instance, Robert Fogelin's article at the end of this anthology.) The following passage, selected by Avrum Stroll from *Zettel*, illustrates Wittgenstein's method of showing that Cartesian skepticism violates ordinary language use.

FROM *ZETTEL*

394. What would it mean for me to be wrong about his having a mind, having consciousness? And what would it mean for me to be wrong about *myself* and not have any? What would it mean to say "I am not conscious"?—But don't I know that there is a consciousness in me?—Do I know it then, and yet the statement that it is so has no purpose?

And how remarkable that one can learn to make oneself understood to others in these matters!

395. A man can pretend to be unconscious; but *conscious*?

396. What would it be like for someone to tell me with complete seriousness that he (really) did not know whether he was dreaming or awake?—

Is the following situation possible: Someone says "I believe I am now dreaming"; he actually wakes up soon afterwards, remembers that utterance in his dream and says "So I was right!"—This narrative can surely only signify: Someone dreamt that he had said he was dreaming.

Imagine an unconscious man (anaesthetised, say) were to say "I am conscious"—should we say "He ought to know"?

And if someone talked in his sleep and said "I am asleep"—should we say "He's quite right"?

Is someone speaking untruth if he says to me "I am not conscious"? (And truth, if he says it while unconscious? And suppose a parrot says "I don't understand a word," or a gramophone: "I am only a machine"?)

397. Suppose it were part of my day-dream to say: "I am merely engaged in phantasy," would this be *true*? Suppose I write such a phantasy or narrative, an imaginary dialogue, and in it I say "I am engaged in phantasy"—but, when I write it down,—how does it come out that these words belong to the phantasy and that I have not emerged from the phantasy?

Might it not actually happen that a dreamer, as it were emerging from the dream, said in his sleep "I am dreaming"? It is quite imaginable there should be such a language-game.

This hangs together with the problem of 'meaning.' For I can write "I am healthy" in the dialogue of a play, and so not *mean* it, although it is true. The words belong to this and not that language-game.

398. 'True' and 'false' in a dream. I dream that it is raining, and that I say "It is raining"—on the other hand: I dream that I say "I am dreaming."

399. Has the verb "to dream" a present tense? How does a person learn to use this?

400. Suppose I were to have an experience like waking up, were then to find myself in quite different surroundings, with people who assure me that I have been asleep. Suppose further I insisted that I had not been dreaming, but living in some way outside my sleeping body. What function has this assertion?

401. "'I have consciousness'—that is a statement about which no doubt is possible." Why should that not say the same as: " 'I have consciousness' is not a proposition"?

It might also be said: What's the harm if someone says that "I have consciousness" is a statement admitting of no doubt? How do I come into conflict with him? Suppose someone were to say this to me—why shouldn't I get used to making no answer to him instead of starting an argument? Why shouldn't I treat his words like his whistling or humming?

402. "Nothing is so certain as that I possess consciousness." In that case, why shouldn't I let the matter rest? This certainty is like a mighty force whose point of application does not move, and so no work is accomplished by it.

403. Remember: most people say one feels nothing under anaesthetic. But some say: It *could* be that one feels, and simply forgets it completely.

If then there are here some who doubt and some whom no doubt assails, still the lack of doubt might after all be far more general.

404. Or doubt might after all have a different and much less indefinite form than in our world of thought.

405. No one but a philosopher would say "I know that I have two hands"; but one may well say: "I am unable to doubt that I have two hands."

406. "Know," however, is not ordinarily used in this sense. "I know what 97×78 is." "I know that 97×78 is 432." In the first case I tell someone that I can do something, that I possess something; in the second I simply asseverate that 97×78 is 432.

For doesn't "97×78 is quite definitely 432" say: I *know* it is so? The first sentence is not an arithmetical one, nor can it be replaced by an arithmetical one; an arithmetical sentence could be used in place of the second one.

407. Can someone *believe* that $25 \times 25 = 625$? What does it mean to believe that? How does it come out that he believes it?

408. But isn't there a phenomenon of knowing, as it were quite apart from the sense of the phrase "I know"? Is it not remarkable that a man can *know* something, can as it were have the fact within him?—But that is a wrong picture.—For, it is said, it's only knowledge if things really are as he says. But that is not enough. It mustn't be just an accident that they are. For he has got to know that he knows: for knowing is a state of his own mind; he cannot be in doubt or error about it—apart from some special sort of blindness. If then knowledge *that* things are so is only knowledge if they *really* are so; and if knowledge is in him so that he cannot go wrong about whether it is knowledge; in that case, then, he is also infallible about things being so, just as he knows his knowledge; and so the fact which he knows must be within him just like the knowledge.

And this does indeed point to one kind of use for "I know." "I know that it is so" then means: It is so, or else I'm crazy.

So: when I say, without lying: "I know that it is so," then only through a special sort of blindness can I be wrong.

FURTHER READINGS

Bogen, J. "Wittgenstein and Scepticism." *Philosophical Review* 83 (1974): 364–73.

De Pierris, Graciela. "Philosophical Scepticism in Wittgenstein's *On Certainty*." In *Skepticism in the History of Philosophy: A Pan-American Dialogue*, edited by Richard H. Popkin, 181–96. Dordrecht: Kluwer, 1996.

Garver, Newton, and S. C. Lee. *Derrida and Wittgenstein*. Philadelphia: Temple University Press, 1994.

Goodman, Russell. *Wittgenstein and William James*. Cambridge: Cambridge University Press, 2002.

Kripke, Saul. *Wittgenstein on Rules and Private Language*. Cambridge, MA: Harvard University Press, 1982.

Sousa Filho, Danilo Marcondes. "Finding One's Way About: High Windows, Narrow Chimneys, and Open Doors. Wittgenstein's 'Scepticism' and Philosophical Method." In Popkin, *Skepticism in the History of Philosophy*, pp. 167–79.

Stroll, Avrum. *Moore and Wittgenstein on Certainty*. New York: Oxford University Press, 1994.

Watson, Richard H. "Wittgenstein and Sextus Empiricus." *Southern Journal of Philosophy* 7 (1969): 229–36.

Wittgenstein, Ludwig. *On Certainty*. Translated by G. E. M. Anscombe. Edited by G. E. M. Anscombe and R. Rhees. Oxford: Blackwell, 1969.

———. *Philosophical Investigations*. Oxford: Blackwell, 1958.

———. *Tractatus Logico-Philosophicus*. London: Routledge, 1922.

40

RUSSELL

B ertrand Russell (1872–1970) was one of the most influential philosophers in Anglo-American analytic philosophy. He developed the theory of logic atomism, according to which all knowledge could be reduced to atomic sentences whose truth or falsehood could be empirically determined. Later he doubted that reality have only the qualities experienced by the senses and was quite concerned with the problem of justifying inferences from sense data. *Human Knowledge: Its Scope and Limits* deals with the skeptical problems related to induction. We have selected the preface to this work where Russell states his famous view—which is a reappraisal of Hume's—that "skepticism, while logically impeccable, is psychologically impossible."

FROM *HUMAN KNOWLEDGE: ITS SCOPE AND LIMITS*

The central purpose of this book is to examine the relation between individual experience and the general body of scientific knowledge. It is taken for granted that scientific knowledge, in its broad outlines, is to be accepted. Skepticism, while logically impeccable, is psychologically impossible, and there is an element of frivolous insincerity in any philosophy which pretends to accept it. Moreover, if skepticism is to be theoretically defensible, it must reject *all* inferences from what is experienced; a partial skepticism, such as the denial of physical events experienced by no one, or a solipsism which allows events in my future or in my unremembered past, has no logical justification, since it must admit principles of inference which lead to beliefs that it rejects.

Ever since Kant, or perhaps it would be more just to say ever since Berkeley, there has been what I regard as a mistaken tendency among philosophers to allow the description of the world to be influenced unduly by considerations derived from the nature of human knowledge. To scientific common sense (which I accept) it is plain that only an infinitesimal part of the universe is known, that there were countless ages during which there was no knowledge, and that there probably will be countless ages without knowledge in the future. Cosmically and causally, knowledge is an unimportant feature of the universe; a science which omitted to mention its occurrence might, from an impersonal point of view, suffer only from a very trivial imperfection. In describing the world, subjectivity is a vice. Kant spoke of himself as having effected a "Copernican revolution," but he would have been more accurate if he had spoken of a "Ptolemaic counter-revolution," since he put Man back at the center from which Copernicus had dethroned him.

But when we ask, not "what sort of world do we live in?" but "how do we come by our knowledge about the world?" subjectivity is in order. What each man knows is, in an important sense, dependent upon his own individual experience: he knows what he has seen and heard, what he has read and what he has been told, and also what, from these data, he has been able to infer. It is individual, not collective, experience that is here in question, for an inference is required to pass from my data to the acceptance of testimony. If I believe that there is such a place as Semipalatinsk, I believe it because of things that have happened to *me*; and unless certain substantial principles of inference are accepted, I shall have to admit that all these things might have happened to me without there being any such place.

The desire to escape from subjectivity in the description of the world (which I share) has led some modern philosophers astray—at least so it seems to me—in relation to theory of knowledge. Finding its problems distasteful, they have tried to deny that these problems exist. That data are private and individual is a thesis which has been familiar since the time of Protagoras. This thesis has been denied because it has been thought, as Protagoras thought, that, if admitted, it must lead to the conclusion that all knowledge is private and individual. For my part, while I admit the thesis, I deny the conclusion; how and why the following pages are intended to show.

In virtue of certain events in my own life, I have a number of beliefs about events that I do not experience—the thoughts and feelings of other people, the physical objects that surround me, the historical and geological past of the earth, and the remote regions of the universe that are studied in astronomy. For my part, I accept these beliefs as valid, apart from errors of detail. By this acceptance I commit myself to the view that there are valid processes of inference from events to other events—more particularly, from events of which I am aware without inference to events of which I have no such awareness. To discover what these processes are is a matter of analysis of scientific and common-sense procedure, in so far as such procedure is generally accepted as scientifically valid.

Inference from a group of events to other events can only be justified if the world has certain characteristics which are not logically necessary. So far as deductive logic can show, any collection of events might be the whole universe; if, then, I am ever to be able to infer events, I must accept principles of inference which lie outside deductive logic. All inference from events to events demands some kind of interconnection between different occurrences. Such interconnection is traditionally asserted in the principle of causality or natural law. It is implied, as we shall find, in whatever limited validity may be assigned to induction by simple enumeration. But the traditional ways of formulating the kind of interconnection that must be postulated are in many ways defective, some being too stringent and some not sufficiently so. To discover the minimum principles required to justify scientific inferences is one of the main purposes of this book.

It is a commonplace to say that the substantial inferences of science, as opposed to those of logic and mathematics, are only *probable*—that is to say, when the premises are true and the inference correct, the conclusion is only *likely* to be true. It is therefore necessary to examine what is meant by "probability." It will be found that there are two different concepts that may be meant. On the one hand, there is mathematical probability: If a class has *n* members, and *m* of them have a certain characteristic, the mathematical probability that an unspecified member of this class will have the characteristic in question is *m/n*. On the other hand, there is a wider and vaguer concept, which I call "degree of credibility," which is the amount of credence that it is rational to assign to a more or less uncertain proposition. Both kinds of probability are involved in stating the principles of scientific inference. . . .

That scientific inference requires, for its validity, principles which experience cannot render even probable is, I believe, an inescapable conclusion from the logic of probability. For empiricism, it is an awkward conclusion. But I think it can be rendered somewhat more palatable by the analysis of the concept of "knowledge" undertaken in Part II. "Knowledge," in my opinion, is a much less precise concept than is generally thought, and has its roots more deeply embedded in unverbalized animal behavior than most philosophers have been willing to admit. The logically basic assumptions to which our analysis leads us are psychologically the end of a long series of refinements which starts from habits of expectation in animals, such as that what has a certain kind of smell will be good to eat. To ask, therefore, whether we "know" the postulates of scientific inference, is not so definite a question as it seems. The answer must be: in one sense, yes, in another sense, no; but in the sense in which "no" is the right answer we know nothing whatever, and "knowledge" in this sense is a delusive vision. The perplexities of the philosophers are due, in a large measure, to their unwillingness to awaken from this blissful dream.

FURTHER READINGS

Eames, Elizabeth R. *Bertrand Russell's Theory of Knowledge*. London: Allen & Unwin, 1969.

Fritz, Charles. A. *Bertrand Russell's Construction of the External World*. London: Routledge & K. Paul, 1952.

Pears, David Francis. *Bertrand Russell and the British Tradition in Philosophy*. London: Collins, 1967.

Russell, Bertrand. *Sceptical Essays*. New York: W. W. Norton, 1928.

Schilpp, Paul Arthur, ed. *The Philosophy of Bertrand Russell*. Evanston and Chicago: Library of Living Philosophers, 1946.

41

POPPER

K arl Popper (1902–1994) was a leading philosopher of science, the most influential in Anglo-American analytical philosophy. His first—and most famous—work was the *Logic der Forschun* (1934), published in English with additions and revisions as *The Logic of Scientific Discovery* (1958). In this work, Popper distinguishes scientific from nonscientific views by the criterion of verifiability. Scientific theories, unlike metaphysical and religious ones, can be empirically refuted. If a verifiable scientific theory survives attempts at refutation, this theory is corroborated by experience but not proved to be true. (This view of Popper's resembles, in broad lines, Pascal's view of scientific knowledge; see chapter 16 in this volume.) Another influential book by Popper is *The Open Society and Its Enemies*. Published at the end of the Second World War (1945), Popper applies his scientific method to social issues, defending liberal democratic societies. Popper's text included in this anthology is selected from a third major book he published: *Conjectures and Refutations* (1963), from which we have selected substantial parts of the article "On the Sources of Knowledge and Ignorance." In this article, Popper presents the view he calls "critical rationalism." Basically, Popper's view is that truth is hidden. Neither the senses (Bacon and the empiricist tradition) nor the intellect (Descartes and the rationalist tradition) can reveal it. Theories (scientific or nonscientific) are thus conjectures (never truths) and the role of reason is to submit them to criticism, that is, to try to refute them. Popper recognizes this position in the Academic philosophical tradition (although he does not identify this tradition as Academic). This tradition holds (see chapter 3 in this volume) that truth is hidden and that the role of reason is not to establish the truth but to refute falsehoods. The Greek philosophers mentioned by Popper: Xenophanes, Democritus, and, above all, the Socrates of the *Apology*, are the main forerunners of the Academic tradition according to Cicero. A number of the modern philosophers Popper cites as belonging to this tradition are included in this anthology. We thank Ricardo Valério Fenati and Patricia Kauark Leite for helping us in choosing Popper's selection.

FROM "ON THE SOURCES OF KNOWLEDGE AND IGNORANCE"

The great movement of liberation which started in the Renaissance and led through the many vicissitudes of the reformation and the religious and revolutionary wars to the free societies in which the English-speaking peoples are privileged to live, this movement was inspired throughout by an unparalleled epistemological optimism: by a most optimistic view of man's power to discern truth and to acquire knowledge.

At the heart of this new optimistic view of the possibility of knowledge lies the doctrine that *truth is manifest*. Truth may perhaps be veiled. But it may reveal itself. [Note omitted] And if it does not reveal itself, it may be revealed by us. Removing the veil may not be easy. But once the naked truth stands revealed before our eyes, we have the power to see it, to distinguish it from falsehood, and to know that it *is* truth.

The birth of modern science and modern technology was inspired by this optimistic epistemology whose main spokesmen were Bacon and Descartes. They taught that there was no need for any man to appeal to authority in matters of truth because each man carried the sources of knowledge in himself; either in his power of sense-perception which he may use for the careful observation of nature, or in his power of intellectual intuition which he may use to distinguish truth from falsehood by refusing to accept any idea which is not clearly and distinctly perceived by the intellect.

Man can know: thus he can be free. This is the formula which explains the link between epistemological optimism and the ideas of liberalism.

This link is paralleled by the opposite link. Disbelief in the power of human reason, in man's power to discern the truth, is almost invariably linked with distrust of man. Thus epistemological pessimism is linked, historically, with a doctrine of human depravity, and it tends to lead to the demand for the establishment of powerful traditions and the entrenchment of a powerful authority which would save man from his folly and his wickedness. (There is a striking sketch of this theory of authoritarianism, and a picture of the burden carried by those in authority, in the story of *The Grand Inquisitor* in Dostoievsky's *The Brothers Karamazov*.)

The contrast between epistemological pessimism and optimism may be said to be fundamentally the same as that between epistemological traditionalism and rationalism. (I am using the latter term in its wider sense in which it is opposed to irrationalism, and in which it covers not only Cartesian intellectualism but empiricism also.) For we can interpret traditionalism as the belief that, in the absence of an objective and discernible truth, we are faced with the choice between accepting the authority of tradition, and chaos; while rationalism has, of course, always claimed the right of reason and of empirical science to criticize, and to reject, any tradition, and any authority, as being based on sheer unreason or prejudice or accident. . . .

The framework of Bacon's theory of induction is this. He distinguishes in the *Novum Organum* between a true method and a false method. . . .

Thus the two methods are (1) "the spelling out of the open book of Nature" leading to knowledge or *epistēmē*, and (2) "the prejudice of the mind that wrongly prejudges, and perhaps misjudges, Nature," leading to *doxa*, or mere guesswork, and to the misreading of the book of Nature. This latter method, rejected by Bacon, is in fact a method of interpretation, in the modern sense of the word. It is the *method of conjecture or hypothesis* (a method of which, incidentally, I happen to be a convinced advocate).

How can we prepare ourselves to read the book of Nature properly or truly? Bacon's answer is: by purging our minds of all anticipations or conjectures or guesses or prejudices (*Nov. Org.* 1.68, 69 end). There are various things to be done in order so to purge our minds. We have to get rid of all sorts of "idols," or generally held false beliefs; for these distort our observations (*Nov. Org.* 1.97). But we have also, like Socrates, to look out for all sorts of counter-instances by which to destroy our prejudices concerning the kind of thing whose true essence or nature we wish to ascertain. Like Socrates, we must, by purifying our intellects, prepare our souls to face the eternal light of essences or natures (cf. St Augustine, *Civ. Dei* 8.3): our impure prejudices must be exorcized by the invocation of counter-instances (*Nov. Org.* 2.16 ff.).

Only after our souls have been cleansed in this way may we begin the work of spelling out diligently the open book of Nature, the manifest truth.

In view of all this I suggest that Baconian (and also Aristotelian) induction is the same, fundamentally, as Socratic *maieutic*; that is to say, the preparation of the mind by cleansing it of prejudices, in order to enable it to recognize the manifest truth, or to read the open book of Nature.

Descartes' method of systematic doubt is also fundamentally the same: it is a method of destroying all false prejudices of the mind, in order to arrive at the unshakable basis of self-evident truth.

We can now see more clearly how, in this optimistic epistemology, the state of knowledge is the natural or the pure state of man, the state of the innocent eye which can see the truth, while the state of ignorance has its source in the injury suffered by the innocent eye in man's fall from grace; an injury which can be partially healed by a course of purification. And we can see more clearly why this epistemology, not only in Descartes' but also in Bacon's form, remains essentially a religious doctrine in which the source of all knowledge is divine authority.

One might say that, encouraged by the divine "essences" or divine "natures" of Plato, and by the traditional Greek opposition between the truthfulness of nature and the deceitfulness of man-made convention, Bacon substitutes, in his epistemology, "Nature" for "God." This may be the reason why we have to purify ourselves before we may approach the goddess *Natura*: when we have purified our minds, even our sometimes unreliable senses (held by Plato to be hopelessly impure) will be pure. The sources of knowledge must be kept pure, because any impurity may become a source of ignorance.

In spite of the religious character of their epistemologies, Bacon's and Descartes' attacks upon prejudice, and upon traditional beliefs which we carelessly or recklessly harbour, are clearly anti-authoritarian and anti-traditionalist. For they require us to shed all beliefs except those whose truth we have perceived ourselves. And their attacks were certainly intended to be attacks upon authority and tradition. They were part of the war against authority which it was the fashion of the time to wage, the war against the authority of Aristotle and the tradition of the schools. Men do not need such authorities if they can perceive the truth themselves.

But I do not think that Bacon and Descartes succeeded in freeing their epistemologies from authority; not so much because they appealed to religious authority—to Nature or to God—but for an even deeper reason.

In spite of their individualistic tendencies, they did not dare to appeal to our crit- ical judgment—to your judgment, or to mine; perhaps because they felt that this might lead to subjectivism and to arbitrariness. Yet whatever the reason may have been, they certainly were unable to give up thinking in terms of authority, much as they wanted to do so. They could only replace one authority—that of Aristotle and the Bible—by another. Each of them appealed to a new authority; the one to *the authority of the senses*, and the other to *the authority of the intellect*.

This means that they failed to solve the great problem: How can we admit that our knowledge is a human—an all too human—affair, without at the same time implying that it is all individual whim and arbitrariness?

Yet this problem had been seen and solved long before; first, it appears, by Xenophanes, and then by Democritus, and by Socrates (the Socrates of the *Apology* rather than of the *Meno*). The solution lies in the realization that all of us may and often do err, singly and collectively, but that this very idea of error and human falli- bility involves another one—the idea of *objective truth*: the standard which we may fall short of. Thus the doctrine of fallibility should not be regarded as part of a pes- simistic epistemology. This doctrine implies that we may seek for truth, for objec- tive truth, though more often than not we may miss it by a wide margin. And it implies that if we respect truth, we must search for it by persistently searching for our errors: by indefatigable rational criticism, and self-criticism.

Erasmus of Rotterdam attempted to revive this Socratic doctrine—the important though unobtrusive doctrine, "Know thyself, and thus admit to thyself how little thou knowest!" Yet this doctrine was swept away by the belief that truth is manifest, and by the new self-assurance exemplified and taught in different ways by Luther and Calvin, by Bacon and Descartes.

It is important to realize, in this connection, the difference between Cartesian doubt and the doubt of Socrates, or Erasmus, or Montaigne. While Socrates doubts human knowledge or wisdom, and remains firm in his rejection of any pretension to knowledge or wisdom, Descartes doubts everything—but only to end up with the possession of *absolutely certain* knowledge; for he finds that his universal doubt would lead him to doubt the truthfulness of God, which is absurd. Having proved that universal doubt is absurd, he concludes that we *can* know securely, that we *can* be wise—by distinguishing, in the natural light of reason, between clear and distinct ideas whose source is God, and all other ideas whose source is our own impure imagination. Cartesian doubt, we see, is merely a *maieutic* instrument for estab- lishing a criterion of truth and, with it, a way to secure knowledge and wisdom. Yet for the Socrates of the *Apology*, wisdom consisted in the awareness of our limita- tions; in knowing how little we know, every one of us.

It was this doctrine of an essential human fallibility which Nicolas of Cusa and Erasmus of Rotterdam (who refers to Socrates) revived; and it was this "humanist" doctrine (in contradistinction to the optimistic doctrine on which Milton relied, the doctrine that truth will prevail) which Nicolas and Erasmus, Montaigne and Locke and Voltaire, followed by John Stuart Mill and Bertrand Russell, made the basis of the doctrine of tolerance. "What is tolerance?" asks Voltaire in his *Philosophical Dictionary*; and he answers: "It is a necessary consequence of our humanity. We are all fallible, and prone to error; let us then pardon each other's follies. This is the first principle of natural right." . . .

The traditional systems of epistemology may be said to result from yes-answers or no-answers to questions about the sources of our knowledge. *They never challenge these questions, or dispute their legitimacy*; the questions are taken as perfectly natural, and nobody seems to see any harm in them.

This is quite interesting, for these questions are clearly authoritarian in spirit. They can be compared with that traditional question of political theory, "Who should rule?" which begs for an authoritarian answer such as "the best," or "the wisest," or "the people," or "the majority." (It suggests, incidentally, such silly alternatives as "Who should be our rulers: the capitalists or the workers?" analogous to "What is the ultimate source of knowledge: the intellect or the senses?") This political question is wrongly put and the answers which it elicits are paradoxical (as I have tried to show in chapter 7 of my *Open Society*). It should be replaced by a completely different question such as *"How can we organize our political institutions so that bad or incompetent rulers* (whom we should try not to get, but whom we so easily might get all the same) *cannot do too much damage?"* I believe that only by changing our question in this way can we hope to proceed towards a reasonable theory of political institutions.

The question about the sources of our knowledge can be replaced in a similar way. It has always been asked in the spirit of: "What are the best sources of our knowledge—the most reliable ones, those which will not lead us into error, and those to which we can and must turn, in case of doubt, as the last court of appeal?" I propose to assume, instead, that no such ideal sources exist? no more than ideal rulers—and that *all* "sources" are liable to lead us into error at times. And I propose to replace, therefore, the question of the sources of our knowledge by the entirely different question: *"How can we hope to detect and eliminate error?"*

The question of the sources of our knowledge, like so many authoritarian questions, is a *genetic* one. It asks for the origin of our knowledge, in the belief that knowledge may legitimize itself by its pedigree. The nobility of the racially pure knowledge, the untainted knowledge, the knowledge which derives from the highest authority, if possible from God: these are the (often unconscious) metaphysical ideas behind the question. My modified question, "How can we hope to detect error?" may be said to derive from the view that such pure, untainted, and certain sources do not exist, and that questions of origin or of purity should not be confounded with questions of validity, or of truth. This view may be said to be as old as Xenophanes. Xenophanes knew that our knowledge is guesswork, opinion—*doxa* rather than *epistēmē*—as shown by his verses (dk, B, 18 and 34):

> The gods did not reveal, from the beginning,
> All things to us; but in the course of time,
> Through seeking we may learn, and know things better.
>
> But as for certain truth, no man has known it,
> Nor will he know it; neither of the gods,
> Nor yet of all the things of which I speak.
> And even if by chance he were to utter
> The perfect truth, he would himself not know it;
> For all is but a woven web of guesses.

Yet the traditional question of the authoritative sources of knowledge is repeated even today—and very often by positivists and by other philosophers who believe themselves to be in revolt against authority.

The proper answer to my question "How can we hope to detect and eliminate error?" is, I believe, "By *criticizing* the theories or guesses of others and—if we can train ourselves to do so—by *criticizing* our own theories or guesses." (The latter point is highly desirable, but not indispensable; for if we fail to criticize our own theories, there may be others to do it for us.) This answer sums up a position which I propose to call "critical rationalism." It is a view, an attitude, and a tradition, which we owe to the Greeks. It is very different from the "rationalism" or "intellectualism" of Descartes and his school, and very different even from the epistemology of Kant. Yet in the field of ethics, of moral knowledge, it was approached by Kant with *his principle of autonomy*. This principle expresses his realization that we must not accept the command of an authority, however exalted, as the basis of ethics. For whenever we are faced with a command by an authority, it is for us to judge, critically, whether it is moral or immoral to obey. . . .

Pessimistic and optimistic epistemologies are about equally mistaken. The pessimistic cave story of Plato is the true one, and not his optimistic story of *anamnēsis* (even though we should admit that all men, like all other animals, and even all plants, possess inborn knowledge). But although the world of appearances is indeed a world of mere shadows on the walls of our cave, we all constantly reach out beyond it; and although, as Democritus said, the truth is hidden in the deep, we can probe into the deep. There is no criterion of truth at our disposal, and this fact supports pessimism. But we do possess criteria which, *if we are lucky*, may allow us to recognize error and falsity. Clarity and distinctness are not criteria of truth, but such things as obscurity or confusion *may* indicate error. Similarly coherence cannot establish truth, but incoherence and inconsistency do establish falsehood. And, when they are recognized, our own errors provide the dim red lights which help us in groping our way out of the darkness of our cave.

Neither observation nor reason is an authority. Intellectual intuition and imagination are most important, but they are not reliable: they may show us things very clearly, and yet they may mislead us. They are indispensable as the main sources of our theories; but most of our theories are false anyway. The most important function of observation and reasoning, and even of intuition and imagination, is to help us in the critical examination of those bold conjectures which are the means by which we probe into the unknown. . . .

Every solution of a problem raises new unsolved problems; the more so the deeper the original problem and the bolder its solution. The more we learn about the world, and the deeper our learning, the more conscious, specific, and articulate will be our knowledge of what we do not know, our knowledge of our ignorance. For this, indeed, is the main source of our ignorance—the fact that our knowledge can be only finite, while our ignorance must necessarily be infinite.

We may get a glimpse of the vastness of our ignorance when we contemplate the vastness of the heavens: though the mere size of the universe is not the deepest cause of our ignorance, it is one of its causes. "Where I seem to differ from some of my friends," F. P. Ramsey wrote in a charming passage of his *Foundations of Mathematics* (p. 29), "is in attaching little importance to physical size. I don't feel in the least humble before the vastness of the heavens. The stars may be large but they cannot think or love; and these are qualities which impress me far more than size does. I take no credit for weighing nearly seventeen stone." I suspect that Ramsey's friends would have agreed with him about the insignificance of sheer physical size; and I suspect that if they felt humble before the vastness of the heavens, this was because they saw in it a symbol of their ignorance.

I believe that it would be worth trying to learn something about the world even if in trying to do so we should merely learn that we do not know much. This state of learned ignorance might be a help in many of our troubles. It might be well for all of us to remember that, while differing widely in the various little bits we know, in our infinite ignorance we are all equal.

There is a last question I wish to raise.

If only we look for it we can often find a true idea, worthy of being preserved, in a philosophical theory which must be rejected as false. Can we find an idea like this in one of the theories of the ultimate sources of our knowledge?

I believe we can; and I suggest that it is one of the two main ideas which underlie the doctrine that the source of all our knowledge is super-natural. The first of these ideas is false, I believe, while the second is true.

The first, the false idea, is that we must *justify* our knowledge, or our theories, by *positive* reason, that is, by reasons capable of establishing them, or at least of making them highly probable; at any rate, by better reasons than that they have so far withstood criticism. This idea implies, I suggest, that we must appeal to some ultimate or authoritative source of true knowledge; which still leaves open the character of that authority—whether it is human, like observation or reason, or super-human (and therefore super-natural).

The second idea—whose vital importance has been stressed by Russell—is that no man's authority can establish truth by decree; that we should submit to truth; that *truth is above human authority.*

Taken together these two ideas almost immediately yield the conclusion that the sources from which our knowledge derives must be super-human; a conclusion which tends to encourage self-righteousness and the use of force against those who refuse to see the divine truth.

Some who rightly reject this conclusion do not, unhappily, reject the first idea—the belief in the existence of ultimate sources of knowledge. Instead they reject the second idea—the thesis that truth is above human authority. They thereby endanger the idea of the objectivity of knowledge, and of common standards of criticism or rationality.

What we should do, I suggest, is to give up the idea of ultimate sources of knowledge, and admit that all knowledge is human; that it is mixed with our errors, our prejudices, our dreams, and our hopes; that all we can do is to grope for truth even though it be beyond our reach. We may admit that our groping is often inspired, but we must be on our guard against the belief, however deeply felt, that our inspiration carries any authority, divine or otherwise. If we thus admit that there is no authority beyond the reach of criticism to be found within the whole province of our knowledge, however far it may have penetrated into the unknown, then we can retain, without danger, the idea that truth is beyond human authority. And we must retain it. For without this idea there can be no objective standards of inquiry; no criticism of our conjectures; no groping for the unknown; no quest for knowledge.

FURTHER READINGS

Artigas, Mariano. "Fallibilism and Skepticism." In *The Ethical Nature of Karl Popper's Theory of Knowledge: Including Popper's Unpublished Comments on Bartley and Critical Rationalism*, edited by Mariano Artigas and Ivan Slade. New York: Peter Lang, 1999.

Miller, David. *Out of Error: Further Essays on Critical Rationalism.* Aldershot, England: Ashgate, 2006.

Musgrave, Alan. *Common Sense, Science and Scepticism: A Historical Introduction to the Theory of Knowledge.* Cambridge: Cambridge University Press, 1993.

Popper, Karl. *The Logic of Scientific Discovery.* London: Hutchinson, 1958.

———. *The Open Society and Its Enemies.* 2 vols. London: Kegan Paul, 1945.

Watkins, John W. *Science and Scepticism.* Princeton, NJ: Princeton University Press, 1984.

42

FEYERABEND

Paul Feyerabend (1924–1994) was an influential and polemical philosopher of science. He was an implacable critic of Popper's critical rationalism. His most well-known book, in which he details his criticism of Popper, is *Against Method*, first published in 1975. Feyerabend argues that scientists do not proceed in the methodical and rational manner claimed by philosophers of science. He opposes, in particular, Popper's view that science can be demarcated from other kinds of traditional knowledge by its openness to criticism and refutations. We could say that Feyerabend—who was initially a follower of Popper—maintains Popper's idea of conjectures (scientific theories are not necessarily established rationally) but rejects Popper's idea of refutations, since for Feyerabend there are no independent empirical or theoretical (rational) standards independent of the conjectures that can either prove (Popper agreed with this point, too) or refute (against Popper) a given theory. The extract below is taken from Feyerabend's later work, *Farewell to Reason*. In this work he disavows *Against Method*, taking a much more radical position. He says that in the former work he was not completely free from the Popperian spell in that, although criticizing Popper's rationalist view of science, he still overvalued Western science. In *Farewell to Reason*, he develops a radical criticism of Western rationalism, in philosophy and in science, defending a skeptical relativism and attacking the prestige and authority that science has acquired in Western societies. We give below Feyerabend's statement of his eleven relativist hypotheses (R1–R11) and his explanation of the last two ones (R10 and R11).

FROM *FAREWELL TO REASON*

R1: [I]ndividuals, groups, entire civilizations may profit from studying alien cultures, institutions, ideas, no matter how strong the traditions that support their own views (no matter how strong the arguments that support these views). . . .

R2: [S]ocieties dedicated to freedom and democracy should be structured in a way that gives all traditions *equal opportunities*, i.e., equal access to federal funds, educational institutions, basic decisions. Science is to be treated as one tradition among many, not as a standard for judging what is and what is not, what can and what cannot be accepted. . . .

R3: Democratic societies should give all traditions *equal rights* and not only equal opportunities. . . .

R4: [L]aws, religious beliefs, and customs rule, like kings, in restricted domains. Their rule rests on a twofold authority—on their *power* and on the fact that it is *rightful* power: the rules are *valid* in their domains. . . .

R5: Man is the measure of all things; of those that are that they are; and of those that are not, that they are not. . . .

R5a: [W]hatever seems to somebody, is to him to whom it seems. . . .

R5b: [T]hat the laws, customs, facts that are being put before the citizens ultimately rest on the pronouncements, beliefs, and perceptions of human beings and that important matters should therefore be referred to the (perceptions and thoughts of the) people concerned and not to abstract agencies and distant experts. . . .

R6: [C]itizens, and not special groups have the last word in deciding what is true or false, useful or useless for their society. . . .

R7: [T]he world, as described by our scientists and anthropologists, consists of (social and physical) regions with specific laws and conceptions of reality. In the social domain we have relatively stable societies which have demonstrated an ability to survive in their own particular surroundings and possess great adaptive powers. In the physical domain we have different points of view, valid in different areas, but inapplicable outside. Some of these points of view are more detailed—these are our scientific theories; others simpler, but more general—these are the various philosophical or commonsense views that affect the construction of "reality." The attempt to enforce a universal truth (a universal way of finding truth) has led to disasters in the social domain and to empty formalisms combined with never-to-be-fulfilled promises in the natural sciences. . . .

R8: [T]he idea of an objective truth or an objective reality that is independent of human wishes but can be discovered by human effort is part of a special tradition which, judged by its own members, contains successes as well as failures, was always accompanied by, and often mixed with, more practical (empirical, "subjective") traditions, and must be combined with such traditions to give practical results. . . .

R9: [T]he idea of a situation-independent objective truth has limited validity. Like the laws, beliefs, customs of R4 it rules in some domains (traditions), but not in others. . . .

R10: [F]or every statement (theory, point of view) that is believed to be true with good reasons *there may exist* arguments showing that either its opposite, or a weaker alternative is true. . . .

Adding the points made in the literature cited in footnote 9 [John H. Bodely, *Victims of Progress*, California, 1983; F. A. von Hayek, *Missbrauch und Verfall der Vernunft*, Salzburg, 1979; M. Rahnema, "Education for Exclusion or Participation?" MS, Stanford, April 16, 1985; I. Illich, *Deschooling Society*, New York, 1970], we arrive at the hypothesis that there exist many different ways of living and of building up knowledge. Each of these ways may give rise to abstract thought which in turn may split into competing abstract theories. Scientific theories, to give an example from our own civilization, branch out in different directions, use different (and occasionally "incommensurable") concepts and evaluate events in different ways. What counts as evidence, or as an important result, or as "sound scientific procedure," depends on attitudes and judgments that change with time, profession, and occasionally even from one research group to the next. Thus Ehrenhaft and Millikan working on the same problem (the charge of the electron) used their data in different ways and regarded different things as facts. The difference was eventually removed but it was the core of an important and exciting episode in the history of science. Einstein and the defenders of hidden variables in the quantum theory use different criteria of theory evaluation. They are metaphysical criteria in the sense that they support or criticize a theory although it is empirically satisfactory and well formulated mathematically. [Note omitted] The same is true of criteria that stretch an empirical subject beyond the reach of its evidence, asserting, for example, that all biology is molecular biology, that botany has no longer any independent claim to truth. T. H. Morgan, preferring direct experimental support to data involving inferences, rejected the study of chromosomes in favor of more overt manifestations of inheritance. In 1946 Barbara McClintock had already noticed the process which today is called transposition. "However she worked alone, she did not work with microorganisms, she worked in the classical manner and stayed away from molecules." Not a single member of the rapidly expanding group of molecular biologists "listened to what she said." Divergences proliferate in psychology: behaviorists and neurophysiologists despise introspection which is an important source of knowledge for gestalt psychology. . . . In medicine a similar antagonism between clinicians and body theoreticians goes back to antiquity, as we have seen. Differences increase when we move on to history and sociology: a social history of the French Revolution shares only names with a description of persons and concrete individual events. [Note omitted] Nature herself can be approached in many ways (the idea that there exists no separation between her and the lives of humans being one of them, the idea of her non-material character being another) and responds accordingly. Taking all this into account I suggest that we strengthen R10 and assert

> R11: For every statement, theory, point of view believed (to be true) with good reasons *there exist* arguments showing a conflicting alternative to be at least as good, or even better.

R11 was used by the ancient skeptics to achieve mental and social peace: if opposing views can be shown to be equally strong, they said, then there is no need to worry, or to start a war about them (Sextus Empiricus, *Hypot.* 1.25f). Statements, theories, arguments, good reasons enter the scene because of the historical situation in which the skeptics made their point: they opposed philosophers who had tried to show that argument would lead to unique conclusions; but argument, the skeptics maintained, has no such power. Including non-argumentative ways of establishing human contact and, possibly, a common purpose further strengthens their position. For now we are dealing not merely with intellectual matters, but with feelings, faith, empathy, and many other agencies not yet catalogued and named by rationalists. A removal of R11 would require detailed empirical/conceptual/historical analyses none of which are found in the customary objections to skepticism and relativism, . . .

But if objectivism while perhaps acceptable as a particular point of view cannot claim objective superiority over other ideas, then the objective way of posing problems and presenting results is not the right way for the relativist to adopt. A relativist who deserves his name will then have to refrain from making assertions about the nature of reality, truth, and knowledge and will have to keep to specifics instead. He may and often will generalize his findings but without assuming that he now has principles which by their very nature are useful, acceptable, and, most importantly, binding for all. Debating with objectivists, he may of course use objectivist methods and assumptions; however his purpose will not be to establish universally acceptable truths (about particulars or generalities) but to embarrass the opponent—he is simply trying to defeat the objectivist with his own weapons. Relativistic arguments are always *ad hominem*; their beauty lies in the fact that the *homines* addressed, being constrained by their code of intellectual honesty, must consider them and, if they are good (in their sense), accept them as "objectively valid." All my arguments in the preceding sections should be read in this manner. [Note omitted]

For example, R7 to R11 are not meant to reveal "objective features" of the world; they are introduced to undermine the objectivist's confidence or to capture outsiders by a vivid historical image. If the objectivist agrees with my arguments, then R1 and R7 become difficulties for his point of view and this quite independently of whether I myself believe in them or not.

FURTHER READINGS

Feyerabend, Paul. *Against Method*. London: Verso, 1975.
———. *Science in a Free Society*. London: Verso, 1978.
Maia Neto, José R. "Feyerabend's Skepticism." *Studies in History and Philosophy of Science* 22, no. 4 (1991): 543–55.
Munévar, Gonzalo, ed. *Beyond Reason: Essays on the Philosophy of Paul K. Feyerabend*. Dordrecht: Kluwer, 1991.

43

DERRIDA

J acques Derrida (1930–2004) was one of the leading exponents of the so-called postmodern or poststructuralist contemporary philosophical movement. Postmodernism has been seen as a kind of skepticism, in particular to the extent that it questions the integrity and validity of reason and the self as they were conjunctly enthroned from Descartes onward as foundational in philosophical inquiry. Derrida's versions of postmodernism is a form of radical skepticism in that he denies that there is anything outside the text and that there is any objective or true interpretation of any text—views that abolish the distinction between fictional and philosophical texts. In the article from which the following passages were extracted—"Cogito and the History of Madness"—Derrida criticizes another exponent of postmodern thought, Michel Foucault's (1926–1984) *History of Insanity*, by taking issue with the latter's interpretation of the apparent abandonment of an argument from madness in Descartes's First Meditation. According to Foucault, Descartes's move is not exactly abandonment but an internment of madness, which he sees as paradigmatic of a large-scale phenomenon that occurs in Western modern societies. Derrida presents his own interpretation of Descartes's doubt and *cogito*, which he sees, contrary to Foucault, not as a rational self-assurance but, on the contrary, as an inaugural moment antecedent to any meaning and rationality, as an arbitrary moment (from the point of view of reason) that makes possible both rationality and madness. In Derrida's view, rather than Descartes's interning madness with his doubt and *cogito*, it is Foucault who interns Cartesian doubt and *cogito* by inscribing them at the center of the historical structure characteristic of modernity that he presents in his *History of Insanity*.

FROM *WRITING AND DIFFERENCE*

[Foucault's] passage devoted to Descartes opens the crucial chapter on "the great internment." It thus opens the book itself, and its location at the beginning of the chapter is fairly unexpected. . . . We are not told whether or not this passage of the first *Meditation*, interpreted by Foucault as a *philosophical* internment of madness, is destined, as a prelude to the historical and sociopolitical drama, to set the tone for the *entire* drama to be played. Is this "act of force," described in the dimension of theoretical knowledge and metaphysics, a symptom, a cause, a language? . . .

Thus the certainty of this simplicity of *intelligible* generalization [Descartes's extension]—which is soon after submitted to metaphysical, artificial, and hyperbolical doubt through the fiction of the evil genius—is in no way obtained by a continuous reduction which finally lays bare the resistance of a nucleus of sensory or imaginative certainty. There is discontinuity and a transition to another order of reasoning. The nucleus is purely intelligible, and the still natural and provisional certainty which has been attained supposes a radical break with the senses. At this moment of the analysis, no imaginative or sensory signification, as such, has been saved, *no* invulnerability of the senses to doubt has been experienced. *All* significations or "ideas" of sensory origin are *excluded* from the realm of truth, *for the same reason as madness* is excluded from it. And there is nothing astonishing about this: madness is only a particular case, and, moreover, not the most serious one, of the sensory illusion which interests Descartes at this point. It can thus be stated that:

. . . The hypothesis of insanity—at this moment of the Cartesian order—seems neither to receive any privileged treatment nor to be submitted to any particular exclusion. Let us reread, in effect, the passage cited by Foucault in which insanity appears. . . .

. . . Descartes has just said that all knowledge of sensory origin could deceive him. He pretends to put to himself the astonished objection of an imaginary non-philosopher who is frightened by such audacity and says: no, not all sensory knowledge, for then you would be mad and it would be unreasonable to follow the example of madmen, to put forth the ideas of madmen. Descartes *echoes* this objection: since I am here, writing, and you understand me, I am not mad, nor are you, and we are all sane. The example of madness is therefore not indicative of the fragility of the sensory idea. So be it. Descartes acquiesces to this natural point of view, or rather he feigns to rest in this natural comfort in order better, more radically and more definitively, to unsettle himself from it and to discomfort his interlocutor. So be it, he says, you think that I would be mad to doubt that I am sitting near the fire, etc., that I would be insane to follow the example of madmen. I will therefore propose a hypothesis which will seem much more natural to you, will not disorient you, because it concerns a more common, and more universal experience than that of madness: the experience of sleep and dreams. Descartes then elaborates the hypothesis that will ruin *all* the *sensory* foundations of knowledge and will lay bare only the *intellectual* foundations of certainty. This hypothesis above all will not run from the possibility of an insanity—an epistemological one—much more serious than madness.

The reference to dreams is therefore not put off to one side—quite the contrary—in relation to a madness potentially respected or even excluded by Descartes. It constitutes, in the methodical order which here is ours, the hyperbolical exasperation of the hypothesis of madness. This latter affected only certain areas of sensory perception, and in a contingent and partial way. Moreover, Descartes is concerned here not with determining the concept of madness but with utilizing the popular notion of insanity for juridical and methodological ends, in order to ask questions of principle regarding only the *truth* of ideas. [Note omitted] What must be grasped here is that *from this point of view* the sleeper, or the dreamer, is madder than the madman. Or, at least, the dreamer, insofar as concerns the problem of knowledge which interests Descartes here, is further from true perception than the madman. It is in the case of sleep, and not in that of insanity, that the *absolute totality* of ideas of sensory origin becomes suspect. . . .

Now, the recourse to the fiction of the evil genius will evoke, conjure up, the possibility of a *total madness*, a total derangement over which I could have no control because it is inflicted upon me—hypothetically—leaving me no responsibility for it. Total derangement is the possibility of a madness that is no longer a disorder of the body, of the object, the body-object outside the boundaries of the *res cogitans*, outside the boundaries of the policed city, secure in its existence as thinking subjectivity, but is a madness that will bring subversion to pure thought and to its purely intelligible objects, to the field of its clear and distinct ideas, to the realm of the mathematical truths which escape natural doubt.

This time madness, insanity, will spare nothing, neither bodily nor purely intellectual perceptions. And Descartes successively judges admissible:

(a) That which he pretended not to admit while conversing with the non-philosopher. To cite Descartes (he has just evoked "some evil genius not less powerful than deceitful"): "I shall consider that the heavens, the earth, colors, figures, sound, and all other external things are naught but the illusions and dreams of which this genius has availed himself in order to lay traps for my credulity; I shall consider myself as having no hands, no eyes, no flesh, no blood, nor any senses, yet falsely believing myself to possess all these things." [Note omitted] These ideas will be taken up again in the second *Meditation*. We are thus quite far from the dismissal of insanity made above.

(b) That which escapes natural doubt: "But how do I know that Hell (i.e., the deceiving God, before the recourse to the evil genius) has not brought it to pass that . . . I am not deceived every time that I add two and three, or count the sides of a square . . . ?" [Note omitted]

Thus, ideas of neither sensory nor intellectual origin will be sheltered from this new phase of doubt, and everything that was previously set aside as insanity is now welcomed into the most essential interiority of thought.

In question is a philosophical and juridical operation (but the first phase of doubt was already such) which no longer names madness and reveals all principled possibilities. *In principle* nothing is opposed to the subversion named insanity, although *in fact* and from a natural point of view, for Descartes, for his reader, and for us, no natural anxiety is possible regarding this actual subversion. (Truthfully speaking, to go to the heart of the matter, one would have to confront directly, in and of itself, the question of what is *de facto* and what *de jure* in the relations of the Cogito and madness.) Beneath this natural comfort, beneath this apparently prephilosophical confidence is hidden the recognition of an essential and principled truth: to wit, if discourse and philosophical communication (that is, language itself) are to have an intelligible meaning, that is to say, if they are to conform to their essence and vocation as discourse, they must simultaneously in fact and in principle escape madness. They must carry normality within themselves. And this is not a specifically Cartesian weakness (although Descartes never confronts the question of his own language), [note omitted] is not a defect or mystification linked to a determined historical structure, but rather is an essential and universal necessity from which no discourse can escape, for it belongs to the meaning of meaning. It is an essential necessity from which no discourse can escape, even the discourse which denounces a mystification or an act of force. And, paradoxically, what I am saying here is strictly Foucaultian. For we can now appreciate the profundity of the following affirmation of Foucault's that curiously also saves Descartes from the accusations made against him: "Madness is the absence of a work." This is a fundamental motif of Foucault's book. Now, the work starts with the most elementary discourse, with the first articulation of a meaning, with the first syntactical usage of an "as such," [note omitted] for to make a sentence is to *manifest* a possible meaning. By its essence, the sentence is normal. It carries normality within it, that is, *sense*, in every sense of the word—Descartes' in particular. It carries normality and sense within it, and does so whatever the state, whatever the health or madness of him who propounds it, or whom it passes through, on whom, in whom it is articulated. In its most impoverished syntax, logos is reason and, indeed, a historical reason. And if madness in general, beyond any factitious and determined historical structure is the absence of a work, then madness is indeed, essentially and generally, silence, stifled speech, within a caesura and a wound that *open up* life *as historicity in general*. Not a determined silence, imposed at one given moment rather than at any other, but a silence essentially linked to an act of force and prohibition which open history and speech. *In general.* Within the dimension of historicity in general, which is to be confused neither with some ahistorical eternity, nor with an empirically determined moment of the history of facts, silence plays the irreducible role of that which bears and haunts language, outside and *against* which alone language can emerge—"against" here simultaneously designating the content from which form takes off by force, and the adversary against whom I assure and reassure myself by force. . . .

The act of the Cogito and the certainty of existing indeed escape madness the first time; but aside from the fact that for the first time, it is no longer a question of objective, representative knowledge, it can no longer literally be said that the Cogito would escape madness because it keeps itself beyond the grasp of madness, or because, as Foucault says, "*I* who think, I cannot be mad"; the Cogito escapes madness only because at its own moment, under its own authority, it is valid *even if I am mad*, even if my thoughts are completely mad. There is a value and a meaning of the Cogito, as of existence, which escape the alternative of a determined madness or a determined reason. Confronted with the critical experience of the Cogito, insanity, as stated in the *Discourse on Method*, is irremediably on a plane with skepticism. Thought no longer fears madness: ". . . remarking that this truth '*I think, therefore I am*' was so certain and so assured that all the most extravagant suppositions brought forward by the skeptics were incapable of shaking it." [Note omitted] The certainty thus attained need not be sheltered from an imprisoned madness, for it is attained and ascertained within madness itself. It is valid *even if I am mad*—a supreme self-confidence that seems to require neither the exclusion nor the circumventing of madness. Descartes never interns madness, neither at the stage of natural doubt nor at the stage of metaphysical doubt. *He only claims to exclude it during the first phase of the first stage, during the nonhyperbolical moment of natural doubt.*

The hyperbolical audacity of the Cartesian Cogito, its mad audacity, which we perhaps no longer perceive as such because, unlike Descartes' contemporary, we are too well assured of ourselves and too well accustomed to the framework of the Cogito, rather than to the critical experience of it—its mad audacity would consist in the return to an original point which no longer belongs to either a *determined* reason or a *determined* unreason, no longer belongs to them as opposition or alternative. Whether I am mad or not, *Cogito, sum.* Madness is therefore, in every sense of the word, only one *case* of thought (*within* thought). It is therefore a question of drawing back toward a point at which all determined contradictions, in the form of given, factual historical structures, can appear, and appear as relative to this zero point at which determined meaning and nonmeaning come together in their common origin. From the point of view which here is ours, one could perhaps say the following about this zero point, determined by Descartes as Cogito.

Invulnerable to all determined opposition between reason and unreason, it is the point starting from which the history of the determined forms of this opposition, this opened or broken-off dialogue, can appear as such and be stated. It is the impenetrable point of certainty in which the possibility of Foucault's narration, as well as of the narration of the totality, or rather of *all* the determined forms of the exchanges between reason and madness are embedded. It is the point at which the project of thinking this totality by escaping it is embedded. By escaping it: that is to say, by exceeding the totality, which—within existence—is possible only in the direction of infinity or nothingness; for even if the totality of what I think is imbued with falsehood or madness, even if the totality of the world does not exist, even if nonmeaning has invaded the totality of the world, up to and including the very contents of my thought, I still think, I am *while* I think. Even if I do not *in fact* grasp the totality, if I neither understand nor embrace it, I still formulate the project of doing so, and this project is meaningful in such a way that it can be defined only in relation to a pre-comprehension of the infinite and undetermined totality. This is why, by virtue of this margin of the possible, the principled, and the meaningful, which exceeds all that is real, factual, and existent, this project is mad, and acknowledges madness as its liberty and its very possibility. This is why it is not human, in the sense of anthropological factuality, but is rather metaphysical and demonic: it first awakens to itself in its war with the demon, the evil genius of nonmeaning, by pitting itself against the strength of the evil genius, and by resisting him through reduction of the natural man within itself. In this sense, nothing is less reassuring than the Cogito at its proper and inaugural moment. . . .

The extent to which doubt and the Cartesian Cogito are *punctuated* by this project of a singular and unprecedented excess—an excess in the direction of the non-determined, Nothingness or Infinity, an excess which overflows the totality of that which can be thought, the totality of beings and determined meanings, the totality of factual history—is also the extent to which any effort to reduce this project, to enclose it within a determined historical structure, however comprehensive, risks missing the essential, risks dulling the *point* itself. Such an effort risks doing violence to this project in turn (for there is also a violence applicable to rationalists and to sense, to *good* sense; and this, perhaps, is what Foucault's book definitely demonstrates, for the victims of whom he speaks are always the bearers of sense, the *true* bearers of the *true* and *good* sense hidden and oppressed by the *determined* "good sense" of the "division"—the "good sense" that never divides itself enough and is always determined too quickly)—risks doing it violence in turn, and a violence of a totalitarian and historicist style which eludes meaning and the origin of meaning. I use "totalitarian" in the structuralist sense of the word, but I am not sure that the two meanings do not beckon each other historically. Structuralist totalitarianism here would be responsible for an internment of the Cogito similar to the violences of the classical age. I am not saying that Foucault's book is totalitarian, for at least at its outset it poses the question of the origin of historicity *in general*, thereby freeing itself of historicism; I am saying, however, that by virtue of the construction of his project he sometimes runs the risk of being totalitarian. Let me clarify: when I refer to the forced entry into the world of that which is not there and is supposed by the world, or when I state that the *compelle intrare* (epigraph of the chapter on "the great internment") becomes *violence itself* when it turns toward the hyperbole in order to make hyperbole reenter the world, or when I say that this reduction to intraworldliness is the origin and very meaning of what is called violence, making possible all straitjackets, I am not invoking an *other world*, an alibi or an evasive transcendence. That would be yet another possibility of violence, a possibility that is, moreover, often the accomplice of the first one.

I think, therefore, that (in Descartes) everything can be reduced to a determined historical totality except the hyperbolical project. Now, this project belongs to the narration narrating itself and not to the narration narrated by Foucault. It cannot be recounted, cannot be objectified as an event in a determined history.

I am sure that within the movement which is called the *Cartesian Cogito* this hyperbolical extremity is not the only element that should be, like pure madness in general, silent. As soon as Descartes has reached this extremity, he seeks to reassure himself, to certify the Cogito through God, to identify the act of the Cogito with a reasonable reason. And he does so as soon as he *proffers* and *reflects* the Cogito. That is to say, he must temporalize the Cogito, which itself is valid only during the instant of intuition, the instant of thought being attentive to itself, at the point, the sharpest point, of the instant. And here one should be attentive to this link between the Cogito and the movement of temporalization. For if the Cogito is valid even for the maddest madman, one must, in fact, not be mad if one is to reflect it and retain it, if one is to communicate it and its meaning. And here, with the reference to God *and* to a certain memory, would begin the hurried repatriation of all mad and hyperbolical wanderings which now take shelter and are given reassurance within the order of reasons, in order once more to take possession of the truths they had left behind. Within Descartes' text, at least, the internment takes place at this point. It is here that hyperbolical and mad wanderings once more become itinerary and method, "assured" and "resolute" progression through our existing world, which is given to us by God as terra firma. For, finally, it is God alone who, by permitting me to extirpate myself from a Cogito that at its proper moment can always remain a silent madness, also insures my representations and my cognitive determinations, that is, my discourse against madness. It is without doubt that, for Descartes, God alone protects me against the madness to which the Cogito, left to its own authority, could only open itself up in the most hospitable way. . . .

FURTHER READINGS

Cascardi, A. J. "Skepticism and Deconstruction." *Philosophy and Literature* 8 (1984): 1–14.

Culler, J. *On Deconstruction: Theory and Criticism after Structuralism.* Ithaca, NY: Cornell University Press, 1982.

Derrida, Jacques. *Margins of Philosophy.* Translated by A. Bass. Chicago: Chicago University Press, 1981.

Foucault, Michel. *Madness and Civilization: A History of Insanity in the Age of Reason.* Translated by R. Howard. New York: Pantheon, 1965.

Garver, Newton, and S. C. Lee. *Derrida and Wittgenstein.* Philadelphia: Temple University Press, 1994.

Hiley, David R. *Philosophy in Question: Essays on a Pyrrhonian Theme.* Chicago: University of Chicago Press, 1988.

44

POPKIN

R ichard H. Popkin (1923–2005) was mainly responsible for the recognition of the crucial role ancient Pyrrhonism played in the history of philosophy, in particular during the Renaissance and the early modern period. His classic book, *The History of Skepticism from Erasmus to Descartes* (1960), later extended to Spinoza (1979) and finally from Savonarola to Bayle (2003), was foundational in establishing a field of research that has been continuously growing worldwide. The text below is unique as the great historian of skepticism presents his own skepticism. The text is in the form of a letter replying to his friend and co-worker Avrum Stroll, an analytic philosopher who proposes a refutation of skepticism based on the commonsense approach of G. E. Moore (1873–1958). Popkin's text shows the centrality he gives to the problem of criterion—first raised by Sextus Empiricus, his sympathy for the skeptical outlook exhibited by Sextus and reappraised by so many early modern philosophers he studied throughout his life, and also his concern with the kind of radical skepticism—unprecedented in the whole skeptical tradition—that he saw in the so-called postmodernist thinkers. Finally, that doubt and skepticism was not merely a philosophical abstract matter for Popkin is clear from his work on the Kennedy assassination, mentioned in passing in the text below.

"SKEPTICISM TODAY: A DEBATE BETWEEN AVRUM STROLL AND RICHARD H. POPKIN" FROM *SKEPTICAL PHILOSOPHY FOR EVERYONE*

The Criterion Problem

The Criterion Problem is for me the heart of the skeptical crisis that everyone has to live with. You're of course right that most of the time, we have criteria that we apply in order to judge the various aspects of our life and we do not question these. We judge what time it is by looking at a watch or a clock. This is sufficient until we find that we've arrived two hours late for an appointment, or when somebody tells us that we have not heard a certain program because we did not realize what time it was. Then we realize that we need a more elaborate criterion. In the example you offered of selecting apples to purchase, if you applied your criterion and then found that the apples you bought were sour or tasteless, you would probably realize you had to find a more elaborate criterion for selecting. If you went back to the store and complained and the grocer asked you why you selected such bad apples and you told him which criterion you used, if he replied that's the wrong way of choosing apples, at this point the skeptical problem begins.

As my hero from ancient times, Sextus Empiricus, pointed out, skeptical questioning begins when there is a controversy about facts, judgments, or opinions. The controversy can be just between what one judges by using one sense versus judging by other senses. It also occurs all the time when we find our judgment differs from other people's. At that point, the issue of what criterion to use to settle our differences becomes preeminent. In many cases the issue is settled pro term by authority or by argument or by force, but are these settlements, to use a word you don't like, justified? If we take the example of the case of the umpires and referees at sporting events who settle differences of opinion about whether a batter is safe or out, whether a basketball player has committed a foul, whether a football player has legally caught a pass—in all these cases, there has to be a temporary judge in order for the game to be playable. Otherwise the game would break down because of the differences in opinion. But the disputants at the game, and the fans and the watchers on TV, do not placidly accept the judgment of the authority. In some cases, they carry grudges for years and years and insist that their team was robbed! They would insist that there is a better criterion if one had the time to examine photographs, make measurements, and so on. But the situation, like many things in life, requires a judgment within a finite time, so temporary criteria are used over and over again even though we know they are faulty. In 1966, in the final match of the World Cup, there was a dispute as to whether West Germany had scored a legal goal against the British team. This dispute, in fact, went on for years as more photographs and eyewitness testimonies were gathered. Now, I think most people would agree that the German goal was legal, but I have met many die-hards who insisted that if one had a photographer directly above the goal or sensors at the goal line, one might be able to reach a truer assessment of what had happened. Of course, then one would need still other criteria for judging the reliability of the photographs, the sensors, and the satellite photos and judging the reliability of the people who gathered the data.

. . . By and large we accept trial by jury and the decisions the jury makes as the best way of deciding in questions of law in the finite time. But as happened with the decision in the O. J. Simpson case, many, many people can say the jury was wrong and had more scientific criteria been applied and if better detective work had been done another decision would have occurred. One can also imagine what would have happened in the Simpson case if the scientist who invented DNA testing had been called to the witness stand. The prosecution thought that it would overwhelm the jury with all the DNA evidence. The scientist who invented the DNA measuring system says he was prepared to testify that his system doesn't work or is unreliable. Apparently, though he is an eminent Nobel Prize winner, he is personally regarded as unreliable. If he had been called as a witness and forced to reveal his substance abuses, this might have led to people judging that he could not be taken seriously. On the other hand, his scientific standing is such that his view would appear to be authoritative. So what criterion does one use?

It is often the case that long after a trial has been held new scientific tests become available which lead to changing the judgment that was made by a jury. Recently a number of people were released from death row because of DNA tests or because of indications that the police had misbehaved. Two major criminal cases indicate that research can go on for a long time in reassessing the decision made by a jury. One is that of Dr. Samuel Sheppard who was convicted of murdering his wife. Dr. Sheppard has now passed away, but his son has been producing evidence based on DNA and other recent chemical tests that would indicate that someone else must have been the actual criminal. Bodies have been exhumed and all sorts of reassessments have been made, and the case is still pending. Another that seems destined to go on indefinitely is that of James Earl Ray, convicted by his own confession of murdering Dr. Martin Luther King Jr. Ray, shortly after being imprisoned, insisted that he didn't do it, and all sorts of evidence indicates that other people must have been involved. Recently, a businessman in Memphis said that he paid someone other than Ray a large sum to kill King. In this case, because of political implications, there are forces pressing to reopen the case and forces pressing to keep it to the original judgment. At what point are we likely to have a satisfactory judgment? The same could be said about John F. Kennedy's assassination, but nobody was ever convicted. Should cases be held in abeyance until all present and all possible future tests have been applied? This would lead to ending the system of trial by jury. However, our system of jurisprudence tries to stop retrying cases or delaying decisions indefinitely because some judgment has to be made in a finite time.

Having said this, I think all of us, including yourself, have qualms at times about the criteria we use. When we get into arguments about our judgments, we would like to be sure we have the right standards, that is, standards that are certain and cannot be challenged. So the problem of justification is not just one that was cooked up by skeptics to badger dogmatists but is a life problem for most people at some time. I don't think that you or Wittgenstein or Popper can really avoid the justification issue. Since we all get into decision problems and we all can get into controversial ones, we often find that we have to justify our means of deciding to satisfy ourselves or others. We are unwilling to accept just arbitrary authority but want some justification for what we are doing—some justification for what we believe. And so the justification problem, it seems to me, grows out of ordinary life situations. When one raises the question asked by Socrates, "Is the unexamined life worth living?" we seem to be forced to make a judgment and if pressed, to justify our judgment. Otherwise it's like the cartoon about the Generation X character who is presented with the Socratic question and replies, "Whatever."

Finale

I am not convinced or impressed by the way that you or G. E. Moore or Wittgenstein dispense with skeptical problems when all is said and done. Taking a long view of the subject, it seems to me that there have only been two or three ways of getting around the skeptical challenges. One is Aristotle's, the other is the Stoic's, and the third is the answer of Mersenne and Gassendi. Aristotle in his great wisdom insisted he would not discuss physics with people who had doubts about whether or not the external world existed. He took it for granted that in order to discuss anything, some principles had to be accepted and he would not deal with skeptical doubts about these principles. The collapse of medieval Aristotelianism is in good part due to a refusal to accept the principles and the doubts cast by skeptics like Francisco Sanchez and his cousin Michel de Montaigne and other renaissance skeptics. Gassendi's withering attack on Aristotle's philosophy on skeptical grounds showed for scholars of the time that Aristotelianism was like the Emperor's New Clothes—that there was nothing that one could accept with any degree of certainty.

The Stoics played on the inability of anyone to live in complete doubt. They also heaped scorn and derision on skeptics and skepticism. But what does this show? As the skeptic Bishop Pierre Daniel Huet replied, "It is one thing to philosophize and another thing to live" [*Treatise on the Feebleness of the Human Mind* (1723), conclusion]. Living goes on undogmatically and philosophizing poses skeptical challenges to any dogmatic theory, whether it be Stoic, Aristotelian, Platonic, or anything else. I have caricatured the skeptical response here as like an anonymous letter. The recipient gets the letter and finds it is full of questions and problems about the philosophy of the recipient. The fact that the sender may also have problems is beside the point—especially if the sender is anonymous and cannot be found.

The Common Sense view of Thomas Reid and then G. E. Moore is a version of the Stoic response and I think fails to meet the challenge. All of us may be forced to believe various things that we cannot explain or justify. So believing is hardly an answer to skepticism and what we believe may in fact be dubious or even false. As Descartes said, "What is true to us may be false to an angel." We may be forced to believe the principles of mathematics and even believe them to be certain but they could still be "pipe dreams."

In light of this, Mersenne and Gassendi, in the first quarter of the seventeenth century, presented a way of dealing with the skeptical crisis. In Mersenne's thousand-page answer to the skeptics, *La Vérité des Sciences Contre les Skeptiques ou Pyrrhoniens*, he puts forth the skeptical arguments from Sextus Empiricus on one subject to another. He then says, "So what?" The skeptical problems do not prevent us from having adequate knowledge to deal with the world around us, even though we are well aware that there are basic doubts and that the principles that we use cannot be justified. The variations in sense experience may prevent us from knowing what is actually happening in the real world but we can have a science of our sensory variations. We can apply the laws of optics, refractions, and so on as ways of connecting our varying experiences. These laws can be stated in mathematical terms even though we cannot justify or prove beyond any doubt that these laws are true. So Mersenne set forth 750 pages of the book, listing what we do in fact know in mathematics and physics, not withstanding the unanswered skeptical problems. His good friend Father Pierre Gassendi said that he was presenting a *Via Media* between skepticism and dogmatism. The skeptical problems raised in antiquity sufficed to undermine the dogmatism of Plato and Aristotle, Descartes, and many other such arrogant philosophers. But the skeptical problems did not prevent the development of a constructive or mitigated skepticism in which one could offer resolutions to the skeptical problems in terms of empirical science. The view of Mersenne and Gassendi has been very influential in modern philosophy of science. It shows a way in which we can carry on our intellectual pursuits while setting aside the skeptical problems but as I have argued for the last forty years, this does not answer the skeptical problems and it leaves our intellectual world without an unshakable foundation. So this way of dealing with skepticism has allowed the modern scientific quest to go on without having to stop at each point and answer the skeptic. I think that I would have to study the matter in much detail. I think that what you and Wittgenstein are proposing is a combination of all of these ways of dealing with skepticism.

Something that I wish we had time to discuss is what I dimly perceive as a radical new version of skepticism, namely, the postmodernist view that is sweeping through various academic circles. Unlike the constructive or mitigated skepticism of Mersenne or Gassendi which accepted mathematics and science as provisionally true for dealing with our experiences, postmodernism seems to offer a form of intellectual anarchy. As far as I understand, it gives up the privileged status of mathematics and science, that any view is as good as any other and one can construct intellectual worlds according to one's tastes. Greek skepticism developed parasitically in terms of the rational frame of reference of Greek dogmatism and so kept within the parameters accepted by all the philosophers. What seems to be emerging now is a forceful skepticism with regard to reason that accepts no privileged framework. What this will lead to I don't know, but it may be that you and I will have to join forces in opposing this skepticism beyond skepticism. I have been told that I am the grandfather of postmodernism, which I hope is not true. But if it is, I may have to consider my actual relations to it.

After a lifetime of skeptical questioning and brooding, I realize that I could not offer a *justification* for why my and other people's questioning ought to go on in terms of accepted science, mathematics, and history rather than in terms of some other framework that satisfies some other people's predilections. Nonetheless, at the present stage of my life I feel that I have to consider things in terms of a "rational scientific framework" even though others can point out that this is just the result of a bad education and too many scientific colleagues. But I see a kind of intellectual disaster blooming if one follows out the implications of the previous sentence. So, *que faire*?

As you probably know, there are now people studying the philosophical classics in terms of the racist and sexist implications of texts rather than in terms of the arguments. There are people studying the texts in terms of the political, social, and religious standings of the authors. A good deal of this throws some new light on the material but if it becomes a sole way of considering the material then we would find ourselves in a radically different milieu in which our arguments would only represent our own sexist, middle-class American values. I don't see that your Wittgensteinian approach will bring us back to a sane and rational world. Instead, as you know, there is much being written about Wittgenstein's sexual life, about his politics, and his problems in adjusting to the position of Jews in the twentieth century in different countries. These kinds of studies may replace reading the texts, and then where are we?

With very best wishes in hopes that you will see the light,
Richard H. Popkin

FURTHER READINGS

Ayers, Michael. "Popkin's Revised Scepticism." *British Journal for the History of Philosophy* 12 (2004): 319–32.

Perter, Dominik. "Was There a 'Pyrrhonian Crisis' in Early Modern Philosophy? A Critical Notice of Richard Popkin." *Archiv für Geschichte der Philosophie* 86 (2004): 209–20.

Popkin, Richard H. *The History of Scepticism from Savonarola to Bayle*. Oxford: Oxford University Press, 2003.

———. *The Second Oswald*. New York: Avon Books, 1966.

Stroll, Avrum. "The Argument from Possibility." In *Scepticism in the History of Philosophy: A Pan-American Dialogue*, edited by Richard H. Popkin, 267–79. Dordrecht: Kluwer, 1996.

45

FOGELIN

R obert J. Fogelin (born in 1932) is an eminent contemporary American philosopher, one of the main experts on the philosophy of Hume and a supporter of a skeptical outlook in epistemology, which he has called Neopyrrhonism. In the text below, Fogelin distinguishes modern Cartesian from Pyrrhonian skepticism and argues that contemporary epistemologists who have been attempting to refute what they simply call "skepticism"—skepticism about the external world—either through "contextualism" or through "coherentism," are in fact Pyrrhonian skeptics.

THE SKEPTICS ARE COMING! THE SKEPTICS ARE COMING![1]

When contemporary epistemologists refer to the skeptic, almost without exception the kind of skeptic they have in mind is a cartesian skeptic, that is, a promoter of skeptical arguments based on skeptical scenarios of the kind found in Descartes' *First Meditation*. (Since Descartes was not himself a skeptic, I spell "cartesian" with a lower-case "c.") Pyrrhonian skepticism, which predates cartesian skepticism by two millennia, gets, by comparison, little attention.[2] This neglect of Pyrrhonian skepticism is illustrated by a recent anthology by DeRose and Warfield entitled *Skepticism: A Contemporary Reader*,[3] whose index contains only two references to Sextus Empiricus. Checking the text, we find that one of the references is a footnote in a piece by Robert Nozick, where Empiricus (as he calls him) is referred to as one member in a long list of writers who have contributed to "the immense literature concerning skepticism." What Sextus's contribution might have been is not indicated. The other reference to Sextus is nothing more than a remark made in passing which, in very short compass, manages to get Sextus's position dead wrong. (Identifying this writer will be worth a footnote later on.)

But even if twentieth- and twenty-first-century epistemologists have tended to ignore the Pyrrhonists, they have, often without explicitly recognizing it, been engaged in a debate with them. What we might call the standard (or old-fashioned) epistemologists shared the assumption that knowledge is at least justified true belief.[4] These epistemologists further assumed that for reasons to be justifying, these reasons themselves must be justified. This, of course, immediately generated the threat of an unacceptable infinite regress. Broadly speaking, there seemed to be only two ways to avoid this unwanted regress: find at least some reasons that are self-justifying or hold that reasons can be mutually justifying. The first is the way of traditional foundationalism, the second the way of traditional coherentism.

Elsewhere I have reflected on the following question: What would happen if a Pyrrhonist were allowed to participate in a three-way discussion with foundationalists and coherentists on the possibility of knowledge?[5] Specifically, how well would representatives of these two brands of epistemology fare when confronted with the five modes leading to the suspension of belief attributed by Sextus to Agrippa?

To describe them briefly, Agrippa's five modes (discrepancy, infinite regress, relativity, hypothesis, and circularity) present a set—or, perhaps, better, a network—of challenges to the dogmatist who claims to be fully justified in the knowledge claims he makes. For expository reasons, I will change the order of the modes and begin with discrepancy and relativity.

> *Discrepancy*: The dogmatist acknowledges that other dogmatists hold competing positions and thereby assumes the burden of showing why his position is justified and competing positions are not.

> *Relativity*: Though general in scope, this mode gets its primary application with respect to claims to possess empirical knowledge. Perceptions, it is conceded, vary relative to the nature of the perceiver and relative to the context in which the perceiving takes place. Therefore, anyone who claims that there can be knowledge based on perception must provide adequate reasons for giving a privileged status to some of these visual perspectives over others.

We can think of these two modes as creating a demand for justificatory reasons—a burden that the dogmatist, *on his own terms*, cannot reject.

The remaining three modes present a trilemma to anyone attempting to satisfy this burden of proof: The justificatory arguments cannot involve an infinite regress, circularity, or hypothesis (i.e., bare, unfounded assertion).

> *Infinite Regress*: If the dogmatist offers reasons to support knowledge claims, he can be challenged to produce reasons for these justifying reasons themselves. Since challenges of this kind can be renewed without limit, we seem to be confronted with an infinite regress.

> *Circularity*: One way to block the infinite regress is to cease presenting ever-new justifying reasons, and, instead, reinvoke a previous reason. That maneuver is, however, banned by the prohibition against circular reasoning.

> *Hypothesis*: Finally, at some point the demand for justifying reasons can simply be set aside or, for that matter, not accepted in the first place. Now,

however, the modes of discrepancy and relativity can be invoked to remind the dogmatist that he is not free to opt out of the justificatory game in this way.

It seems, then, that the dogmatist has no way of sidestepping the trilemma and no way of resolving it once he addresses it. This, in broad outline, is how I understand the way Agrippa's five modes function.

The strategy for most twentieth-century coherentists and foundationalists was to take Agrippa's trilemma head on and then argue that one of the members of the triad is not objectionable—indeed, when properly understood or transformed, provides the *basis* for epistemic justification. There was a general consensus that infinite regress was not the way to go, indeed, the problem was often called the *infinite regress problem*. With infinite regress out of the way, the question became this: Which provides the best exit route for escaping the trilemma, circularity or hypothesis? Some elevated the mode of circularity into coherentism—attempting to avoid the problem of emptiness by invoking a totality of mutually intertwined judgments leaning on each other for support. Others transformed the mode of hypothesis into foundationalism, attempting to avoid arbitrariness by invoking basic or fundamental judgments that needed no support because they carried their justifying force within themselves. In *Pyrrhonian Reflections on Knowledge and Justification*, I suggest that each position gains most of its force from the weaknesses of its competitor, and that, if a Pyrrhonist were made party to the discussion, both the twentieth-century foundationalists and coherentists would emerge losers. Hands down. No contest. Or so it seems.[6]

But many of our New Epistemologists (as I will call them) have foresworn this large-scale attempt at validation through reason-giving, either by severing the connection between knowledge and reason-giving, or by dispersing reason-giving into a plurality of procedures, giving no preeminence to one procedure over all others. Severing the connection with reason-giving is the way of *externalism* (early Alvin Goldman); dispersing reason-giving is the way of *contextualism* (perhaps the very late Wittgenstein). Hybrid theories employ both strategies, combining them in various proportions (Michael Williams and David Lewis). How, I now want to ask, would a Pyrrhonist deal with these New Epistemologists? But before turning to this, I want to say some things about Pyrrhonian skepticism, contrasting it with cartesian skepticism.

A central difference between cartesian skepticism and traditional Pyrrhonian skepticism is that cartesian skepticism, but not Pyrrhonian skepticism, deals in strong negative epistemic evaluations. For example, taking claims to perceptual knowledge as their target, cartesian skeptics typically present arguments purporting to show that perception cannot provide us with knowledge of the external world. The Pyrrhonian skeptic makes no such claim. Instances of perceptual variability—from one perceiver to another, from one setting to another, etc.—can, as already noted, be used to challenge empirical claims made from a particular perspective. But even if no suitable answer to this challenge can be brought forward in response, this does not show that empirical knowledge is *impossible*. Reaching this negative conclusion would depend on establishing a strong claim to the effect that no perceptual perspective is epistemically privileged. No Pyrrhonist who knows his business would accept the burden of establishing such a claim. Pyrrhonian skeptics are adept at avoiding burdens of proof. Since they are not out to prove that knowledge is impossible, they have no burden of proof to bear. For Pyrrhonian skeptics, the claim that a certain kind of knowledge is impossible amounts to a form of negative dogmatism. This charge, which they brought against their ancient rivals, the Academic Skeptics, applies to cartesian skeptics as well.[7]

Another difference between the cartesian and the Pyrrhonian skeptic is that the cartesian skeptic, but not the Pyrrhonian skeptic, raises doubts that call into question our most common beliefs about the world around us. If I am no more than a brain in a vat on a planet circling Alpha Centuri so wired that all I seem to see around me is nothing but a dream induced in me by a malicious demon, then I do not know—as I think I know—that I am sitting at my computer revising this essay. For the cartesian skeptic, if an adequate response to this challenge is not forthcoming, I am then obliged to reject even my most common, ordinary claims to knowledge. In contrast—though, as we shall see, this is a disputed point—the Pyrrhonian skeptic does not target common, everyday beliefs for skeptical assault. The primary target of Pyrrhonian skepticism is dogmatic philosophy—with secondary sallies into other fields where similar dogmatizing is found. The Pyrrhonists presented themselves as therapists treating a particular malady: the unease or cosmic jitters created by the quest for philosophical understanding. This is an occupational hazard of "Professors"—not of common people pursuing the honest (or, for that matter, not-so-honest) business of daily life. The Pyrrhonian skeptic leaves common beliefs, unpretentiously held, alone.

I should acknowledge that this account of Pyrrhonian skepticism—in particular, the claim that it leaves common belief undisturbed—has been the subject of sharp controversy in the recent literature on Pyrrhonism. Borrowing the distinction from Galen, Jonathan Barnes contrasts two ways of interpreting late Pyrrhonist texts as either *rustic* or *urbane*. Treated as rustic, the Pyrrhonist is pictured as setting aside subtlety and flatfootedly seeking suspension of belief on all matters whatsoever, including the practical beliefs concerning everyday life. This is the interpretation adopted by Jonathan Barnes, Miles Burnyeat, and a number of other distinguished British scholars.[8] The rustic interpretation does have the charm of giving Pyrrhonian skepticism some of the zip of cartesian skepticism and for this reason, I suppose, makes it seem more arresting. On the other side, it also opens the Pyrrhonian skeptic to the charge made by Burnyeat (and Hume before him) that Pyrrhonian skepticism, genuinely embraced, is unlivable, perhaps suicidal. If so, the professed Pyrrhonist can only survive by living in epistemic bad faith. Since, following Michael Frede,[9] I adopt the urbane interpretation of the text, this choice does not come up. I think that the root mistake here is to think that the Pyrrhonists adopt or share the dogmatists' standards of epistemic evaluation. If that were so, then Pyrrhonists' attacks on dogmatic philosophy would generalize to undermine common belief as well. The Pyrrhonist adopts the dogmatists' standards only dialectically to show how, on their own terms, the dogmatists are bound up in difficulties they cannot resolve. More should be said on this. The defenders of the rustic interpretation should be given their due. There is not time to do this here. In any case, I want to make it clear that when I speak of Pyrrhonism, I mean Pyrrhonism urbanely understood.

I am inclined to think that the ancient Pyrrhonists were trying to show (or exhibit) more than that the dogmatists' epistemological programs fail on their own terms. Beyond this they were, I think, trying to show that pursuing such a program actually generates a radical skepticism rather than avoids it. I confess that I have found no text in the writings of Sextus that says just this, though Sextus, I think, might be pleased with this further critique of epistemic dogmatism. Hume, whom I take to be an urbane Pyrrhonist, explicitly makes this move in the *Treatise* when he tells us:

> It is impossible, upon any system, to defend either our understanding or senses; and we but expose them further when we endeavour to justify them in that manner. As the sceptical doubt arises naturally from a profound and intense reflection on those subjects, it always encreases the further we carry our reflections, whether in opposition or conformity to it.[10]

Since Hume adopted a rustic interpretation of ancient Pyrrhonism, he distanced himself from it in these words:

> But a Pyrrhonian cannot expect, that his philosophy will have any constant influence on the mind: or if it had, that its influence would be beneficial to society. On the contrary, he must acknowledge, if he will acknowledge any thing, that all human life must perish, were his principles universally and steadily to prevail. All discourse, all action would immediately cease; and men remain in a total lethargy, till the necessities of nature, unsatisfied, put an end to their miserable existence.[11]

Adopting a rustic interpretation of Pyrrhonism, Hume recommends a philosophical tonic containing "only a small tincture of Pyrrhonism."[12] If he had interpreted Pyrrhonism as urbane, he could have counseled a richer draft.

The notion that "skeptical doubt arises naturally from profound and intense reflection" finds a parallel expression in Wittgenstein, who, by my lights, is also an urbane Pyrrhonist. These passages come from *On Certainty*.

> 481. When one hears Moore say, "I know that that's a tree," one suddenly understands those who think that that has by no means been settled.
> The matter strikes one all at once as being unclear and blurred. It is as if Moore had put it in the wrong light. . . .
> 482. It is as if "I know" did not tolerate a metaphysical emphasis.[13]

It seems that when we view even the most ordinary knowledge claims in a philosophical light, a sense of their fragility becomes almost unavoidable.

The suggestion here is that the epistemological enterprise, when relentlessly pursued, not only fails in its efforts, but also, Samson-like, brings down the entire edifice of knowledge around it.[14] I make a fuss over this in *Pyrrhonian Reflections*. I am inclined to think that this doctrine is at least implicit in the writings of ancient Pyrrhonists. But however matters stand with the traditional Pyrrhonists, the Samson principle—I'll call it that—is a central tenet of urbane Pyrrhonism, a standpoint adopted at least by Hume, Wittgenstein, and me. (Here I engage in *catacosmesis*. For those not fully up to speed on rhetorical terms, catacosmesis involves the ordering of words from the greatest to the least in dignity. Cf., "For God, for country, and for Yale.")[15]

One final difference between cartesian skepticism and Pyrrhonian skepticism is that skeptical scenarios play a central role in cartesian skepticism but not in Pyrrhonian skepticism. Cartesian skeptics hold that we do not know something (that is, do not really know it) unless it is completely bulletproof against possible defeators however remote. Skeptical scenarios are introduced to show that, in principle, this standard cannot be met—at least for a particular class of knowledge claims, typically those concerning perceptual knowledge of the external world. Since Pyrrhonists will suspend judgment concerning the appropriateness of this criterion for knowledge— just as they suspend judgment on the appropriate criterion of truth—they will not play the cartesian game in an attempt to establish the strong negative epistemic judgment that perceptual knowledge is not possible. For the Pyrrhonist, such skeptical scenarios are simply science-fiction variations on the mode of relativity. The Pyrrhonist can, however, take pleasure in the confusion that besets epistemologists in their efforts to respond to the challenges to knowledge raised by skeptical scenarios. For decades, now, there has been what amounts to an obsession with this problem. Indeed, theories of perceptual knowledge stand or fall relative to their ability to deal with skeptical scenarios. Here I will invite a Pyrrhonist to the party.

There seem to be two main options for replying to the challenges of skeptical scenarios. The first is to argue that skeptical scenarios are conceptually incoherent, and, for this reason, the challenges they present are lacking in meaning, contentless, otiose—or something like that. They are, it is sometimes said, pseudo-challenges. This is the transcendental (sometimes verificationalist) response to skeptical scenarios. This response faces hard going, for skeptical scenarios seem, on their face, to be perfectly intelligible; thus a heavy burden falls on anyone who wishes to persuade us otherwise.[16] There is a deeper worry. Suppose, for whatever reason, we acknowledge that if we are brains in vats, then our words may not mean what we think they mean, or perhaps may not mean anything at all. If that is correct, then the skeptic's doubt—so the argument sometimes goes—undercuts the very expressability of his doubts. It is hard to see, however, how this threat of semantic (instead of epistemic) nihilism provides solace. Perhaps we just *are* brains in vats and so deeply fuddled semantically that no sense attaches to the skeptical scenarios we formulate—or to anything else either. Standard cartesian doubt pales in comparison with the threat of semantic nihilism. But I won't ask the reader to peer into that abyss, at least not here.

On the assumption that skeptical scenarios are at least intelligible, what response can be made to them? More specifically, what responses do our New Epistemologists make to them? Externalism/reliabilism in its many forms represents one popular approach. The story goes something like this: If our beliefs stand in the right sort of relationship to the things they are about (for example, if they reliably track the truth—and perhaps track it in the right sort of way), then we can be said to know them to be true. The important point, for this approach, is that a relationship of this kind can hold even if the person possessing the knowledge is not in a position to produce adequate reasons that show this. So the cartesian skeptic's claim that, for example, we cannot know things on the basis of sensory evidence is met with the response, "For all we know we do know such things." Notice that, if correct, this is all that is needed to refute the *cartesian* skeptic's strong claim that we *cannot* know.[17] It has no tendency to refute Pyrrhonian skepticism, not even in its rustic form. Neither the urbane nor the rustic Pyrrhonist would *deny* the existence of perceptual knowledge.

The contextualist line in its most straightforward form rests on the following idea: What you know or do not know is a function of the epistemic standards governing the context in which you are operating. For example, if the context is governed by cartesian standards, the possibility that one is a brain in a vat is a relevant defeator to the claim that you can, just by looking, come to know you have a hand. In contrast, in a non-epistemological setting you can usually make it known that you have a hand simply by making an appropriate Moorean gesture while at the same time saying, "Here is a hand."[18] So, for the contextualist, if the context is rigidly epistemological, then you do not know that you have hands; if the context is ordinary, or in Thompson Clarke's lingo, "plain," then you do (or at least can) know this.[19] Moore's mistake, so the response goes, was to make a plain response in a philosophical context. The skeptic's mistake is to demand a philosophical response in a plain context. Contextualist theories are usually more complex than this—they are often supplemented by an externalist component—but this gives the rough form that such theories take.

How would an urbane Pyrrhonist, suitably briefed on these maneuvers, respond? As a way of approaching this question, we can imagine someone encountering Descartes' *Meditations* and becoming sore perplexed. Finding the discussion of the deceiving spirit genuinely disturbing, he turns to more recent writings, only to discover stories concerning brains in vats. Since he can think of no way of showing that he is not a brain in a vat, he succumbs, in Berkeley's phrase, to a "forlorn skepticism" concerning the world around him. Since he is an earnest seeker of a way out of his perplexities, we will call him Ernest. We will imagine various representatives of the New Epistemology appearing before Ernest much as the comforters appeared before Job. We will allow an externalist, a contextualist, and then an urbane Pyrrhonist to address him in turn.

We can begin with an externalist (or proto-externalist). When Ernest expresses his anxiety about not knowing whether he has hands or not, because he can come up with no good reasons for thinking he is not a brain in a vat, the externalist comforter expresses no surprise and candidly admits that, with respect to producing reasons of this kind, he is in precisely the same boat (or vat) that Ernest is. But not to worry. The inability to produce justifying reasons does not show that either he or Ernest is lacking in *knowledge* concerning the possession of such things as hands. To suppose otherwise, he tells Ernest, is to be a captive of an archaic internalist conception of knowledge, where the possession and command of justificatory reasons is held to be a necessary condition for knowing something. Emancipation occurs, he continues, through severing the connection between knowledge and justification. At first dazzled, upon reflection Ernest feels dissatisfied. Down deep what he was looking for were good *reasons* for thinking that he has hands, given the fact that he might be a brain in a vat. In response, the externalist tells him that the possession of good reasons is not a necessary condition for knowing something. Ernest might candidly admit that before encountering externalism he believed—perhaps naively—that knowledge involved the possession of justifying reasons. Corrected on that point, his basic yearnings remain. Even if he grants that it is possible to know something without possessing reasons justifying our claim to know (and possible to know something without knowing that one knows), he is still looking for good reasons for believing he is not a brain in a vat. So far, at least, the externalist comforter has done nothing to help him in this regard. Of course, real externalists are not usually flat-footedly committed to externalism as my proto-externalist is. They can, for example, combine their positions with some form of contextualism and then argue that we often do have good reasons to believe that our cognitive faculties are reliable. So let's turn to contextualism to see what aid it may provide.

At first sight, the contextualist (or proto-contextualist) seems to do better in satisfying Earnest's yearnings for reasons. The contextualist comforter assures Ernest that often both he and Ernest possess adequate, sometimes clearly statable, reasons for believing they are not brains in vats. The contextualist comforter might argue as follows: "Given the present state of technology, it is wholly unlikely that brains can be supported in vats in the way described in the skeptical scenario. Thus we know that we are not brains in vats just as we know that there are no anti-gravity machines. With this knowledge, the skeptical doubts that were supposed to flow from this hypothesis are nullified." Ernest has qualms. "But even so," he replies, "if I am a brain in vat, couldn't my beliefs about the present state of technology be brain-probe-induced falsehoods?" Let's suppose that the contextualist puzzles it out and admits that yes, these beliefs could have been induced by electric stimulation—that is, he makes no move in the direction of declaring the skeptical hypothesis unintelligible or incoherent. Acknowledging the coherence of the skeptical hypothesis, the contextualist argues that taking this possibility seriously shifts the context, and in this new, more demanding, or at least different context, Ernest does not know, for in this new context his reasons are no longer adequate. So to Ernest's original question, "Are there adequate reasons for my believing that I am not a brain in a vat?" the answer is: "It all depends—it all depends on context."

The key move in the contextualist response to skepticism is to refuse to assign a privileged status to epistemological contexts. That is, the contextualist rejects the view that *strictly speaking* we do not know something unless it meets the demand that all possible defeators have been eliminated, a view, the contextualist can point out, that almost automatically generates strong skeptical conclusions. What the contextualist says instead is something like this: In the context of an informed understanding of present technology, we do know that we are not brains in vats, whereas in a context governed by traditional epistemological demands we do not. There is no contradiction here because the standards of relevance and rigor are different in the two cases.

"What about the fruitcakes?" This is Ernest's next question. He has noticed that the world is filled with people who hold wildly different views about the general disposition of the world around them. They seem to have only one thing in common: a deep intolerance for views other than their own. There is, for example, a brisk competition among various Pentecostals. Can they be said to know things—each in his or her own Pentecostal way? Will a thoroughgoing contextualist have to say yes? The contextualist does not hold that anything goes, for whether something "goes" or not depends upon the constraints of the context in which the claim is made. But does the contextualist hold that any context goes? I do not know, for the contextualist, when pressed on this matter, tends to brush it aside—dismissing it as tedious and sophomoric. It seems, however, that what the contextualists have done is this: They have tried to find a way of avoiding the Old Epistemologists' trilemma by seeking refuge in the mode of relativity.

I do not know of any contextualist who can deal adequately with Ernest's problem with the fruitcakes of this world. Keith DeRose's version of contextualism is a case in point. His position is an elaboration of what he calls the "Basic Strategy."

> According to the contextualist solution, . . . the skeptic's present denials that we know various things are perfectly compatible with our ordinary claims to know those very propositions. Once we realize this, we can see how both the skeptic's denials of knowledge and our ordinary attributions of knowledge can be correct.[20]

Now, for DeRose, responding to the skeptical challenge is a matter of finding some way to neutralize arguments of the following kind:

The Argument from Ignorance

1. I don't know that not-H,
2. If I don't know that not-H, then I don't know that O.
   So,
C. I don't know O.

Specifically, DeRose takes H to be the skeptical hypothesis that I am a brain in a vat and O the observationally based claim that I have hands.

DeRose notes something that others have noted before him: the fact that (1) and (2) validly imply (C) has no tendency by itself to establish the truth of (C). A valid inference is neutral with respect to *modus ponens* and *modus tollens*. DeRose thinks this presents us with four options.

1. The Skeptical Option: accept both premises, and from them draw the strong skeptical conclusion (C).
2. Moore's Option: Argue that we are more certain of the falsehood of the conclusion than we are of the truth of the premises and leave it at that.
3. The anti-closure move: Deny (2).
4. The DeRose Ploy: Both affirm and deny (1) as needed.

Roughly (very roughly), where Nozick (for example) used possible-world semantics as a basis for denying the closure principle expressed in the second premise,[21] DeRose invokes possible-world semantics in order to reject the first premise. I do not find either use of possible-world semantics persuasive because I do not see how appeals to possible worlds can, in general, provide non-arbitrary truth-conditions for subjunctive conditionals. That, however, is a complicated matter that I do not want to go into here. One thing worth noting, however, is that DeRose speaks as if there are just *two* sorts of contexts: the philosophical (with its "very high standards") and the ordinary (with its "more relaxed standards"), whereas contexts can differ in the *kinds* of standards they employ and not simply in the stringency with which they are employed. The result is that a plurality of possible contexts can exist, each with its associated structure on possible worlds and each autonomously determining epistemic evaluations on its own terms. Pentecostals can avail themselves of possible-world semantics too. By restricting his attention to just two contexts—the philosophical and the ordinary—DeRose, along with other contextualists, fails to address the fruitcake problem. A contextualism of this kind seems to make it unsolvable.

So it seems that neither our externalist comforter nor our contextualist comforter will provide comfort for Ernest. If he is seeking *reasons* for thinking that he is not a brain in a vat, being told that knowledge is possible in the absence of justificatory reasons hardly helps. Even setting aside the problem of fruitcakes (but not forgetting it), the contextualist meets Ernest's demands for reasons but overdoes things by telling him that he both does and does not possess them. If the context is ordinary (or plain) then he does have adequate—or at least very good—reasons for believing that he is not a brain in a vat. If the context is epistemological, well, then he does not. But Ernest's present context is epistemological, so his conversation with the contextualist seems to reinforce, rather than resolve, his skeptical doubts.

What will the Pyrrhonian skeptic say to Ernest? Pretty much what was said in the last few paragraphs. If we epistemologize in earnest, then we will be led into skepticism. If we turn to epistemologists for help, they will provide none, perhaps make things worse—or so it seems.

But perhaps I have been too hard on the New Epistemologists. I have tended to treat them as close to Old Epistemologists maintaining the family business, though under straightened conditions. On that reading, they remain targets—though diminished targets—of Pyrrhonian attack. There is a more generous way of viewing our New Epistemologists: they are newly emerging urbane Pyrrhonists: They simply have not faced up to this fact. The central concern of the Pyrrhonists was the claimed capacity of their dogmatic opponents to present adequate reasons in behalf of their dogmas as, following their own standards, they pretended to do. The central maneuver of Pyrrhonists was to challenge the dogmatists to produce such reasons. The externalists, who sever the connection between knowledge and reason-giving justification, should have no quarrel with this, for their central reason for rejecting internalism is its persistent failure to produce the justificatory reasons the theory demands. The contextualists, for their part, simply reject the ideal of traditional epistemology by embracing the Pyrrhonian mode of relativity.

An image from Samuel Beckett's *Watt*, illustrates what I have in mind. Beckett describes Watt's method of locomotion in these words:

> Watt's method of advancing due east, for example, was to turn his bust as far as possible towards the north and at the same time to fling out his right leg as far as possible towards the south, and then to turn his bust as far as possible towards the south and at the same time to fling out his leg as far as possible towards the south . . . and so on, over and over again, many many times, until he reached his destination, and could sit down.[22]

We can add a further element of absurdity. As described, by placing one foot at least slightly ahead of the other, Watt manages to move very slowly forward. But suppose we let his leg swing even a longer arc so that one foot comes down slightly in back of the other. (Though admittedly not easy, this stride is actually possible.) The result is that Watt, though apparently striving to move forward, is, instead, slowly backing up.

Now change the perspective and view this activity from the rear. We then get the image of someone seemingly making every effort to flee, but backing up instead. This is how the skeptics are coming: They are the New Epistemologists who, with what seem to be elaborate efforts to the contrary, are backing up—incremental step by incremental step—into skepticism. Pyrrhonian skepticism.

NOTES

1. This piece is an extended—and somewhat more formal—version of a talk I presented at a conference on Pyrrhonism in October 2001 celebrating my retirement. The original version appears in the proceedings of the conference, *Pyrrhonian Skepticism*, edited by Walter Sinnott-Armstrong (New York: Oxford University Press, 2004), pp. 161–73.

2. Some heroic efforts have been made to present Pyrrhonism in a forceful and sympathetic light. Pride of place goes to Richard Popkin for his groundbreaking work, *The High*

SKEPTICISM: AN ANTHOLOGY

Road to Pyrrhonism (San Diego, CA: Austin Hill Press, 1980). More recently, Michael Frede has presented Pyrrhonism in a way that immunizes it against the long-standing—and misplaced—criticism that Pyrrhonism, taken seriously, is unlivable. See the appropriate essays in his *Essays in Ancient Philosophy* (Oxford: Clarendon Press, 1987).

3. Keith DeRose and Ted A. Warfield, eds., *Skepticism: A Contemporary Reader* (New York: Oxford University Press, 1999).

4. The qualifying phrase "at least" is a nod in the direction of so-called Gettier problems. I will not discuss them here.

5. Robert J. Fogelin, *Pyrrhonian Reflections on Knowledge and Justification* (Oxford and New York: Oxford University Press, 1994).

6. I try to make a plausible case for this claim in Part II of *Pyrrhonian Reflections on Knowledge and Justification*. The five modes attributed to Agrippa appear in Sextus's *Outlines of Pyrrhonism*, bk. 1, pp. 164–77. See Benson Mates's translation in *The Skeptic Way: Sextus Empiricus's Outlines of Pyrrhonism* (New York and Oxford: Oxford University Press, 1996), pp. 110–12.

7. Even though Sextus is perfectly clear in his commitment to a thoroughgoing noncommitalism, people get him wrong on this point. Christopher Hill, in the DeRose/Warfield anthology cited earlier, attempts to embarrass a skeptical critic with the following maneuver:

Let us suppose that process reliabilism is true, and that the skeptic *does* have an obligation to consider this question. . . . Well, since questions of reliability are empirical questions, the skeptic would be under an obligation to appeal to empirical data. An appeal of this sort would of course be something of an embarrassment to the skeptic, holding as he does that no empirical beliefs are empirically justified. But, what is worse, it seems that it would be impossible for him to come up with empirical data of the required sort. [Then this!] Thus, pace Sextus Empiricus, it seems that it would be impossible to find empirical data that would establish that perceptual processes are globally unreliable. (125)

This certainly seems to attribute to Sextus the view "that no empirical beliefs are justified," precisely the negative dogmatism that Sextus explicitly rejects.

8. See, for example, Jonathan Barnes, "The Beliefs of a Pyrrhonist" in *Proceedings of the Cambridge Philological Society*, ed. E. J. Kenny and M. M. MacKenzie (1982), and Myles Burnyeat, "Can the Sceptic Live His Scepticism?" in *Doubt and Dogmatism*, ed. M. Schofield, M. Burnyeat, and J. Barnes (Oxford: Clarendon Press, 1980).

9. See Michael Frede, "The Skeptic's Beliefs," in *Essays in Ancient Philosophy* (Minneapolis: University of Minnesota Press, 1987), pp. 179–200.

10. David Hume, *A Treatise of Human Nature*, 2nd ed., ed. L. A. Selby-Bigge and P. H. Nidditch (Oxford: Oxford University Press, 1978), p. 218.

11. David Hume, *Enquiries concerning Human Understanding and concerning the Principles of Morals*, 3rd ed., ed. L. A. Selby-Bigge and P. H. Nidditch (Oxford: Clarendon Press, 1975), p. 159.

12. Ibid., p. 161.

13. Ludwig Wittgenstein, *On Certainty*, trans. G. E. M. Anscombe, ed. G. E. M. Anscombe and R. Rhees (Oxford: Basil Blackwell, 1969).

14. David Lewis recognizes this threat in "Elusive Knowledge," *Australasian Journal of Philosophy* 74, no. 4 (1996): 549–67. There is not time here to discuss this subtle and com-

plex article, but I discuss it in detail in "Two Diagnoses of Skepticism," in *The Skeptics: Contemporary Essays*, ed. Steven Luper (Aldershot, England: Ashgate, 2003).

15. I owe my arcane knowledge of catacosmesis to Richard A. Lanham's *A Handlist of Rhetorical Terms*, 2nd ed. (Berkeley: University of California Press, 1990).

16. See Michael Williams, *Unnatural Doubts: Epistemological Realism and the Basis of Skepticism* (Oxford: Basil Blackwell, 1991), particularly pp. 149–55.

17. Indeed, if our second-order beliefs about what we know also track the truth, then, for all we know, we know that we know certain things. In principle, nothing except cognitive overload stops us from nesting knowings endlessly. Contrary to the cartesian skeptic's claim, for all we know (and for all he knows) we may know a heck of a lot.

18. This might be a useful thing to do if, for example, you are trying to assure someone (perhaps yourself) that a feared amputation has not been performed. For Moore's argument, see "Proof of an External World," *Proceedings of the British Academy* 25 (1939). It is reprinted in *Philosophical Papers* (London: George Allen and Unwin, 1959).

19. See Thompson Clarke, "The Legacy of Skepticism," *Journal of Philosophy* 69 (1972): 764–69.

20. Keith DeRose, "Solving the Skeptical Problem," *Philosophical Review* 104, no. 1 (1995): 5.

21. See Robert Nozick, *Philosophical Explanations* (Oxford: Oxford University Press, 1981), chap. 3, pt. 2.

22. Samuel Beckett, *Watt* (New York: Grove Press, 1959), p. 28.

FURTHER READINGS

Fogelin, Robert J. *Pyrrhonian Reflections on Knowledge and Justification*. Oxford and New York: Oxford University Press, 1994.
———. *Walking the Tightrope of Reason: The Precarious Life of a Rational Animal*. Oxford: Oxford University Press, 2005.

BIBLIOGRAPHY

Entries are arranged alphabetically, in the following order: books, as author or editor; articles, essays, or material that is part of an anthology or a collection; and journal articles.

Adam, Michel. *Etudes sur Pierre Charron*. Talence: Presses Universitaires de Bordeaux, 1991.

Agrippa von Nettesheim, Heinrich Cornelius. *De incertitudine et vanitate scientiarum atque artium declamation*. Anversa: Johannes Grapheus, 1530.

———. *Of the Vanity and Uncertainty of Arts and Sciences*. Translated by James Sanford. London: Henry Wykes, 1569. (New edition by Catherine M. Dunn. Northridge: California State University, 1974.)

Alven, M. N. *Augustine: Skepticism and Philosophy*. Notre Dame, IN: University of Notre Dame Press, 1978.

Annas, Julia. "Doing without Objective Values: Ancient and Modern Strategies." In *The Norms of Nature*, edited by M. Schofield and Gisela Striker, 3–29. Cambridge: Cambridge University Press, 1986.

———. "Plato the Skeptic." In *Methods of Interpreting Plato and His Dialogues*, edited by J. Klagge and N. Smith, Oxford Studies in Ancient Philosophy, Supplementary Volume. Oxford: Clarendon Press, 1992, pp. 43–72.

Annas, Julia, and Jonathan Barnes. *The Modes of Skepticism*. Cambridge: Cambridge University Press, 1985.

Apel, Karl-Otto. *From a Transcendental-Semiotic Point of View*. Edited by Marianna Papastephanou. Manchester: Manchester University Press, 1998.

Araujo, Marcelo de. *Scepticism, Freedom and Autonomy: A Study of the Moral Foundations of Descartes' Theory of Knowledge*. Berlin: De Gruyter, 2003.

Armour, Leslie. "Simon Foucher, Knowledge and Idealism: Philo of Larissa and the Enigmas of a French 'Skeptic.'" In Lennon, *Cartesian Views*, pp. 97–115.

Arnauld, Antoine. *Des vrais et des fausses idées*. Paris: Fayard, 1986.

Artigas, Mariano. "Fallibilism and Skepticism." In *The Ethical Nature of Karl Popper's Theory of Knowledge: Including Popper's Unpublished Comments on Bartley and Critical Rationalism*. Edited by Mariano Artigas and Ivan Slade. New York: Peter Lang, 1999.

Artigas-Menant, Geneviève, and Antony McKenna, eds. "Le Doute Philosophique: Philosophie Classique et Littérature Clandestine. Dossie Thématique." *La Lettre Clandestine* 10 (2001).

Augustine. *Against the Academics*. Translated by J. J. O'Meara. Westminster, MS: Newman Press, 1950.

————. *Confessions*. Translated by F. J. Sheed. Indianapolis, IN: Hackett, 1993.

————. *The Trinity*. Translated by Edmund Hill. New York: New City Press, 1991.

Ayers, Michael. "Popkin's Revised Scepticism." *British Journal for the History of Philosophy* 12 (2004): 319–32.

Backus, Irena. "The Issue of Reformation Skepticism Revisited: What Sebastian Castellio Did or Did Not Know." In Paganini and Maia Neto, *Renaissance Skepticisms*.

Bacon, Francis. *The Works*. 14 vols. Edited by James Spedding, Robert L. Ellis, and Douglas D. Heath. London: Longman and Co., 1858.

Bailey, Alan. *Sextus Empiricus and Pyrrhonian Skepticism*. Oxford: Oxford University Press, 2002.

Baldi, Marialuisa. *Verisimili, non vero: Filosofia e politica in Andrew Michael Ramsay*. Milan: Franco Angeli, 2002.

Barnes, Jonathan. *The Toils of Skepticism*. Cambridge: Cambridge University Press, 1990.

————. "The Beliefs of a Pyrrhonist." *Elenchos* 4 (1983): 5–43.

Bayle, Pierre. *Dictionnaire historique et critique*. 16 vols. Geneva: Slatkine Reprints, 1969. Reprint of the 1820–1824 Paris edition.

————. *Historical and Critical Dictionary: Selections*. Edited and translated by Richard H. Popkin. Indianapolis, IN: Hackett, 1991.

————. *Oeuvres diverses*. 4 vols. Hildesheim: Olms, 1964. Reprint of the 1727–1731 La Haye edition.

Beaude, Joseph. "Amplifier le dixième trope, ou la différence culturelle comme argument sceptique." In *Recherches sur le XVII siècle* 5, edited by André Robinet, 21–29. Paris: Editions du CNRS, 1982.

Belin, Christian. *L'Oeuvre de Pierre Charron, 1541–1603: Littérature et théologie de Montaigne à Port-Royal*. Paris: Honoré Champion, 1995.

Bénatouil, Thomas. *Le scepticisme: Textes choisis et présentés*. Paris: Flammarion, 1997.

Benitez, Eugenio, and Lívia Guimarães. "Philosophy as Performed in Plato's *Theaetetus*." *Review of Metaphysics* 47 (1993): 297–328.

Berkeley, George. *Philosophical Works*. Edited by Michael R. Ayers. London: Everyman, 1st ed. 1975, revised edition, 1993.

Bernier, Marc André, and Sébastien Charles, eds. *Scepticisme et Modernité*. Saint-Étienne: Publications de l'Université de Saint-Étienne, 2005.

Besnier, Bernard. "Sanchez à moitié endormi." In Moreau, *Le Scepticisme au XVIe et au XVIIe Siècle*, pp. 102–20.

Bett, Richard. *Pyrrho, His Antecedents, and His Legacy*. Oxford: Oxford University Press, 2000.

————. "Carneades' Distinction between Assent and Approval." *Monist* 73, no. 1 (1990): 3–20.

————. "Carneades' *Pythanon*: A Reappraisal of Its Role and Status." *Oxford Studies in Ancient Philosophy* 7 (1989): 59–94.

————. "Nietzsche on the Skeptics and Nietzsche as Skeptic." *Archiv für Geschichte der Philosophie* 82 (2000): 62–86.

Beuchot, Mauricio. "Some Traces of the Presence of Scepticism in Medieval Thought." In Popkin, *Scepticism in the History of Philosophy*, pp. 37–43.

Bianchi, Lorenzo. *Tradizione libertine e critica storica: Da Naudé a Bayle*. Milan: Franco Angeli, 1988.

Blackwell, Constance W. T. "Skepticism as a Sect, Skepticism as a Philosophical Stance: Johann

Jakob Brucker versus Carl Friedrich Stäudlin." In Van der Zande and Popkin, *The Skeptical Tradition around 1800, Skepticism in Philosophy, Science, and Society*, pp. 343–63.

Bloch, Olivier. *La Philosophie de Gassendi*. The Hague: Martinus Nijhoff, 1971.

Bogen, J. "Wittgenstein and Scepticism." *Philosophical Review* 83 (1974): 364–73.

Bolton, Martha B. "Locke and Pyrrhonism: The Doctrine of Primary and Secondary Qualities." In Burnyeat, *The Skeptical Tradition*, pp. 353–75.

Bourdin, Jean-Claude. "Matérialisme et scepticisme chez Diderot: Diderot, philosophie, matérialisme." *Recherches sur Diderot et sur l'Encyclopédie* 26 (1999): 85–97.

Boyle, Robert. *The Sceptical Chymist: The Classic 1661 Text*. Mineola, NY: Dover Publications, 2003.

Bracken, Henry M. *Berkeley*. London: Macmillan, 1974.

———. *Descartes*. Oxford: Oneworld, 2002.

———. *The Early Reception of Berkeley's Immaterialism: 1710–1733*. Rev. ed. The Hague: Martinus Nijhoff, 1965.

———. "Bayle's Attack on Natural Theology: The Case of Christian Pyrrhonism." In Popkin and Vanderjagt, *Skepticism and Irreligion in the Seventeenth and Eighteenth Centuries*, pp. 254–66.

———. "Bayle Not a Sceptic?" *Journal of the History of Ideas* 25 (1964): 169–80.

Brahami, Frédéric. *Le Scepticisme de Montaigne*. Paris: Presses Universitaires de France, 1997.

———. *Le travail du scepticisme: Montaigne, Bayle, Hume*. Paris: Presses Universitaires de France, 2001.

Brittain, Charles. *Philo of Larissa: The Last of the Academic Sceptics*. Oxford: Oxford University Press, 2001.

Brochard, Victor. *Les Sceptiques grecs*. Paris: Vrin, 1969.

Broughton, Janet. *Descartes's Method of Doubt*. Princeton, NJ: Princeton University Press, 2002.

Brown, Stuart. "Foucher's Critique and Leibniz's Defense of the 'New System.'" In *Leibniz: Reason and Experience*, edited by Stuart Brown, 96–104. Milton Keynes: Open University Press, 1983.

———. "The Leibniz-Foucher Alliance and Its Philosophical Basis." In *Leibniz and His Correspondents*, edited by Paul Lodge. Cambridge: Cambridge University Press, 2004.

———. "Leibniz as Platonist and Academic Skeptic." *Skepsis* 9 (1998): 111–38.

Brucker, Jacob. *Historia critica philosophiae*. 6 vols. Hildesheim: Olms, 1975. Facsimile reproduction of the 1742–1767 Leipzig edition.

Bruès, Guy de. *Dialogues: A Critical Edition with a Study in Renaissance Scepticism and Relativism by Panos Paul Morphos*. Baltimore: John Hopkins University Press, 1953.

Brush, Craig. *Montaigne and Bayle: Variations on the Theme of Skepticism*. The Hague: Martinus Nijhoof, 1966.

Burnyeat, Myles, ed. *The Skeptical Tradition*. Berkeley: University of California Press, 1983.

———. *The Theaetetus of Plato*. Indianapolis, IN: Hackett, 1990.

———. "Can the Sceptic Live His Scepticism?" In Schofield, Burnyeat, and Barnes, *Doubt and Dogmatism*, pp. 20–53.

———. "Idealism and Greek Philosophy: What Descartes Saw and Berkeley Missed." *Philosophical Review* 91 (1982): 3–40.

———. "Protagoras and Self-Refutation in Later Greek Philosophy." *Philosophical Review* 85 (1976): 44–69.

Busson, Henri. *La Pensée religieuse française de Charron à Pascal*. Paris: J. Vrin, 1933.

———. *Le Rationalisme dans la littérature française de la Renaissance (1533–1601)*. Paris: J. Vrin, 1957.

Caccia, N. *Note sulla fortuna di Luciano nel Rinascimento: Le versioni e I dialoghi satirici di Erasmo da Rotterdam e di Ulrico Hutten*. Milan: Signorelli, 1914.

Caizzi, Fernanda Decleva, ed. *Pirrone Testimonianze*. Naples: Bibliopolis, 1981.

Camus, Albert. *The Myth of Sisyphus and Other Essays*. Translated by Justin O'Brien. New York: Vintage Books, 1955.

Cao, Gian Mario. "L'eredità pichiana: Gianfrancesco Pico tra Sexto Empirico e Savonarola." In *Pico Poliziano e l'Umanesimo di fine Quattrocento*, edited by P. Viti, 231–45. Florence: Olschki, 1994.

———. "Gianfrancesco Pico and Skepticism." In Paganini and Maia Neto, *Renaissance Skepticisms*.

———. "The Prehistory of Modern Skepticism: Sextus Empiricus in Fifteenth-Century Italy." *Journal of the Warburg and Courtauld Institutes* 64 (2001): 229–79.

Carabin, Denise. *Henri Estienne, érudit, novateur, polémiste*. Paris: Honoré Champion, 2006.

Carraud, Vincent. *Pascal et la philosophie*. Paris: Presses Universitaires de France, 1992.

Carraud, Vincent, and Jean-Luc Marion, eds. *Montaigne: Scepticisme, métaphysique, théologie*. Paris: Presses Universitaires de France, 2004.

Carrithers, D. W. *Joseph Glanvill and Pyrrhonic Skepticism: A Study in the Revival of the Doctrines of Sextus Empiricus in Sixteenth and Seventeenth Century Europe*. New York: New York University Press, 1972.

Cascardi, A. J. "Skepticism and Deconstruction." *Philosophy and Literature* 8 (1984): 1–14.

Castellio, Sebastian. *Concerning Heretics*. Translated by Roland H. Bainton. New York: Columbia University Press, 1935.

———. *De arte dubitandi et confidendi, ignorandi et sciendi*. Edited by Elisabeth F. Hirsch. Leiden: Brill, 1981.

Cavaillé, Jean-Pierre. "Scepticisme, tromperie et mensonge chez La Mothe Le Vayer et Descartes." In Paganini, *The Return of Skepticism from Hobbes and Descartes to Bayle*, pp. 115–31.

Cavel, Stanley. *The Claim of Reason: Wittgenstein, Skepticism, Morality, and Tragedy*. Oxford: Oxford University Press, 1979.

Charles, Sébastien. *Berkeley au Siècle des Lumières: Immatérialisme et Scepticisme au XVIIIe Siècle*. Paris: J. Vrin, 2003.

Charron, Jean D. *The "Wisdom" of Pierre Charron: An Original and Orthodox Code of Morality*. Chapel Hill: University of North Carolina, 1961.

Charron, Pierre. *Oeuvres*. 2 vols. Geneva: Slatkine Reprints, 1970. Reprint of the 1635 Paris edition.

———. *Of Wisdom*. Translated by Samson Lennard. London: Edward Blount & William Aspley, 1608.

Chouillet, Jacques. "Le personnage sceptique dans les premières oeuvres de Diderot." *Dix-Huitième Siècle* 1 (1969): 195–211.

Cicero, Marcus Tullius. *De Natura Deorum and Academica*. Translated by H. Rackham. (Loeb Classical Library) Cambridge, MA: Harvard University Press, 1994.

Clarke, Thompson. "The Legacy of Skepticism." *Journal of Philosophy* 69 (1972): 764–69.

Comparot, Andrée. "Montaigne et Sanchez ou les exigences de la pensée scientifique." In *Montaigne et la Grèce: 1588–1988: Actes du colloque de Calamata*, edited by K. Christodoulou, 206–16. Paris: Aux Amateurs des Livres, 1990.

Conche, Marcel. *Pyrrhon, ou l'apparence*. Paris: Presses Universitaires de France, 1994.

Cossuta, F. *Le Scepticisme*. Paris: Presses Universitaires de France, 1994.

Couissin, Pierre. "L'origine et l'évolution de l'*époche*." *Revue des études grecques* 42 (1929): 373–97.

———. "The Stoicism of the New Academy." In Burnyeat, *The Skeptical Tradition*, pp. 31–63.

Courtenay, William. "John of Mirecourt and Gregory of Rimini on Whether God Can Undo the Past." *Recherches de théologie ancienne et médiévale* 39 (1972): 224–56.

Crousaz, Jean-Pierre de. *Examen du pyrrhonisme ancien et moderne*. 2 vols. Paris: Fayard, 2003–2004.

———. *La Logique ou système de réflexions qui peuvent contribuer à la netteté et l'étendue de nos connaissances*. Seconde édition revue, corrigée et augmentée. 3 vols. Amsterdam: L'Honoré et Chatelien, 1720.

Culler, J. *On Deconstruction: Theory and Criticism After Structuralism*. Ithaca, NY: Cornell University Press, 1982.

Curley, Edwin. *Augustine's Critique of Skepticism: A Study of "Contra Academicos."* New York: Bern, P. Lang, 1997.

———. *Descartes against the Skeptics*. Cambridge, MA: Harvard University Press, 1978.

Curtis, James. "Shestov's Use of Nietzsche in His Interpretation of Tolstoy and Dostoievsky." *Literature and Language* 27 (1974): 289–302.

Cusa, Nicholas. *On Learned Ignorance: A Translation and an Appraisal of De docta ignorantia*. Translated by Jasper Hopkins. Minneapolis, MN: A. J. Benning Press, 1981.

Davidson, H. M. *The Origins of Certainty: Means and Meanings in Pascal's 'Pensées.'* Chicago: University of Chicago Press, 1979.

Davies, Richard. *Descartes: Belief, Scepticism and Virtue*. London: Routledge, 2001.

De Pace, Anna. *La scepsi, il sapere e l'anima: Dissonanze nella cerchia laurenziana*. Milan: Led, 2002.

De Pierris, Graciela. "Philosophical Scepticism in Wittgenstein's *On Certainty*." In Popkin, *Skepticism in the History of Philosophy*, pp. 181–96.

Demonet, Marie-Luce, and Alain Legros, eds. *L'Écriture du scepticisme chez Montaigne: Actes des journées d'étude (15–16 novembre 2001)*. Geneva: Droz, 2004.

DeRose, Keith. "Solving the Skeptical Problem." *Philosophical Review* 104 (1995): 1–50.

DeRose, Keith, and Ted A. Warfield, eds. *Skepticism: A Contemporary Reader*. New York: Oxford University Press, 1999.

Derrida, Jacques. *Margins of Philosophy*. Translated by A. Bass. Chicago: Chicago University Press, 1981.

———. *Writing and Difference*. Translated by A. Bass. London: Routledge, 1978.

Descartes, René. *The Philosophical Writings*. Translated by John Cottingham, Robert Stoothoof, and Dugald Murdoch. 2 vols. Cambridge, MA: Cambridge University Press, 1985.

———. *Meditations on First Philosophy*. Translated by John Veitch. In Popkin, *The Philosophy of the 16th and 17th Centuries*, pp. 122–87.

Desilets, André. *Léon Chestov: Des paradoxes de la philosophie*. Québec: Éditions du Beffroi, 1984.

Dostoevsky, Fiodor. "Notes from the Underground." In *Existentialism from Dostoevsky to Sartre*, edited by Walter Kaufmann, 52–82. Cleveland and New York: Meridian, 1956.

Diderot, Denis. *Oeuvres Complètes*. 20 vols. Critical and annotated edition by John Lough and Jacques Proust. Paris: Hermann, 1976.

———. "La Promenade du sceptique." In *Oeuvres*. 5 vols. Edited by Laurent Versini, 1:65–132. Paris: Robert Laffont, 1994.

Diderot, Denis, D'Alambert, et al. *Encyclopedia*. Translated by N. S. Hoyt and Thomas Cassirer. Indianapolis, IN: Bobbs-Merrill, 1965.

Diogenes Laertius. *Lives of Eminent Philosophers*. 2 vols. Translated by R. D. Hicks. Cambridge, MA: Harvard University Press, 1943.

Dumont, J-P. *Le scepticisme et le phénomène*. Paris: Vrin, 1972.

Eames, Elizabeth R. *Bertrand Russell's Theory of Knowledge*. London: Allen & Unwin, 1969.

Engstler, Achim. "Commentary: Reading Schulze's *Aenesidemus*." In Van der Zande and Popkin, *The Skeptical Tradition around 1800*, pp. 159–72.

Erasmus, Desiderius. *In Praise of Folly*. Translated by Leonard Dean. In Popkin, *The Philosophy of the 16th and 17th Centuries*, pp. 32–36.

Evans, C. Stephen. *Kierkegaard's Fragments and Postscript: The Religious Philosophy of Johannes Climacus*. Atlantic Highlands, NJ: Humanities Press, 1983.

Ferreira, Jaime. "Locke's 'Constructive Skepticism'—A Reappraisal." *Journal of the History of Philosophy* 24 (1986): 211–22.

Feugère, F. *Essai sur la vie et les ouvrages de Henri Estienne*. Paris: J. Delalain, 1853.

Feyerabend, Paul. *Against Method*. London: Verso, 1975.

———. *Farewell to Reason*. London: Verso, 1987.

———. *Science in a Free Society*. London: Verso, 1978.

Flintoff, Everard. "Pyrrho and India." *Phronesis* 25 (1980): 88–108.

Floridi, Luciano. *Sextus Empiricus: The Transmission and Recovery of Pyrrhonism*. Oxford: Oxford University Press, 2002.

———. "The Diffusion of Sextus Empiricus' Works in the Renaissance." *Journal of the History of Ideas* 56 (1995): 63–85.

Fogelin, Robert J. *Hume's Skepticism in the "Treatise of Human Nature."* London: Routledge and Kegan Paul, 1985.

———. *Pyrrhonian Reflections on Knowledge and Justification*. Oxford: Oxford University Press, 1994.

———. *Walking the Tightrope of Reason: The Precarious Life of a Rational Animal*. Oxford: Oxford University Press, 2005.

———. "Two Diagnoses of Skepticism." In Luper, *The Skeptics*, 137–48.

Force, James E., and David S. Katz, eds. *Everything Connects: In Conference with Richard H. Popkin*. Leiden: Brill, 1999.

Forster, Michael N. *Hegel and Skepticism*. Cambridge, MA: Harvard University Press, 1989.

Foucher, Simon. *Critique [of Nicolas Malebranche's] Of the Search for the Truth*. Translated by Richard A. Watson. Carbondale and Edwardsville: Southern Illinois University Press, 1995. (Journal of the History of Philosophy Monograph Series)

———. *Dissertation sur la Recherche de la Vérité contenant l'Apologie des Académiciens, où l'on fait voir que leur manière de philosopher est plus utile pour la religion, & la plus conforme au bon sens, pour servir de Réponse à la Critique de la Critique, & avec plusieurs remarques sur les erreurs des sens & sur l'origine de la philosophie de Monsieur Descartes*. Paris: Estienne Michallet, 1687.

———. *Dissertation sur la Recherche de la Vérité contenant l'histoire et les principes de la philosophie des Académiciens, avec plusieurs réflexions sur les sentiments de Monsieur Descartes*. Paris: Jean Anisson, 1693.

Foucault, Michel. *Madness and Civilization: A History of Insanity in the Age of Reason*. Translated by R. Howard. New York: Pantheon, 1965.

Frankfurt, Harry G. *Demons, Dreamers, and Madmen: The Defense of Reason in Descartes' Meditations.* Indianapolis, IN: Bobbs-Merrill, 1970.

Frede, Michael. "The Sceptic's Beliefs." In Michael Frede, *Essays in Ancient Philosophy*, chap. 10. Minneapolis: University of Minnesota Press, 1989.

———. "The Sceptic's Two Kinds of Assent and the Question of the Possibility of Knowledge." In *Philosophy in History: Essays on the Historiography of Philosophy*, edited by Richard Rorty, J. B. Schneewind, and Quentin Skinner, 255–78. Cambridge: Cambridge University Press, 1984.

Fritz, Charles A. *Bertrand Russell's Construction of the External World.* London: Routledge & K. Paul, 1952.

Funkenstein, Amos. "Scholasticism, Scepticism and Secular Theology." In Popkin and Schmitt, *Scepticism from the Renaissance to the Enlightenment*, pp. 45–54.

Garfagnini, Gian Carlo, ed. *Giovanni Pico della Mirandola: Convegno internazionale di studi nel cinquecentesimo anniversario della morte (1494–1994).* Florence: Olschki, 1997.

Garver, Newton, and S. C. Lee. *Derrida and Wittgenstein.* Philadelphia: Temple University Press, 1994.

Gassendi, Pierre. *Disquisitio metaphysica seu dubitationes et instantiae adversus Renati Cartesi metaphysicam et responsa.* Bilingual edition and translation to French by Bernard Rochot. Paris: J. Vrin, 1962.

———. *Exercitationes Paradoxicae adversus Aristoteleos.* Bilingual edition and translation to French by Bernard Rochot. Paris: J. Vrin, 1959.

———. *Opera omnia.* 6 vols. Edited by Tulio Gregory. Stuttgart: Frommann, 1964. Reprint of the 1658 Lyon edition.

———. *The Selected Works.* Edited and translated by Craig B. Brush. London and New York: Johnson Reprint, 1972.

———. *Vie et moeurs d'Epicure.* Translated and annotated by Sylvie Taussig. Paris: Alive, 2001.

Giannantoni, Giovanni, ed. *Lo Scetticismo antico: Atti del convegno organizzato dal Centro di studio del pensiero antico del C.N.R., Roma 5–8 novembre 1980.* 2 vols. Naples: Bibliopolis, 1981.

———, ed. *Sesto Empirico e il pensiero antico. Elenchos* 13 (1992).

Giocanti, Sylvia. *Penser l' irrésolution: Montaigne, Pascal, La Mothe Le Vayer.* Paris: Honoré Champion, 2001.

Glanvill, Joseph. *Essays on Several Important Subjects in Philosophy and Religion.*

Granville, Joseph, and Bernard Fabian. *Collected Works of Joseph Granville.* 9 vols. Hildesheim: G. Olms, 1970–1985.

Hildesheim: Olms, 1979. Facsimile of the 1676 London edition.

———. *Skepsis Scientifica.* New York: Garland, 1978. Facsimile of the 1665 London edition.

Glucker, J. *Antiochus and the Late Academy.* Göttingen: Vandenhoeck & Ruprecht, 1978.

Goodman, Russell, ed. *Pragmatism: Critical Concepts in Philosophy.* 4 vols. London: Routledge, 2005.

———. *Wittgenstein and William James.* Cambridge: Cambridge University Press, 2002.

Gouhier, Henri. "Doute méthodique ou négation méthodique?" *Etudes Philosophiques* 9 (1954): 135–62.

Gouverneur, Sophie. "La Mothe Le Vayer et las politique, ou l'usage libertin du scepticisme antique." *Libertinage et philosophie* 7 (2003): 189–201.

Granada, Miguel. "Apologétique platonicienne et apologétique sceptique: Ficin, Savonarole,

Jean-François Pic de la Mirandole." In Moreau, *Le Scepticisme au XVIe et au XVIIe Siècle*, pp. 11–47.

Gregory, Tulio. *Genèse de la raison classique de Charron à Descartes*. Paris: Presses Universitaires de France, 2000.

———. *Scetticismo ed empirismo: Studio su Gassendi*. Bari: Editori Laterza, 1961.

———. "Dio ingannatore e genio maligno." *Giornale Critico della Filosofia Italiana* 53 (1974): 477–516. French translation published in T. Gregory, *Genèse de la raison classique de Charron à Descartes*. Paris: Presses Universitaires de France, 2000, pp. 293–347.

Grimsley, Ronald. *Søren Kierkegaard and French Literature*. Cardiff: University of Wales Press, 1966.

Groarke, Leo. *Greek Scepticism: Anti-realist Trends in Ancient Thought*. Montreal: McGill-Queen University Press, 1990.

———. "Descartes' First Meditation: Something Old, Something New, Something Borrowed." *Journal of the History of Philosophy* 22 (1984): 281–301.

Groarke, Leo, and Graham Solomon. "Some Sources for Hume's Account of Cause." *Journal of the History of Ideas* 52 (1991): 645–63.

Grundmann, Thomas. "Polemic and Dogmatism: The Two Faces of Skepticism in Aenesidemus-Schulze." In Van der Zande and Popkin, *The Skeptical Tradition around 1800*, pp. 133–41.

Guellouz, S., ed. *Pierre-Daniel Huet (1630–1721)*. Actes du Colloque de Caen (1993). Paris: Biblio 17, 1994.

Guillemin, J. J. *Le Cardinal de Lorraine, son influence politique et religieuse au XVIe siècle*. Paris: Joubert, 1847.

Haag, Éliane M. "Diderot et Voltaire lecteurs de Montaigne: Du jugement suspendu à la raison libre." *Revue de Métaphysique et de Morale* 3 (1997): 365–83.

Hamlin, William M. *Tragedy and Scepticism in Shakespeare's England*. Hampshire: Plagrave/St. Martin's Press, 2005.

Hankinson, R. J. *The Skeptics*. London: Routledge, 1995.

Harowitz, Maryanne. "Pierre Charron's View of the Source of Wisdom." *Journal of the History of Philosophy* 9 (1971): 443–57.

Häseler, Jens. "Formey et Crousaz, ou comment fallait-il combattre le scepticisme?" In Paganini, *The Return of Skepticism from Hobbes and Descartes to Bayle*, pp. 449–62.

Hegel, Georg W. F. *The Encyclopedia Logic*. Translated by T. F. Geraets, W. A. Suchting, and H. S. Harris. Indianapolis, IN: Hackett, 1991.

———. *Lectures on the History of Philosophy*. 3 vols. Translated by E. J. Haldane. Lincoln: University of Nebraska Press, 1995.

———. *Phenomenology of Spirit*. Translated by A.V. Miller. Oxford: Oxford University Press, 1977.

———. "Verhältnis des Skeptizismus zur Philosophie." *Kritisches Journal der Philosophie* 2 (1802): 1–74.

Henderson, George. D. *Chevalier Ramsay*. Edinburgh: Thomas Nelson & Sons, 1952.

Herbert, Lord Edward of Cherbury. *De Veritate*. Translated by Meyrick H. Carré. Bristol: J. W. Arrowsmith Ltd., 1937.

Hiley, David. R. *Philosophy in Question: Essays on a Pyrrhonian Theme*. Chicago: University of Chicago Press, 1988.

House, D. K. "The Life of Sextus Empiricus." *Classical Quarterly* 30 (1980): 227–38.

Huet, Pierre-Daniel. *Against Cartesian Philosophy*. Translated by Thomas M. Lennon. Amherst, NY: Humanity Books, 2003.

———. *An Essay concerning the Weakness of Human Understanding*. Translated by Edward Combe. London: Matthew de Varenne, 1725.

———. *Mémoires*. Translated by Charles Nisard, revised and annotated by Philippe-Joseph Salazar. Toulouse: Société de Littératures Classiques, 1993.

———. *Nouveaux mémoires pour servir à l'histoire du cartésianisme*. Rezé: Séquences, 1996.

Hull, Robert. "Skepticism, Enigma and Integrity: Horizons of Affirmation in Nietzsche's Philosophy." *Man and World* 23 (1990): 375–91.

Hume, David. *A Treatise of Human Nature*. Edited by L. A. Selby-Bigge. Oxford: Oxford University Press, 1964.

———. *Dialogues concerning Natural Religion*. Edited with an introduction by Richard H. Popkin. Indianapolis, IN: Hackett, 1980.

———. *Enquiries concerning Human Understanding and concerning the Principles of Morals*. Edited by L. A. Selby-Bigge and P. H. Nidditch. 3rd edition. Oxford: Clarendon Press, 1975.

Ioppolo, A. M. *Opinione e Scienza: Il dibattio tra Stoici e Accademici nel III e nel II secolo a . c.* Naples: Bibliopolis, 1986.

James, William. "The Will to Believe." In William James, *Essays on Faith and Morals*, selected by Ralph Barton Perry, 32–62. Chicago: Meridian Books, 1962.

Janácek, K. *Sextus Empiricus' Sceptical Methods*. Prague: Karlova University, 1972.

Joukovsky, F. "Le Commentaire d'Henri Estienne aux *Hypotyposes* de Sextus Empiricus." In *Henri Estienne*, 129–45 (Paris: Presses de l'Ecole Normale Supérieure, 1988).

Joy, Lynn. *Gassendi, the Atomist: Advocate of History in an Age of Science*. Cambridge: Cambridge University Press, 1987.

Kamboucher, Denis. *Les Méditations Métaphysiques de Descartes*. Vol. 1: Introduction general. Première Méditation. Paris: Presses Universitaires de France, 2005.

Kant, Immanuel. *Critique of Pure Reason*. Translated by J. M. D. Meiklejohn. London: J. M. Dent and New York: E. P. Dutton, 1950. First edition 1934.

———. *Prolegomena to Any Future Metaphysics*. Translated and edited by Gary Hatfield. Cambridge: Cambridge University Press, 1997.

Karger, Elizabeth. "Ockham and Wodeham on Divine Deception as a Skeptical Hypothesis." *Vivarium* 42 (2004): 225–36.

Kennedy, Leonard. *Peter of Ailly and the Harvest of Fourteenth-Century Philosophy*. Lewiston, NY: Edwin Mellen Press, 1986.

Kierkegaard, Søren. *Concluding Unscientific Postscript*. Translated by David F. Swenson and Walter Lowrie. Princeton, NJ: Princeton University Press, 1974.

———. *Fear and Trembling*. Edited and translated by Howard V. Hong and Edna H. Hong. Princeton, NJ: Princeton University Press, 1983.

———. *Philosophical Fragments*. Edited and translated by Howard V. Hong and Edna H. Hong. Princeton, NJ: Princeton University Press, 1985.

Kirwan, Christopher. "Augustine against the Skeptics." In Burnyeat, *The Skeptical Tradition*, pp. 205–23.

Kripke, Saul. *Wittgenstein on Rules and Private Language*. Cambridge: MA: Harvard University Press, 1982.

Kuehn, Manfred. "Skepticism: Philosophical Disease or Cure?" In Van der Zande and Popkin, *The Skeptical Tradition around 1800*, pp. 81–100.

La Mothe Le Vayer, François. *De la vertu des païens*. Paris: Augustin Courbe, 1647.

———. *Dialogues faits à l'imitation des anciens*. Paris: Fayard, 1988.

———. *Hexameron Rustique*. La Versanne: Encre Marine, 2005.

———. *Oeuvres*. 14 vols. Dresden: M. Groell, 1756–59.

———. *Petit traité sceptique sur cette commune façon de parler: N'avoir pas le Sens commun*. Mayenne: Le Promeneur, 2003.

Labrousse, Elizabeth. *Pierre Bayle*. 2 vols. The Hague: Martinus Nijhoff, 1963–64.

Lactantius. *Divine Institutes*. Translated by Sister Mary Francis McDonald. Washington: Catholic University of America Press, 1964.

Landesman, Charles, and Roblin Meeks, eds. *Philosophical Skepticism*. Malden, MA: Blackwell, 2003.

Laursen, John Christian. *The Politics of Skepticism in the Ancients, Montaigne, Hume and Kant*. Leiden: J. Brill, 1992.

———. "Crousaz." In *Grundriss der Geschichte der Philosophie, 18 Jhr.*, edited by Friedrich Ueberweg. Band 2/1-2 (forthcoming).

———. "Kant in the History of Scepticism." In *John Locke und Immanuel Kant: Historische Rezeption und gegenwärtiger Relevanz*, edited by Martyn P. Thompson, 254–68. Berlin: Duncker & Humblot, 1991.

———. "Skepticism and the History of Moral Philosophy: The Case of Carl Friedrich Stäudlin." In Van der Zande and Popkin, *The Skeptical Tradition around 1800*, pp. 365–78.

———. "Skeptics, Unconvincing Anti-Skepticism, and Politics." In Bernier and Charles, *Scepticisme et modernité*, pp. 167–88.

Laursen, John Christian, and Richard H. Popkin. "Sources of Knowledge of Sextus Empiricus in Kant's Time: A French Translation of Sextus Empiricus from the Prussian Academy, 1779." *British Journal for the History of Philosophy* 6 (1998): 261–68.

Legros, A. "La Dédicace de l'*Adversus Mathematicos* au Cardinal de Lorraine, ou du bon usage de Sextus Empiricus selon Gracien Hervet et Montaigne." *Bulletin de la Société Internationale des Amis de Montaigne* 8 (1999): 15–16, 41–72.

Leibniz, G. W. *Discourse on Metaphysics and Related Writings*. Edited and translated by Martin Niall and Stuart Brown. 2nd edition. Dordrecht: D. Reidel, 1969.

———. *Die Philosophischen Schriften*. 7 vols. Edited by C. J. Gerhardt. Berlin: Weidmann, 1875–99.

———. *Theodicy: Essays on the Goodness of God, the Freedom of Man and the Origin of Evil*. Edited by Austin Farrer and translated by E. M. Huggard. London: Routledge & K. Paul, 1952.

Lennon, Thomas. *The Battle of the Gods and Giants: The Legacies of Descartes and Gassendi*. Princeton, NJ: Princeton University Press, 1993.

———, ed. *Cartesian Views: Papers Presented to Richard A. Watson*. Leiden: Brill, 2003.

———. *Reading Bayle*. Toronto: University of Toronto Press, 1999.

———. "Foucher, Huet, and the Downfall of Cartesianism." In Lennon, *Cartesian Views*, pp. 117–28.

———. "Huet, Descartes, and the Objection of the Objections." In *Skepticism in Renaissance and Post-Renaissance Thought: New Interpretations*, edited by José R. Maia Neto and Richard H. Popkin, 123–42. Amherst, NY: Humanity Books, 2004.

———. "Huet, Malebranche and the Birth of Skepticism." In Paganini, *The Return of Skepticism from Hobbes and Descartes to Bayle*, pp. 149–65.

———. "The Skepticism of Huet's *Traité philosophique de la foiblesse de l'esprit humain.*" In Bernier and Charles, *Scepticisme et Modernité*, pp. 65–75.

———. "Bayle's Anticipation of Popper." *Journal of the History of Ideas* 58 (1997): 695–705.

Levy, Carlos. *Cicero Academicus: Recherches sur les Académiques et sur la philosophie cicéronienne.* Rome: École Française de Rome, 1992.

Lewis, David. "Elusive Knowledge." *Australasian Journal of Philosophy* 74 (1996): 549–67.

Limbrick, Elaine. "Franciscus Sanchez 'Scepticus': Un médecin philosophe précurseur de Descartes (1550–1623)." *Renaissance and Reformation* 6 (1982): 264–72.

———. "Was Montaigne Really a Pyrrhonian?" *Bibliothèque d'Humanisme et Renaissance* 39 (1977): 67–80.

Locke, John. *An Essay concerning Human Understanding.* Edited with an introduction by Peter H. Nidditch. Oxford: Clarendon Press, 1975.

Lom, Petr. *The Limits of Doubts: The Moral and Political Implications of Skepticism.* Albany: State University of New York Press, 2001.

Long, A. "Timon of Phlius: Pyrrhonist and Satirist." *Proceedings of the Cambridge Philosophical Society* 24 (1978): 68–91.

Long, A., and David Sedley, eds. *The Hellenistic Philosophers.* 2 vols. Cambridge: Cambridge University Press, 1997.

Luper, Steven, ed. *The Skeptics: Contemporary Essays.* Aldershot, England: Ashgate, 2003.

Lupoli, Agostino. "*Humanus animus nusquam consistit*: Doctor Sanchez's Diagnosis of Incurable Human Unrest and Ignorance." In Paganini and Maia Neto, *Renaissance Skepticisms.*

Lux, David S. *Patronage and Royal Science in Seventeenth-Century France: The Académie de Physique in Caen.* Ithaca, NY, and London: Cornell University Press, 1989.

Maia Neto, José. R. *The Christianization of Pyrrhonism: Skepticism and Faith in Pascal, Kierkegaard and Shestov.* Dordrecht: Kluwer, 1995.

———. "Bayle's Academic Skepticism." In Force and Katz, *Everything Connects*, pp. 264–75.

———. "Charron's Academic Skeptical Wisdom." In Paganini and Maia Neto, *Renaissance Skepticisms.*

———. "Charron's *epoche* and Descartes's *cogito*: The Skeptical Base of Descartes's Refutation of Skepticism." In Paganini, *The Return of Skepticism from Hobbes and Descartes to Bayle*, pp. 81–113.

———. "*Epoche* as Perfection: Montaigne's View of Ancient Skepticism." In Maia Neto and Popkin, *Skepticism in Renaissance and Post-Renaissance Thought: New Interpretations*, pp. 13–42.

———. "Foucher's Academic Cartesianism." In Lennon, *Cartesian Views*, pp. 71–95.

———. "Academic Skepticism in Early Modern Philosophy." *Journal of the History of Ideas* 58 (1997): 199–220.

———. "Feyerabend's Skepticism." *Studies in History and Philosophy of Science* 22 (1991): 543–55.

———. "Hume and Pascal: Pyrrhonism versus Nature." *Hume Studies* 17 (1991): 41–49.

Maia Neto, José R., and Richard H. Popkin, eds. *Skepticism in Renaissance and Post-Renaissance Thought: New Interpretations.* Amherst, NY: Humanity Books, 2004.

Magnus, Bernd. "Nietzsche's Mitigated Skepticism." *Nietzsche-Studien* 9 (1980): 260–67.

Makkreel, Rudolf A. "Kant's Responses to Skepticism." In Van der Zande and Popkin, *The Skeptical Tradition around 1800*, pp. 101–109.

Malbrail, German. "Descartes censuré par Huet." *Revue philosophique* 116 (1991): 311–28.

Malebranche, Nicholas. *De la Recherche de la Vérité*. 3 vols. Paris: Vrin, 1991.

Margolin, Jean-Claude. "D'Érasme à Montaigne: l'écriture de l'opionion et la double voie de la croyance." In Demonet and Legros, *L'Écriture du scepticisme chez Montaigne*, pp. 109–30.

Mates, Benson. *The Skeptic Way*. Oxford: Oxford University Press, 1996.

McDowell, John. *Plato: Theaetetus*. Oxford: Clarendon Press, 1973.

McKenna, Antony. *The Return of Skepticism from Hobbes and Descartes to Bayle*, pp. 249–65.

———. "Skepticism at Port-Royal: The Perversion of Pyrrhonian Doubt." In Paganini, *De Pascal à Voltaire: Le rôle des Pensées de Pascal dans l'histoire des idées entre 1670 et 1734*. 2 vols. Oxford: Voltaire Foundation at the Taylor Institute, 1990.

Mersenne, Marin. *L'Impiété des déistes, athées, et libertins de ce temps, combattue, et renversée de point en point par raisons tirées de la philosophie et de la théologie*. Paris: P. Bilaine, 1624. Facsimile reprint, Stuttgart: Frommann, 1975.

———. *La Vérité des sciences contre les sceptiques ou pyrrhoniens*. Paris: T. du Bray, 1625. Facsimile reprint, Stuttgart: Frommann: 1969.

Meyers, R. G. "Meaning and Metaphysics in James." *Philosophy and Phenomenology Research* 31 (1971): 369–80.

Miller, David. *Out of Error: Further Essays on Critical Rationalism*. Aldershot, England: Ashgate, 2006.

Montaigne, Michel de. *The Apology for Raymond Sebond*. In Popkin, *The Philosophy of the 16th and 17th Centuries*, pp. 70–81.

———. *The Complete Essays*. Translated by Donald M. Frame. Stanford, CA: Stanford University Press, 1965.

Moore, G. E. "Proof of an External World." *Proceedings of the British Academy* 25 (1939). Reprinted in G. E. Moore, *Philosophical Papers*. London: George Allen and Unwin, 1959.

Moreau, Joseph. "Doute et savoir chez Francisco Sanchez." *Portugiesische Forschungen des Gorrespgesellschaft*, erste reihe, *Aufsatze zur Portugiesischen Kulturgeschichte* 1 (1960): 24–50.

Moreau, Pierre-François, ed. *Le Scepticisme au XVIe et au XVIIe Siècle*. Paris: Albin Michel, 2001.

Mori, Gianluca. *Bayle philosophe*. Paris: Honoré Champion, 1999.

———. "Pierre Bayle on Skepticism and 'Common Notions.'" In Paganini, *The Return of Skepticism from Hobbes and Descartes to Bayle*, pp. 393–413.

———. "Scepticisme ancient et moderne chez Bayle." *Libertinage et philosophie* 7 (2003): 271–90.

Mosher, D. "The Arguments of St. Augustine's *Contra Academicos*." *Augustinian Studies* 12 (1981): 89–113.

Mosser, Kurt. "Should the Skeptic Live His Skepticism? Nietzsche and Classical Skepticism." *Manuscrito* 21 (1998): 47–84.

Mothu, Alan, and Antonella del Prete, eds. *Révolution scientifique et libertinage*. Turnhout: Brepolis, 2000.

Munévar, Gonzalo, ed. *Beyond Reason: Essays on the Philosophy of Paul K. Feyerabend.* Dordrecht: Kluwer, 1991.

Murr, Sylvia, ed. *Gassendi et l'Europe, 1592–1792.* Paris: Vrin, 1997.

Musgrave, Alan. *Common Sense, Science and Scepticism: A Historical Introduction to the Theory of Knowledge.* Cambridge: Cambridge University Press, 1993.

Naess, Arne. *Scepticism.* London: Routledge, 1968.

Naudé, Gabriel. *Apologie pour tous les grands personnages qui ont été faussement soupçonnés de magie.* Farnborough: Gregg International, 1972. Facsimile of the Paris 1625 edition.

Nadeau, Christian. "Sagesse 'sceptique' de Charron? L'articulation de scepticisme et du stoïcismedans *La sagesse* de Pierre Charron." *Libertinage et philosophe* 7 (2003): 85–104.

———. *Considérations politiques sur les coups d'Etat.* Edited by Frédérique Marin and Marie-Odile Perulli, followed by *Naudaena*, edited by Lionel Leforestier. Paris: Le Promeneur, 2004.

Naya, Emmanuel. "Renaissant Pyrrhonism: A Relative Phenomenon." In Paganini and Maia Neto, *Renaissance Skepticisms.*

———. "*Quod nihil scitur*: La parole mise en doute." *Libertinage et philosophie* 7 (2003): 27–43.

———. "Sextus à Genève: La Réforme de doute." *Libertinage et Philosphie au XVlle siècle* 8 (2004): 7–30.

Nehels, B. "Erasmus von Rotterdam: Das für und wider die Skepsis." In *Renaissance-Humanismus, Jugäng zur Bildungstheorie der frühen Neuzit.* Edited by Jörg Ruhloff. Essen: Die Blaue Eule, 1989.

Norton, David F. *David Hume: Common-Sense Moralist, Skeptical Metaphysician.* Princeton, NJ: Princeton University Press, 1982.

Nozick, Robert. *Philosophical Explanations.* Oxford: Oxford University Press, 1981.

O'Connell, Robert J. *William James on the Courage to Believe.* New York: Fordham University Press, 1984.

Olaso, Ezequiel de. "Leibniz and Skepticism." In Popkin and Schmitt, *Scepticism from the Renaissance to the Enlightenment*, pp. 133–67.

———. "Skepticism and the Infinite." In *L'infinito in Leibniz: problemi e terminologia*, edited by Antonio Lamarra, 95–118. Rome: Edizioni dell'Anteneo, 1990.

——— "The Two Scepticisms of the Savoyard Vicar." In Watson and Force, *The Skeptical Mode in Modern Philosophy*, 43–59.

Oliveira, Bernardo J. de, and José R. Maia Neto. "The Skeptical Evaluation of *Techné* and Baconian Science." In Paganini and Maia Neto, *Renaissance Skepticisms.*

Osler, Margaret. *Divine Will and the Mechanical Philosophy: Gassendi and Descartes on Contingency and Necessity in the Created World.* Cambridge: Cambridge University Press, 1994.

———. "Baptizing Epicurean Atomism." In *Religion, Science and Worldview.* Edited by Margaret Osler and P. L. Farber. Cambridge: Cambridge University Press, 1985.

Owen, John. *The Skeptics of the French Renaissance.* London: S. Sonnenschein & New York: Macmillan, 1893.

Paganini, Gianni. *Analisi della fede e critica della ragione nella filosofia di Pierre Bayle.* Florence: La Nuova Italia, 1980.

———, ed. *The Return of Skepticism From Hobbes and Descartes to Bayle.* Dordrecht: Kluwer, 2003.

————. *Scepsi Moderna: Interpretazioni dello scetticismo da Charron a Hume*. Cosensa: Busento, 1991.

————. "Hume, Bayle et les *Dialogues concerning natural religion*." In *Pierre Bayle dans la République des Lettres: Philosophie, Religion, Critique*, edited by Antony McKenna and Gianni Paganini, 527–67. Paris: Honoré Champion, 2004.

————. "'Pyrrhonisme tout pur' ou 'circoncis'? La dynamique du scepticisme chez La Mothe Le Vayer." *Libertinage et Philosophie au XVIIe siècle* 2 (1997): 7–31.

Paganini, Gianni, Miguel Benitez, and James Dybikowski, eds. *Scepticisme, Clandestinité et Libre Pensée*. Paris: Honoré Champion, 2002.

Paganini, Gianni, and José R. Maia Neto, eds. *Renaissance Skepticisms*, forthcoming.

Panichi, Nicola. "A Skepticism That Conquers the Mind: Montaigne and Plutarch." In Paganini and Maia Neto, *Renaissance Skepticisms*.

Pascal, Blaise. *Pensées*. Translated by A. J. Krailsheimer. London: Penguin, 1966.

————. "Reply to Father Noel," "Preface to Treatise on the Vacuum," and "Conversation with Sacy." In *Pascal Selections*, edited and translated by Richard H. Popkin, 49–55, 62–66, 79–89. New York: Macmillan, 1989.

Patterson, David. "Shestov, Kierkegaard, and the Origins of Nothingness: Reflections of the Fall." *American Benedictine Review* 39 (1988): 15–30.

Pears, David Francis. *Bertrand Russell and the British Tradition in Philosophy*. London: Collins, 1967.

Penelhum, Terence. *God and Skepticism*. Dordrecht: D. Reidel, 1983.

Perez Ramos, Antonio. *Francis Bacon's Idea of Science and the Maker's Knowledge Tradition*. Oxford: Clarendon Press, 1988.

Perler, Dominik. "Was There a 'Pyrrhonian Crisis' in Early Modern Philosophy? A Critical Notice of Richard Popkin." *Archiv für Geschichte der Philosophie* 86 (2004): 209–20.

Perreiah, Alan. "Modes of Skepticism in Medieval Philosophy." In *Studies on the History of Logic: Proceedings of the III. Symposium on the History of Logic*, edited by Ignacio Angelelli and María Cerezo, 65–77. Berlin: De Gruyter, 1996.

Pico della Mirandola, Gianfrancesco. *Examen vanitatis doctrinae gentium et veritatis christianae disciplinae*. Mirandola: I. Maciochus Bundenius, 1520.

Pintard, René. *Le Libertinage érudit en France dans la première moitié du 17éme siècle*. Nouvelle édition augmentée d'un avant-propos et de notes et réflexions sur les problèmes de l'histoire du libertinage. Réimpression de l'édition de Paris, 1943. Geneva: Slatkine, 2000.

Plato. *Apology*. Translated by H. N. Fowler. (Loeb Classical Library) Cambridge, MA: Harvard University Press, 1995.

————. *Theaetetus*. Translated by H. N. Fowler. (Loeb Classical Library) Cambridge, MA: Harvard University Press, 1996.

Poellner, Peter. *Nietzsche and Metaphysics*. Oxford: Clarendon Press, 1995.

Popkin, Richard H. *The High Road to Pyrrhonism*. Edited by Richard A. Watson and James E. Force. San Diego: Austin Hill, 1980.

————. *The History of Scepticism from Savonarola to Bayle*. Oxford: Oxford University Press, 2003.

————, ed. *The Philosophy of the 16th and 17th Centuries*. Toronto: Collier-Macmillan, 1966. (Readings in the History of Philosophy series, general editors: Paul Edwards and Richard H. Popkin)

————, ed. *Scepticism in the History of Philosophy: A Pan-American Dialogue*. Dordrecht: Kluwer, 1996.

———. *The Second Oswald*. New York: Avon Books, 1966.

———. "Bishop Pierre-Daniel Huet's Remarks on Malebranche." In *Nicolas Malebranche: His Philosophical Critics and Successors*, edited by Stuart Brown, 10–21. Assen: Van Gorcum, 1991.

———. "The 'Incurable Scepticism' of Henry More, Blaise Pascal and Søren Kierkegaard." In Popkin and Schmitt, *Scepticism from the Renaissance to the Enlightenment*, 169–84.

———. "Pierre Bayle's Place in 17th Century Skepticism." In *Pierre Bayle, le philosophe de Rotterdam*, edited by P. Dibon, 1–19. Amsterdam: Elsevier, 1959.

———. "Some Thoughts about Stäudlin's 'History and Spirit of Skepticism.'" In Van der Zande and Popkin, *The Skeptical Tradition around 1800*, pp. 339–42.

———. "L'Abbe Foucher et le problème des qualités premières." *Bulletin de la Société d' Etudes du XVIIe Siècle* 33 (1957): 633–47.

———. "Berkeley and Pyrrhonism." *Review of Metaphysics* 5 (1951): 227–31.

———. "Berkeley in the History of Scepticism." In Popkin, Olaso, and Tonelli, *Scepticism in the Enlightenment*, pp. 173–186.

———. "Charron and Descartes: The Fruits of Systematic Doubt." *Journal of Philosophy* 51 (1954): 831–37.

———. "David Hume and the Pyrrhonian Controversy." *Review of Metaphysics* 6 (1952): 65–81.

———. "David Hume: His Pyrrhonism and His Critique of Pyrrhonism." *Philosophical Quarterly* 1 (1951): 385–407.

———. "Hume and Kierkegaard." *Journal of Religion* 31 (1951): 274–81.

———. "Joseph Glanvill: A Precursor of Hume." *Journal of the History of Ideas* 14 (1953): 292–303.

———. "Joseph Glanvill's Continuation of the *New Atlantis*: Mitigated Skepticism and the Ideal of the Royal Society." *Actes du XIIe. Congrès International d'Histoire des Sciences*. Paris: Albert Blanchard, 1968, pp. 89–94.

———. "Kierkegaard and Skepticism." *Algemeen Nederlands Tijdschrift voor Wijsbegeerte en Psychologie* 51 (1959): 123–41.

———. "Leibniz and the French Skeptics." *Revue internationale de philosophie* 76–77 (1966): 228–48.

———. "New Views on the Role of Scepticism in the Enlightenment." *Modern Language Quarterly* 53 (1992): 279–97.

———. "Prophecy and Skepticism in the Sixteenth and Seventeenth Century." *British Journal for the History of Philosophy* 4 (1996): 1–20.

———. "Sources of Knowledge of Sextus Empiricus in Hume's Time." *Journal of the History of Ideas* 54 (1993): 137–41.

Popkin, Richard H., and José R. Maia Neto. "Bishop Pierre-Daniel Huet's Remarks on Pascal." *British Journal for the History of Philosophy* 3, no. 1 (1995): 147–60.

Popkin, Richard H., Ezequiel de Olaso, and Georgio Tonelli, eds. *Scepticism in the Enlightenment*. Dordrecht: Kluwer, 1997.

Popkin, Richard H., and Charles Schmitt, eds. *Scepticism from the Renaissance to the Enlightenment*. Wiesbaden: O. Harrassowitz, 1987.

Popkin, Richard H., and Avrum Stroll. *Skeptical Philosophy for Everyone*. Amherst, NY: Prometheus Books, 2002.

Popkin, Richard H., and Arjo Vanderjagt, eds. *Scepticism and Irreligion in the Seventeenth and Eighteenth Centuries*. Leiden: J. Brill, 1993.

Popper, Karl. *Conjectures and Refutations: The Grow of Scientific Knowledge*. London and New York: Routledge, 1989, first edition 1963.

———. *The Logic of Scientific Discovery*. London: Hutchinson, 1958.

———. *The Open Society and Its Enemies*. 2 vols. London: Kegan Paul, 1945.

Porchat Pereira, Oswaldo. *Vida comum e ceticismo*. São Paulo: Brasiliense, 1993.

———. "Ainda é preciso ser cético." *Discurso* 32 (2001): 9–30.

Powell, J. G. F., ed. *Cicero the Philosopher: Twelve Papers*. Oxford: Clarendon Press, 1995.

Radrizzani, Ives. "Le scepticisme à l'époque kantienne: Maimon contre Schulze." *Archives de philosophie* 54 (1991): 553–70.

Ramsay, Andrew Michael. *The Philosophical Principles of Natural and Revealed Religion Unfolded in a Geometrical Order*. Glasgow: Robert Foulis, 1748.

Rapetti, Elena. *Percorsi anticartesiani nelle lettere a Pierre-Daniel Huet*. Florence: Olschki, 2003.

———. *Pierre-Daniel Huet: Erdizione, filosofia, apologetica*. Milan: Vita e Pensiero, 1999.

Redgrove, H. S., and I. M. L. Redgrove. *Joseph Glanvill and Psychical Research in the Seventeenth Century*. London: William Rider & Son, 1921.

Richter, Raoul. *Der Skeptizismus in der Philosophie*. 2 vols. Leipzig: Dürr'sche Buchhandlung, 1904, 1908.

Robin, L. *Pyrrhon et le scepticisme grec*. Paris: Presses Universitaires de France, 1944.

Rogers, G. A. J. "John Locke and the Skeptics." In Paganini, *The Return of Skepticism from Hobbes and Descartes to Bayle*, pp. 37–53.

———. "Boyle, Locke and Reason." *Journal of the History of Ideas* 27 (1966): 205–16.

Roth, M. D., and G. Ross, eds. *Doubting: Contemporary Perspectives on Scepticism*. Dordrecht: Kluwer, 1990.

Rousseau, Jean-Jacques. *Emile or Education*. Translated by Barbara Foxley. London & Toronto: J. M. Dent & E. P. Dutton, 1911.

Russell, Bertrand. *Human Knowledge: Its Scope and Limits*. London: George Allen and Unwin, 1961 (first edition, 1948).

Sanchez, Francisco. *Opera philosophica*. Edited by Joaquim de Carvalho. Coimbra: Inedita Ac Rediviva, Separata da *Revista da Universidade de Coimbra*, vol. 18 (1955).

———. *That Nothing Is Known*. Introduction, notes, and bibliography by Elaine Limbrick. Translation by Douglas Thomson. Cambridge: Cambridge University Press, 1988.

Sandberg. Karl C. *At the Crossroads of Faith and Reason: An Essay on Pierre Bayle*. Tucson: University of Arizona Press, 1966.

Santayana, George. *Skepticism and Animal Faith: Introduction to a System of Philosophy*. Dover: New York, 1955.

Sarasohn, Lisa T. *Gassendi's Ethics: Freedom in a Mechanistic Universe*. Ithaca, NY: Cornell University Press, 1996.

Schiffman, Z. S. "Montaigne and the Rise of Scepticism in Early Modern Europe: A Reappraisal." *Journal of the History of Ideas* 45 (1984): 499–516.

Schilpp, Paul A., ed. *The Philosophy of Bertrand Russell*. Evanston and Chicago: Library of Living Philosophers, 1946.

———, ed. *The Philosophy of George Santayana*. Evanston and Chicago: Northwestern University Press, 1940. Second edition: La Salle, IL: Open Court, 1971.

Schmitt, Charles B. *Cicero Scepticus: A Study of the Academica in the Renaissance*. The Hague: Martinus Nijhoff, 1972.

———. *Gianfrancesco Pico della Mirandola (1469–1533) and His Critique of Aristotle*. The Hague: Martinus Nijhoof, 1967.

Schneider, Ulrich J. "Commentary: Stäudlin and the Historiography of Philosophy." In Van der Zande and Popkin, *The Skeptical Tradition around 1800*, pp. 379–84.

Schofield, M., M. Burnyeat, and J. Barnes, eds. *Doubt and Dogmatism: Studies in Hellenistic Epistemology*. Oxford: Oxford University Press, 1986.

Schoockius, Martinus (Martin Schook). *De Scepticismo Pars Prior, sive Libri Quatuor*. Groningen: H. Lussinck, 1652.

Schulze, Gottlob Ernst. *Aenesidemus oder uber die Fundamente der von dem Herrn Prof. Reinhold in Jena gelieferten Elementar-Philosophie; nebst einer Vertheidigung des Skepticismus gegen die Anmaasungen der Vernunft*. Neudrucke seltener philosophischer Werke, vol. 1. Berlin, 1991.

———. *Kritik der Theoretischen Philosophie*. Hamburg: C. E. Bohn, 1801.

Schwartz, Jerome. *Diderot and Montaigne: The "Essais" and the Shaping of Diderot's Humanism*. Geneva: Droz, 1966.

Scribano, Emanuela. "Foucher and the Dilemmas of Representation: A 'Modern' Problem?" In Paganini, *The Return of Skepticism from Hobbes and Descartes to Bayle*, pp. 197–212.

Sedley, David. "Three Platonist Interpretations of the *Theaetetus*." In *Form and Argument in Late Plato*, edited by C. Gill and M. M. McGabe, 79–103. Oxford: Oxford University Press, 2000.

Senchet, Emilien. *Essai sur la méthode de Francisco Sanchez*. Paris: V. Giard et E. Brière, 1904.

Sextus Empiricus. *Against the Ethicists*. Translated by Richard Bett. Oxford: Clarendon Press, 1997.

———. *Against the Grammarians*. Translated by David Blank. Oxford: Clarendon Press, 1998.

———. *Contra gli astrologi*. Translated by Emidio Spinelli. Naples: Bibliopolis, 2000.

———. *Contra gli Etici*. Translated by Emidio Spinelli. Naples: Bibliopolis, 1995.

———. *Esquisses pyrrhoniennes*. Translated by Pierre Pellegrin. Paris: Seuil, 1997.

———. *Outlines of Pyrrhonism*. Translated by Julia Annas and Jonathan Barnes. Cambridge: Cambridge University Press, 1994.

———. *Outlines of Pyrrhonism and Adversus Mathematicos*. 4 vols. Translated by R. G. Bury. (Loeb Classical Library) Cambridge, MA: Harvard University Press, 1933–34.

———. *Selection from the Major Writings on Scepticism, Man, & God*. Edited by P. Hallie. Indianapolis, IN: Hackett, 1985.

Shein, Louis L. "The Philosophy of Infinite Possibility: An Examination of Lev Shestov's *Weltanschauung*." *Ultimate Reality Meaning* 2 (1979): 59–68.

Shelford, April. "Thinking Geometrically in Pierre-Daniel Huet's *Demonstratio evangelica* (1679)." *Journal of the History of Ideas* 63 (2002): 599–617.

Shestov, Lev. *Athens and Jerusalem*. Translated with an introduction by Bernard Martin. New York: Ohio University Press, 1966.

———. *In Job's Balances: On the Sources of the Eternal Truths*. Translated from German by Camilla Coventry and C. A. Macartney. Athens: Ohio University Press, 1975.

Sihvola, Juha, ed. *Ancient Scepticism and the Sceptical Tradition*. Helsinki: Acta Philosophica Fennica, 2000.

Silhon, Jean de. *De la certitude des connaissances humaines*. Paris: Fayard, 2002.

Sinnott-Armstrong, Walter, ed. *Pyrrhonian Skepticism*. New York: Oxford University Press, 2004.

Smith, Norman Kemp. *The Philosophy of David Hume: A Critical Study of Its Origins and Central Doctrines*. London: Macmillan, 1941.

Sorbière, Samuel. *Discours sceptiques*. Paris: Honoré Champion, 2002.

Sousa Filho, Danilo Marcondes. "Finding One's Way About: High Windows, Narrow Chimneys, and Open Doors—Wittgenstein's 'Scepticism' and Philosophical Method." In Popkin, *Skepticism in the History of Philosophy*, pp. 167–79.

Sprigge, Timothy L. S. *Santayana*. London: Routledge, 1999.

Stamm, Marcelo. "Skepticism and Methodological Monism: Aenesidemus-Schulze versus Arcesilaus-Erhard." In Van der Zande and Popkin, *The Skeptical Tradition around 1800*, pp. 143–58.

Stough, Charlotte L. *Greek Skepticism*. Berkeley: University of California Press, 1969.

Stroll, Avrum. *Moore and Wittgenstein on Certainty*. New York: Oxford University Press, 1994.

———. *The Significance of Philosophical Skepticism*. Oxford: Oxford University Press, 1984.

———. "The Argument from Possibility." In Popkin, *Skepticism in the History of Philosophy*, pp. 267–79.

Stroud, Barry. *Hume*. London: Routledge and Kegan Paul, 1977.

Struve, Nikita, ed. *Leon Chestov: Un philosophe pas comme les autres?* Paris: Institut d'Etudes Slaves, 1996.

Talaeus, Audomarus (Omer Talon). *Academia. Eiusdem in Academicam Ciceronis fragmentum explicatio*. Paris: M. David, 1547.

Talmor, Sascha. *Glanvill: The Uses and Abuses of Skepticism*. Oxford: Pergamon, 1981.

Taranto, Domenico. *Pirronismo ed assolutismo nella Francia del '600: Studi sul pensiero politico dello scetticismo da Montaigne a Bayle (1580–1697)*. Milan: Franco Angeli, 1994.

Tarrant, H. *Scepticism or Platonism? The Philosophy of the Fourth Academy*. Cambridge: Cambridge University Press, 1985.

Tonelli, G. "Kant and the Ancient Sceptics." In Popkin, Olaso, and Tonelli, *Scepticism in the Enlightenment*, pp. 69–98.

———. "The Weakness of Reason in the Age of Enlightenment." *Diderot Studies* 14 (1971): 217–44. Reprinted in Popkin, Olaso, and Tonelli, *Scepticism in the Enlightenment*, pp. 35–50.

Unger, Peter. *Ignorance: A Case for Scepticism*. Oxford: Clarendon Press, 1975.

Valentia, Petrus (Pedro de Valencia). *Academica sive de iudicio erga verum, ex ipsis primis fontibus*. Antwerp: Viduam et J. Moretum, 1596. Bilingual Spanish/Latin edition translated by José Oroz Reta. Badajoz: Diputación Provincial de Badajoz, 1987.

Van der Zande, J., and Richard H. Popkin, eds. *The Skeptical Tradition around 1800: Skepticism in Philosophy, Science, and Society*. Dordrecht: Kluwer, 1998.

Van Leeuwen, Henry G. *The Problem of Certainty in English Thought 1630–1690*. The Hague: Martinus Nijhoff, 1963.

Verneaux, R. "L'essence du scepticisme selon Hegel." *Histoire de la philosophie et métaphysique. Recherches de philosophie* I. Paris: Desclée de Brower, 1955.

Villey, Pierre. *Les Sources et l'évolution des* Essais *de Montaigne*. Paris: Hachette, 1908.

Vives, Juan Luis. *Opera omnia*. Edited by Gregorio Mayans y Siscár. Valencia: Monfort, 1782–90. Reprinted, London: Gregg Press, 1964.

Voelke, A-J., ed. *Le Scepticisme antique: Actes du colloque international sur le scepticisme antique, Cahiers de la revue de théologie et de philosophie* 15 (1990).

Voltaire. *Philosophical Dictionary.* Translated by Peter Gay. New York: Basic Books, 1962.

Walker, Ralph. "Gassendi and Skepticism." In Burnyeat, *The Skeptical Tradition,* pp. 319–36.

Washburn, Michael C. "Dogmatism, Scepticism, Criticism: The Dialectic of Kant's Silent Decade." *Journal of the History of Philosophy* 13 (1975): 167–76.

Watkins, John W. *Science and Scepticism.* Princeton, NJ: Princeton University Press, 1984.

Watson, Richard A. *The Breakdown of Cartesian Metaphysics.* Atlantic Highlands, NJ: Humanities Press, 1987.

———. *The Downfall of Cartesianism 1673–1712: A Study of Epistemological Issues in Late 17th Century Cartesianism.* The Hague: Martinus Nijhoff, 1966.

———. "Wittgenstein and Sextus Empiricus." *Southern Journal of Philosophy* 7 (1969): 229–36.

Watson, R. H., and J. E. Force, eds. *The Skeptical Mode in Modern Philosophy.* Dordrecht: Kluwer, 1988.

Wetsel, David. *Pascal and Disbelief.* Washington, DC: Catholic University of America Press, 1994.

———. "La Mothe Le Vayer and the Subversion of Christian Belief." *Seventeenth-Century French Studies* 21 (1999): 183–93.

Whelan, Ruth. *The Anatomy of Superstition: A Study of the Historical Theory and Practice of Pierre Bayle.* Oxford: Voltaire Foundation at the Taylor Institute, 1989.

———. "The Wisdom of Simonides: Bayle and La Mothe Le Vayer." In Popkin and Vanderjagt, *Scepticism and Irreligion in the Seventeenth and Eighteenth Centuries,* pp. 230–53.

Wiley, Margaret L. *The Subtle Knot: Creative Scepticism in Seventeenth-Century England.* Cambridge, MA: Harvard University Press, 1952.

Williams, Bernard. *Descartes: The Project of Pure Inquiry.* Harmondsworth, England: Penguin, 1978.

Williams, Michael. *Unnatural Doubts: Epistemological Realism and the Basis of Skepticism.* Oxford: Basil Blackwell, 1991.

Wittgenstein, Ludwig. *On Certainty.* Edited by G. E. M. Anscombe and R. Rhees. Translated by G. E. M. Anscombe. Oxford: Blackwell, 1969.

———. *Philosophical Investigations.* Oxford: Blackwell, 1958.

———. *Tractatus Logico-Philosophicus.* London: Routledge, 1922.

———. *Zettel.* Edited by G. E. M. Anscombe and G. H. von Wright. Translated by G. E. M. Anscombe. Berkeley: University of California Press, 1967.

Wright, John P. *The Skeptical Realism of David Hume.* Minneapolis: University of Minnesota Press, 1983.

Yhap, Jennifer. *The Rehabilitation of the Body as a Means of Knowing in Pascal's Philosophy of Experience.* Lewiston, NY: Edwin Mellen Press, 1991.

Yolton, John. *Locke and the Compass of Human Understanding.* Cambridge: Cambridge University Press, 1970.

———. *Locke and the Way of Ideas.* Oxford: Oxford University Press, 1956.

Yrjönsuuri, Mikko. "Self-Knowledge and Renaissance Sceptics." In Sihvola, *Ancient Scepticism and the Sceptical Tradition,* pp. 225–53.

Zanin, Seguey. "L'entremise du scepticisme: Jean-Jacques Rousseau et la composition du *Discours sur les sciences et les arts.*" In Bernier and Charles, *Scepticisme & Modernité,* pp. 155–66.